THE MUSICAL WORKSHOP

FREDERICK DORIAN

THE

MUSICAL

WORKSHOP

GREENWOOD PRESS, PUBLISHERS
WESTPORT, CONNECTICUT

To my dear wife

CONTENTS

SUMMARY

MUSICAL EXAMPLES

ILLUSTRATIONS

These illustrations will be found in a group following page 176

AUTHOR'S NOTE
AND ACKNOWLEDGMENT

The Musical Workshop is an attempt to show how great composers of past centuries saw their task and created their music. Due to its content—based upon the self-analysis, sketches and manuscripts of the masters—this book is one single acknowledgment in itself: an acknowledgment to the documents which have inspired this study and provided the substance of its material.

The author plans an inquiry into the creative technique of contemporary composers at a later date. Obviously, the proximity in time and space to the living artist suggests an approach different from the one which prevails in this present volume.

✿   ✿

✿

I am deeply indebted to Dr. Robert E. Doherty, President of Carnegie Institute of Technology, for his generous encouragement of this research.

As in my other work during the past decade, I was guided by the world-wide and lifelong experience of Professor Curt Sachs of New York University. It was during a discussion with Dr. Sachs that the idea for this book first came to light.

Dr. Max Schoen, Head of the Department of Psychology of Carnegie Institute of Technology, gave most liberally of his time: I was indeed fortunate to have the constant counsel of a scientist who combines his specific interest with a profound love of music. Dr. Schoen has examined the psychological material of this study and greatly helped me through his careful reading of the entire manuscript. I am particularly grateful to him.

I wish to thank my friends and colleagues, Professors Charles A. H. Pearson and Nikolai Lopatnikoff: their companionship and advice was the source of strong stimulation. Professor Pearson helped me with his profound historical knowledge and with his conscientious examination of the complete material. The reading of the manuscript on the part of so distinguished a composer as Nikolai Lopatnikoff was of great value.

I also had the advantage of a critical appraisal of my work by Gladys Schmitt, the noted writer, and by Simon Goldfield whose numerous suggestions were extremely beneficial. I am also indebted to Dr. Yale David Koskoff for his friendship and advice. My colleague, Roland J. Leich, has kindly assisted me in the correction of the final proofs.

Miss Irene Millen, Head of the Music Department of the Carnegie Library of Pittsburgh, was most helpful in procuring rare research material. Miss Esther Fawcett of the Fine Arts Library of Carnegie Institute of Technology has offered her assistance in many ways.

My special thanks to Mrs. Catharine K. Miller, acting chief of the Music Division of the New York Public Library, as well as to the entire staff for their co-operation and patience. I would also like to express my appreciation to Miss Eva Judd O'Meara, Curator of the Music Library of Yale University, for the permission to study rare manuscripts belonging to her division.

Mr. Joseph Breitenbach was unsparing in his time and great skill in preparing the photographs for this book.

Last but not least, I would like to acknowledge the great professional debt I owe to those writers from whose works I have drawn special guidance and orientation: first of all to Dr. Max Graf and to Dr. Ernst Buecken. As to their special contribution to this work and to the contribution of other scholars, I have endeavored in my notes and bibliographical references to make proper acknowledgment wherever it is appropriate.

It is likewise in this bibliographical appendix that due acknowledgments are made for quotations, reprints and translations.

FREDERICK DORIAN

New York, September 16th, 1946

PROLOGUE

THE INNER LIFE OF MUSIC

> He who considers things in their
> first growth and origin will obtain
> the clearest view of them.
>
> ARISTOTLE

ART AND CRAFT

THESE pages tell the inner story of great music. "To write the history of Beethoven's inner and outer life would be a wonderful task," asserted Schumann in a letter from the year 1838. This provocative suggestion implies a study of the growth of Beethoven's scores, a search for the ideas integrated in the master's lifework—a biography of musical style, stuff and substance.

What occurred in the creator's world of sounds to inspire his work? What were its driving forces? What went on in Beethoven's inner workshop that finally resulted in the Eroica or the Ninth, in his only opera *Fidelio* and in the four different overtures for it, in his piano works and chamber music, or in the crown of his vocal art, the *Missa Solemnis*?

In regard to Beethoven and all other masters in the history of music, this fascinating problem challenges our search for knowledge with the ever-present question: how did these scores come into being? That enchanting play of sounds called music—how was it put together?

Our book is an attempt to answer these questions by tracing the creative process in music from the first inspirational vision of a work to its finished score. The intrinsic truth of Aristotle's observation that "he who considers things in their first growth and origin will obtain the clearest view of them,"[1] necessarily holds true also for the genesis of music. Moreover, an inquiry into the basis of musical creation has not only been suggested by the great composers; it is they who have made it possible. In words as well as in tones, they have offered testimony which clarifies their creative procedure for posterity. The composers have left us amazing records of self-analysis which appear as a precious counterpart to our heritage of their musical wealth. For the purpose of a study of diverse creative techniques in music, we shall explore the authentic material surrounding this crucial and dramatic topic of genesis: scores and sketches, treatises and essays, autobiographies and letters—all written by the masters themselves. Engrossed in the study of these authentic documents, we shall eavesdrop, as it were, on music as it is being made in the workshop of the artist.

The chief purpose of the following pages, then, is to learn more about the genesis and nature of music. Contrary to other works of appreciation, of history and aesthetics, our book is not concerned with a formal analysis or minute dissection of the finished art product. Rather it is the story of its embryonic life, prior to its fulfillment in the score, that will comprise the content of these chapters.

We start with a thrust inward, deep into the roots of the artistic events.

Like all works of art, a musical score evolves from several distinct stages. The development is intrinsically threefold: inspiration, elaboration and synthesis. This division readily suggests the broad outline of our book. In its simple strokes, it is designed to follow the course of the composer's creative procedure.

The chief center of our observation will remain at all times a musical one, for tones are the material of the musician and their permutation is his task. How he deals with this material in early phases of his work is strikingly revealed in the composer's sketches. The study of these drafts enables us to go beyond the registration of the artistic phenomena as we find them in the finished masterpieces. Delving into the deeper strata below the surface of the

[1] Footnote references will be found beginning on p. 343.

score script, we can examine the relationship that exists between the embryonic phase of artistic creation and its completed result. Particularly, where there are numerous sketches for a work or even a particular section of it, the reasoning powers and motivating forces of the masters come to the fore and fulfill musically the desire of the philosopher, Georg Christoph Lichtenberg, who said: "In certain works of glorious men, I would rather read what is scratched out than what is left in."

An examination of complex working methods obviously cannot be limited to technical problems alone. "The most important in music is not the notes," claimed Gustav Mahler in reference to those forces determined by the composer's spiritual and emotional life and by his cultural associations, all of which are inevitably integrated into his music. To what extent is the personality of the composer, his taste and temperament responsible for the motivation and synthesis of his musical material? "I shall try to see in various compositions, the various forces which have contributed to their creation and that which they contain of the inner life,"[2] reads the promise of Debussy when he added to his activities as a composer that of a writer, appraising and evaluating the work of his fellow musicians.

If one could watch a composer at his work as apprentices watch a painter at his drawing and sketching (his use of the palette in front of the canvas, and the gradual transformation of all preliminary work to its final shape), then a great deal could be learned at its very source about the technique of creating music. But watching a musician improvise, sketch, arrange and correct his scores can show nothing except the external motion; it obviously cannot convey any real insight into the working procedure as it does in the case of other artists. The development of the composer's work is always incomprehensible without the thought process behind it.

It is enlightening, however, to trace the approach to composition with the help of the authentic documents on which our study is based. The title, *The Musical Workshop*, has been chosen because it places emphasis on the great variety of working methods by which music has been made through history as an art and as a craft. The term "musical workshop" is used here in a dual sense. We shall speak of it metaphorically, implying the inner workshop of the musician. Here we refer to the inner process of music in the making, to the production of work in all its spiritual and technical ramifications. We shall also examine the external workshop of great masters, the tools and supplies which were necessary to produce their scores. Whatever furnishings the composer chooses for his workshop, even mere decoration, may perhaps offer a clue to his inner world. Everything counts in the study of a great creative artist. Consideration must be paid to whatever may add to an understanding of the musical workshop in its total setting.

With all its findings, this book does not intend to present a thesis with sweeping conclusions. After all, the creative phenomenon is deeply seated in the uniqueness and originality of individual genius. But *The Musical Workshop* attempts to bring remote creative phenomena closer to our understanding by reducing as many effects to as few causes as possible. This can be done: music, in spite of the veils which cover its genesis, is not all mystery. Composition is based on the rules of craft as well as on the laws of art. Whatever pertains to craft can be explained, and much of what pertains to art does not have to remain inexplicable.

No one can fail to reap the moral from the documentary harvest which shows the great and noble struggle for perfection that is inherent in every artistic endeavor. Behind the work appears the soul of its maker, the conscious and subconscious forces of the creative drive. Goethe has interpreted perhaps more succinctly than anyone else the meaning of the creative process when he says: "The beautiful has already reached its highest purpose in its genesis and in the development that follows. Our after-enjoyment is only a consequence of its existence." The same Olympic thinker declared that one must go into the poet's land in order to understand him: "Wer den Dichter will verstehen, muss in Dichter's Lande gehen." And it is to this remote land, to the creative realm of fantasy with its enchantment, wonders and mysteries, but also to its cool and detached aspect of craft, technique and sheer reasoning that the following pages will take the reader.

INSPIRATION FROM BEYOND

How is music born? Is it heaven-sent? Can we think of musical inspiration in the light of the antique myth in which the Muse descends to the artist? Her kiss is the spark that sets afire the composer's fantasy, and conjuring up his music in a romantic way, the fairy guest from Mount Parnassus leaves the composer glowing with a mysterious force, able to envision, to plan and to complete his tonal work.

Ever since Homer called upon the goddess to sing his epic, *The Odyssey*, artists have longingly invoked the graces of the Muse to foster their inspiration. Even Plato, inaugurator of all rationalistic philosophy, believed that "poets do not write by wisdom, but by a kind of genius and inspiration." This genius stems from direct divination. Inspiration occurs in a creative trance. Such is the source of poetry and likewise that of music: it is art sent from beyond, a divine utterance inexplicable like the revelations of the Hebrew prophets.

In exalted moments of inspiration, the musician hears new motifs and envisions beautiful forms—perhaps even a whole work in one single lightning flash. The creative trance lifts the clouds of inertia and reveals to his imagination the sudden vision of a still unborn score. Something which is not written down in the script and signs of musical notation, something not yet captured on the staves of note paper, suddenly sounds at the composer's inner ear, is tangibly existent in his musical mind. And from this inspirational moment on, the music becomes gradually his own—now he can seize it!

Imagination—the faculty which creates—permits the composer to hear the tone rows of his embryonic art work and even to read its yet unwritten notes. Music streams from his mind to his fingers ready to be played on an instrument or to be jotted down on note paper. What the imagination reads and hears is now captured forever. Music has been born!

This is the work of inspiration: a lightning flash of the subconscious, the mining of an idea from its hidden shafts to the level of consciousness and craft. It is this subconscious factor of the creative power that has enticed many artists to seek all sources of imagination beyond earthly vistas. Musicians of every era have indulged in the antique metaphor of the Muses and their inspiring mission. Everywhere there is expression of the artist's belief in the inexplicable role of fantasy. The enlightened Beethoven, in a mellow mood, poetically entreated the force that hewed his destiny:

Apollo and the Muses are not going to deliver me yet to the door of Death. I still owe them much, and before my departure to the Elysian fields, I must bestow upon them what the Spirit has endowed me to complete. I feel as if so far I had written just a few notes.

These words were written in a letter to the publisher Schott, September 17, 1824; and if we think of what Beethoven achieved in the remaining three years of his life, the Muses indeed granted him their favor. Beyond such mythical notions, Beethoven could not tell the true source of his inspiration:

From where do I take my ideas? That I cannot say with certainty. They come uncalled, directly and indirectly. I could grasp them by my hands in the freedom of nature, on walks in the silence of the night or in the early morning through moods which turn into tones which sound, blow, storm until the notes are standing before me.[3]

Weber, with the religious undertone characteristic of the composer of Der Freischütz, calls all products of imagination "a gift from above." And those heaven-sent gifts are held in just as great astonishment by the artist who receives them as by the world which comes to appreciate their beauty.

"How did you find the beautiful theme of your Seventh Symphony?" Anton Bruckner was asked by an admiring pupil. "The good Lord sent it to me," was the sincere answer of the devout old master.

Within such firm beliefs, creation evolves as a mystery not to be solved by human beings. It is something that cannot be either taught or learned. No power of will, no industry, no discernment nor analysis, no concerted effort of intellect, of mind and ear can synthetically fabricate in the workshop the heaven-sent products of a transcendental faculty. They are the precious diamonds mined only in rare and lucky finds. It is only the simulated stone that can be hewn in a factory at a workman's will.

"I emphatically deny that the mere will is enough to give flight to the imagination. This is equally impossible as it is impossible for the human soul to command emotions according to will alone. Our human sensations are not a clock-work which one can wind up at will and whose hands can be set according to personal fancy."[4] Thus spoke Rossini—a composer who had fully experienced the blessings of heaven-sent gifts as well as the tortures of denials. He

had written *The Barber of Seville* in a true trance, requiring for
its completion the incredibly short time of only thirteen days. But
years later, after he had brought his *William Tell* to paper under
exhausting difficulties, Rossini was really never able to reawaken
his inspirational powers from their deep slumber.

Work, then, seems a small task if the artist drifts along on the
magical tide of his flowing fantasy. Carried on such a stream, he
fancies that his music has been dictated to him.[5] He brings ideas
to paper that were perfected in his subconscious mind and were
waiting to be delivered.

Thus, we see that inspiration is regarded by a certain type of
composer as a force which transcends all rational determination.
The beautiful tunes that enchant our ears and hearts are gifts and
dreams from beyond. They are but lucky apparitions born like the
golden Aphrodite from the foam of the waves.

CRAFT AS CREATIVE SOURCE

Music is a craft as well as an art. In contrast to all mystic beliefs,
to all notions of an inspiration from beyond, artists have sought the
answer to the creative enigma in realistic formulas. They found
them in the intrinsic laws of the material and in rules extracted by
reason and empiricism. Why could not sheer craft yield the tonal
products to the musician of skill and knowledge? After all, great
composers achieved their results by wise and conscientious craftsmanship as well as by inspiration and vision. The theory of composition has for ages shown how music was made according to
specified rules and regulations. Aesthetics traced the blueprints of
tonal beauty which have guided the masters in the construction of
their scores. The process of composing was regarded as an activity
controlled by law and logic, just as any other kind of productive
thinking. And the working method of many composers is not only
comparable but intrinsically related to that of the mathematician.

A strictly mathematical approach to music is attributed to the
Greek scientist, Pythagoras (500 B.C.), though by indirect evidence
since none of his musical writings have been preserved. If his followers claimed him to be "the father of music," they alluded primarily to his mathematical, acoustical theories. Things are numbers.

Music, too, Pythagoras held, is in essence a play of numbers, for tonal relationships can be numerically expressed. The profound influence of the Pythagorean school was not limited to antiquity; medieval followers continued its teachings. St. Augustine[6] described the nature of God as a circle: its center was everywhere, its periphery nowhere. Significantly, St. Augustine's main work, the six volumes, *De Musica*, deals primarily with the problems of rhythm and meter. Tonal art is viewed as fully controlled by mathematical regulation. This theory paved the way for Boethius,[7] the author of the most influential work on music that the Middle Ages produced. In the first book of his *De Institutione Musica*, Boethius defines the musician as one "who examines (his problems) by reason."

The essence of such rational teaching never lost its grip on musicians for centuries to follow. Reason as the guiding star reoccurs with modifications and variations in every period. Those who adhere to the rational approach resort to musical mathematics, to the use of numbers, and emphasize the exclusive role of craft. No matter how much their method may differ individually, reason appears as the dominant factor of the approach. There is nothing mysterious nor secretive about the creative process. It can always be reduced to the scientific. And so, as centuries pass, the antique and medieval attempts to enter the musical realm through the door of numerical speculations live on. In 1706, Alessandro Scarlatti, in a letter to Ferdinand de Medici, refers to his music specifically as "the daughter of mathematics." Composition was a science to this Sicilian musician in romantic Naples. In eighteenth century Germany, J. S. Bach's pupil, Lorenz Christoph Mizler, discarded imagination altogether for the sake of a strictly rational procedure. The Leipzig Society of Musical Science, which Mizler founded in 1738, dedicated its efforts to an exclusively scientific exploration of the laws controlling musical construction.

The scientific composer believes in work that springs from inventive skill and technique alone. To his mind music results from a very specialized craft rather than from a dramatic wonder bestowed upon the composer by the grace of the Muses. Miracles belong to the sphere of religion. All activities of human beings must be ordered, controlled by conscious planning. Significantly, the Latin word, *compositio*, is a term connoting craft. The German *Künstler* (artist) is a noun derived from the verb *können,* to know, to be able to do. The composer, then, is the artisan who knows his craft, who is well equipped and prepared to put tones together. Much more promising than relying upon inspirational ideas is the composer's capacity to plan and organize his tonal material, to proceed logically toward a clearly fixed direction. Just as the cabinetmaker who converts his wood into chairs and tables is guided by the rules of his trade, so the maker of music follows intrinsic laws of his craft while working on his tonal substance. The natural material of music—tones—supplies the concrete stuff of composition like wood, marble or any other substance in the hands of a fine craftsman. The artisan-composer aims at his accomplishments through knowledge, workmanship and industry. And it is in the workmanlike atmosphere and constancy of his production that he feels the strongest impulse for work. "Inspiration," or whatever other fancy term may represent that waiting for the Muse, is a romantic notion at which the inveterate craftsman will only smile. He, for his part, depends only on his métier. Work, to the craftsman, is sheer knowledge, the "knowing how" to arrive methodically at the coolly-set goal.

CONSTRUCTION VERSUS INSPIRATION

Throughout history, one of the two opposing principles—inspiration or craft—have dominated the musician's pursuit of composition. The one he follows will infallibly reveal his working procedure. There is the type of artist who interprets composition mystically: the genesis of his work seems to him irrational, inexplicable, evading analysis. Then there is the musical craftsman who approaches the problems of his work on a strictly rational basis of construction. To him, even the initial approach to composition and all the results thereafter spring from craft and detached observation. He brings the creative phenomenon down to earth.

But there is no pure approach: great art never stems exclusively from either inspiration or craft alone. Craft on its highest level is unthinkable without inspiration. On the other hand, the further elaboration of all the raw material first mined by inspiration is necessarily controlled by reason, by the composer's artistic intellect

and his technical knowledge. Whether a composer takes a mystic
or rationalistic view on his road to creation depends upon his own
intrinsic disposition. It is true the ideology of his era, the association
with a school, all factors of the spiritual climate will influence his
decision. Yet the final conclusion rests in the specific psychological
make-up of the individual artist.

Inevitably, the two approaches to musical creation have been
often viewed as opposing principles. This is shown by Verdi in his
letter of December 7, 1869 to Camille du Locle:

I believe in inspiration; you people believe in construction. I don't
object to your criterion, for the sake of the argument, but I desire the
enthusiasm that you lack in feeling and in judging. I strive for art, in
whatever form it may appear, but never for the amusement, artifice or
system which you prefer. Am I wrong? Am I right? However it may be,
I have reason enough to know that my ideas are completely different
from yours, and furthermore, my backbone isn't pliable enough for me to
give way and deny my convictions, which are profound and deeply
rooted in me.

This creed is manifest everywhere in Verdi's philosophy of art.
It permeates his entire life and finds repeated expression throughout
his correspondence. To Countess Clarina Maffei (January 30, 1876)
Verdi complains about the contemporary trend in music: "No one
thinks of following his own inspiration any more." Years later, on
December 17, 1884, again to the same confidante, Verdi writes: "An
art without naturalness and simplicity is no art. Inspiration in the
very nature of things, produces simplicity."

This inspiration, in which Verdi so strongly believes as opposed
to construction, is the creative faculty beyond the approach of the
calculating intellect. Inspiration is whatever moves the artist. It is
the source of all true expression. Intellect alone breaks the creative
spell. Construction without enthusiasm can produce only a make-
shift which is not inwardly felt by the composer, a music which
has no soul. By contrast, the inspirational is a primary utterance of
the inner life. It is romantic in its aloofness from the prosaic and is
carried by that enthusiasm which is antithetical to all cool calculation. As to its origin, the creative flash itself might be veiled in
secrecy. Yet the finished result, with Verdi no less than with any
other real master, is rational in the sense that it appears orderly,

self-understood and coherent. Only the inspirational aspect, how it first happened, remains a mystery. It seems mysterious that one man is singled out to conceive great works to which other mortals can only listen with awe.

THREE STAGES OF COMPOSITION

The previously mentioned threefold scheme of composition is common to all creative enterprise. Inspiration, organization and synthesis are the main stages through which the artist proceeds on his road to the final goal. This scheme broadly marks his way—whether his aesthetic guidepost is classical or romantic, whether the specific aim is a small piano piece or a grandiose symphony, a song or a four-night opera cycle. Yet within these three stages of work, a great variety of procedure appears which exposes the artistic ideology of a specific era as well as the creative technique of an individual composer.

We are already acquainted with the term "inspiration" defined as any impulse which sets the musician's mental activity into motion. Whatever this impulse may be and from whatever it may stem, to the musician, its end result is tones. The composer's productive response to the stimulus is tonal: he hears a motif, a chord or rhythm; he envisions a specific musical form. The fruits of such initial inspiration are regarded by a certain type of composer as ripe. He will accept as satisfactory the form in which the musical idea first occurs to him. This is particularly true of the romantic artist with his stress on subjectivity. For him, the product of the inspirational phase takes on remaining significance.

In the second stage of work, that of elaboration, all the technical equipment of the composer swings into full action. This is the stage of musical tectonics; it is dominated by the art of tonal construction. Now the work's fundamental concept must be assured. The blueprint of the score is drawn, but still in adjustable lines.

It is particularly in this phase of work that the great complexity of the creative problem becomes apparent. Once conceived, music lives a willful life of its own. Following the inner laws of its existence, the composer tests the forces of the newly created tonal life, weighing and balancing their qualities in constant view of his final goal. Frequently the reasoning powers of the composer are in conflict with the life forces of the embryonic tonal material: hence this second stage is still an experimental one, full of tests and trials. New plans appear which might necessitate a change of the original course, invoke adjustments of the blueprint or even exclude thoughts which were destined originally for use in the final work. Thus, while a score is being composed along a given pattern, its substance might change again and again.

In this second stage, the role of inspiration is by no means terminated. A clairvoyant vision continually lightens the composer's way through every phase of his work. In this sense, no great musician ever writes a single note without being truly inspired. In fact, the inspirational spell may well be maintained throughout the whole work and not be limited to its original conception. Yet at the same time, the creative impetus is blended with constructive thinking. If this were not so, the art work would lack its logical organization. Free fantasy, unchecked by reason, endangers workmanship. A certain degree of aesthetic speculation and architectural planning following the stage of conception must be taken for granted. If the full creative emphasis is laid on craft, then all subjective impulse is overshadowed by the accomplishment through workmanship and architectural organization. In the cool air of strict tonal building, the inspirational flash loses much of its sovereignty. Not a romantic rapture, but enlightened procedure, carried safely by laws of composition, organizes the tonal material on the sound basis of musical craft.

The third and final stage is that of creative synthesis. Here, in the literal meaning of the term *compositio*, all parts of the score are put together. Whatever has been separate is now combined: a development joins a preceding exposition, a first or second theme is set against a bridging episode, a coda is affixed at the end of a movement. This movement, in turn, joins the total cycle of a sonata or a symphony. All work that was tentative before now becomes final. All that germinated and sprang from inspiration and was thoroughly tested in elaboration must be ordered by the objectifying reason of synthetic work. Setting the score in its totality, the role and place of every detail must be explored. The final shape of the score, though visible before, takes on clear contours.

In the first stage of composition, genius is manifest by inspiration. In the second, it is displayed by the superb mastery of the musical craft. Here, in the third and final stage, it emerges as the blend of craft and talent with the unfatigued perseverance of genius: it truly appears as the capacity of taking infinite pains.

PART ONE

INSPIRATION

CHAPTER ONE

CREATION IN THE LIFE CURVE

Art is intimately connected with
life.

WAGNER

EVERYTHING is inspiration to the born musician. The voice
of his mother. The smile of his friend. The muffled tread of
human passions—life on earth from the cradle to the grave.
The curses of hell and the glory of God.

There is no vision and no experience which has not been turned
into an inspirational impulse by creative musicians. Inner and outer
events, the whole gamut of psychic and physical experiences to
which the human being is exposed or which his imagination can
conjure up—they all have been the springboard of inspirational
impulses in the music of thousands of years. "There is a song," in
Eichendorff's beautiful words, "which slumbers in all things that
dream endlessly, and the world will begin to sing if thou findest the
key word."

Life itself is the most potent force of artistic creation. Many of the
artist's problems are born with him: when and where he first sees
the light of day, which music he hears and to which spiritual and
artistic climate he is exposed in childhood, inevitably affect his
creative direction.

Fate, setting the artist in his time and place, emerges as the first molding factor of his style and expression. Every artist would have expressed himself differently had he been born in a different time and place. Thus, the date of his birth sets an all-important point of departure for his artistic endeavors. Even the greatest revolutionary of all—even Beethoven, whose demoniacal genius eventually shattered all bars of contemporary expression—had to start his creative enterprise in close connection with the music of his time. This could not have been otherwise. Inevitably in the youthful works of every composer, the influences and artistic implications of the sphere in which he lives appear as his subconscious guideposts. Only gradually can a style emerge which the composer pursues when he develops into a freely choosing and gradually maturing artist. Maturing means that the artist learns to understand and express himself with increasing honesty and depth. As life flows onward, his basic and youthful style undergoes change. His technique may develop to such a point that it advances far ahead of his generation. Nevertheless, at some advanced point even genius is bound to reach the limit which determines the course and end of all human enterprise. The Renaissance composer, he of the baroque or of the classical era—they all speak the language of their time as well as that of their creative individualities.

At birth all those traits of an individual human nature are implanted which later emerge as driving forces in the creative work. No artist can escape himself, nor can he ever change himself completely. Every human being, every musician is born with a psychosomatic set-up which will determine his inclinations, his taste and temperament, and in turn, his reactions to the tonal experience.

CHILDHOOD

The life curve of the composer is the rail upon which the creative enterprise rides searching for its ideal terminal. It is in childhood that impressions of lifelong importance are made. The artistic manifestations of these impressions might not occur until much later, perhaps not until he reaches his maturity. But with some of the greatest, those traits which characterize their masterworks were evident in their earliest years. Some of them were born into an atmosphere laden with music. This rich heritage, laid in the cradle by fate, seemed to Schumann the true and earliest foundation of musical mastery. And so he praised the good fortune of all "whose fathers were simple musicians, who with their mother's milk drank music and learned it in their childish dreams."

Mozart's father, Leopold, in a letter of February 16, 1778, tells Wolfgang how he behaved in early years: "As a child you were more serious than childish. When sitting at the piano or otherwise busy with music, no one was permitted the slightest fun. Yes, even your facial expression was so serious that many prudent people were deeply concerned for your life." Wolfgang's grave countenance meant fanatical concentration on his inner music which sounded in his mind since childhood and remained with him forever. There are also those documents referring to the gayety, to the playfulness of the prodigious child. Johann Andreas Schachtner, the Salzburg court trumpeter, speaks in a letter to Mozart's sister, April 24, 1792, of the grave as well as of the frolicsome moods of "Wolfgangerl."[1] His phenomenal prematurity explains how it is possible that the music composed in boyhood already displays unmistakable characteristics of what we know today as Mozart's style: particularly the ambivalence of serenity and melancholy belongs in this picture. Not even Mozart's last word, the *Requiem,* is one of unbroken gravity. Up to *The Magic Flute,* his music is full of children's playfulness which affects us like the fragrance of bygone happy days.[2]

The child Handel, although discouraged in his love for music by his surgeon father, lived and played in tones only. It is said of the infant Georg Friedrich that he started to make music before he was able to walk. And after he was old enough to utter wishes, all he desired for Christmas was musical instruments. And so trumpets, horns, a flute and a drum became his favorite childhood toys.[3] Well known is the story that tells how he would steal out of bed at night and teach himself how to play on his clavichord. Here, on the keyboard, his infantile imagination found its first outlet in an improvising manner. And this remained the method in which the mature man pursued many of his ideas throughout his long creative life.

Every composer's biography shows how the experiences of early years play their irrefutable part in the work of the mature artist. We have only to read the biographies of Haydn, Weber, Chopin,

Mendelssohn, Tchaikovsky to find highly illustrative material which tells how the budding of creativeness in childhood coincides with the early unfolding of the emotional and psychological activity of human nature.

Among more recent composers, there is Gustav Mahler whose childhood memories of military music, trumpet signals, marches and drumbeats turn up frequently in the works of the mature man. A lasting impression was left on the young boy's mind when his nurse took him for walks around the military barracks in his native Moravia. In Mahler's symphonies, these military fanfares and drum rhythms of the old Austrian army occur in such a way that their significance cannot be understood on the basis of the symphonic blueprint alone. These effects belong to the realm of musical surrealism. They lead to a world of dreams, of symbols and childhood recollection where the laws of tonal logic are canceled.

STYLE ABSORPTION AND PERSONAL STYLE

As composers grow older, their personalities naturally take on more definite shape and are revealed more clearly in their music. What a difference in technique and what a contrast in style is there in the initial and the last work of every master! What a way has been traveled by the truly great from their initial opus to their opus ultimum!

Early works necessarily bespeak the young composer's search for a style: he is eager to learn, to absorb and finally to throw tradition overboard. The young artist feels himself to be striving, searching, groping, never reaching complete fulfillment. Stops at different stations open new vistas and outlooks. To reach his creative goal, a high degree of receptivity is indispensable: often the young composer cannot find his own style unless he has gained a thorough knowledge of the music written up to his time and has consumed whatever appears useful to him in contemporary techniques. As we shall show, the recourse to the technique of others is an intermediary stage even with those composers who later achieve the highest degree of originality.

The young Bach sought and found direction in the works of Frescobaldi, Froberger, Kerll, Pachelbel, Fischer, Strungk, Buxtehude, Reinken, Bruhns, Böhm and some old French organists, who, according to the fashion of those times, were all great masters of harmony and of the fugue.[4] As Forkel reports, Vivaldi's concertos for the violin, which were then just published, also guided his approach to his own music:

> He conceived the happy idea of arranging them all for his clavier. He studied the chain of the ideas, their relation to each other, the variations of the modulations, and many other particulars. The change necessary to be made in the ideas and passages composed for the violin, but not suitable to the clavier, taught him to think musically; so that after his labor was completed, he no longer needed to expect his ideas from his fingers, but could derive them from his own fancy. Thus prepared, he wanted only perseverance and unremitting practice to reach a point where he could not only create himself an ideal of his art, but might also hope, in time, to attain it. In this practice he was never remiss. He labored so constantly and so assiduously that he frequently even took the nights to his aid. What he had written during the day, he learned to play in the succeeding night.[5]

Mozart's correspondence with his father shows that imbibing of wisdom at the springs of his contemporaries was by no means a subconscious procedure. It is just another stop on the road which leads to the final goal of artistic independence: "As you know, I can more or less adopt or imitate any kind and any style of composition." (February 7, 1778.) And adopt he did—first the Salzburg and older Viennese masters. Later he imitated whatever he heard on his travels: Italian and French music as well as various German styles. It was in Mannheim that he became acquainted with the *Medea* by Benda and reported to his father, November 12, 1778: "Do you know what my opinion is? That one should treat most recitatives in the opera in such a way (as treated in the *Medea* score) and that one should only occasionally sing the recitatives, namely when the words can be well expressed in the music." Mozart's zeal for this newly discovered mode of dramatic expression did not cease until he himself tried a melodrama of his own, in *Zaïde*.

No youthful composer—not even one endowed with Mozart's genius and its seemingly inexplicable sources—can in reality create fully out of himself. As long as spiritual independence is beyond the reach of the prodigious artist, his gifts are primarily manifest in the astonishing capacity to absorb and thus to acquire the sureness of a technique of his own. He combines the insatiable urge to imitate with the talent to conquer any style he chooses.

It was on the tree of absorbed wisdom that Mozart's own style fully blossomed. In maturity his own creation, the primeval experience, comes to the fore in place of the deducted experience: the latter one he shared with those whose art he had to overcome and conquer. The primeval experience belongs to himself, and it is from now on that his creative technique achieves the highest originality.

In the unending stream of inspirational impulses, Mozart is a link: he takes from those who came before and gives to those who come later. It is of specific interest to observe that almost a century after Mozart, Edward Elgar, twenty-one years old, was instinctively drawn to Mozart's music for guidance. Supplementing his study of heavy theoretical treatises, Elgar decided to copy the classical architecture of Mozart's G Minor Symphony by writing and instrumentating a symphony in the same style and key. He modulated where Mozart modulated. He subdivided the form and arranged the parts in close observation of Mozart's model while avoiding a slavish adherence to the original.

Our Illustrations I and II aim at a comparison of Mozart's G Minor Symphony, the source of Elgar's inspiration, and its imitation on the part of the young English composer. A few realistic and somewhat humorous remarks indicate Elgar's approach. Mozart's woodwind section contained originally only flutes, oboes and bassoons. Elgar, observing how Mozart had supplanted the original woodwind scoring with two oboes and two clarinets which were to take the place of the original oboe parts, copies this procedure.[6]

We see, then, how a young composer absorbs a masterwork of the past. The admired score serves as a model furnishing the groundwork from which the apprentice proceeds to learn and to grow. He traces the form in all details. Just as a painter copies pictures in the gallery for the purpose of retracing a master's method for his own benefit and guidance, so the young composer studies and outlines great music that particularly appeals to his artistic imagination.

The mature composer whose personal style is already set never copies in the sense of mere imitation. If enthusiasm for the music of another artist acts as a springboard for his own creative impulse, the outcome is inevitably something new.

Mozart, whose creativeness began at such a prodigiously early age, passed the stage of absorption in the works of his boyhood. At an age when others are still seeking their style, he had long since discovered himself creatively. Thus, when he intensively studied the music of others in the last ten years of his life, he did so with a fully mature artist's never ceasing desire for new orientation. Genius never stands still. Burning artistic curiosity, an ever searching quest for knowledge prompted Mozart to ask his father, April 10, 1782:

I wish you would send me Handel's six fugues and the toccata and fugues by Eberlin. I go every Sunday morning to the Baron van Swieten, and nothing is played there but Handel and Bach. I am making a collection of the Bach fugues, Sebastian's as well as Emanuel's and Friedemann's, and also of Handel's, and I want just these six. Also, I should like to let the Baron hear Eberlin's.

For Mozart, intimate acquaintance with the baroque masters proved to be a decisive experience in his creative life.[7]

Mozart's last opera, *The Magic Flute,* particularly its small ensembles, proved to be true stimulation for Schubert. He spent happy hours of music-making in the house of the Fröhlich sisters where he accompanied their singing of Mozart's opera. The lovely blend of three women's voices, here for the Ladies-in-Waiting of the Queen of the Night, there for the Trio of the Genii enchanted Schubert: "O God, what a treat this is," he exclaimed.[8] After such an evening of singing and playing of *The Magic Flute,* Schubert went home ringing with Mozart's music. A few days later, he surprised his friends with the finished manuscript of his vocal quartets, Gott ist mein Hirt and Gott in der Natur.

The composer, inspired by the work of another, may first assume an experimental or imitative attitude. Yet, in the case of a master, such experiments frequently lead to a new working method of his own, to music which only distantly recalls the model from which it stems inspirationally. Thus Berlioz embarked on a methodical study of the opera by making regular visits to the theater.[9] He relates in his memoirs how he would take the score of the announced work with him and follow it attentively during the performance from a seat where he had sufficient light. In this practical way, Berlioz grew to understand the handling of an orchestra, and recognized the function and timbre of most of the instruments, even if he could not yet grasp their mechanism. By a careful comparison of the means used by an admired master with their end results, Berlioz "perceived the subtle connection which exists between musical expression and the special art of instrumentation." Among all the scores he analyzed in this way, the works of Gluck were dearest to him: "I read them again and again. I memorized them. They deprived me of sleep, made me forget food and drink. I was enchanted with them."

Berlioz, in turn, exerted powerful stimulation for young Wagner, who heard some of the French master's important scores in Paris between 1840 and 1842. Wagner commented on his impression of the Romeo and Juliet Symphony:

At first the grandeur and masterly execution of the orchestral part almost overwhelmed me. It was beyond anything I could have conceived . . . I was simply all ears for things of which till then I had never dreamed and which I felt I must try to realize. . . . In fact at that time I felt almost like a little schoolboy by the side of Berlioz.

As late as October 7, 1859, and after the completion of such a strikingly original work as Tristan, Wagner confided to Hans von Bülow that he had, after acquaintance with the works of Liszt, become an "altogether different fellow in regard to harmony."

The analysis of works by other artists can influence the working process, not only by a desire to imitate and to achieve related results, but also negatively: from such studies a composer may learn what to reject and avoid in his own music. Full appreciation for the high achievements of another musician does not necessarily mean that the observer takes over wholeheartedly his model or even certain of its features. After studying the score of Lohengrin Tchaikovsky records this reaction in a letter to Madame von Meck (May 17, 1879):

I want to study this score very closely, and to decide whether to adopt some of its methods of instrumentation. His (Wagner's) mastery is extraordinary, but for reasons which would necessitate technical explanations, I have not borrowed anything from him. Wagner's orchestration is too symphonic, too overloaded and heavy for vocal music. The older I grow, the more convinced I am that symphony and opera are in every respect at the opposite poles of music. Therefore the study of *Lohengrin* will not lead me to change my style although it has been interesting and of negative value.

Verdi's occupation with Wagner's music led to analogous conclusions and to their expression in almost identical words (letter of July 14, 1889).

With a great master the intense absorption of the work of others is as a rule only a transitory stage to the complete unfolding of his own originality. In contrast, there is the composer who consumes, perhaps with equal success, past and contemporary expression. But his style never develops beyond the stage where his mind functions like a prism through which the rays of the already existing music constantly fall in new refractions. The whole problem can also be interpreted in terms of genius and talent. Genius creates anew. Talent absorbs with great skill. In terms of the eighteenth century, Hasse, Graun, Jommelli and Telemann were composers of striking talent. Worshiped by their contemporaries, they were evaluated even higher than those upon whom posterity bestowed the attribute "genius."

There was the celebrated Georg Philipp Telemann, much more esteemed in his day than his contemporary, J. S. Bach. Telemann was a brilliant craftsman: Even Handel asserted that Telemann could write a motet in eight parts as easily as someone else could write a letter. Moreover he worked with comparable facility in every other branch of composition, but never deviated from the tracks of his predecessors. His extraordinary talent was manifest in craft, in the power of absorption. But simultaneously this advantage led to artistic doom—from the point of view of posterity. If the judgment of posterity on Telemann differs from the adoration of his contemporaries to the extent of reversing their appraisal, it is because his technical excellence has lost much of its significance today, and his accomplishments appear somehow dated. Yet the depth and character of the music of Bach is still new today. It is timeless, like all works of genius.

The greatest original genius of the nineteenth century, Beethoven, was no exception to the inevitable process of style absorption through which all masters must pass. This process of assimilating past and contemporary expression can be readily demonstrated in any phase of Beethoven's technique. But nowhere is it more strikingly in evidence than in the evolution of the fugal style of Beethoven and his growth from apprenticeship with Haydn and Albrechtsberger to independent mastery.

With the exception of a small organ fugue in D major, no score in Beethoven's total production materialized as an independent fugal composition. The rich fugal work, which his creations display, consists either of completed fugues (which are only part of cyclical work such as sonatas, symphonies) or of fugues built into the otherwise harmonic frameworks of individual movements. This is in principle the status of the fugue in the various works of Haydn and Mozart.

With the baroque masters, the fugue is a purpose in itself. With the Viennese masters, the fugue functions differently: it appears as the strongest carrier of polyphony within complex compositions. Haydn and Mozart adjusted essential features of their technique to the new functions of their fugues. Their fugal themes show a tendency to symmetric periodization; they display a distinct disposition into fore and after phrases. The baroque masters, on the other hand, recognized in such periodization of the fugal theme a handicap for later developments. And consequently they usually avoided the periodic building of their fugal themes. The "Cum Sancto Spiritu" in Mozart's third (C major) and in Beethoven's first Mass (also in C major) shows an obvious similarity in the building of the themes. (Cf. Example 1.)

The new application of the fugue in the service of the sonata scheme on the part of the Viennese masters led also to an intrinsic change of the fugal groundplan. In contrast to the baroque fugue, the modulating middle sections of the Vienna fugue grew at the expense of the main exposition. With this increase in size, the middle section assumed added contrapuntal importance. The introductory exposition is usually exhausted with the round of the theme through all parts.[10]

Mozart

cum san‧cto   spi ‑ ri ‧ tu

Beethoven

EXAMPLE 1

By contrast, the baroque fugue allows more room for the opening section in the main key and likewise for the final section prior to the last cadence. A tie-up of two expositions in the tonic is nothing unusual. Thus Bach's Fugues in F Major and F Minor (Well-Tempered Clavier, Vol. 1), broadly enunciate on the main key in their exposition and counterexposition before the modulating development section starts. Furthermore, the primarily contrapuntal features in the baroque fugue considerably outweigh all other factors.

The Vienna masters reversed this situation: the harmonic aspect of the fugal form takes on great importance. Again, the works of Haydn and Mozart mark a clear transition to those of Beethoven, who co-ordinates the role of modulations with that of counterpoint. This fact emerges already from a mere quantitative comparison of the different sections in Beethoven's fugues. We have only to think of the giant fugues in his last scores in which the total circle of the fifth is repeatedly traversed. Such a technique is antithetical to that of Bach who, as exemplified in works such as the C Major Fugue (Well-Tempered Clavier, Vol. I), made the most extensive use of contrapuntal combinations with a minimum of modulations.

In place of a strict reality of part-writing in the baroque fugue and the resulting independence of voices, there appeared in classical polyphony a new manner of counterpoint: the melodic lead shifts constantly from one voice to another. The other parts accompany the thematic voice. The melody is made more prominent. Yet the accompaniment is *obligato*;[11] it always participates keenly in the contrapuntal development. The reason for the transfer of this device into the frame of the fugue is its integration into the sonata form. As a result, the style of the fugal section is assimilated to the lesser polyphonic parts of the sonata movement. All this Beethoven learned from Haydn and Mozart. In terms of the fugue, this was his classical heritage.

In later years, Beethoven turned to an intense inquiry into baroque polyphony. One of his notebooks contains numerous examples taken from Bach's Art of the Fugue which Beethoven had obviously copied for the purpose of intense study. Czerny relates his master's profound acquaintance with the Well-Tempered Clavier and Beethoven's repeated playing of the preludes and fugues. According to Beethoven's own statement, the fugal style of Handel inspired the conception of the Overture in C, Op. 124.

Beethoven's last fugues show—in their plans as well as in technical details—the powerful influence of Bach and Handel. Certain features in Op. 106 and Op. 133 point to Bach's great organ fugues. The thematic unity in the fugue of the Hammerklavier Sonata, Op. 106, does not result from the predominance of one single subject. It rather stems from the manner in which all contrapuntal substance is derived from the main theme itself, upon which also the episodes are based. Such a technique is suggested by Bach's E Major Fugue (Well-Tempered Clavier, Vol. II). Again, the climax and complications of Beethoven's triple fugue in Op. 106 are reminiscent of the polyphonic technique in Bach's C-sharp Minor Fugue (Well-Tempered Clavier, Vol. I). The blueprint of the triple fugue is not derived from an exposition of three subjects of equal importance; instead it stems from a combination of three subjects which serve as counterpoints of the main theme.[12]

Another baroque feature in Beethoven's fugal style is the frequent aggregation of expositions which gives Beethoven's Grand Fugue, Op. 133, the impression of truly baroque dimensions. There is a similarity between the somewhat rondolike groundplan of Bach's C-sharp Major Fugue with its six interludes (Well-Tempered Clavier, Vol. I) and those of Beethoven's fugues in Op. 106 and Op. 133.

Of striking significance is the difference between Beethoven's adherence to strict fundamental rules in his last fugues and his free treatment of fugal counterpoint in his earlier works. Obviously, this purification of style is another important result of Beethoven's intense occupation with baroque music. Approximately one hundred violations of strict counterpoint occur in the scores of the young Beethoven. By contrast, transgressions of rigid fundamental rules are a rarity in scores where Beethoven was engaged in the most intricate polyphonic problems. This, too, throws light on Beethoven's artistic personality: at the very time that he wrote his most complex scores, he also achieved his purest style.

A survey of Beethoven's scores containing fugal works shows about twenty-five instances of fugues (fugatos) throughout his different style periods.[13] It is in his last period that strict fugal work occurs most frequently. It is found in the following scores: Op. 101, 102, 106 (twice), 110, 120 (twice), 123 (three times), 125, 131, 133, 136, 137. It was during the composition of these works that Beethoven was creatively inspired by Bach's linear counterpoint as well as by Handel's polyphony, which placed such great emphasis on the predominance of the melodic elements.

The result of Beethoven's occupation with the masterworks of Bach and Handel led, however, to something new. This newness was derived from Beethoven's blend of the fugal techniques of the Vienna and baroque masters. His own polyphonic technique grew, then, through constant absorption: from higher and different levels of craft new contrapuntal features were conquered and new wisdom was reached.

Beethoven acquired full independence only after divesting himself of all borrowed raiment. If we compare the style of these youthful years with that of the last Beethoven, it seems as though there never has been an inner development like this in music. What a conquest of techniques! Yet the technical development is unthinkable without its spiritual corollary. Its inner cause is hidden in the grandiose development of his creative personality—of Beethoven the man, his character and his noble creative goals. At the time of his first visit to Vienna in 1787, young Beethoven suffered the first great shock of his life. The death of his mother in July of that year terminated his initial studies in the Austrian capital. At twenty-eight he was forced to become a philosopher to bear his life.[14] In everything he wrote appeared an element of that early acquired philosophy, of sublimation, of suffering and of a humor which is but the counterpart of a tragic soul. The tragic experience of oncoming deafness and his distress over it had turned into the source of greatest introspection.

To prove the existence of parallels between life and art was a favorite task of Schumann's. He frequently gave himself as an example to show the tie-up between life's experiences and its artistic counterpart. "You will easily discover what is immature and incomplete," he explains to a friend in reference to his own music. "These are the mirror-pictures of my wildly moving earlier life. For it is the human being as well as the musician who sought herein simultaneous expression." In the works of every artist, such contrasts of youth and maturity are apparent.

Again, what a remarkable development in Wagner's lifework from youth to age, from the amorality of the *Liebesverbot* and the untamed sensuality of the first version of *Tannhäuser* (first performed in Dresden, 1845), to the renunciation of life and love in *Tristan*, and to the final religious asceticism in *Parsifal*. Engrossed in work on his second *Tannhäuser* (first performed in Paris, 1860), Wagner recognizes the long way he has gone in more than fifteen years. His attitude to the same problem which he had already approached as a younger man must now undergo a profound change. He writes, in a letter of September 30, 1860:

Already I have been working a bit at the music of my new scene. Remarkable: all the inward impassionate, what I might term feminine-ecstatic I could do absolutely nothing with at the time I wrote the original *Tannhäuser*; there I had been compelled to throw down everything and build anew, in fact, I am horrified at my earlier props-Venus![15]

The rebuilding occurs with new musical material. There is a new instrumentation affecting particularly the trumpets, horns and a new treatment of the strings. With the altered score of the Paris Bacchanale, a new land of chords is entered. The ninth chord and that of the major seventh anticipate the harmonious sphere of the *Nibelungen*. Numerous other musical corollaries of Wagner's artistic growth tell of his changed outlook in craft and aesthetics.

The "inward impassionate" and "feminine-ecstatic" of the second *Tannhäuser* yields to the religious ecstasy of Wagner's last confession in the "Bühnenweihfestpiel," *Parsifal*. We see, then, in his lifework[16] from *Liebesverbot* to *Parsifal*, the mirror picture of a man's evolution from his third to his seventh decade. It has been argued that the spirituality of his opus ultimum, *Parsifal*, was the mere result of old age and that it lacked the true sublimation which emerged from the works of the old Bach, Haydn or Verdi. Even if the charge were correct, the creation of *Parsifal* still shows how art runs parallel with life. This observation of course, is not only true of the musician. A deeper understanding of the genesis of any art work is possible only through its projection against the life curve of its maker. Tolstoi's personal and creative life shows a curve from uninhibited youthful indulgence in the pleasures of the flesh to the asceticism of his late novel, *The Kreutzer Sonata*. Youth sins. Maturity reflects, while old age thinks in terms of life eternal.

Between such creative beginnings and ends, there is a perpetual striving for a permanent ideal. In Wagner's lifework, one single motif unites all his creative substance—the ideal of redemption. In his earlier creative period, this motif is interpreted as self-sacrifice on the part of a loving woman. In later works, redemption is fulfilled through mercy, through the moral strength of kindness. Wagner's life struggle with his dramatic and musical substance, his striving to blend philosophy, art and religion all dissolved in this human leitmotif: atonement and longing for liberation and for salvation.

Such constancy in the pursuit of a creative mission and substance also explains why the artist's approach may defy external order and logical procedure. Wagner relates that when preparing the script for the third act of *Tristan*, he had the sudden vision of a youth who, with a spear in his hand, stepped toward the sickbed of the dying Tristan. This knight, clad in armor, was Parsifal. What had this flash of the religious hero of Wagner's last work to do with Tristan? We know, today, from the finished scores, that there is no connection between the *Tristan* and *Parsifal* dramas, not even in a faint tie-up as it exists in *Lohengrin* (who mentions Parsifal as his father) or in *Meistersinger* where Hans Sachs refers to the sad story of Tristan and Isolde.

But the sick Tristan and the suffering Amfortas are both longing for relief from pain. They both are hopelessly wounded, doomed to die. Tristan, in Wagner's vision, is approached by the youth Parsifal, elected to bring Amfortas that relief which could stem only from touching his wound with the holy spear. In this interplay of conscious work with involuntary subconscious interruption through a vision (seemingly extraneous to the immediate goal), we realize an inner continuity of the creative stream. Yet the connection of the *Parsifal* vision during the genesis of *Tristan* lies in the subconscious continuity of the artist's lifework which is unbroken: in such perpetual striving, work does not end with one score and start with the next. Creation is a continuous stream from opus primum to opus ultimum. Its current can promote more substance than the composer utilizes at the particular time. Nothing that the subconscious brings to light is worthless, even if the purpose cannot be recognized at the moment. Parsifal's appearance during Wagner's occupation with *Tristan* proved to be important substance for a later creative enterprise.

It is the inner continuity of pursuit in the life curve which explains how it is possible for a composer to work simultaneously on different scores, perhaps of even conflicting character. His imagination can shift back and forth from past and present to future projects without any danger of confusion. In the multiplicity of endeavors, the life curve continues to function as the basic rail, leading to goals that are inwardly related—no matter how varied their outer appearance may become. In this sense, all isolated works are but the individual manifestations of the same creative search.

Beethoven's notebooks frequently show new thoughts occurring in an environment of sketches with which they have no external connection whatsoever. On June 29, 1800, Beethoven writes to Wegeler: "I live only in my notes, no sooner is one here than the next one is already started. The way I am working now, I frequently do three or four things simultaneously."[17] Instances of such simultaneous work on different scores are the string quartets, Op. 59, 130, 131 and 133. And even when working on one single score, Beethoven did not necessarily take up the composition in its finished order. The first sketches for the Sonata Pathétique, Op. 13, occur during work on the finale of the Trio in G major, Op. 9, No. 1, and on the scherzo of the Trio in C minor, Op. 9, No. 3. Sketches for the Sonata, Op. 14, No. 1, occur at several places: for instance on the last pages of a leaf which already contained music for the second and third movements of the Piano Concerto in B-flat. Working on the Seventh Symphony, Beethoven sketched the scherzo movement while also writing the two preceding movements. Preparing the Ninth Symphony, Beethoven tackled the second and third movements simultaneously. In fact, the genesis of the Ninth Symphony shows a yearlong—no, a lifelong pursuit of that tonal vision of a choral scene with orchestra which haunted the master since his youth and remained unsolved until the last years of his searching life. In consequence of such a method of work, where different tasks are started at the same time, the sketches overlap each other. But Beethoven's mind, equipped with the uncanny memory that is one of the marks of genius, was well able to cope with such seeming irregularities of notation.

From 1815 to 1826, for eleven years, Schubert sought a satisfactory musical expression of Goethe's poem, "Nur wer die Sehnsucht kennt." In no less than six versions, he had tackled the problem until he arrived at the version (A) quoted in our example.

An extremely interesting aspect of Schubert's long and intensive pursuit of this one small song is the tieup it has melodically with another song based on the poem, "In's stille Land," by Salis (B) quoted in our example:

EXAMPLE 2

This song was written ten years earlier; yet the comparison of both melodies shows a high degree of similarity in their shape and latent harmonies. Obviously, Schubert never rid himself of a favorite idea which seemed to fit different compositions. An inner bond linked the two songs, ten years apart in origin and based on different texts.

Glimpses into the workshops of other composers likewise show a persistence of musical substance which leads the composer to new and different results. A notebook of Brahms with drafts for the Love Song Waltzes as well as the Alto Rhapsody suddenly brings, between sketches on these neighboring works, Op. 52 and Op. 53, a rather lengthy draft of the Tragic Overture which was completed along with the Academic Festival Overture in 1880-81.[18] The idea of the Tragic Overture was revived at this time because of the composer's desire to write a companion piece for the Academic Festival Overture.

It is usually in the subconscious that the tie-up of ideas lies. Later in the totality of the conscious production, all thoughts line up with amazing order. From the watchtower of lifelong experiences, composers look back at the endeavors of their youth and see their early strivings anew in the dimmer light of life's oncoming evening. As they re-think former thoughts, they also relive creatively former experiences. This may culminate in practical reoccupation with scores of earlier years. Thus Beethoven, Berlioz, Bruckner, Brahms, Wagner and Mahler rewrote some of their youthful works as they grew older. The enlightenment of maturity falls on the product of their youth. Brahms, at the end of his life, completely revised the Trio for Violin, Cello and Piano, Op. 8. No less than thirty-three years lie between the two versions of this chamber music work. Different guideposts direct the approach of the young and mature composer. Youth is romantic. Age is classic.

CHAPTER TWO

THE ARTIST IN HIS ART WORK

> This is not a book; who touches it,
> touches a human being.
>
> WALT WHITMAN

PERSONALITY AND MUSIC

MAN himself emerges as the first and final source of inspiration. All human forces freely flow into the man-made art work. Eros, the overflow of life, love of beings as well as of things are elementary sources: happiness inspires the composer to write, to endow the passing events of ephemeral bliss with lasting music. Yet composers have found strong stimuli for creation not only in the infinite enjoyment which life may provide. Great scores have also been the fruit of tragedy, of sorrow and losses, of loneliness and lack of appreciation.

The shift from a man's experiences and personality to its integration into the art work is one of the most fascinating spectacles in creation. Obviously it is not a problem that can be reduced to the precision of a mathematical equation. But we may certainly accept those leads which the artists themselves have given us when they showed how dominant traits in their disposition as well as their inner experiences became part and parcel of their artistic impulse.

"Art is intimately connected with life," Wagner asserts and he maps out the route by which the traits of his personality traveled to reach the points of contact and transformation into the art work.

"Extreme moods in strong conflict with each other" are in Wagner's words the underlying force of his own character and subsequently of his work. "The extreme and great moods of life are brought to an understanding in my dramas. This understanding can be accomplished only through the decided and forceful motivation of transitions—upon which my whole art work is based."[1]

In Wagner's own opinion, then, the essence of his musical form stemmed from his character. Wagner, the man, detested the abrupt and the sudden. And so the artist applied in his scores every means of expression to achieve the desired shadings of transition. It was this act of gradual and most subtle change that Wagner claimed as the finest and deepest feature in his compositions. And he singled out the second act of *Tristan* as his masterpiece in this technique: the opening scene displays the overflow of life in its most violent emotion. With this erotic exuberance as a starting point, there is developed a constant decrescendo until the other extreme of the curve is reached in the lover's inward desire to die. The intrinsic formal design of the love act displays, then, a transition and most gradual decrescendo of emotion, feelings, states of soul. Only the very end of it bears the bloody accent of the fatal stab aimed at the hero's heart.

The fantastic nature of Hector Berlioz, swinging from the tragic to the delirious and the grotesque, is decisively manifest in his art. "The chief characteristics of my music are passionate expression, inner glow, rhythmic swing and surprising turns," he writes in his memoirs. "By passionate expression, I mean a perseverant tendency . . . to exhaust the most innocent of the sources, even where the contrast of passion is concerned, such as gentle, tender feelings or perfect peace." In these lines we have a passport to Berlioz's personality, a portrayal of the inner man. At the same time, his words give us a clue to the transposition of his character into works like the Symphonie Fantastique which in turn inaugurated the whole concept of modern program music. Berlioz tells of his physician father and of his suffering from

an incurable internal disease which often brought him to death's door. Keeping himself alive by constant and ever-increasing doses of opium, once he was so desperate from pain that he took thirty-two grains at a dose. "I don't mind telling you," he said to me afterwards, "it was not to cure myself that I took it." Instead of killing him, however, so large a dose relieved him instantly of his pain.

Such unhappy experiences with a suffering father would have left their imprint on any sensitive son. In Berlioz, these trials were bound to proclaim themselves creatively. Their connection with the Symphonie Fantastique is obvious: the young artist (of the Symphonie program), longing to die, takes a dose of opium which does not kill him, but puts him into a feverish slumber. Once more, in the dream, his distressing love story unfolds itself and comes to a fantastic conclusion.

The music of Brahms is full of ambivalent expression: bright colors are apt to be dimmed by shadows of somberness, like the heavy gray mists of the North Sea over his native Hamburg, which Brahms forsook for the warm serenity of the Vienna skies. His friends were well aware of this peculiar bent of feelings in the man and his music. Clara Schumann complained: "Sometimes it seems as though he does not want his listener to feel too happy."

Happiness was never unmixed in Brahms' life. At work on a cheerful overture, he cannot help writing a tragic one, too, immediately following, as he confesses in a letter of September 6, 1880: ". . . I had to say 'yes' for January 6 to the people in Breslau[2] and I agreed to write a very gay Academic Festival Overture with 'Gaudeamus' and all sorts of things. Yet I couldn't help, with my melancholy disposition also writing an overture for a tragedy." Thus the Academic Festival and Tragic overtures were written as companion pieces.[3] As to their composer, he appears quite conscious of this mixture in his temperament and can even poke fun at it.

The two devout sons of the Catholic church, César Franck and Anton Bruckner, poured their religious imagination not only into scores of primarily liturgical character: everywhere in their music an expression of religiosity is latent. Both composers came from small provincial towns to worldly capitals—the Belgian Franck to Paris, the Upper-Austrian Bruckner to Vienna. These changes in environment had no influence on their unchangeable personalities, which speak so directly in their music of creed, submission and humility. Franck and Bruckner were both supreme organists. Their orchestra conveys the sound and mode of the organ with its ecclesiastical timbre, registrations, and canonic patterns. Medieval textures and old polyphonic formulas shine through the web of their counterpoints. Frequently there is an afterglow of the liturgical service in their scores. The musical symbols of religion are turned, as it were, into a cantus firmus, into a directive for melos and expression. In spite of this, neither Franck nor Bruckner eschewed the romantic language of their time.

The frequent pauses in Bruckner's symphonies (puzzling to many who seek the motivation of all symphonic happenings in the form-scheme alone) are the recollections of the transubstantiation in the Mass. In these fermatas, however, Bruckner hearkens to the ritual in the church. This points to the musician's pious habits: when the chimes rang out for vespers, Bruckner used to stop teaching, and let his pupils wait while he said his prayers. His Ninth and last symphony bears the dedication, "To the Good Lord," but Bruckner worried whether He would accept it. He did: He took the musician to Him after the completion of the adagio. And the finale went with Bruckner to the infinite.

SUBLIMATION

"Unhappiness alone has created the Winterreise," Schubert confessed at the end of his tragic life. This last of his song cycles was written in a state of immense depression. And in his diary Schubert states, March 27, 1824: "My works owe their existence to my musical intelligence as well as to my suffering. Those (works) which were created through pain alone the world seems to enjoy least."

Sublimated in the art works are the narratives of men. Their spirit and thinking, their happiness and suffering, their heights and depths—and everything that lies between—lives on in the music of the true artist, reflected, recreated and translated into tonal forms of beautiful sensations. Schubert confesses how sadness made him turn to his lyre. In tones, he dreamed himself into a better world where he could forget the one in which he was doomed to live. "Thou gracious Art, how often in hours of sadness, Wherein life's fever'd battle round me press'd, Hast thou my heart—recalled to love and gladness, And borne it high into a world more blest, borne it into a world more blest." Thus in his song, "An die Musik," Schubert speaks for all who in their art have sought refuge from the bleakness of their earthly existence. They did not seek it in vain. They turned the tables through the enchantment of creative work. Art becomes the artist's true reality and life remains but a sad dream. A merciful Muse has shown the artist the way out of his misery: the dark forces of destruction which endanger his psychic existence can be fought through the creative act. A cunning device of nature helps her creatures; it forces tragedy to serve its own victim. Enslaved by his unhappiness, threatened with doom, the artist revolts and sets himself free through work. This act of liberation originates from the inspirational moment itself, when a struggling human being forces all of his strength and energies into paths of productivity. All this is the act of sublimation: in his music the composer honors his experiences recording them beyond the fleeting hour for times to come.

Throughout history, the curtain never falls on the tragedy of human suffering and its sublimation in creative deeds. The composer of the music drama is by inclination and temperament a man with a strong sense for the tragic. His traits and feelings are sometimes further accentuated by experiences which show life itself much more dramatic than the theater can ever be. Unhappiness lay deeply embedded in the heart and mind of Monteverdi. His life was filled with sorrow: the loss of his beloved wife, who left him a widower with two small sons, intensified the tragic trait in his character. And so his creative energy was constantly directed toward the sublimation of his sad experience. The man whose daily life was that of a church composer and conductor at St. Mark's in Venice found his consummate self-expression in the almost unbroken creation of musical tragedies.

A dual drama, the one which he himself experienced and the one which his imagination conjured up, was the world of Giuseppe Verdi. This greatest master of Italian opera two centuries after Monteverdi, lost his wife and two children within a few months— in the midst of writing a comic opera! Verdi's life, from that time forth, became a volcanic outpouring of musical tragedies, of operas in which the force of destiny is felt in its relentless fury, where death reigns and sorrow never ceases. Not until the late evening of his life could the old master amuse himself and the world in tones: smiling throughout an opera carried by the precious wit of Shake-

speare's Falstaff and his merry wives, Verdi bade farewell to the
tragic stage with a laugh at life as a comedy only—"Tutto nel mondo
è burla."

Every time and land sees the pilgrimage of musicians to the altar
of their art: beaten in life, they appear as victors in their work.
Suffering has led them to the utmost intensification of all creative
forces. Loneliness results in fruitful artistic consequences. Beethoven, Tchaikovsky, Berlioz, Smetana, Delius had to learn in
grim lessons indifference to a fate of seemingly unsurmountable
handicaps or personal suffering. Wagner spoke from personal
experience when pointing to suffering as the deepest among the
sources of creation. This is the meaning of his words: "Fortunate
is the genius on whom Fortune never smiled."[4]

Resigned to the mishaps of their earthly life, great masters were
lured out of their misery by their distant creative goal. And fanatic
concentration of all expressive energies emerged victoriously
into lasting works. This is the process of *catharsis* as the antique
thinkers interpreted it. It is the act of purification in which the artist
liberates himself from the grip of his emotions and creates pure
forms of beauty.

TO THE MEMORY

After the loss of a loved one, creativeness frequently asserts
itself in the form of a memorial. The more the artist suffers from a
loss of those whom he loves, the stronger becomes his urge to
regain their souls from death—to meet them again in his creative
works. This urge, in close tie with the liturgical purpose of the
Requiem, is the impulse in the creation of the Mass for the dead.
The Requiem is commemoration as well as consolation. Listening
to the music, human beings may gain added strength to bear the
cruel stroke of fate. Music may console "like a mother comforteth
her child."[5]

Perusing the great memorial music of the past four centuries, we
arrive at an observation of an almost mystical scope. It seems as
though the composer detached himself from life on earth in the
creation of his Requiem; his Mass for the dead turns out to be
his opus ultimum or his last major creative effort. When Vittoria
composed his *Missa pro Defunctis*—the most important Requiem

written in the seventeenth century—for the Empress Maria in 1603, the work proved to be the late creative climax of his life: Vittoria, himself, called it his swan song. Cherubini wrote his great *Requiem* in D in his seventy-seventh year (1836). No major task of his was completed afterward. He composed only two minor chamber music works following the completion of the Requiem.

The genesis of Mozart's unfinished *Requiem* is surrounded by mystery. The score was completed posthumously by his pupil, Franz Xaver Süssmayer. On December 4, 1791, the day before his death, Mozart went over the score for a last time, with a few singers at his sickbed. At the first few bars of the Lacrimosa, Mozart realized that he would not be permitted to finish it. And he gave Süssmayer, who came in the evening, directions for the completion of the score. Thus Mozart's last thoughts were devoted to the work which was to become his own Requiem. About midnight, his head fell to one side in death and he appeared to be asleep . . .

A significant recent instance of a composer writing a Requiem for another, which fate, however, turns into his own, concerns Alban Berg and his Violin Concerto. The composer, retarded in his progress on the work, was shocked by the death of a beautiful young girl who had borne a long illness with angelic patience. The experience so stirred him that he suddenly saw the score anew, conceiving it now as a memorial "dedicated to the memory of an angel." This remained his last score; Alban Berg died a few weeks later.

In all these works there is a foretaste of the composer's own death: he creates, it seems, between his earthly existence and what comes after. Confronted with death, his art becomes the torchbearer of eternity. But all this happens only with the artist who truly experiences the shudder of death. In contrast, there is that type of Requiem composer in whose work we feel only an official sorrow. Throughout musical literature, we find a legion of composers who wrote their Masses as commissions and for special occasions. Their craftsmanship cannot be denied, but they composed without the spark of inner glow, without the dreaded sternness and divine clemency of the truly inspired artist.

The power of inspirational impulse is overwhelmingly felt in the two most important Requiems that the nineteenth century produced,

those of Verdi and Brahms. And it is the genesis of both scores
which bears out our belief in the truly inspirational foundation of
the immortal Mass for the dead.

Shortly after the passing of Rossini in November, 1868, Verdi conceived the unusual idea that the leading Italian musicians should
jointly compose a Requiem honoring the memory of the departed
master. In pursuit of the plan, the different parts of the traditional
Requiem were assigned to various composers outstanding in their
day:

Requiem:	Buzzola	Confutatis:	Boucheron
Dies irae:	Bazzini	Lacrimosa:	Coccia
Tuba mirum:	Pedrotti	Domine Jesu:	Gaspari
Quid sum miser:	Cagnoni	Sanctus:	Platania
Recordare:	Ricci	Agnus Dei:	Petrella
Ingemisco:	Nini	Lux aeterna:	Mabellini
		Libera me:	Verdi

It so happened that the last part, the prayer for delivery from
eternal death, was assigned to Verdi. After its proposed premiere
at the Cathedral of Bologna, the Requiem was not to be performed
until the centenary of Rossini's death and always thereafter at this
same cathedral. While nothing ever came of this joint undertaking,
Verdi's Libera me developed in a way which he himself would
never have suspected.

Alberto Mazzucato, director of the Milan Conservatory, asked
Verdi—three years after the plan for the Rossini Requiem had been
abandoned—whether he would not write all preceding parts which,
with his Libera me, would comprise a complete Requiem. But
Verdi's answer was "No! I have no love for useless things. Requiem
Masses exist in plenty, plenty, plenty! It is·useless to add one more
to their number." Verdi, the inspirational artist, missed the inner
incentive for such a memorial work. Yet on May 22, 1873, Alessandro Manzoni, the poet whom Verdi adored and loved as a friend,
had died. After a visit to his grave, the idea flashed through Verdi's
mind to write the Requiem in Manzoni's honor: "It is a heartfelt
impulse, or rather a necessity," he confided to the Mayor of Milan
(June 3, 1873), "which prompts me to do honor as best I can to
that Great One whom I so much admired as a writer and venerated

as a man." Fate pushed aside all inhibitions which Verdi harbored against composing a Requiem. The spark was lit for the creation of one of the most beautiful works in devotional literature. Out of the germ of the finale to the Requiem dedicated to Rossini, grew the score honoring Manzoni's memory, which we know today as Verdi's *Requiem*.

The thought of a Requiem was ever latent in Brahms since the tragic passing of Schumann, his noble sponsor, who had taken such a deep and affectionate interest in him for two decisive decades. With the death of Brahms' mother in 1865, the vision took on new significance, and the composer interpolated a fifth part into the already finished score. Here he beautifully expressed his deep-seated love for his lost mother.

Six weeks after his closest friend, Clara Schumann, died, Brahms wrote to her daughters, Marie and Eugenie (July 7, 1896):

When you receive a volume of serious songs, please do not misunderstand the gift. These songs pertain also very directly to you. I wrote them in the first week of May. Similar words often occupied my mind. I did not think I had to expect worse news about your mother. But deeply inside of a human being something often speaks and acts, almost not conscious to us, and this something may at times, sound as a poem or as music . . . I beg you to regard these songs as a memorial to your beloved mother.

The trio of lives which surrounded Brahms' existence in the most meaningful way—his mother, Clara and Robert Schumann—turns up in his works in a very tangible way. Brahms also utilized the themes of Schumann's last creative effort—a set of four-hand variations—for the Piano Duet in E-flat, Op. 23, and dedicated it to Schumann's daughter, Julie.

Many composers found forms other than the Requiem to honor the memory of departed ones. When Queen Mary II died at Kensington, December 28, 1694, Purcell wrote the music for the funeral, which is described as one of the most imposing that had ever been accorded to an English monarch.[6] French composers lean toward the form of a musical apotheosis where they bestow high honor upon a revered predecessor. Couperin's L'Apothéose de Lulli is such a memorial to the great founder of the French musical tradition.

Ravel's Le Tombeau de Couperin upholds this same custom centuries later.

Mozart's Maurische Trauer Musik (K. 477) was written in July,
1785, to honor the passing of the two freemasons, Duke George
August von Mecklenburg and Count Franz von Esterházy.[7] This
short composition is without equal in its sublime instrumental expression and in the condensation of its symbolic content. Beethoven's
Elegischer Gesang in E major, Op. 118, was written in 1814 when
the wife of Baron Pasqualati died. A slow and gentle theme evokes
the spirit of the departed. Just as in Mozart's Maurische Trauer
Musik, the instrumentation is one of somber and simple colors.[8]

FROM THE DIARY

There is, then, an interdependence of the creative imagination
with the personal experiences of life as the composer lives them
from day to day; his work points to a specific state of the soul, to
the uniqueness of the moment as a springboard of inspiration. This
at least is true of the romantic composer who integrates wholeheartedly his emotions into his music. Such mutual action between
his inner life and art is repeatedly demonstrated by Schumann.
In reference to his Overture, Scherzo and Finale, Op. 52, composed
in 1841, one year after his marriage, he says: "The whole has a light
and friendly character. I wrote it in a quiet and serene mood."
In contrast, the Fantasy, Op. 17, composed in 1836 during great
difficulties in his courtship of Clara, is associated with sadness:
"You can understand the Fantasy only if you imagine yourself back
in the unhappy summer in which I gave you up. Now I have no
reason to compose so unhappily and with so much melancholy."
Clara, his alter ego, his artistic confidante, is the source of all these
sad and happy states. The Sonata in F-sharp minor, Op. 11, is
called "a single heart cry for Clara whose theme occurs in all
possible features." After the seemingly unsurmountable obstacles to
their union were overcome, their happiness together led to the
lyric outpouring of the year 1840, the year of their marriage which
Schumann himself calls the "year of song."[9]

Schumann's letters and prose writings reduce the inspirational
problem to a plain and direct formula: the whole scale of moods,

all the experiences of life are transferable into music. Anything from buoyancy to depression is directly transposed into the tonal language. "Nothing inspires the imagination more than tension and desire," is the composer's comment referring to the Novelletten. Eliminating all doubts as to the creative tie-up between the man and his music, Schumann warns that "it would be a small art which displays only sounds and does not express the state of the soul."[10]

In Schumann's creative life, such romantic convictions are apparent from youth. At the age of eighteen, in a letter of August 5, 1828, he rejects the intellectual approach to composition, and warns that "the hard paws of the lion of reason must not mangle the soft hands of the lyric tone-muse who plays on the keyboard of our feelings." Feelings and emotions are the keynote of artistic conception. Indicative of this romantic approach are Schumann's prose remarks interjected among his musical sketches. These intimate comments give his notes the appearance of a musical diary, where thoughts are tied down to a precise date and to the hour of a certain day. Thus Schumann interprets a joyous melody: "On November 30, 1836, when blissfully delirious . . . ," or he explains a sad invention: "On April 28, 1838, as no letter came from you." All such diary remarks betray, if not the specifically musical spring of imagination, at least, the mood which led to a definite composition.

Still more light on the inseparable interrelationship of the personal and artistic is shed by Schumann's rejection of the music of those "whose life is not in harmony with their work."[11] As to himself, he confesses that he enjoys best to create "so very much out of family life." Equally revealing is Schumann's letter to his father-in-law, Wieck, commenting on Schubert's creative procedure: "What is for others a diary to which they confess their momentary feelings, became for Schubert unmistakably his note paper to which he entrusted his moods and his innermost musical soul." And Schumann reads the music of Schubert as a chronicle of his inner life. Certain characteristics of Schubert's personal style are explained on the basis of such an approach, particularly that seeming lack of formalistic logic in Schubert's style. His ideas are directed by psychological associations and frequently evade the bars of rigid schemes. Only a few have "like Schubert succeeded in forcing a singular individuality upon his tonal pictures and only a few have written so much for themselves and for their heart."

"Since yesterday morning, I have written about twenty-eight pages of music and I can tell you nothing more than that I laughed and cried over them with delight," writes Schumann in February, 1840, to Clara. His music flows from an exalted, highly emotional state. As he writes, the composer is excited, overcome with feeling, delirious, in tears.

Is such emotional behavior limited to the composer labeled as romantic? We are told that many great masters displayed excitement and tears in the stage of inspiration. Sheffield relates that Handel was often surprised by the valet bringing his chocolate for breakfast when he was weeping over the paper on which he wrote. And Hawkins asserts that Handel "had no sense for what was going on around him. What exultation and streams of tears when he worked! He cried while composing the aria, 'He was reviled.'"

We can assume, however, that the composer's behavior will change from the emotionalism of the inspirational stage to the indispensable calm of work in the synthetic stage. Moreover, the type of creative task is decisive for the composer's behavior at work. Obviously, composing a score of objective character requires a builder's calm rather than emotional excitement. A composer, mathematically calculating his structure for architectural music, will as little work with tears and excitement as an engineer will plan the blueprint of his bridge under emotional stress.

By contrast, the emotional spring as well as the emotional state during hours of work points to romantic creation. While composing, the artist may feel an emotion appropriate to the content of his music. The intensity of feeling which the hearer later experiences corresponds to the emotional intensity which the composer put into his work. Schubert says of his "Ave Maria":

People are also wondering about my religiosity which I have expressed in my "Hymn to the Holy Virgin," which seems to touch all souls and stimulate devotion. I think that this comes about because I never force myself into devotion unless I am overcome by it involuntarily, since I never compose hymns or prayers; but if I do, it is usually the right and true reverence.

The composer holds the sincerity of emotion during the act of composing responsible for this genuine appeal in his "Ave Maria."

Mendelssohn firmly believes in the emphasis on the subjective mood. On January 26, 1842, he writes to a young composer who had asked his advice concerning the correct approach to coi..-position: "Do work it out yourself! Express whatever lives in you by way of moods and sensations, what no other one but you know. Let reason decide external questions. But your heart (must decide) the basic ones—and by the true moods that you feel!"

Yet Mendelssohn admits that perfection in musical form can never be attained as the composer strives for an expression of his moods and feelings. This clear piece of self-criticism amounts to the realization of the proverbial romantic split between form and the subjective content.

From all the foregoing, we learn that the emotional factor functions twofold: the composer not only creates in the state of emotion but he also tries to express emotional content in his music. In important treatises in the second part of the eighteenth century, the explicit relationship between tonal tools and specific emotions is taken for granted. How it happens that the emotions serve as the springboard of musical inspiration we learn from the dissertation, On Musical Poetry by Christian Gottfried Krause, published in 1752. The author observes that

the tone of sadness is weak and trembling, its expression short and slow. In anger the slow alternates with the fast, gasping with trembling. Broken tones express fear. In the state of fright, the blood and the spirits of life recede and are contracted, hence (in the musical corollary) the mouth for a time is speechless and the tone thereafter is broken. Just as a man filled with insecurity is apt to separate his words or syllables, one can similarly express such a state of fear in music. Regret is identified by a sighing, sometimes complaining voice. Shame speaks through vacillating tones, sometimes short and broken, sometimes long and sustained. Despair does not have a definite tone; its speech is disconnected, confused and exaggerated. An enraged being screams, roars and splits exalted words.

The famous *Versuch einer Anweisung die Flöte traversiere zu spielen* by J. J. Quantz, court composer and flute master of Frederick the Great, shows at length how the emotions are tied to definite tonal symbols. The hard key (major) is used for the expression of the gay, fresh, serious or profound. By contrast, the soft key (minor) is used for the expression of the flattering, sad and gentle. As to the employment of intervals, the slurred and closed ones convey the flattering, sad and gentle. The gay and fresh on the other hand is expressed by short notes or by more distant leaps of notes, particularly of such figures where the dots appear behind the second note. Dotted and sustained notes suggest the serious and pathetic. The intermingling of long notes, of half and whole values, between quick notes express the grandiose and profound. The affinity between these prescriptions of Quantz and the observations on musical poetry by C. G. Krause is self-evident. Significantly both works were publicized in the same year of 1752.

We see then how the composer goes about the task of expressing emotional experiences in music. His perception is tied to a certain emotion which, in turn, is associated with a tonal picture. This procedure corresponds with that all-important contemporary theory, the elaborate *Affektenlehre*—The Doctrine of Emotions.[12] No composer of the eighteenth century could fully escape the spell of this all-embracing discipline. In essence, the Doctrine of Emotions expounded that all music expressed human emotion—be it by naturalistic imitation or by a symbolic transformation into tones. First, there are the categories of happy and sad states of the soul which are easily conveyed in tones. But as we have seen, the *Affektenlehre* also aims at the artful representation of more complex emotions.

Of decisive interest is the integration of these doctrines into great works of art. Bach blended human emotions with sacred expression. He applied the contemporary doctrine of affections to the religious realities of his devotional music.[13] Mozart discusses the secular aspect of the problem in the correspondence with his father. A letter of September 26, 1781, shows Wolfgang speculating on certain scenes of his opera, *Abduction from the Seraglio.* How to express emotion and anger in tones is the specific question:

The anger of Osmin is brought into the comic because Turkish music is employed with it. (The passage) "At the Beard of the Prophet" is in the same tempo, yet with quicker notes and since his (Osmin's) anger is constantly growing, the allegro assai must be in altogether different tempo and in a different key, which makes an excellent effect since one believes the aria is already at its end. A man in utmost anger is beyond any control, measure and aim—he does not even know himself. Hence, the music, too, must not know itself. . . . Since the emotions must be expressed violently, yet never ad nauseam, the music too must never offend the ear, even in the most terrible situation. It must at the same time give pleasure, that is to say, it must always remain music . . .

What a perfect condensation of an aesthetic theory! Music must, as Mozart pronounces, remain unconditionally true to its intrinsic laws. No matter what it symbolizes and what emotional extreme it represents, musical beauty must be derived from within. Again, referring to an aria in *Abduction* (the opening scene of Belmonte), Mozart shows how he has characterized the emotional state of anxious love. "It is the heartbeat of love which must be expressed . . . the second violins play in octaves—and one can see trembling, hesitation; the breast heaves and sighs which is expressed through a crescendo; one hears whispers and sighing—which is expressed through the first violins with mutes and a flute in unison." This approach of Mozart to the tone-psychological portrayal of an emotion is obviously closely akin to the Doctrine of Emotions.

HUMOR

Wit and humor are rooted in specific faculties of the human mind. Ever since there has been music, composers have indulged in buffoonery in connection with a comic text, chanson or light opera.

Musicians are also humorous in their abstract play of tones. In certain cantatas, Bach is facetious. Truly humorous music came from the imagination of men such as Haydn, Mozart, Beethoven, Rossini, Verdi, Offenbach, Johann Strauss or Debussy—all blessed with an intrinsic sense of humor, inventors of a wit which found immediate points of contact in the tonal realm. Haydn, with his deeply rooted humor truly conquered musical wit. Sometimes his jokes are only for the connoisseur: for instance, Haydn sets The Ten Commandments into music in the form of canons. But while composing the Seventh Commandment, "Thou shalt not steal," he cannot resist "stealing" the melody of another composer. Usually Haydn's humor is mere whimsical play with sounds, a merriment of counterpoints, the jeu d'esprit of instruments, such as the second movement of the Surprise Symphony.

Already as a child, Mozart longed for fun and pranks. His father describes the jokes he had to tell little Wolfgang every evening at bedtime. In later years, his innate humor was bound to manifest itself creatively. One of his scores written exclusively in a witty spirit, the Musikalischer Spass (K. 522), pokes fun at incompetent colleagues. The Musical Fun is scored for strings and two horns, a divertimento which, true to its title, diverts and entertains. Mozart's parody aims chiefly at those vain musicians who foolishly proclaim themselves to be composers. Probably Mozart's targets were the actual shortcomings of certain composers of his time. But as in a work of fiction, in which the characters seem to be portrayals of people in real life (who are, however, not identified), so the composer permits the victims of his wit to remain incognito.

The whole score is a lesson in composition negatively stated, namely, how not to do it. The opening movement exposes the typical pitfalls of the would-be composer. He cannot organize; his plans are hopelessly muddled. Hence, all we hear is a statement of themes, but no development, no convincing connection between first and second subject. This the composer cannot do, since he completely lacks technique and is ignorant of modulation. One clearly sees what he wants to do, but he just cannot do it at all. The poor composer has learned some rules, and knows, for instance, that the second theme should appear in C major, the key of the dominant. Audaciously he jumps into the adventure of that modulation, using B-natural in the key of F. But alas, two measures later, back to F major he goes and finally falls into C major, like the bull into the china shop!

The wittiest attack is made on those musicians who try to replace true inspiration by dry skill. Thus, the finale becomes a parody on dull academicians. Suddenly in the midst of the rondo, a fugato appears.

The bass introduces the theme, which helplessly breaks in the fourth measure. The viola brings a "real" answer but the counter-

EXAMPLE 3A

point does not move away from the fifth. The next entrance of the theme occurs without any link, while the two lower voices simply pause in embarrassment. At the entrance of the first violin, the three other voices, instead of participating in the polyphonic play, just keep still.

We see that the would-be composer wants to appear scholarly, a learned contrapuntalist. The outcome is only dry, boring—empty phrases. How paperlike is the fugal theme; still poorer are the counterpoints. It all smells of hard but futile work at the desk. After a few measures, the thread does not hold. The presto concludes with a joke which sounds as nonsensical in performance as it looks on staves.

EXAMPLE 3B

The title given to the work after Mozart's death, the Dorfmusi-
kanten or the Peasant Symphony does not evaluate its finer points.
The famous false tones of the horns and fiddlers are almost incidental to the "technical" humor of the tone play.

Beethoven's humor was for a long time not sufficiently recognized: thus Nietzsche spoke of his "seriousness of a bear." Reading
Beethoven's letters, we gain insight into his brand of wit and
discover how much he enjoyed the opportunity to joke. Musical
corollaries are found, just as in the case of Haydn and Mozart,
throughout Beethoven's entire lifework. Although the tragic experiences of his later years turned him into an introvert, his humor
comes to the fore creatively even in his last works, such as the
String Quartet, Op. 135.

The main stage for Beethoven's comic tone play, however, is the
form which he invented: the scherzo, although his wit found
countless other outlets—even in movements of slower character.
In the scherzo of the Pastoral, there occur the famous syncopations
in which Beethoven pokes fun at the village musikants. The oboist
commits an error in counting, and starts to blow his solo too early.
As a result the whole dance tune is out of line. Because of the
wrong syncopations, melody and accompaniment are never together;
everybody seems to come too late for his cue and the musicians of
the village do not seem to be able to find each other again.

THE SUBCONSCIOUS AND DREAMS

The true consciousness is the knowledge of our unconscious.
Wagner recognized the importance of the unconscious mental
processes half a century before Sigmund Freud's psychoanalytical
penetration into the hidden recesses of the mind. Moreover, the
reference does not occur as an isolated thought in the writings of
Wagner. His sporadic correspondence with Eduard Hanslick shows
amazing insight into the blend between the subconscious and conscious creative powers.[14]

On October 5, 1858, Wagner wrote to Mathilde Wesendonck:

My fantasy makes me always again a poet, an artist. In the moment in
which I capture it, a picture stands before me of the most vivid soulful
clearness—a picture that enchants me. I have to view it always closer

and closer, still more intensely to see it, firmer and deeper to execute it and finally to enliven it as a creation of my own.

In these lines, Wagner describes how the imagination takes possession of an idea and employs it for the creative purpose. A specific technique, however, is required to grasp the tone pictures which are derived from the subconscious.

How particularly the dream enters into the creative realm is illustratively told in Wagner's autobiography. The Prelude for his *Rheingold* was conceived in the drowsiness of somnolence. Wagner, as always in pursuit of a congenial environment suited to new creations, took a boat to Spezia in search of absolute calm. But the overnight trip turned into a nightmarish experience—he was attacked by seasickness. Utterly exhausted, Wagner arrived in the Mediterranean port scarcely able to drag himself another step. He made for the best hotel, discovering to his horror that it was located in a noisy narrow street:

After a night spent in fever and sleeplessness, I forced myself to take a long tramp the next day through the hilly country, which was covered with pine woods. It all looked dreary and desolate, and I could not think what I should do there. Returning in the afternoon, I stretched myself, dead-tired, on a hard couch, awaiting the long-desired hour of sleep. It did not come; but I fell into a kind of somnolent state, in which I suddenly felt as though I were sinking in swiftly flowing water. The rushing sound formed itself in my brain into a musical sound, the chord of E-flat major, which continually reechoed in broken forms; these broken chords seemed to be melodic passages of increasing motion, yet the pure triad of E-flat major never changed, but seemed by its continuance to impart infinite significance to the element in which I was sinking. I awoke in sudden terror from my doze, feeling as though the waves were rushing high above my head. I at once recognized that the orchestral overture to *Das Rheingold*, which must have long lain latent within me, though it had been unable to find definite form, had at last been revealed to me. I then quickly realized my own nature; the stream of life was not to flow to me from without, but from within. I decided to return to Zurich immediately, and begin the composition of my great poem. I telegraphed to my wife to let her know my decision, and to have my study in readiness.

Thus it happened that this dream, like so many of Wagner's life experiences, was integrated into his *Nibelungen* music. Elsewhere dreams function on the Wagnerian stage as dramatic content, such as Elsa's tale in *Lohengrin*, Act I. The scene between Walther and Hans Sachs in the third act of *Meistersinger* revolves around a dream: during his sleep, a tune has occurred to Walther. It is the Preislied in its embryonic stage. The kind poet and shoemaker, Hans Sachs, aids his young friend to shape this tonal vision into the song which in the final scene of the opera gains the bride.

Berlioz describes in his memoirs how, awakening from a deep slumber, he is unable to recall a valuable invention that came to him during a dream. Unhappy about this failure, his instinct tells him: "Go for a walk." He does so and the rhythm of his step accidentally coincides with the rhythm of the forgotten musical idea and thus brings it back to his memory. "Great Lord," he cries, "this time I am not going to lose it," and he wildly searches for a notebook in his pockets. Unable to find one, he runs home, brushing past people on the street who curse him, a wild-looking man who had obviously gone mad! Arriving home, he rushes to his room, grabs a piece of paper, writes down the fugitive thought in the greatest haste. Exhausted, but happy, he sinks into a chair. At last the musical dream is his.

Tartini relates the origin of his Violin Sonata in C Minor (1713) in the following manner:[15] he dreamed that he had sold his soul to the devil. Wondering whether the evil spirit was a good musician, the composer handed him his fiddle, upon which the devil played a piece surprisingly well. Awakening breathlessly, Tartini tried in feverish haste to hold onto the enchanting music he had just dreamed. Though he could not fully reproduce the music as he heard it, the inspiration was still strong enough to lead him on to the composition of the Sonata Trillo del Diavolo, which Tartini considered the best piece he ever wrote. Among other composers who tell of the tie-up between their musical invention and their dream life are Chopin, Bruckner and César Franck. Czerny's description of Beethoven's work during hours of interrupted sleep suggests a similar link.

Dreams, then, are fertile soil for the growth of new music, provided that the composer can reproduce the musical images which have passed through his mind during sleep. The free forces of the subconscious continue to bring forth valuable raw material. This fact includes dreams among the important sources of tonal inspiration.

PERSONAL RELATIONSHIPS

What could be more human than the reflection of the composer's personal ties in his creative work? The pen overflows with that which fills the heart. It overflows not only in the writing of notes, but frequently in words telling the great part which the artist's loves and friendships have played as inspirational source in the creation of his music.

How much initial stimulation has been drawn from the intimate spheres of a composer's life can only be understated. Most references surrounding the emotional spring of great music is familiar material: there is no need to add a word to the biographies that treat such historic instances as Beethoven and his immortal beloved, Wagner and Mathilde Wesendonck or Tchaikovsky and the sublimation of his friendships. Certain writers have concentrated on this particular phase in the composer's life and have stressed the personal aspect at the expense of the purely musical one. Yet the fact remains that personal relationships create all-important psychological premises for work and progress. Mozart's voluminous letters bear witness to the heart-warming directness and uninhibited naturalness of his affections and friendships, all of which are expressed with the most delightful frankness. At twenty-one, he wrote the *Abduction from the Seraglio* in the glow of his love for Constanze. The abducted bride in the opera bears the name of his betrothed. And he refers to his marriage as the abduction from the "Auge Gottes"—from the house in which the bride was given away.

The D Minor Quartet (K.421), Geburtswehen-Quartet, originated when Constanze lay in labor pains, and Mozart would interrupt his writing as often as he was needed to help in the sickroom and then always return to his table to continue this melancholy, beautiful and anxiously tense score. But this is a story[16] typical of the pitfalls of a sentimentalizing interpretation of the creative process. From all we know (and will show in later chapters) of Mozart's working procedure, the plan of the quartet must have been firmly established in his mind before the writing of the score during Constanze's confinement. The sad undertone is not necessarily the sole consequence of the trying circumstances under which Mozart brought the music to paper. On the other hand, we have no right to reject entirely the possibility of a quasi-extemporaneous tie-up of mood and expression.

Mozart's dependency on Constanze for his equilibrium during working hours is beyond doubt. Her well-being is required for calm at work. So he confesses to Michael Puchberg in a letter of July 12, 1789: "Now that my dear wifey is doing better from day to day, I will be able to work again—for last night she slept so well—and so I, too, will start to be disposed toward my work." And to Constanze, who had left for Baden to take the cure, he writes (July 7, 1791): ". . . Even my work gives me no pleasure, because I am accustomed to stop working now and then and to exchange a few words with you. Alas! this pleasure is no longer possible." In 1782, Constanze reproaches her husband for neglecting the writing of fugues, which she considered one of the most beautiful forms in music. She insists that he should devote more effort to it. On April 20, 1782, Mozart acknowledges the origin of a new score (Three Part Fugue, K.394): "The reason why this fugue came into the world is only my dear Constanze."

Taking these statements at their face value, they tell the simple story of Mozart's emotional reliance on his wife in certain aspects of his work. Its flow is stimulated by her presence. Her absence or illness discourages and blocks progress. Herein, genius is not different from the ordinary mortal. And it is exactly in these simple traits that Mozart appears so lovably human.

As it could not be otherwise, the tie between the artist and his parents often plays a varied and complex role in his productivity. This bond may even prove to have greater significance than the matrimonial relationship. We speak elsewhere of the deep-seated import of the parental bond in the creative life of the composer.

Where friends hold a dominant place in the artist's heart, they easily assume an inspirational role: dedications on many scores point to the personalities responsible for the origin of the music. The Variations on an Original Theme (Enigma Variations), Op. 36, by Elgar bears the dedication, "To my friends pictured within." Thus, the music is a portrayal of the composer's companions. The main theme is interchangeably viewed through the eyes of their different personalities. Even the inspirational impulse may stem from the names of friends or from places that have a significance in their lives. Particularly Schumann enjoyed musical games with motifs based on such meaningful letters and names. Already his Op. 1, Variations on the name of Abegg, is a musical play on the name of a friend's fiancée. Op. 5 is the Impromptu on a Romance by Clara Wieck.[17] In Carnival, Op. 9, the letters of the name Asch—the native town of his friend Ernestine—lend themselves to the four "lettres dansantes" in the waltz rhythm of the "scenes mignonnes." The meaning of Schumann's mystifications emerges from the coincidence of letters in the German alphabet with certain musical notes:

German	English
B	B-flat
H	B
S	E-flat

Hence, the name of Asch suggests the motif A E♭ C B:

EXAMPLE 4

Yet such thematic stimulation derived from names of friends and admired persons is by no means known only to the romantic composer. Already the music of the Middle Ages shows the trend. The great Netherland master of the late fifteenth century, Josquin Deprès, was inspired in the thematic conception of one of his Masses by the vowels contained in the name of Hercules, dux Ferrarae. From Heinrich Isaac's theme, La-mi-la-sol and the numerous tone plays on the name B-A-C-H up to the nineteenth century mystifications of Schumann and countless other composers, we find inventions running the whole gamut from deeply mysterious symbolism to mere tonal playfulness.

THE ROLE OF THE ACCIDENT

Inspiration is willful, sporadic, unpredictable. It is freakish, beyond the control of the composer who may seek the most conducive environmental conditions in his attempt to induce the flow of his fantasy with every means at his disposal. He may surround himself with things he loves, and avoid whatever distracts him from work. He may travel or throw himself into adventures and passions. Yet no matter how forceful the attempt, inspiration retains the role of a mistress who cannot be called upon by sheer will. The composer appears rather as her servant obeying her summons whenever and wherever they occur. Memoirs and letters tell us of many capricious and seemingly queer cases in which the composer is the helpless victim of a whim, completely under the spell of inspiration, sacrificing his comfort, rest, meals, sleep and, along with all this, his health.

Beethoven had summed up his inspirational plight with the following answer to a friend: "From where do I take my ideas? . . . They come uncalled, directly and indirectly." This picture of obedience to the unpredictability of inspiration is rounded out by two of Beethoven's close associates. Thus Schindler refers to the moments of sudden enthusiasm which so often overcame his master in serene company. On the street, he would arouse the curiosity of passers-by. What went on in him was stamped on his lightened-up eyes as well as all over his face. Czerny asserts that his master would often get up in the middle of the night, awakening and frightening his neighbors by pounding on the piano, by stamping his feet and screaming. One might feel sorry for the neighbors, but inspiration had no consideration for them, had no time to wait. The sparks did not ignite the Eroica or *Fidelio* according to the domestic routine and regular sleeping hours of Viennese burghers, but on the obscure and unpredictable timetable of a mysterious force.

VERDI'S NABUCCO

Inspiration comes as an unforeseen event. Its cause is unknown. It is accidental. And composers recognize the role of the accident as a factor of inspiration. They know and readily admit the part accidents play in the lucky findings of their musical ideas.

No false pride, no desire to appear as a superhuman inventor could induce the scrupulous Verdi to give a glorified report of his tonal discoveries. Describing in his autobiographical sketch the genesis of his important youthful opera, *Nabucco,* the composer underlined the role of the accident: Verdi met Merelli, the manager of La Scala in Milan. He urged the composer to consider a libretto written by Solera. But Verdi was not set for work; for about a year, he had been a desperate man who had lost his wife and children. His Muse was silent. Yet Merelli forced the manuscript into his hands, and Verdi went on his way with it:

As I was walking back, I was seized with a sort of vague anxiety, a profound sadness, an anguish that gripped my heart! . . . Back home, I threw the manuscript on the table with an almost violent gesture, and remained standing before it. In falling, it had opened of itself; without my realizing it, my eyes clung to the open page and the one special line: "Va, pensiero, sull' ali dorate."

These were fateful words: "Fly, oh thought, on golden wings." And they shaped themselves, in the composer's mind, into the melody of the great nostalgic chorus of the Jews. None of all his powerful inventions proved to be more fateful for Verdi. It was this chorus in *Nabucco* which laid the foundation of his lasting fame. It was also this chorus that was spontaneously sung by the crowd at Verdi's funeral . . .

EXAMPLE 5

We learn from Verdi's tale that inspiration may come at the most unexpected time—when the composer is least prepared for it. Yet what seems to happen without cause has been prepared by that force which governs our lives—the force of destiny.

THE FLYING DUTCHMAN

Life has many ways of setting the stage for the play of the artist's fantasy. He might experience a tumultuous, nerve-shattering event in which his inner and outer existence hangs in the balance. Certain pages in the exciting chapters of Richard Wagner's auto-biography *My Life* show how at such times clearly defined shapes and forms emerge from dark strata of the subconscious into the firm grip of an organizing artistic will. Rarely has a great artist offered such insight into the genesis of his work as Wagner has given us in the unique report of the means by which his romantic opera, *The Flying Dutchman,* came into being.

During his tempestuous flight from Pillau to London, a series of images were conjured up surrounding the old legend of the cursed captain. The turmoil of Wagner's inner and outer struggles and his despair at the time of this escape from the Continent were strangely matched by the tempest encountered on the North Sea during his passage. It happened in the year of 1839. Wagner was forced to escape debtors' prison in Riga, and stole away with his wife Minna, like thieves at night, without passports to the Russian frontier. Crawling on hands and knees over the borderline, in danger of being fired upon in case of discovery by the lurking border guards, they finally reached the harbor of Pillau. Here the captain of the little boat, *Thetis,* England bound, accepted the exhausted fugitives without the obligatory passports. The hunted couple felt great relief when at last the anchor was weighed.

Wagner, daydreaming on deck, is intrigued by the stories of the sailors, a crew of only seven, who were preparing for an approaching storm. In the midst of his own dangerous adventure on the wild waves of the ocean, the old legend of the Flying Dutch-man takes on new meaning for Wagner and occupies more and more of his fantasy. At a Norwegian fjord, the enormous granite walls echo the hail of the crew. And the sharp rhythm of this call shapes itself, in Wagner's mind, into the theme of the Song of the Sailors as we know it from the opera's first act today.

With unheard of violence, the storm finally breaks. Crew and

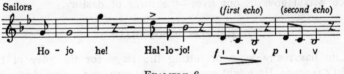

EXAMPLE 6

passengers fight with the elements for their very lives. At the mercy of the sea-monster which appears now as a fathomless abyss, now as a steep mountain peak, the small vessel is hurled up and down with terrible force. The malignant glances of the superstitious crew point to Wagner and Minna as the cause of the disaster. They evidently brought bad luck for the otherwise familiar and rather harmless passage to England.

Yet Wagner himself appeared insulated from the turmoil and confusion around him: inspiration had seized him. It made him see the phantom picture of the Flying Dutchman ship. Engrossed in the dreadful and fantastic ocean scene, the artist identified himself with the Flying Dutchman. He, himself, is the wanderer in the tempest, the unlucky fugitive on the dreadful ocean who looks in vain for love and final peace.

When the storm subsides, Wagner is exhausted from his vision and struggles. Yet a music drama is born; and Wagner knows that the Dutchman has met his redemption at last. Where and when will he find his own liberation? . . .

ROMANCE CONCEIVED UNROMANTICALLY

A more exciting frame for the springboard of a romantic opera than that of *The Flying Dutchman*—where life itself appears immensely more dramatic than any fiction—can hardly be imagined. And we could not have asked for a more explicit interpretation of the tie-up between the inner and outer struggle of a man, of the victorious sublimation of his experiences in creative work than the one which Wagner has provided in his autobiography.

Yet not every creation is born amid the fury of the elements or from an exultant state of the soul. A stirring idea may well be the product of the searching imagination only. It may result in a manner completely independent of external circumstances, of what happens to the artist as a person and of what goes on around him.

In a charming paradox, Berlioz discloses how some of his sweepingly romantic creations originated most unromantically. The Archduke of Weimar, moved by the beauty of the love music of Berlioz's last work, *Béatrice et Bénédict*, inquired about the circumstances surrounding the composition of the love duet, "You are sighing, my

Lady." The Duke took for granted that such music could only have been conceived in the moonlight, in a very romantic landscape. But the composer's answer disillusioned his German host: "Your Highness, those are impressions of nature which every artist has stored within him. At the proper time, it flows out of his soul, regardless of where he may happen to be. As to the duet, I sketched it one day at the Institute when one of my colleagues gave a talk." "Indeed," said the Archduke laughingly, "this speaks for the lecturer. He must have been eloquent."

Berlioz displays the same sense of humor when he recognizes in his memoirs the chance play of inspiration during the writing of a choral cantata. He could not make any headway with its last and most important verse, "Poor Soldier, I am going to see France again." In vain, the composer tried to find an appropriate melody but finally gave up. Two years later (after not giving the matter any further thought) Berlioz went for a walk in Rome on the Possin Promenade along the steep embankment of the Tiber. "The ground gave in," he relates in his memoirs, "and I toppled over into the water. When I fell, I had only one thought—that I might drown. But when I emerged from the water, all of a sudden, the melody, 'Poor Soldier' which I had been hunting for two years, rushed into my mind. 'Alas, you came just in time, better late than not at all.' "

The march in the finale of Weber's opera, *Oberon*, originated most unexpectedly through a curious scene in a Dresden bathhouse, as told by Weber's friend, Roth. Weber had stopped there with his friend for a cup of coffee. Because of heavy rain, tables and chairs were placed on top of each other. Yet the composer's imagination reacted to the jumble of piled up furniture, wet and shiny with rain, in a purely musical way. Weber happened to be occupied with the composition of incidental music for the tragedy of *Henry IV*. When he returned in the evening to the theater, the composer sketched the big march for wind instruments from an idea conceived at the bathhouse. Years later, he integrated the same march into the finale of *Oberon*.

Busy working on his *Freischütz*, Weber sought a characteristic expression for the laughing chorus in the first act, in which people, in a gay and mocking way, poke fun at the unlucky hunter. By sheer accident, he found the solution while visiting a chapel in the small Saxon town of Pillnitz. A number of old women had joined the afternoon service, but their group singing was considerably out of tune. The effect was comic. It sounded as though auxiliaries were placed, in seconds, next to the original notes, causing a dissonance while permitting the melody to be perceived distinctly. This grotesque impression suggested to Weber the splendid choral scene of *Freischütz* Act I.

EXAMPLE 7

Wagner's anger over the blacksmith in front of his house who deafened his ears the whole day with ceaseless hammering gave him the cue for the motif of Siegfried's outburst of rage against the stubborn hammering smith Mime. "Immediately I played it for my sister (Clara)," Wagner relates, in his autobiography, "and sang angry words and everyone had to laugh heartily." What turned the accident into a musical find was the coincidence of the composer's own rage with the anger he was about to compose. Of course, the rhythmical noise also played its part.

Deeply steeped in the dream world of *Tristan*, Wagner returned late at night to his Venetian home on the gloomy Canale Grande. The moon, he relates, appeared suddenly and illuminated the marvelous palaces:

The tall figure of my gondolier towering above the stern of the gondola slowly moved his huge sweep. Suddenly, he uttered a deep wail, not unlike the cry of an animal; the cry gradually gained in strength, and formed itself after a long-drawn "Oh" into the simple musical exclamation "Venezia!" This was followed by other sounds of which I have no distinct recollections as I was so much moved at the time. Such were the impressions that to me appeared the most characteristic of Venice during my stay there, and they remained with me until the completion of the second act of *Tristan*, and possibly even suggested to me the long drawn wail of the shepherd's horn at the beginning of the third act.

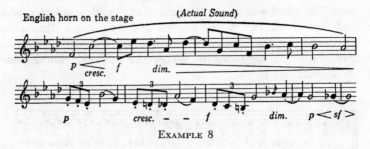

EXAMPLE 8

CHAPTER THREE

THE VOICE OF NATURE

> Sometimes I copy a tree, a bird
> or a cloud.
>
> HAYDN

NATURE, mother source of all living things, has given the musician infinite impulses: her cycles and rhythm, her seasons, the hours of the day from dawn to dusk.

Nature sounds! In the mountains where the wind storms from wide horizons and roars around the rocks. On the surging sea where the sport of waves whirls in tossing rhythm against high cliffs or splashes toward the softness of sandy beaches.

Everywhere the bells of nature's mysterious music ring. In the fall of the raindrops and the mild rustlings of leaves in the autumn. On meadows and fields where grasshoppers dance a scherzo in the warming rays of the midday sun.

The good earth bears all creatures that sound or sing—beasts and birds and human beings. To the artist, nature is inspiration as well as comfort, refuge, escape from man-made life. Nature consoles him as a mother comforts her son. And his heart opens up through an inner sympathy with all animate and inanimate things. His fantasy becomes stimulated through an inner kinship with animals, with trees and flowers, with rocks and water. Here his inspiration blossoms; here is the beginning of a tonal idea, a melody, a rhythm.

How gratefully Beethoven acknowledges this dual bliss of nature which has offered him boundless inspiration and comfort: "If you stroll through the mysterious pine forests, think that Beethoven poetized here often or that he, as one says, composed." And again, to Therese von Malfatti, probably May, 1810: "What happiness I shall feel in wandering among groves and woods and among trees and plants, and rocks! No man on earth can love the country as I do!" In his diary from the year 1812, he writes: "On the Bare Mountain. End of September. Almighty! In the forest, I am transfigured. Happy everything in the forest. Every tree speaks, through thee, my Lord. What magnificence!"

Like Beethoven, composers of all times have listened with enchantment to the voice of nature. Their statements often refer to nature as a favorite workshop. The preference for the out of doors is expressed by Haydn. On his walks he carried with him a little blackboard, and wrote upon it musical thoughts as they occurred to him: "Other composers sit down at the piano until there is no way out of their confusion. I rather seek my ideas on the street or in the fresh air. Sometimes I copy a tree, a bird, or a cloud."

Nature plays her part in the creative procedure of every romantic artist. Throughout their letters and diaries, we find acknowledgment of her contribution. Many composers collect their sketches on walks. Hugo Wolf, returning home in the evening from long tramps in the woods, elaborates on what he has jotted down out of doors. Often he would sing for friends from such pencil sketches. "I let my ideas come to me as I hike around," Brahms writes to Elizabeth Herzogenberg, January 15, 1887. The Second Symphony originated on an Austrian Lake, the Fourth Symphony in the Alps. His Violin Sonata, Op. 78, uses a motif playing on the sound of raindrops.

Mahler writes in reference to his Third:

My symphony will turn into something that the world has not heard yet. All of nature has a voice in it and she tells a deep secret as one can guess it only in a dream. It strikes me rather curiously that most people when referring to nature think only of flowers, birdies, the fragrance of the forest. Nobody knows the god, Dionysos, the great Pan. There you have a program already, that is to say, a sample of how I make music. Music is always and everywhere only the voice of nature. . . . But it is the world, nature as a whole, which, as it were, is being awakened to sound and clangs out of its inexplorable silence.[1]

The joint experience with animals and plants, his closeness to the "great Pan" takes on productive significance for the composer. He puts his heart into everything he hears and sees. He humanizes nature, and nature in turn speaks back to him. Ear and mind register dual sensations. The musician knows the secret language of flowers, clouds and rocks and understands what birds tell him. He knits himself deeply into the mysterious web of the world. His senses seem widely increased, even beyond their natural limits. The artist's imagination conjures up the fantastic inhabitants of nature: fauns and nymphs, ghosts and demons, beings both lovely and terrifying. The borders between dream and reality disappear. Subconscious forces of creation stream freely out of their hiding places. His fantasy overflows.

Nature's eternal music has remained unchanged throughout the ages, unchangeable by time, by fate and history. Yet man's response to the polyphony of her voices shows an infinite variety of expression reflecting in his music the development of his art, the growth of technique, the varying ways in which the nerves of new generations respond to the stimuli of nature. We will come to understand the reason for this multiformity as we learn more about the factors which enter into the composition of a musical score. As we delve into the strata of the composer's inspiration derived from nature, the problem will unfold itself in all its complexity.

THE SONG OF BIRDS

The court musicians of nature are the birds. They are always performing, from sunrise to sunset, but perhaps their most brilliant concerts can be heard on beautiful spring mornings in budding forests. Rocking in the light green of young branches, they happily whistle their allegro of rapid trills or they gently sigh in an adagio of a melting, fluting and melancholy quality.

Men have never tired of translating the performances of nature's adorable musicians into their tone language: they have tried to capture in signs of script and notation the main motifs and characteristic embellishments of bird songs, integrating them as thematic raw material into works of tonal art. The list of these integrations into master scores throughout history must include music of many lands and many styles. Everywhere, however, there is an obvious partiality toward the calls of certain birds.

Among all of them, it is the cuckoo with his marked motif that is most frequently heard in important scores of many centuries and countries. Dating back to the Middle Ages, there is that historic quadruple canon, "Sumer is icumen in." Its four tenor parts were supported by a pes^2 consisting of two bass parts in canon, over whose measured tread that light melody danced along. It is the breezy current of folk-made music that lends life to this cuckoo round. Ever since the coming of summer has been heralded by the cuckoo, the characteristic rhythm and intervals of its call have attracted composers as thematic substance. The survey of important utilizations of the cuckoo's call in centuries to follow must include scores such as the Chant des oiseaux, by Clément Jannequin (probably published 1529). There is the German collection of Kurzweiligen guten frischen teutschen Liedlein (1570) whose "entertaining, good, fresh little German songs" contained the tune "Der Gutzbauch auf dem Baume sass, Kuckuk, Kuckuk es regnet nass." The seventeenth century score, Hortulus Chelicus, by Johann Jakob Walther (1688) displays a Scherzo d'angeli con il cuccu among its twenty-eight pieces for string instruments. Still another instance occurs in Capriccio Cucu of Johann Kaspar Kerll.[3] The treatise, Musurgia, published in 1650 by Athanasius Kircher, contains many interesting details regarding bird and fowl calls. The author, a natural scientist as well as a musician, combined his two interests in the notations of these various voices which we find in our Illustration III.

A noteworthy example from the eighteenth century is the Rite of Spring, an overture by J. J. Fux, which captured Bach's interest to the extent that he made a copy of the music for himself. The organization of Fux's overture occurs according to the different birds whose voices flutter through the music: "pour le rossignol," "pour le coucou," "pour la caille." More representative examples of bird music in the eighteenth century bring the Kukuk's Minuett (London, 1570), a collection of pieces for flute, and Boccherini's bird quintet, L'Uccelleria. The cuckoo also happily calls in Haydn's

Children's Symphony but he plays his most important symphonic role in Beethoven's Pastoral. Significant is the integration of the cuckoo motif in a symphony written at the end of the same century —the First in D major, by Gustav Mahler. In still another symphonic work, the title suggests its inspirational impulse: "On Hearing the First Cuckoo in Spring," an impressionistic tone poem written by Delius in 1913.

Our musical illustration shows that the call of the cuckoo does not create the same sensation in various composers' minds. They differ in the registration of the cuckoo motif as much as from a minor third to a fourth. J. K. Kerll hears the call of the bird in his Capriccio Cucu as a minor third. Jannequin as well as Beethoven uses a major third. Delius, in typical impressionistic manner, vacillates from a minor third to a major third. Mahler hears the interval as a fourth, admonishing the player of the clarinet to whom the motif is entrusted "to imitate the call of the cuckoo."

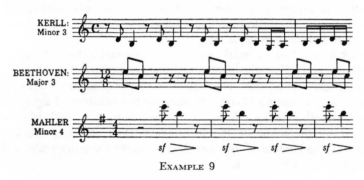

EXAMPLE 9

Three different intervals, then—a minor third, a major third and fourth—represent the cuckoo in musical scores from several centuries. And it is with this array of his musical portrayals that the cuckoo teaches us a first lesson about the problem of nature's reflection and imitation in art: sounds of nature as exemplified in the call of a bird do not lend themselves to an exact musical reproduction within the limits of musical expression.

Mahler gives a clue to his artistic intent by keeping the characteristic cuckoo rhythm, but augmenting the melodic interval to a fourth. To him the call of the cuckoo is the very voice of nature.

Not a specific bird is to be recognized and identified by the listener. It is nature herself that speaks to him. The ornithologist is concerned with subtle objective nuances audible in bird calls. The composer (on the higher art level) seeks no objectification of the sensory reaction. Acoustic reality is no content for musical imagery. It is true, the composer borrows certain sounds from nature; but once they become part of his music, reality loses its significance. The inner life of music comes to the fore and directs the course of the tonal fantasy.

Only the composer on a more primitive level aims at sheer imitation of natural phenomena. He may resort to various devices in his effort to come as close as possible to the original effect. Ottorino Respighi, in his tone poem, The Pines of Rome, employs in the orchestra at the end of the second movement, the Catacombs, an actual record of the song of the nightingale, in order to convey a realistic impression of the bird call. Here, the gramophone becomes an orchestral instrument: Nature, on the disc, enters the concert hall. The little nightingale sings from the cage and pleads to us to believe that all is real.

But it is rather in tonal reflections (comparable to that of the cuckoo's call) that the poetic nightingale attained her place in master scores of all eras. The little prize singer of nature is likewise heard in Jannequin's Chant des oiseaux. The ornamental figure of the sixteenth century referred to as the *ribattuta* is obviously inspired by the motif of the nightingale. It is contrived from a gradual acceleration of two neighboring notes until the main and auxiliary notes form a fast trill:

EXAMPLE 10

In this form the shake of the nightingale is integrated into vocal scores of the sixteenth and seventeenth century. It lives on in Beethoven's Pastoral, his Lied der Nachtilgal and in numerous poetic scores up to the Love Song Waltzes by Brahms.

Not as frequently quoted as the nightingale or cuckoo, but still a favorite with musicians, is the quail. This little musician whistles a characteristic rhythm ♩. ♪ ♩ which entertained the old Romans, who translated the motif into the Latin syllables of *Dic Cur Hic.* Where the other two birds appear, the quail is usually not far away, as in Haydn's Children's Symphony and the *Seasons.* In Boccherini's L'Uccelleria, a duo between quail and cuckoo is entrusted to the violin and cello. The same birds are represented by oboe and clarinet in Beethoven's Pastoral.

"The yellowhammer up there, the nightingales and cuckoos all around composed with me."[4] Thus reads Beethoven's acknowledgment of the birds' collaboration in the Pastoral. The year 1808, in which this symphony was composed, had also brought on a new attack of Beethoven's deafness. Nevertheless, bird motifs did not vanish from his scores after this dreaded affliction had prevented him from the enjoyment of listening to his favorite little singers— Beethoven had preserved their music in his memory. At the end of the Scene on the Brook, Beethoven introduced the famous little trio of birds, a nightingale, quail and cuckoo. This is the most realistic quotation of nature's sounds in which the master ever indulged. But he himself asserted that the passage from the Pastoral had a humorous connotation: "Mit denen soll es nur Scherz sein."[5] And it is only in the light of this remark—that the whole ought to be taken with a sense of humor—that we must interpret Beethoven's "literal" portrayal of the three birds. Everywhere else in the symphony—in keeping with its motto, "more expression of feeling than painting"—the composer was guided by the intent to reproduce his inner impressions rather than to imitate the voice of nature.

The terzetto of a cuckoo, quail and nightingale, which starts its performance in the eighth measure of the coda, does not by any means comprise the complete personnel of bird scenes in the Sixth Symphony. Other ornithological specimens participate in the tonal play of nature, and one of the birds (to whom no acknowledgment is made in the score) is a little inhabitant of the Vienna woods who on sultry summer days, before the onset of storm and rain, constantly warbles his triplet-like motif. The timing of his performance seemed prophetic to the peasants who nicknamed him the "rain whistler." Beethoven made the prophecy of the bird come true in the course of the Pastoral: already in the scherzo, rain is predicted by the whistling of this bird, and it certainly pours in the fourth movement!

Along with the tunes of the already mentioned birds, still others are heard in the Pastoral such as the oxeye. And in the second movement, the shake in the first violins suggests the flutter and trilling of the lark. Schindler relates how, in the summer of 1823, Beethoven who was entirely deaf by this time,

seating himself on the turf, and leaning against an elm, asked if there were any yellowhammers to be heard in the tree above us. But all was still. He then said, "this is where I wrote the Scene on the Brook, while the yellowhammers were singing above me, and the quails, nightingales and cuckoos calling all around." I asked why the yellowhammer did not appear in the movement with the others; on which he took his sketchbook and wrote the following phrase:

EXAMPLE 11

"There's the little composer," he said, "and you'll find that he plays a more important part than the others; for they are nothing but a joke.

When Schindler asked his master

why he had not mentioned the yellowhammers with the others, he said that to have done so would only have increased the number of ill-natured remarks on the andante, which had already formed a sufficient obstacle to the symphony in Vienna and elsewhere. In fact, the work was often treated as a mere jeu d'esprit on account of the second movement, and in many places had shared the fate of the Eroica. In Leipzig, they thought it would be more appropriately called a fantasia than a symphony.[6]

NATURE AS CONTENT

The great allurement of singing birds has served us well to display the variety in which composers have echoed the voice of nature. Beethoven's utilization of bird calls shows that it is primarily the artful application and development of the symphonic motifs which matters. Schindler asserts that the motif of the yellowhammer was also the origin of the tremendous theme which opens the Fifth Symphony. Is it credible that these fateful and mighty notes (which have been interpreted to connote "the knock of fate") were inspired by a bird call? The answer to this question is not very important since it is not the sequence of thirds which makes the opening movement of the Fifth what it is, and it is not the motif of the birds, the cuckoo, quail, nightingale or oxeye, which creates the enchantment of the various scenes in the Pastoral. In both symphonies, the Fifth and the Sixth, it is the ingenious artistry of thematic development rather than the theme itself which accounts for the incomparable results in this great music.

Not only in his symphonies, but throughout his whole lifework, Beethoven utilized nature-given material for the purpose of high art. The use of nature's motifs in music prior to Beethoven's occurred in a rather playful manner. It is no coincidence that it was Beethoven, in his historic position on the threshold of classicism and romanticism, who developed this technique.

The relationship of the true romanticist to nature takes on new meaning. He hears music everywhere: all things living have captivated the musician's ear and mind. But he has also established contact with inanimate nature charged with the sound of elementary forces—the wind and rain, thunder and lightning, the waves of the ocean. It is from primitive but suggestive beginnings that composers have developed the method of expressing natural phenomena in tonal art. As in the case of the birds, the attempt to attain such musical images started early in history. Already in the first operas such as Monteverdi's *Orfeo,* the orchestra comments on the scenery. In the prelude to Cavalli's *Giasone,* when the coast of the ocean is visible, the orchestra plays a short Sinfonia navale which reproduces the even breathing of waves with primitive means but with distinction and atmospheric resonance. Such techniques develop in a space of more than two centuries into the powerful colors and striking effects with which the romantic dramatist painted the scenes of his operas. The ghostly midnight in *Freischütz,* the threatening storm opening *Othello,* the brilliant sun in *Siegfried* are contents of the drama—like the human beings exposed to the forces of these elements.

With this development in the scores of the great masters, there has come about a certain conventionality of instrumentation, a sort of orchestral glossary of nature's sounds: no one ever fails to grasp the meaning of the roaring tympani roll as the substitute for thunder preceded by a wild cymbal crash for lightning. All such effects are suggested by the acoustic proximity of the artificial to the natural sound. The composer counts on the listener's understanding of these effects. Long before the use of program notes, audiences were trusted to have enough imagination to envision murmuring waters when hearing instrumental combinations such as gentle trills of woodwinds and divided strings playing alternately rippling intervals. Musicians strove to bring to the listener as exact a reproduction of nature's sounds as they could accomplish on instruments—a photography in tones, as it were. Thus certain composers aimed at, and succeeded in achieving, an astonishing degree of imitation. Liszt in his symphonic poem, Mazzeppa, alluded to the snorting of the horse by the *col legno* of violins, of violas and celli, letting the stick of the bow fall on the strings. He paved the way for those highlights of realism which followed in the scores of the naturalistic school.

Yet nature's reflection in music is as varied as human nature's capacity to respond to the manifestations of the outside world. Hence we face such a great difference in the translation of the natural phenomena into formed products of art. If the simple call of the bird is registered by composers in contradictory intervals, the more complex phenomena of nature necessarily lead to a wide range of reflections from rationalistic-naturalistic imitation to impressionistic symbolism.

Consequently, there is the symphonic record of a highly personal reaction to nature's elements and inhabitants. Herein the composer attempts to represent nature in the abstract vocabulary of the tonal language and not to reproduce her in a literal manner.

At the turn of our century, the most challenging attempts to integrate nature into the symphonic world were made by Mahler and Debussy. Mahler's symphonies conjure up the sound of the universe and seek in music pantheistic answers to the problem of life and death. Debussy's artistic position is that of a superbly refined tone painter who communicates primarily the tonal response of his nerves and senses to the sea and landscape. Composing his symphonic sketches, La Mer, he explains to Durand, August 8, 1906: "Here I am again with my old friend, the sea; it is always endless and beautiful. It is really the thing in nature which restores one best to one's place." From such an inspirational level, the modern impressionist created his resonances to nature with the unsurpassable finesse of his tonal colors, hues and shades. But as usual the contemporary criticism lagged behind in the understanding of the composer's intent. "I neither hear, nor see, nor feel the sea," wrote Pierre Lalo in Le Temps after the première of La Mer. And Gaston Carraud declared that "the sketches" were misnamed in that they neither "gave any complete idea of the sea nor expressed its essential characteristics." These words point to the clash between two ways of interpreting nature in music. The reactionary critics went astray because they wanted to hear the voice of nature in the external and antiquated terms they could understand. Debussy's work was beyond their reach; he had approached the problem from his highly personalized place to which, as he says, only nature could restore him.

JOURNEYS

Artistic imagination is captured by the distant and the remote, by the unknown and the exotic. Many composers refer to the enjoyment of journeys whether by coach and four or by more modern means of transportation. The romance of travel opens new horizons to the artist. Though a journey cannot always be to foreign countries and people, even a small trip is greatly welcomed when it provides at least an illusion, variety and the new. But as it happened, some composers who were eager to travel lacked the opportunity. Others who had the chance spurned it. We cannot always know the causes of their behavior; yet we see how travel— or the lack of it—affected their musical work.

There is a parallel in the lives of Orlando di Lasso and Handel, masters of the sixteenth and eighteenth centuries, and of their respective contemporaries, Palestrina and Bach. The latter composers spent their days close to their homes; journeys were few and short. Both were keenly aware, however, of the national art of other countries.

Lasso and Handel, on the other hand, traveled extensively, lived long and decisive years of maturity in foreign countries, absorbing foreign style and taste through direct influence and personal assimilation. The Netherland master, Lasso, born in Mons, visited Italy and England, settled for years in Antwerp, and was later appointed court conductor in Munich. From the Bavarian capital, he visited France, and finally returned to Munich to spend his remaining years. Decisive traces of international influences and of the stylistic peculiarities acquired in his foster countries are abundant in his scores. Handel's journeys in young years to Italy and his assimilation of the English world in maturity resulted in a truly cosmopolitan art: the highlights within these influences point to Italian opera, to Corelli's instrumental music, to Purcell's choral style and, of course, to Handel's native affiliation with the early German baroque. All these heterogeneous styles were studied and absorbed through firsthand acquaintance with the workshops of foreign masters. Their art was imbibed at the places where it was created, performed and preserved by a living tradition.

With both Lasso and Handel, their journeys led inevitably to their taking new roots in foreign soil. And similar was the fate, to the advantage of their art, of many other great musicians of all times such as the two great Italians, Lully and Cherubini, in France, the Spaniard Vittoria who settled in Palestrina's Italy, the Germans, Beethoven and Brahms, who accepted the universal spirit of a bygone Austria as an aesthetic guide.

Haydn, born in the Austrian Burgenland, regretted that he could not travel to Italy, a country which artistically held great attraction for him. He realized, however, certain compensations resulting from the long years spent in Esterház:

My Prince was always satisfied with my works; I not only had the encouragement of constant approval, but as conductor of an orchestra, I could make experiments, observe what produced an effect and what weakened it, and was thus in a position to improve, alter, make additions or omissions, and be as bold as I pleased; I was cut off from the world, there was no one to confuse or torment me, and I was forced to become original.

This statement is a piece of illuminating self-analysis. The two journeys Haydn made in later years to London, in December, 1790,

and July, 1792, left innumerable impressions on his still extremely
active creative mind. He listened with greatest interest to the performance of English music. He was deeply moved by the Handel
commemoration in Westminster Abbey—a performance of the
Messiah on a grand scale. Perhaps the first impulse for Haydn's
great oratorios, the *Creation* and *Seasons,* was received in England.
He brought from London to Vienna Lidley's text based on Milton's
Paradise Lost, which had been originally written for Handel, who
died before he was able to turn to the composition of the poem.

Mozart from childhood was exposed to the influences of foreign
music, languages, art and people. He was as much at home in
Bologna, Paris, Munich or Mannheim as he was in Vienna or his
native Salzburg.[7] The frequently quoted letter in which he allegedly
attributes his best work to the stimulus of traveling in a coach
is not authentic.[8] But he wrote to his father on September 11, 1778:

I assure you that if people do not travel (those at least who are concerned with art and science) they are indeed poor creatures. . . . A man
of second-rate ability remains always second-rate, whether he travels or
not, but a man of superior talent (and I cannot deny myself this without injustice) would go wrong if he stayed always in the same place . . .

For a more specific record of the interaction between visual
impressions and composition, we turn to documents where such
a tie-up is expressly stated. Max von Weber records his father's
statement: "The viewing of a landscape is for me the performance
of a musical work. I feel it as an entity and do not dwell on the
details which caused it. The landscape stretches itself out in time.
Funeral marches, rondos, furiosos and pastorals rush in somersaults
as nature rolls out before my eyes." This translation of space into
time occurs with Weber through the traditional forms of music.
The composer hears, as it were, the landscape. But the shift from
the optical to the auditory sensation does not yield to him the
vision of new tonal shapes and impressions. It depends on those
established patterns with which he has already worked and has
become familiar. Weber's approach is further elucidated by his
son, Max, who asserts that his father, "clear thinker and observer
that he was," frequently commented upon this process himself.
Particularly when he was sitting in a traveling coach, his musical

thoughts blended with external impulses. The landscape rolled on before his ear symphonically, and melodies emerged from the rising and lowering of the terrain, from every bush, from the wheat fields. Weber's landscape hearing, then, is the adaptation of visual impressions into the formal symbols of tonal art.

Mendélssohn's romantic sensitivity translated his experiences gained on traveling into visual as well as tonal art works. His hands were skilled in sketching here a landscape, there a piece of music. On his repeated journeys to the British Isles, Switzerland and Italy, he took dual advantage of what his eyes and ears experienced (Illustration IV). Not always did Mendelssohn's principal talent, that of a composer, sway him to the writing of a tonal score. At times, he vacillated between recording an impression visually or aurally. He might even follow both bents, and draw and compose the same subject. In a letter of August 11, 1831, to his sisters, Mendelssohn speaks of his double intention "to sketch the view from this window with my pen on the back of my letter and also to write out my second Lied. The Untersee will soon also belong to my reminiscences." The record of the trip is made both in tones and lines.

"I also have to be grateful for so much that is not actually music: to the monuments, the paintings, the serenity of nature, which itself is mostly music." This acknowledgment to his teacher, Carl Friedrich Zelter, is eloquent enough.[9] And in the same letter (December 1, 1830), Mendelssohn distinguishes between an inspiration received through the visual in contrast to the "musical music" which is derived from tonal impressions only. To further intensify the impulse, Mendelssohn chooses a specific environment for the composition of a particular music. He informs his sister Fanny from Rome of the progress of the Italian Symphony, but since he cannot find a solution for the slow movement, he decides to leave its composition for a different environment—for Naples. As it turned out, the exuberant atmosphere of the southern port made its most obvious tonal contribution, not in the adagio, but in the finale of the Fourth Symphony whose fiery saltarello so vividly portrays a typical Neapolitan dance scene. The Third Symphony, as its popular appellation indicates, was inspired by a journey to Scotland.

In all these traveling experiences, the visual impulse blended with the tonal. As in his composing, the desire of self-expression in the visual arts started in Mendelssohn's boyhood. With oncoming maturity, the quantity of his drawings and water colors matched their quality. Twenty-seven large drawings were brought back from his first journey to Switzerland in 1822. The last journey in 1847 resulted in fourteen large water colors. Thus, there is a creative reflection of the Italian and Scotch journeys not only in those master scores which echo these experiences, but also in ample work by the painter, Mendelssohn. The same characteristics which distinguish Mendelssohn's musical style are also evident in his drawings and paintings. The sense of form and proportion, the fine lines and delicate details are typically Mendelssohn. In his musical tonepainting, Mendelssohn creates new formal media to hold the individual content of that which he portrays in sea and landscape. All this is progress from Weber's technique of translating the visual into traditional patterns of older forms. Here with Mendelssohn are the beginnings of an impressionistic treatment of nature's phenomena. How significant that this step was made by a great composer who was also a painter![10]

Like other traits of the creative personality, a deep-seated interest in foreign countries and their people points back to childhood. Berlioz shows in his memoirs how the dreams and wishes of his early years were creatively transformed by his romantic imagination in maturity. The composer's father had often reproached young Berlioz because he knew the name of every one of the Sandwich Islands, Moluccas and Philippines and the Straits of Torres, Timor, Java and Borneo, but at the same time was ignorant of French geography. "My interest in foreign countries was whetted by reading all the books of travel, both ancient and modern, which I could lay hands on at home. Had I chanced to live in a seaport, I should certainly have run away to sea."

Just as Mozart and Weber, so Berlioz enjoyed composing during the long hours of traveling or at the different stations of his journey. His dramatic oratorio, *Damnation de Faust*, originated on a trip through the Austrian-Hungarian monarchy. He wrote it in the coach, in the railroad stations in all towns where he stopped over. The Round of the Peasants was written on the spur of the moment, by gaslight in Budapest. It was also in the Hungarian capital that Berlioz heard for the first time the fiery melody and rhythm of the Rakoczy March.

The extraordinary impression which the march made upon me induced me to integrate it into the *Faust* score, taking the liberty of placing my hero at the beginning of the action in Hungary and making him witness the march of the Hungarian army. A German critic found it rather curious, but I simply do not see what should have prevented me from taking him anywhere.

This, then, is the reason why Berlioz's *Damnation* starts on a plain in Hungary with Faust alone in the fields (instead of the original opening of Goethe's tragedy which places the scholar, weary with learning and science, in his study). It is sunrise: "Winter has departed, spring is here!" We hear the Round of the Peasants until the first fanfare of the Rakoczy March breaks in. The composer did not hesitate to indulge in the liberty of transferring the locale of Goethe's drama from medieval Germany to the Hungary of fiery and vigorous music and even comments on it (as just quoted) quite naïvely. Inspired by the romantic environment of the Danube landscape, Berlioz, otherwise such a strict guardian of artistic purity, threw overboard his usual scruples in dealing with the work of another artist.[11]

Wagner's whole life was a continuous journey in the literal sense, and by no means always a voluntary one. Exciting experiences did not in every instance permit him the pleasure of self-chosen trips. But fate compensated the composer in the form of powerful inspiration derived from truly dramatic journeys which were in reality flights from persecution, from mortal danger and ill health. More serene settings were pleasure outings like the excursion to Bohemia, where the atmosphere of the beginning of the first act of *Tannhäuser* was derived: "Mounting the Wostrai Mountain, near Aussig on the Elbe River, I was surprised when turning the corner of a valley to hear a gay dance tune whistled by a shepherd—and I found myself immediately in a chorus of the pilgrims which passed by the shepherd into the valley."[12]

In contrast to the accidental inspiration which easily springs from the romance of journeys, there is the pursuit of a specific stimulation which only a particular environment can yield. Thus, Verdi, approaching the composition of *Aïda*, went to Egypt to acquaint himself with the atmosphere of his opera and its scenes of Egyptian temples, the embankment of the Nile, the graves of the kings in Luxor.

Viewing the Nile with its softly rippling waters and its deserted banks, the idea of the third act and the scene of its action full of secrecy and hidden desires came to my mind. Also musical folklore which gave local color in characteristic mood to my tone, specific musical thoughts which only the hot climate of the high noon could suggest to me. The view of the obsolete grandeur of the country and the wild melancholy affected me amidst the ruins of the colossal architecture.

Mussorgsky attributes his consciousness of the Russian world to his first trip to the capital:

At last I have seen Moscow! From the very outset I realized its original character. The towers, the cupolas of the churches positively reek of bygone times. The Red Gates are very quaint; I beheld them with delight. . . . How beautiful the Kremlin! I could not help being struck with awe. . . . My impressions of the Church of Vassili Blajemmi were altogether enjoyable and strange: I felt that any moment the boyars of yore in their long coats and high headgears, might appear before my eyes. . . . You know I was a cosmopolitan; but having seen Moscow, I am so to speak reborn, and everything Russian is very close to me now.

The great impression led subsequently to a decisive turn in Mussorgsky's art. The abandonment of Western orientation became inevitable and the composer started on his pursuit of the specifically national Russian element in his music.

WEATHER

A beautiful spring day and a happy creative thought easily spell unison. Most artists claim dependence on pleasant weather for their inspiration as well as for a satisfactory procedure in later phases of work. Bad weather hampers and at times fully dams the flow of ideas. "I somehow try to write again but it is almost impossible to know something in this nasty climate." Thus Beethoven, unable to make any headway on a composition, blames it on the weather.

There were probably, as always in the complex strata of the human mind, more hidden reasons inhibiting the progress of work. But often composers seek the cause on the surface, in the weather, particularly in the lack of sunshine. Schubert complains: "The Almighty seems to have abandoned us. The sun just doesn't want to shine. Now in May one cannot yet sit in the garden. Terrible!" On the benches in the public parks with which Vienna abounds, Schubert frequently meditated and sketched. These gardens were his second workshop, for here he could write under trees, looking at the flower beds and fountains, thus escaping the bareness of his room.

Not only in Vienna, but elsewhere, too, spring and sun are some-times behind schedule, and so is the progress of the composer. Wagner badly misses the sun in a letter of April 26, 1859: "The heavy curtain is finished, only the sun is missing against which it is supposed to protect me. Today, however, the sun is here and so everything will proceed better." In the following, too, cause and effect is evident: "Horrible weather! The brain refused persistently to function." Many other references to weather and its effect upon work are to be found in Wagner's writings.

A beautiful day in connection with the significance of a specific date of the calendar adds up to a powerful stimulation. Wagner writes from Zurich in 1857:

On Good Friday I awakened to find the sun shining brightly for the first time in this house: the little garden was radiant with green, the birds sang, and at last I could sit on the roof and enjoy the long-yearned-for peace with its message of promise. Full of this sentiment, I suddenly remembered that the day was Good Friday, and I called to mind the significance this omen had already assumed for me when I was reading Wolfram's *Parsifal*. . . . Now its noble possibilities struck me with over-whelming force, and out of my thoughts about Good Friday I rapidly conceived a whole drama of which I made a rough sketch with a few dashes of the pen, dividing the whole into three acts.

Schumann completed his Spring Symphony (the First) in 1841. In a letter to Spohr (November 23, 1842), the composer made the following and self-explanatory comment:

I finished the symphony . . . at the end of winter and, if I may say so, under that vernal impulse which sweeps all men along, even the most aged, and every year carries them away anew. My purpose was not to describe or to paint. I am convinced, however, that the season in which the symphony was composed influenced its formation and helped make it exactly what it is.

In spite of the powerful stimulus which spring uniquely provides, summer proved to be the most prolific time for many composers—partly for external reasons. Their occupational schedule as teachers, performers, conductors did not permit sufficient concentration for creative work in the frame and distractions of city life during the season. Some of them had to store their creative energies until vacation time. Gustav Mahler, the opera director with all his absorbing duties, wrote his nine symphonies between opera seasons during the summer months. Other artists who did not lack the leisure for work during the winter months depended on the warmth of summer to incubate their embryonic thoughts. This is true for instance of Brahms, who wrote the bulk of his orchestral compositions and many other important works between spring and autumn.[13]

ANIMALS

Many composers are passionately fond of animals. Pets play their friendly part not only in the hours of their master's relaxation; they are admitted through the otherwise guarded doors into his workshop. In fact, the attachment of a musician to his four-legged friend can be so great that the absence of the pet during working hours can be very disturbing. Thus, Verdi informed his friend, Arrivabene, on December 29, 1867: "My poor Black is very sick; he hardly moves about any longer and will not live very long. I've ordered another Black who is being made in Bologna, for in case I should get the idea of composing another *Don Carlos*, I could not do it without such a collaborator." This, of course, Verdi said with a twinkle in his eye. But more credit could hardly be given to the little companion of his workshop.

The playfulness and refreshing primitivity of dogs relax the tense mind of the complex brainworker. There seems to be a silent understanding between these two nature-given instincts: between the composer's instinct which leads him to find solutions beyond the grasp of the intellect and the animal's instinct which stimulated from within feels its way through life and always knows what suits him best.

While Verdi writes his operas of human passion, a favorite dog lies at his feet. In spite of their genial role in his life, Verdi did not accord any important part to his pets on the opera stage; and herein, as everywhere, a psychological difference between Verdi and his antagonist, Wagner, comes to the fore. With the Bayreuth composer, animals played a dual role—in his life as well as on his stage. Wagner always cared for the company of dogs and required them for companions. Even on his dangerous flight to London, he refused to part with his big Dane. The loss of a favorite dog, Peps, was bemoaned as a major mishap and turned into a true crisis in his childless marriage with Minna. Other animals, too, were the source of great joy and relaxation during working hours, particularly the clever parrot in the Zurich days. This little gray fellow learned to whistle themes from Beethoven's symphonies, and his repertoire climaxed in motifs from his master's works which the bird first performed before they were introduced to the musical world. The roster of animals which Wagner introduced to the stage of his eleven music dramas could make up a small zoo. There are horses in *Rienzi, Tannhäuser, Walküre, Götterdämmerung*; a swan and a dove in *Lohengrin*; a ram in *Walküre*; a bear, a dragon and a bird in *Siegfried*; ravens in *Götterdämmerung*.

As to the killing of the swan in *Parsifal*, the composer explains how this scene is related to a traumatic experience of his own youth. On a hunting trip with a party of comrades, young Wagner shot a rabbit. The dying look of the animal moved him to such pity and remorse that ever afterward, the mere thought of a hunt made him shudder. The trauma in his early life haunted Wagner until he sublimated it in his last work through the reproaches of old Gurnemanz to the pure fool, Parsifal, who had just senselessly murdered the swan:

Gurnemanz: Here, Behold! thy arrow struck . . . extinguishes his eye . . . mark'st thou its look?

Art thou not conscious of thy trespass? Say, boy, perceivest thou thy heinous sin? How could'st thou have acted thus?

Parsifal: I knew not 'twas wrong. I know not . . .

To analyze the symbolism of all the other animals in Wagner's world would be a worthwhile study in itself. And obviously, such a study could be fruitfully extended to other composers. The kindly Dvořák loved the company of peaceful pigeons and kept great numbers of them in his garden. He found great relaxation in their feeding hour. Ravel considered his Siamese cats the chief members of his household. And the most human of all composers, Mozart, could not be missing among those who have an affinity with animals. The correspondence of the Mozart family gives a vivid picture of the role their pets played in their lives. And so Bimperl, the favorite dog of the Mozarts, acquired a little bit of immortality, too.

CHAPTER FOUR

CYCLES OF INSPIRATION

> Our human mind is not a clock-work which one can wind up at will.
>
> ROSSINI

CONSTANT AND INTERRUPTED PRODUCTIVITY

IF WE project the periods of creative activity against the total life curve of the artist, two types of composer emerge. There is the musician whose workshop never closes: his whole life appears as one constant pursuit of the creative goal. The gigantic output of Palestrina, Orlando di Lasso, Bach, Handel, Haydn, Mozart, Beethoven or Schubert gives the impression of a single drive which started in early youth and stopped only when death took the pen out of the composer's hand.

This does not imply that there were never any breathing spells in the intense forward march of these imperturbable workers toward their envisioned aims. Obviously, there were also periods of greater and lesser productivity. They took sick like other human beings. Paralyzing experiences or heavy professional obligations as performers might have forced them to forsake their writing temporarily. Yet planning and a certain amount of sketching did not come to a full stop. And in this sense it appears that these composers were always in touch with their workshops.

In contrast to this type, there is the composer who knows complete breaks in his creative activity. Major stoppages in his production may last a long time. Productivity can be limited to a few years altogether, particularly to years of youth, followed by a damming up of the creative flow which, in some cases, has even disappeared forever. Such cessation of work has been regarded as an enigma. Men of erratic productivity have become the object of attacks on the part of unsympathetic critics who fail to understand how an artist can give up his work after illustrious proof of genius, after achievements of spectacular success. Moreover, it is claimed that the artist's obligation to contribute to the world never ceases!

No one was more bitterly reproached and besieged than Rossini following his withdrawal from the writing of operas in 1829. Was it really true that the artist who had enraptured Europe with his *Barber of Seville* had retired to a smug life of epicurean pleasures? Did the cooking of exquisite dishes and the artful seasoning of salads or sauces really take the place of making melodies, for which, since the success of *L'Italiana in Algeri* and the series of brilliant operas up to *William Tell,* the whole of Europe had developed such an insatiable appetite? When the impatience and scorn of so-called admirers had reached a peak, Rossini embarked upon an eloquent defense of his case. His plea was addressed to the lawyer, Micotti, his friend and executor of his will:

I am asking the question whether a man who loves sincerity should make others believe that he really could at any time force his imagination to that height of enthusiasm which is required to create the forms of fantasy. . . . I emphatically deny that the mere will is enough to give flight to the imagination. This is equally impossible because it is impossible for the human soul to command emotions according to will alone. Our human mind is not a clockwork which one can wind up at will and whose hands can be set according to personal fancy.[1]

This self defense of Rossini's amounts to a strong and genuine plea for a more sympathetic understanding of his own predicament. It also serves to vindicate all artists who have suffered as he did from the failing grace of their inspirational disposition. The composer is not an automaton! His mental machinery cannot be wound up at will and at any desired hour. When Rossini sketched *The Barber of Seville* in the amazing period of less than two weeks, he was only twenty-four, "in the prime of life, easily stimulated, and the ideas automatically came to him." Compared with such record-breaking productivity, the five months which he required for the writing of *William Tell* seemed to him an "eternity." Yet thirteen years had passed since the prodigious feat of writing the *Barber*, and Rossini as a human being had greatly changed. After he had put parts of the score of *William Tell* on paper, in 1829, he "felt physically exhausted and unable to awaken further inspiration. This state lasted very long." In fact, his true inspirational powers were never fully restored again. In the remaining thirty-eight years of his life, Rossini wrote nothing but his *Stabat Mater* and a few insignificant scores.[2]

Not many artists accept periods of unproductivity with the rationalistic renouncement of which Rossini was capable. Instead, a reaction of melancholy, even of despair frequently sets in. The victim of mental sterility often loses the desire to live. Thus, the letters of Hugo Wolf, dating from the crucial time of his waning inspiration speak a desperate language. After the composer had completed the great song cycles, the Lieder based on the poems of Mörike, Goethe and Eichendorff, his productivity seemed hopelessly blocked. What had happened? The Spanisches and Italienisches Liederbuch had been the fruits of an uninterrupted and blissful harvest.[3] Yet at the very time the second volume of the Italienisches Liederbuch was announced, Wolf broke down: "I am at the end. May it soon be a complete one." And in June, 1891, he asks for a friend's sympathy: "Do pity your Hugo Wolf—lost to art." A long period followed during which all the rich resources of Wolf's invention seemed to have disappeared forever. A letter as late as January 7, 1895, shows how the composer is still plagued by the loss of his productivity: "If only the desperately longed for inspiration would return. I have been unable to find the correct magic formula whereby to awaken from its slumber that mysterious force."

But out of the darkness and despair of stagnation, after four long years of silence, the light of inspiration flashes, and once more the stream of fantasy flows: the mysterious force has been awakened at last. The worst fears of the plagued genius were unjustified—at least for the time being!

With this fresh "heaven-sent impulse," the now deliriously happy

Wolf throws himself violently into a veritable orgy of creation. The opera, *Corregidor*, his only one, takes possession of him: "I work like a madman from six in the morning until dawn without any let-up, continuously." With such white heat and top speed of creation, Wolf's librettist, Rosa Mayreder-Obermayer cannot cope. The poetess is admonished, threatened, beseeched when her verses do not arrive rapidly enough for the onrush of the composer's musical flood. Now no dam can hold it back: "Music is haunting my whole body!" the enraptured composer shouts with joy. No obstacles, no hurdles can be tolerated. Recesses are dreaded: "For heaven's sake," he warns Frau Rosa, "you are not going to stop working because of the holiday and bring me to despair. You couldn't be so cruel!" But when the expected script fails to arrive on time, Wolf composes the music anyway. For years, he was stalled; now he cannot stop for a minute. When the verses finally arrive, Wolf remarks with good humor: "They do not fit my music which I have composed *anticipando*."

But the up and down spiral of Hugo Wolf's creativeness led soon after the climax of *Corregidor* to another low of sterility. The white heat of composing cooled off. The tragic end, first of the great musical mind (1897), later of its human carrier (1902), was near.

CREATIVE PAUSES IN COMPOSING

Stoppage of the inspirational flow, dreaded as a threat to the *élan vital* by some composers, has been turned by others, who had an amazing capacity for adjustment, into productive channels. Between the completion of Wagner's *Lohengrin* and the conception of *Siegfried* lie almost seven fallow years: not a single music dramatic score came forth during this long period. Instead, with the revitalizing instinct of genius, Wagner utilized this "general pause" in his composing for study and aesthetic reflection. A reorientation at this stage had become indispensable to the composer as preparation for further creative enterprises. New ideas had to be tested. New working methods had to be organized. In a letter to Liszt, from Zurich on November 25, 1850, Wagner explains:

I had to abandon the entire life lying behind me, to bring into full consciousness everything dawning in it, to conquer any rising reflection by its own means in order to throw myself once more with clear and cheerful consciousness into the beautiful unconsciousness of artistic creation. I shall spend the winter in completing this abandonment. I want to enter a new world unburdened, free and happy, bringing nothing with me but a glad artistic conscience.

Inevitably, this leave of absence from composing, which is spent on important aesthetic research, leads to major changes in the composer's style. In this way, the artist gains a more objective distance from his creative projects. This is necessary if, in Wagner's words, "a dramatic work is to have concentrated importance and originality. A higher step in life cannot be gained with every half year. Only several years bring concentrated maturity."

Long pauses between spells of overwhelming production occur even with composers of a generally robust creative power. We realize the uneven rhythm of their work by comparing the dates referring to the origin and the completion of their different scores. Opus numbers are often misleading: they may be determined by the order of publication rather than by the chronology of production. Thus neither Beethoven's opus numbers nor his enumeration of works within a certain genre (Leonore overtures, Piano Concertos) indicates the order in which the works were written. But the time between the end of the so-called second period and the first works of the so-called third period of Beethoven's lifework points to the issue: it is unthinkable that he could have made the great step to the sublimity and spirituality of the final period without a thorough aesthetic reorientation.

PATTERNS OF PRODUCTION

Various factors govern the pattern of production. The composer might desire to exhaust a certain technique in all its possibilities. He may feel that the space of one single score does not suffice for the exploration of the problem which occupies his interest at a particular time. As a result, he may write several works immediately following each other dealing with the tectonic task in all its various aspects. Thus Brahms wrote in almost immediate succession the two serenades, Op. 11 and 16, two concertos, Op. 77 and 83, two overtures, Op. 80 and 81 and two symphonies, Op. 90 and 98. He was challenged by the chance to develop a newly acquired technique further than he could have done within the limit of one work. The Liebeslieder, Op. 52, closely follow the composition of the two string quartets, Op. 51. This amounts to three continuous essays in quartet writing; the vocal quartets of the Love Song Waltzes and the two chamber music scores all deal with the creative exploitation of four-part counterpoint.

Schumann also concentrated on particular forms and types during a certain period of creation. His inspiration revolved around either instrumental or vocal spheres. He started out as an instrumental composer. His opus one to twenty-three are piano works exclusively. In the decade from 1829 to 1839, piano works predominate. The year of his marriage, 1840, is the famous year of songs. The year of 1842 is one of chamber music resulting in three quartets, Op. 41—all written in slightly more than a month. The same year also brings forth the piano quintet, Op. 44, and the piano quartet, Op. 47. Three overtures, Op. 100, 128, 136, were written in 1850-51. The change from one domain of music to another is not accidental. That it occurred consciously is proven in a letter to Clara in which Schumann speaks of his farewell to vocal writing: "Now the instruments have their turn."

Composers of different centuries and styles, Purcell, Bach, Haydn, Tchaikovsky, Debussy, Reger, worked in close succession on scores of a tectonically related character. Beethoven's remark to Wegeler, June 29, 1800, "the way I am working now, I frequently do three or four things simultaneously," is a clue not only to his capacity to shift back and forth from one work to another, but also to his favorite method of solving problems somehow connected in form and technique. Examples of such simultaneous composition of different but inwardly allied scores are Piano Sonatas, Opus 2, Nos. 1, 2 and 3; Opus 14, No. 1 and 2; Opus 31, No. 1, 2 and 3 and Opus 49, Nos. 1 and 2. Likewise in the composition of chamber music, such a pattern of work emerges. Beethoven concentrated on three Rasumofsky Quartets, Op. 59 in May, 1806 and finished them by the end of the year. Among the last quartets, the scores Op. 130, 131, and 133 likewise owe their existence to a co-ordinated effort.

The eternal sequel of tension and relaxation plays its unmistakable part in the pattern of creation. Thus the alternating rhythm of strong excitement followed by a serene diversion can be observed in the familiar order of Beethoven's symphonies. The Eroica is followed by the idyll of the Fourth. The classic drama of the Fifth is succeeded (1808) by the summer day's dream of the Pastoral. The year 1812 produces the serenity of the Eighth, which was preceded by the dithyrambic Seventh. In turn, the humor of the Eighth is the prelude to the monumental Ninth.

TEMPO AND QUANTITY OF WORK

"Genius is industry"—when Lessing reduced the mystery of creative power to such a realistic and simple formula, he did not intend to dismiss the spiritual source of creation. But the great poet knew from his own experience the all-importance of a never fatiguing capacity for work. In this sense industry is also the key word to the achievements of most great composers. Yet this aspect of ceaseless effort is often overlooked for the sake of a rather mystical interpretation of the composer's work.

The enormous creative output of certain composers is in itself an irrefutable indication of how industriously and intensely they must have written their scores. Look on the shelves of the great libraries at the array of their collected works, volume after volume! The mere physical expenditure required to do all this writing forced the masters of music to be also master economists of their time and of all their available strength. Palestrina created over one thousand works. Orlando di Lasso, Bach and Handel produced comparably in sheer quantity of achievement. The Köchel catalogue cites over six hundred of Mozart's different scores. Over six hundred happens to be the number of songs alone in Schubert's fruitful harvest. Haydn wrote one hundred and four symphonies. Wagner turned out two thousand pages of prose-writing and nine thousand pages in full score of music. Verdi completed a prodigious number of operas, but he was blessed, like few human beings, with long years of health, yielding fruit at the age of eighty-five.

If we project, by contrast, the creativeness of other musicians against the briefness of their life span, does not the accomplishment of Purcell, Pergolesi, Mozart and Schubert appear little short of miraculous? Frequently, these great composers, with their seemingly superhuman achievements, have been portrayed as musical wonder men. Obviously, it was their miraculous inspirational drive that made the seemingly impossible possible: the invention of the musically beautiful as well as its astonishing multiplication in a profusion of scores written in so short a time. These feats are the secret of genius. Music is found like a gem. It is turned out transcendentally, without effort and toil. Not the conquest of work as the exertion of human will is the miracle, but the transcendental trance in which the whole creative act is believed to occur.

But the self-analysis of the great composers who worked that "miracle" brings the problem much closer to earth. The composers show their gigantic output, not only in the light of inspiration, but equally as a testimony of unfatiguing, relentless labor. Thus, Haydn destroys the illusion of the mere rapidity of production which is so frequently attributed to him: "I was never a fast writer and always composed with thoughtfulness and industry." To his publisher, Brietkopf and Härtel, Haydn writes in reference to his *Creation:* "No one will believe how much pain and effort I had to exert."

Mozart commented on his string quartets dedicated to Haydn: "Essi sono è vero, il frutto d'uno lunga e laboriosa fatica." These words asserting that the quartets were "the fruit of long and laborious work" are to be taken literally. There is no exaggeration in such a confession made by one great craftsman to another. And Mozart leaves no doubt about the difficult character of a specific task. He explains to his father: "You can't believe how hard it is to put a thing like this into harmony—that it should be appropriate to the blowing instruments and yet no effect lost. Well, I have to use the night for that, otherwise it won't work out. I will try to work as rapidly as possible and yet to write well, hurry permitting." In Mozart's short life, many nights were thus spent, adding to the working hours of the days which proved too short for him.

Mozart's wife relates[4] the origin of the Overture to *Don Giovanni.* Two days before the premiere of the opera in Prague, exhausted from rehearsals, Mozart explained to Constanze that he had not yet written the overture. He would have to write it that very night! And so he asked his wife to make him punch and stay with him to keep him awake while he wrote. Constanze solved her part of the task by telling him fairy tales such as "Aladdin and His Lamp" and others, which made him shed tears for laughter. Yet the punch was apparently not the proper stimulant; it made Mozart so sleepy that he dozed off the moment Constanze stopped talking and worked only as long as she recited her tales. Finally sleepiness made progress impossible; Constanze insisted that he sleep on the couch but promised to awaken him in an hour. He slept so deeply that she did not have the heart to disturb his rest and let him sleep on for two full hours—until five o'clock. At seven o'clock the copyist was due. And at seven the *Don Giovanni* overture was finished.

The story of the origin of the famous overture reads like one of the fairy tales which Constanze told Mozart during the night. But the realistic explanation of such phenomenal work lies obviously in Mozart's procedure: he had the music fully in his head. What he accomplished in the crucial night was the mere physical part of writing out the score. This task, due to his prodigious memory, was so mechanical that he could even listen "with one ear" to the fairy tales of his wife during the occupation of score writing.

The tempo of Mozart's work depended also on the actual pleasure he derived from his task. Certain commissions were the source of difficulties which Mozart described in letters referring to the Bardengesang and the Adagio for the watchmaker. The latter task bored him very much. How pathetic that Mozart should have to struggle with a composition to earn a few ducats which he hoped to present to his wife. On the other hand, if Mozart was stimulated, work progressed very lightly, a fact which is borne out by various letters.[5]

Gluck stated that his preparation for a new work usually required "one entire year; and not rarely did I contract a severe disease from such effort—yet people call this composing light tunes." The struggles of Beethoven for perfection are proverbial. As we shall see later, many of his compositions took years to mature and were the result of seemingly endless toil and labor. This, however, does not mean that he was incapable of producing rapidly. The Sextet, Op. 71, was composed in one single night. Likewise the *Fidelio* overture owes its existence to such phenomenal effort in tempo and concentration.

Handel often marked the date when he completed a main

section of a score. Due to this habit, we are able to trace his progress almost step by step. The first part of the *Messiah* was composed between August 22nd and 28th (1741): it took him only six days to complete a manuscript of one hundred pages. The second part, longer than the first, bears the final date, September 6th, and the final and shortest part, fifty-one pages in all, was concluded on September 12th. Even if we assume that Handel had the music already in his head, and that he wrote his scores in a manner that left much for the copyist to complete,[6] he must have worked at white heat. The completion of the great score from August 22nd to September 12th is a colossal achievement, even as far as the physical effort of mere writing is concerned. It is a deed of unbroken will power as well as of unbroken inspiration.

Schubert's personal notes, like those of Handel, help to trace the astonishing intensity and tempo of his production. On one single day, October 15, 1815, he accomplished the colossal task of writing no less than eight songs. On several occasions, the answer to how much time was required for an individual score was supplied by the composer himself. At the end of the first movement of the Quartet in B-flat major, Schubert noted, "written in four and a half hours." The manuscript of the four-hand overture in F bears the remark: "In November (1819) in the room of Mr. Joseph Huettenbrenner in the Civic Hospital—written in three hours and skipped lunch because of it."

Such achievements of speed and inspiration must not make us overlook the fact that Schubert knew truly Beethovenian struggle for the completion of some of his most important works. Such was the case with certain songs, the perfection of which was achieved only through repeated settings of the tonal substance.

Schumann completed one hundred and fifty works in the space of twenty-five creative years. In productive spells, his music erupted like the fiery lava of a volcano. In the happy equilibrium which followed his marriage he poured out no less than one hundred and thirty-eight songs in a single year (1840). And what songs, how inspired, how novel in their artistic features! The First Symphony was speedily sketched in no more than three days, from January 23rd to January 26, 1841. Schumann still had a decade of creative though gradually deteriorating power before him. And even threatening mental disorder permitted isolated flickerings of the sadly doomed creativeness.

Berlioz, either spellbound by lightning flashes or desperately left void, must follow the freaks of moods of inspiration through thick and thin, through day and night. Yet in contrast to the creative type of a Rossini (with whom he shared these traits) Berlioz was more fortunate in another respect: his creative powers did not abandon him in the later years of his life. At the peak of inspiration, the tempo of work is always fast. Yet what is conquered in rapid work calls later for elaborate alterations and sometimes for complete revisions. Thus, Berlioz states in his memoirs:

Under the constant influence of Goethe's *Faust*, I wrote the fantastique —some movements with great difficulty, others with incredible easiness. The adagio, The Scene in the Country, gave me trouble for three weeks. Yet I composed in one single night The March to the Scaffold. Therefore I had to change considerably . . .

With Wagner, everything spells lengthiness and quantity. As a rule he did not work at a fast tempo on his voluminous scores. But once he settled down to work, Wagner progressed with a certain steadiness, turning out at times a regular number of score pages per day with the dependability of a true craftsman. The composer relates that while working on *Die Walküre*, he completed six pages as a daily self-assignment. As a young man, and under trying circumstances, he finished *The Flying Dutchman* in seven weeks, exclusive of the instrumentation. In April, 1859 Wagner commented himself on the quantity and quality of his achievements: "Next November it will be six years since I have started to compose again. In those six years, I have written four, I say four great operas." (He included *Siegfried* which was only half finished.) For such periods of extraordinary creativeness, Wagner paid in equally long periods of silence, at least as far as the actual composition of music was concerned. But as we have seen, such periods were wisely turned into other productive channels.

Bruckner required much time, worked cautiously and was most conscientious in the setting of every note. In composing, he believed that there could be as little hurry as there is in a church service. Since his music was not particularly in demand, worries over deadlines were beyond his concern. By contrast, his contemporary Brahms was frequently rushed by publishers to finish a manuscript for print. In 1870, however, Brahms warned his publisher, Simrock: "Give up driving your composers—it may become dangerous. Some colleagues have spoiled the world—Bach, Mozart, Schubert. But if we cannot emulate them in writing beautifully, we must guard ourselves against trying to emulate them in writing rapidly."

THE DAILY SCHEDULE

One is not apt to think of composers as men of habit and regularity. Inspiration, as we have seen in so many instances, is a freakish and willful force evading all law and order. Would it not then be absurd to expect from an artist, with his proverbial moods and temperamental disposition, the regularity and normality of the average person's way of living and working?

Biographical data, however, do not necessarily lend themselves to a Bohemian picture of a composer's daily life, where the only rule is the absence of rule—a life without schedule, routine and punctuality. The daily habits of many composers display much more regularity than popular notion presumes. The reason lies first of all in the fact that composing is an act calling for high organization. It is unthinkable without strict order. Master scores are intricate constructions, works of high craft, often based on complex plans. Their intimate mechanism, the closely interrelated parts must be put together with utmost precision, like the parts of a fine clock. To assemble the components of such intricate work requires intense planning, great effort, lasting energy, controlling will, and above all, time and again time! Voluntarily placing themselves under these hard conditions, facing their tasks, and mastering them, the great composers have learned early to be hard workers also, gearing the highest degree of their life energies toward the creative goal.

The previously mentioned gigantic output of certain masters, the immensity of their total work, all accomplished in the span of a single lifetime belies the brevity of their earthly pilgrimage: Mozart and Schubert were taken in the prime of their lives. Purcell, Weber, Mendelssohn, Chopin, Schumann—all prolific writers—did not reach the half century mark. They all worked with a superhuman intensity as though they knew they were living on borrowed time.

Those who lived to old age, such as Rameau, Handel, Haydn, Cherubini and Verdi were equally untiring workers. How could they otherwise have conquered their self-imposed life task, so immense in quantity and quality, if they permitted themselves major detours from an unbroken and steady line of the creative task?

A cross section through the daily schedules of some masters will acquaint us with the arrangement of their time. Haydn according to his own statements[7] "arose at six-thirty in the morning in the summer; during the winter at seven." Thus starts the work day, extremely busy in the morning and gradually relaxing toward the evening. While getting dressed, he also listens to the playing of early pupils; at eight o'clock he has breakfast. The hours after are spent improvising at the piano, searching for specific thoughts that suit a particular score. What he finds, he immediately writes down. In these morning hours at the piano, many first sketches originated. Dinner, the main meal in the middle of the day (following the traditional Austrian style) is usually taken from two to three. The meal is followed by reading music or books. At four o'clock, composing is taken up again. Haydn would test the sketches he had rapidly written in the morning and put them carefully into score, allowing for this procedure considerable time, usually three to four hours. In the evening, preferably from eight to nine, he went out. Upon his return, if no social obligations kept him away, he would either continue to write or read until supper time—usually about ten. The remainder of the evening belonged to relaxation with friends. Naturally this schedule was not typical of Haydn's earlier years, when his duties as conductor involved a different routine of rehearsing and directing the court orchestra in Lukavec and Esterház.

Mozart, less fortunate than Haydn in the free disposal of his time, had to adjust his daily routine to extraneous factors depending upon where he lived, with whom, whether he had the whole day for himself or was tied up with lessons at the apartments or palaces of his various pupils. Much of his composing was done whenever he could fit it in between such professional and social obligations.

That is the reason his statements concerning favorite hours for composing do not coincide and even contradict each other. Once the evening, another time the morning is mentioned as first choice. From Mannheim, December 20, 1777, he communicated to his father a daily schedule full of complicating circumstances:

I am writing this at eleven o'clock at night, for it is the only time I am free. We can't get up before eight o'clock, as until half-past eight there is no daylight in our room which is on the ground floor. I dress in haste and at ten, I sit down to compose until about twelve or half-past twelve. Then I go to Wendling's, where I again compose a little until half-past one when we have lunch. Thus the time passes until three when I go off to the Mainzischer Hof (an inn) to give a Dutch officer a lesson in galanterie and thoroughbass for which I receive, if I am not mistaken, four ducats for twelve lessons. At four I must be home again to instruct the daughter of the house. We never begin our lessons before half-past four, as we have to wait for the lights. At six I go to Cannabich's and give Mlle. Rosa her lesson. I stay there for supper after which we talk or occasionally someone plays. If it is the latter, I always take a book out of my pocket and read—as I used to do in Salzburg.[8]

Three months later, from Mannheim, February 14, 1778, Mozart again tells of adverse circumstances which force him to compose at night:

. . . It is not surprising that I have not been able to finish them for I never have a single quiet hour here. I can only compose at night, so that I can't get up early as well; besides, one is not always in the mood for working. I could, to be sure, scribble off things the whole day long, but a composition of this kind goes out into the world and naturally I do not want to have cause to be ashamed of my name on the title page.[9]

Mozart became, however, fully accustomed to composing after dark; in fact, writing to his father on December 13, 1780, from Munich, he refers to the evening as his favorite time for work.

Yet two letters from Vienna tell of Mozart composing in the early part of the day. "In the morning I write in my room and in the afternoon I am rarely in the house," Mozart informs his father on July 25, 1781. And again on December 22, 1781: "Every morning at six o'clock my friseur arrives and wakes me and by seven I have finished dressing. I compose until ten when I give a lesson to Frau von Trattner and at eleven to the Countess Rumbeck . . ." Typical of how external circumstances, be it teaching, social obligations or concerts, affect his composing schedule is the account he gives to his sister, on February 13, 1782, from Vienna:

My hair is always done by six o'clock in the morning and by seven I am fully dressed. I then compose until nine. From nine to one I give lessons. Then I lunch, unless I am invited to some house where they lunch at two or three o'clock, as for example today and tomorrow at Countess Zichy's and Countess Thun's. I can never work before five or six o'clock in the evening and even then I am often prevented by a concert. If nothing intervenes, I compose until nine. I then go to my dear Constanze though the joy of seeing one another is nearly always spoilt by her mother's bitter remarks. I shall explain this in my next letter to my father. For that is the reason why I am longing to be able to set her free and to rescue her as soon as possible. At half past ten or eleven I come home—it depends on her mother's darts and on my capacity to endure them! As I cannot rely on being able to compose in the evening, owing to the concerts which are taking place and also to the uncertainty as to whether I may not be summoned now here and now there, it is my custom (especially if I get home early) to compose a little before going to bed. I often go on writing until one—and am up again at six.[10]

Beethoven's favorite working time, according to Dr. Wawruch, his last physician, was the lonely, quiet peace of night. Schindler, whose account is not limited to the last period of Beethoven's life, relates that his master, winter and summer alike, got up at dawn and went right to his desk. He worked until two or three P.M., at which time he had his main meal. In the meantime, however, he would run once or twice into the open air. Beethoven particularly favored working and planning on his walks.

Schubert habitually spent the time from nine in the morning until two o'clock composing or studying. Yet we read also about work on the spur of the moment, which occurred at any time of the day or night. There is, as in the case of Mozart, no irreconcilable conflict in these varied reports. We must interpret Schubert's submission to regularity as a routine devoted to the sketching and working out of large compositions. But inspiration seized the artist beyond all schedules and timetables. Thus some of his most beautiful songs were jotted down in one single flash. With a letter to Joseph Huettenbrenner, February 21, 1818, Schubert encloses a

Lied: "I am sending here, another one which I have just written here at Anselm Huettenbrenner's at twelve o'clock midnight." This song was "The Trout." And in his sleepiness, he grabbed the ink bottle instead of the sand pourer and spilled it all over the new music. To his brother Ferdinand, Schubert writes in the same year: "It is night, half-past eleven, and finished is your *Mourning Mass.*"

Weber's working day was strictly organized as indicated in a letter to his friends, the Türk family, October 2, 1812. He tells them that he rises at six o'clock in the morning and works at his desk or piano continuously from seven to one. Then he has his lunch. At four he resumes work again until nine o'clock. After the evening meal, he reads in bed from ten until twelve o'clock. Six hours of sleep suffice.

Berlioz distributed work almost equally throughout the night and day depending on changing inclination: "I have spent whole nights over my score and the strenuous work of instrumentation keeps me sometimes eight hours without interruption at my table— immovable—without my being tempted even to change my position."[11]

Much of the romantic music of Wagner originated on a steady schedule once the initial inspiration had set into full motion his mental machinery. A great deal of work occurred in the forenoon: "In Venice (1858-1859) my schedule was kept with the utmost regularity throughout the whole time (seven months). I worked until four or five o'clock, stepped into an already waiting gondola in order to ride along the Canale Grande to the Piazetta. There I went into my favorite restaurant."[12] Generally, what he sketched before noon, he tested on the piano in the afternoon. If he did not go out, the hours between five and six (particularly when dusk fell at this time), were his favorite hours for this purpose. And with his brand of humor, the creator of *Twilight of the Gods* called himself the "twilight man."[13]

The composer of light music may be a hard worker, too: that which makes one smile takes serious effort to create. Johann Strauss worked with utmost concentration every day from ten to two in his safely guarded study to which he referred as his "factory."[14] Once in a while, he would leave the room for a few throws at the billiard table. The clicking and rhythmic tones of the brightly colored ivory balls, their smooth gliding on the green surface had a fascination for Strauss as well as for Mozart who equally loved the relaxation of billiards and other games, and with whom Strauss had characteristic traits of musical playfulness in common. Locked in his workshop, Strauss permitted himself another interruption, that of a visit of his favorite barber, Scharff. Yet the business of shaving did not stop that of composing: "When I shaved Herr von Strauss, he would jump out of his seat and rush to the piano to play a few measures, then take one of the pencils that were lying around and make a few notations." No doubt with such an inspirational client, the barber had to be a master of his craft, too.

Just as in every other aspect of creation, the individuality of the composer enters into his choice of working hours. External circumstances, over which the composer has no control, are likewise reflected in his schedule. Often there is a conflict between the hours the composer would choose (if he were master of his time and situation) and those that he is forced to accept. Thus, Mozart's conflicting statements are to be interpreted as having their roots more in the external set-up than in his individual preference.

From most sources, quoted and others, we learn that many composers work in the early morning. The mind is fresh after the rest of sleep. Thoughts come quickly, the imagination is vivid, the rested physique can easily tackle the by-tasks of composition—score reading, writing, playing. Hours of the afternoon are given only second preference: many composers followed the old-world routine of eating the main meal in the early afternoon after which relaxation and perhaps a little nap were in order. Such after-dinner rest, in midday, helped them to keep very late hours at night—hours which certain composers found as productive as the early hours of dawn. Night work is even first choice with some: the stillness and quiet of the environment, the darkness where the only light is that of the lamp focused on the note paper, is conducive to utmost concentration. Many great works were written at night alone, a few of them in one single night.[15]

MUSIC MADE TO ORDER

> I being sure of that commission
> would work with greater peace of
> mind.
>
> MOZART

COMMISSIONS AND INSPIRATION

MUSIC has been made to order at all times. For thousands of years, composers both of true genius as well as of mere craftsmanship have been commissioned to write for various purposes: sacred and secular scores, oratorios and operas, symphonies, chamber music and scores for the modern electrical media of performance. Just as the architect builds to order, so the composer copes with the specified wishes of his sponsor. And as any artisan, the composer carries out his commissions according to the rules of his specific craft. Under contract, he completes and delivers the work at a particular date. He is paid for it like the artisan for his piece of handiwork.

What are the artistic results of commissions? What effect do they have upon the creative attitude of the composer? Can a commission truly inspire in the sense of other impulses which we have come to know as inspirational sources, or does it rather inhibit the productive flow? Are the artistic results of commissioned music below the standards of those works which do not seem to have any tie-up with a specific occasion or demand from the outside world?

No doubt, the "business" angle in the composer's workshop

destroys the romantic illusion of the musician as a free creator who listens only to his inner voice and proudly spurns all monetary offers. The believer in an aloof art will not grant the same honor to the composer of commissions as he would bestow wholeheartedly upon the artist who is his own commissioner. The only order to which the latter answers is that of his inspiration and artistic conscience. All measurements of work are dictated by his inner vision and not by the caprice or fancy of a sponsor. His yardstick is the envisioned ideal, his art is aloof, disinterested. His schedule is the timetable of imagination, not a deadline set by a contract. His music cannot be purchased. Composing for money means selling oneself. His kingdom is not of this earth . . .

But the world we are living in has by no means permitted even the great composer to take such an attitude: to listen to his inner voice alone, to disdain offers of work coming to him under various titles. On the contrary, great masters considered commissions most desirable—if it were only for the feeling of security derived therefrom.

Moreover, the relationship of art patron to the composer has assumed various forms throughout history and so has the procedure of commissioning music. A commissioned work is one where the composer is engaged to write for compensation, frequently according to certain specified conditions. These conditions may permit the composer wide freedom of self-expression. They may, on the other hand, tie him down to rather rigid requirements of style and form.

In the wider sense of the term, the bulk of music in the Middle Ages was commissioned. Medieval composers worked as employees of the church, serving creatively the ideals of Catholic liturgy. Hence their scores had to meet definite stylistic specifications imposed by the church. Medieval doctrines did not yield living space to a free artistic expression in a manner which the modern artist has come to take for granted. The medieval composer expressed the spiritual ideology of his religion just as the medieval architect integrated the Catholic theology into the Gothic cathedral. The Catholic ideal of universality called musically speaking for broad expression of the collective spirit, for an all-embracing intelligibility. Palestrina, the "savior of church music," stands out as the greatest representative of this trend in the sixteenth century. His music put the ecclesiastical aestheticism into tonal reality. And we learn from his example how the guideposts of a music for all can cope with the highest artistic standards.

If Palestrina followed the guideposts of Catholic liturgy, German church musicians of the seventeenth century composed along lines which Luther had promulgated. This tradition lived on and culminated in the greatest representative of Protestant service: Johann Sebastian Bach. Most of the immortal music which the cantor at St. Thomas in Leipzig wrote was born from the need of the community. With his passions, oratorios and cantatas, the master supplied the demands of the church calendar and its regular holidays. But also smaller works, organ preludes and numerous other scores; were written to meet a specific purpose within Bach's duties at his church.

Theatrical music, since its inception and up to the present day, was usually commissioned. Monteverdi's operas, Lully's ballets, Purcell's incidental music were written for specific festivities and occasions at court.

Haydn, from his thirtieth to his fifty-eighth year, was in the service of Prince Esterházy.[1] The contract with his employer contained the following clause: ". . . by order of His Highness, the Vice Conductor (Haydn) is obliged to compose such musical matters as are commanded of him and thereafter new compositions must not be commercialized to anybody else, nor be copied, etc." This formulation amounts to a business contract in the legal connotation of the term. All music involved therein was made to order for the prince.

MOZART WRITES COMMISSIONED MUSIC

Unfortunately, sponsorship did not play a constant part in the life of Mozart. If it had, his plight not only would have been easier but posterity would have greatly profited. This is proven by the fact that Mozart's operas, for instance, were all written to order. But in the years from 1787 to 1789, Mozart wrote no operas for the simple reason that none were commissioned.[2] No musician's life could have started out more auspiciously than that of Wolfgang Amadeus: six years old, a little man with sword and peruke, he appeared before the almighty Austrian Empress Maria Theresia, and moved the whole court of Hapsburg-Lorraine with his incredible gift at the clavier. To what this appreciation amounted on the part of his Empress, at a crucial time in Mozart's life, can be judged by a letter which Maria Theresia wrote nine years later[3] to her son, Maximilian. The Archduke had considered employing the then fifteen-year-old Mozart as court composer in Milan but hesitated to do so without his mother's advice which reads:

You ask me about taking into your services the young Salzburg musician. I do not know in what capacity, believing that you have no need for a composer or for useless people. . . . What I say is intended only to urge you not to burden yourself with useless people, and not to give such people permission to represent themselves as belonging to your service. It gives one's service a bad name when such people run about like beggars; and besides, he has a large family.

Thus spoke the worshiped and glorified benefactress from her throne. And with such sponsorship, Mozart spent the thirty-six years of his life in constant struggle.

To be sure, commissions came to Mozart, too, but they were sporadic and uncertain. Always in desperate need of money, he had to write little tidbits for whatever they could bring. At the same time, he tried to make money as a performer on the piano. His letter of November 13, 1777, relates of the compensation for a concert at court:

It was just as I had expected. No money, but a fine gold watch. At the moment, ten carolins would have suited me better than the watch, which including the chain and the mottoes has been valued at twenty. What one needs on a journey is money; and let me tell you, I now have five watches. I am therefore seriously thinking of having an additional watch pocket on each let of my trousers so that when I visit some great lord, I shall wear both watches (which, moreover, is now the fashion), so that it will not occur to him to present me with another one.

His collection of gold watches did not help to pay Mozart's bills. What was still worse, he could not pawn them either because of the "honor" attached to these gifts from highborn donors.

Since royalty did not condescend to employ Mozart or at least to remunerate his services with cash and currency, he was forced to turn to other sources. Toward the end of 1777, a Dutchman promised Mozart two hundred florins for a series of compositions. Optimistically, Wolfgang reported on the hopeful venture to his father, and referred to Monsieur de Jean (the Dutchman) as a gentleman of means, a lover of all arts and sciences and a great friend and admirer of his. In short, he seemed really a first-rate fellow, willing to pay two hundred gulden for such bagatelles as three short concertos and several quartets for flute. Yet the outcome of this enterprise turned into just another of many disappointments that Mozart had to take throughout his life. Three months later (February 14, 1778), Mozart admitted to his father that the Dutchman had sent him only ninety-six florins because he had finished only two concertos and three quartets.[4] (Mozart adds that he was unable to finish the other scores: he never had a single quiet hour in which to compose.) Ninety-six florins! One hundred minus four was the amount the "lover of all the sciences" sent to his greatly admired protégé. He would not even make it the round figure of one hundred! This was in February, 1778. Eight years later in his short life, the sad spectacle of Mozart begging for commissions because of pressing debts continued. This time (August 8, 1786) he resorted to approaching the former valet and friseur of the Mozart family who was now in the service of the Prince Fürstenberg:

I venture to make a little musical offer to His Highness which I beg of you, my friend, to put before him. As His Highness possesses an orchestra, he might like to have works composed by me for performance solely at his court, a thing which in my humble opinion would be very gratifying. If His Highness would be so gracious as to order from me every year a certain number of symphonies, quartets, concertos for different instruments, or any other compositions which he fancies, and to promise me a fixed yearly salary, then His Highness would be served more quickly and more satisfactorily, and I, being sure of that commission, would work with greater peace of mind.[5]

A position comparable with that of Haydn's (in economic security) or at least a small but fixed salary is the dream of Mozart. But an inexorably cruel fate selected him for the earthly paradox of a world-famous and at the same time a poor struggling musician—a tragedy in which one can see no sense other than that of an indictment against the self-contented society which permitted it.

Mozart did not receive the desired commission from Prince Fürstenberg. He worked along on other tasks, some large, some small, but never simple undertakings. Whatever he touched constituted for him an intricate artistic problem. Thus he pondered over a seemingly indifferent small commission and as usual described the problem to his father (December 12, 1782):

I am engaged in a very difficult task, the music for "The Bard's Song" of Denis on Gibraltar. But this is a secret, for it is a Hungarian lady who wishes to pay this compliment to Denis. The ode is sublime, beautiful, anything you like, but too exaggerated and pompous for my fastidious ears. But what is to be done? The golden mean of truth in all things is no longer either known or appreciated. In order to win applause one must write stuff which is so inane that a cabdriver could sing it, or so unintelligible that it pleases precisely because no sensible man can understand it. This is not what I have been wanting to discuss with you; but I should like to write a book, a short introduction to music, illustrated by examples, but I need hardly add, not under my own name.[6]

The letter is remarkable: it shows how Mozart finds difficulties in a task which, to a mere craftsman, would have been a trivial and routine job. But Mozart could work only on a high art level. He even tried to find a particular style for this score ordered by the anonymous Hungarian lady. Notwithstanding its banality, the subject led Mozart's mind to important aesthetic reflections. He created, as it were, his own inspiration.[7]

But Mozart's imagination went on strike when the commission held no artistic challenge for him. Mozart, the supreme musical craftsman, was caught in a deadlock by another craftsman, a watchmaker. All of Mozart's technique could not conquer that small task because he could not stimulate the necessary interest and thus lacked the driving force of work. Yet a letter written on October 3, 1790 from Frankfurt am Main toward the close of his life plainly shows the reason why Mozart could not quit an unpleasant job:

. . . I have now made up my mind to compose at once the adagio for the watchmaker and then to slip a few ducats into the hand of my dear little wife. And this I have begun; but as it is a kind of composition which I detest, I have unfortunately not been able to finish it. I compose a bit of it every day—but I have to break off now and then as I get bored. And indeed, I would give the whole thing up if I had not such an important reason to go on with it. But I still hope that I shall be able to force myself gradually to finish it. If it were for a large instrument and the work would sound like an organ piece, then I might get some fun out of it. But, as it is, the work consists solely of little pieces which sound too high-pitched and too childish for my taste.[8]

Other commissions in Mozart's workshop led to truly immortal works. The two most significant examples occurred in the last four years of his life: the opera, *Don Giovanni*, and his opus ultimum, the *Requiem*.

The beginning of the year 1787 found Mozart in Prague and in gay spirits. He reported to his friend, Gottfried von Jacquin (January 15, 1787): "The one subject of conversation here is *Figaro*; nothing is played, sung or whistled but *Figaro*; nobody goes to any opera but *Figaro*; everlastingly *Figaro*." Greatly encouraged by such success of the comic opera, Mozart expressed his eagerness to write another score for the intelligent and appreciative public of the Bohemian capital. The impresario of the theater, Bondini, commissioned him to compose an opera for the next year. The contract called for the fee of one hundred ducats and the librettist was to receive fifty.

Lorenzo da Ponte who had already furnished the libretto for *Figaro* (based on Beaumarchais' comedy, *La folle journée*) joined Mozart again in the teamwork of the new opera. Its story was to be that of *Don Giovanni*, of the romantic seducer, his adventures, sins and final punishment. In the middle of plans and preparations for the new work, Mozart suffered the loss of his father on May 28, 1787. Engrossed in the scenes and figures of the brilliant opera, Mozart felt a growing and deep affinity with the paternal figure of the Commandant, who is mortally wounded in the opening scene of the opera but lives on as a statue and even returns as the stony guest in the finale—a human symbol of justice and righteousness. Mozart, sublimating the loss of his father in his creative work, lent the figure of his Commandant all the dignity and paternal majesty which his late father took on in his memory. When the statue of the Commandant starts to speak in the graveyard scene, death is overcome: the father has gone, but his righteous soul lives, speaks, is truly immortal.

It is impossible to believe in the opinion of the biographer Jahn that Mozart was "too busy"[9] with the composition of *Don Giovanni* to think too much about his father's death. How could Wolfgang have been too busy to mourn his closest friend,[10] his teacher, his guide, of whom he said, "Next to God comes Papa." Certainly the problem was not so close to the surface. On the contrary, it clearly points to the deeper strata of artistic sublimation: the explanation of the tie-up between the two great paternal figures in Mozart's real and creative life must be sought in the composer's subconscious. Mozart mourned his father in his creative deed. He strove to fulfill the artistic goal of the great opera as his father himself would have wanted him to do. This happens with great creative natures at a time of such fateful blows. Shakespeare lost his father while deep in work on *Hamlet*. The symbolism of the scene in the tragedy—where the ghost of Hamlet's dead father appears to lead the son on to the fulfillment of his mission—reveals the secret of the creative procedure. In both cases—in Shakespeare's *Hamlet* as well as in Mozart's *Don Giovanni*—our knowledge of the artist's experience throws light on the genesis of these great works.[11]

Three and a half years after father Leopold's death, a haggard man dressed in gray appeared at Mozart's sickbed. It was late in 1791. The solemn man was a messenger of Count Walsegg who had just lost his wife and wanted to honor her memory through a specially composed Requiem. When the count's choice fell on Mozart, he had unknowingly selected a man already marked himself for death. Thoughts of dying, never foreign to Mozart, were now uppermost in his mind. The last half year of his short life had arrived. Mozart was fully attuned in mind and body for the conception of a Mass for the Dead. And so out of a commission grew a work truly immortal in its austere beauty and in its mission to immortalize the soul of its creator. Mozart's *Requiem* became his own.

ARTISTIC IDEALS AND COMMISSIONS

Beethoven explained to his troublesome nephew Karl on August 16, 1823: "Nous sommes trop pauvre, et il faut écrire ou n'avoir pas de quoi." This remark, though not formulated in the most flawless French, has nevertheless an unmistakable meaning. Even the greatest composer writes for a living as well as for creative expression.

He must find some means of income from his scores. If the publisher's fees do not provide adequately, the only hope is to receive orders from private sponsors. Documents show that many of Beethoven's most important works were the result of commissions.

A score of such infinite inspiration as the Ninth Symphony was ordered by the Philharmonic Society of London. On April 6, 1822, Beethoven wrote to Ries, his pupil in the British capital: "How much is the Philharmonic Society likely to give me for a symphony?" When the directors of the Society met on November 10, 1822, they decided to offer Beethoven fifty pounds for the manuscript of a symphony and the rights of the first performance.[12] This sum was satisfactory to Beethoven. He sent his approval on December 20, 1822: "With pleasure I accept your commission to write a new symphony for the Philharmonic Society."

If we compare these dates with those in the section on the genesis of the Ninth Symphony (Chapter X), we realize that this correspondence coincides with the time in which Beethoven was wrestling with various symphonic plans. No doubt, the commission from England hastened the crystallization of his music. After all, Beethoven had to deliver the manuscript for performance and therefore could not indefinitely postpone the decision as to the form of the new symphony. Of course, the commission did not inspire the Ninth, but it would be unfair to underestimate the role of London's sponsorship in this great creative struggle.

A year later (March 20, 1823), Beethoven wrote to the publisher, Peters: "My condition demands that I must be guided more or less by what is to my advantage. It is different, however, with the work itself, because then, God be thanked, I never think of gain, but only of how I compose." In these few sentences, Beethoven states concisely the principle which governs his work on commissions. He admits that he could not afford to remain aloof from material compensation, but his artistic ideals could never be touched by a material offer; this principle is evident in such scores as the string quartets, Op. 127, 130, 132—all works commissioned by Prince Galitzin. This music remains the unequivocal expression of Beethoven's uncompromising spirituality.

There were, however, occasional instances when Beethoven was ready for certain allowances or adjustments in the scores ordered from his workshop: "I do not only write what I should like most, but for the sake of the money which I need."[13] And Beethoven does not hesitate to make the following commitment: "The lady may have a sonata from me. I am willing generally to follow her plan along general lines, also in aesthetic respects." The clue to the astonishing degree of Beethoven's conciliatory attitude must be sought in the different tasks: in cases like the latter one, the urge of self-expression was not involved. Beethoven considered these products made to order in the literal sense, as pieces of mere craft. Hence, his willingness to go along with the specifications of the lady "in aesthetic respects." It was work for money and nothing else. Such a state of affairs might disillusion the naïve believer in Beethoven's high artistic ideals, but he must remember that with deteriorating health and increasing deafness, the master's income from concertizing and teaching had greatly dwindled. Moreover, in Beethoven's last years, his annuity from sponsors like the Archduke Rudolph, Prince Lobkowitz and Count Kinsky had shrunk very much in value. Beethoven had to depend more than ever on income derived from composing. With a sigh he confided to his pupil Ries, on February 25, 1823, that "almost always to live by one's pen is not easy." It certainly was not! Prince Galitzin who had commissioned the previously mentioned quartets was delinquent in his payments to Beethoven. It was in these crucial times that Beethoven turned again for help from Vienna to London. And once more, he was not disappointed. He received a letter from Moscheles sending him one hundred pounds as advancement on a benefit concert which the London Philharmonic Society was planning to give in the near future. Twenty-six days after the date of Moscheles' letter, Beethoven was dead. His high sponsors felt justifiably embarrassed by the generosity of the British Society which had "meddled" in Austrian affairs by relieving the last days of the great master. It was up to the noblemen to convince the Viennese people that Beethoven had not died in want. Archduke Rudolph used the imperial veto power with the official Austrian newspaper and assured the public that Beethoven had had no reason to worry.[14] The press release, however, did not hinder anyone from believing what he chose. And it did not make any difference to Beethoven any more.

FOR AND AGAINST COMMISSIONS

Many works which posterity might have highly evaluated and treasured as lasting contributions to art were never written because of the lack of commissions. In his memoirs Berlioz tells the story of such a frustration:

Before my wife's health had become hopeless and when it was the cause of great expense to me, I dreamt that I was composing a symphony. On awakening next morning, I recollected nearly the whole of the first movement which I can still remember was an allegro in two time, in the key of A minor. I had gone to my table to begin writing it down when I suddenly reflected: "If I write this part I shall let myself be carried on to write the rest. The natural tendency of my mind to expand the material is sure to make it very long. I may perhaps spend three or four months exclusively upon it (I took seven to write *Romeo and Juliet*); meantime I shall do no feuilletons, or next to none, and my income will suffer. When the symphony is finished I shall be weak enough to allow my copyist to copy it out and thus immediately incur a debt of one thousand or twelve hundred francs. Once the parts are copied I shall be harassed by the temptation to have the work performed; I shall give a concert, in which, as is sure to be the case in these days, the receipts will barely cover half the expenses; I shall lose what I have not got; I shall want the necessaries of life for my poor invalid, and shall have no money either for myself or for my son's keep on board ship!" These thoughts made me shudder. I threw down my pen, saying, "Bah! I shall have forgotten the symphony tomorrow." But, the following night the obstinate symphony again presented itself, and I distinctly heard the allegro in A minor, and what was more, saw it written down. I awoke in a state of feverish agitation, and hummed the theme. The form and character of it pleased me extremely: I was about to rise . . . but the reflections of the preceding night again restrained me. I hardened myself against temptation. I clung to the hope of forgetting. At last I fell asleep again, and when I awoke the next day, all recollection had vanished forever.

If a commission had come along at this time, posterity might hear today a work equal in quality to the Symphonie Fantastique or Harold in Italy. But the composition of a symphony was, during these crucial months, a luxury Berlioz could not afford. What a commission could do for him is shown in his grandiose *Requiem*.

He was encouraged to write it, when the Minister of the Interior, de Gasparin, had set up a budget of three thousand francs yearly to stimulate the production of church music in France. Again for the symphony, Harold in Italy, Berlioz received the sum of twenty thousand francs from Paganini who had commissioned the score and expected to play the solo viola part at its first performance. The Mourning and Triumph Symphony are also the result of commissions.

The commissioned artist, as we have seen, may have carte blanche in the execution of his work. Under such conditions, the composer works practically as a free entrepreneur. He expresses himself creatively without any interference on the part of his patron. On the other hand, there is the type of commission which imposes definite conditions upon the artist. Such superimposed orders can have a repressing effect on the creative flow. There seems to be an element, intangible and psychological in essence, which inhibits inspiration: artistic ideals may suffer from a sponsor's order as well as from the mere thought of material compensation and success. An externality like an approaching deadline, a hurry due to pressure for time, may obviously have a deteriorating effect, create blind spots and detract from the high standard of execution of the score. From such ramifications and doubts evolves the negative attitude which is taken by the esoteric composer who claims disinterestedness from worldly and monetary entanglements. He is unconditionally against commissions.

Typical of this attitude is Mendelssohn who rejected anything resembling commissions, along with prize-winning contests or competitions. In 1835, Spohr had called Mendelssohn's attention to a contest and suggested that he should participate with one of his new works. But Mendelssohn refused with the following explanation:

The announcement brought most markedly to my mind how impossible it would be for me to compose anything whatsoever with a thought of a contest. I would not even be able to get started. . . . In fact, if to become a musician one would have to pass an examination, I am convinced I would have to be rejected. The thought of a prize as well as a decision upsets me.

Mendelssohn also declined with firm politeness a commission coming from the Prussian king. In careful diplomatic phrasing, artistic considerations serve to reject the honorable order from King Friedrich Wilhelm, which most contemporary composers would have felt privileged to accept. On October 12, 1842, the king invited Mendelssohn to write a score for the *Medea* of Euripides. But Mendelssohn pointed to the various difficulties of the task: "I do not trust myself with the solution and therefore cannot accept the commission." Likewise, he turned down the offer to write the music for another Greek tragedy, for *Agamemnon*, by Aeschylus. This time the king seemed very eager that Mendelssohn, with his established prestige and proven sense for the classical milieu, should be the one to compose the music for the planned performance in the royal playhouse. But again the composer's decision remained negative: "I could not promise to deliver the composition . . . the task is beyond all my strength." The problem could not be just to write music somehow fitting to the Greek choruses (which every experienced composer could do), but rather to shape the choruses of Aeschylus into the musical forms in the contemporary sense, expressing and reinforcing musically the message of the drama. Mendelssohn's rejection of these most tempting commissions for incidental music in the theater is significant, for it was in this very medium that he achieved such enchanting results as in his unmatched music for Shakespeare's *Midsummer Night's Dream*. The secret is that here the composer felt an affinity with the task. He had already written the overture at the age of seventeen.

On the other hand, these quoted comments, coming as they do from one of the most affluent and independent composers in history, give still another secret away. Mendelssohn could very well afford to take a negative attitude and to refuse whatever did not suit his taste. This, however, does not alter the issue which points to Mendelssohn's aloofness from all practicalities and also to a disinterestedness in external honors. After all, there was glory connected with a king's repeated offers to which Mendelssohn remained indifferent for artistic reasons.

While Mendelssohn was born wealthy, other great composers had to arrange their lives with compromise. For them, the commission fulfilled its essential function as an economic necessity. And since some of the greatest artists were also the most impoverished ones, we cannot be surprised that they not only accepted commissions of all sorts, but at times were forced to beg for them. The commission fulfilled also another purpose: it might give the latent inspiration a chance to seize the artist if he is ready for a specific task—as the genesis of Mozart's *Don Giovanni* and the *Requiem* proves. Specific circumstances and a particular psychological attunement to the commission were all-important factors. Inner affinity with the content of the composition, along with complete freedom in execution, can lead to overwhelming results whereby the commission, as the springboard of a work, remains invisible in the background and does not influence the composer's artistic attitude in any phase of work. By contrast, certain commissions with specified requirements can present, even to a great master, difficulties which he does not easily conquer. Lacking interest, his imagination is stalled. Such commissions are viewed in frank admission only as a source of income.

In the light of all quoted documents, we see that a commission can never directly take the place of inspiration. Tchaikovsky says: "For commissioned works one must sometimes create one's own inspiration." He differentiates between two categories of compositions, the ones he writes on his own initiative because of sudden inclination and urgent need, and compositions inspired from the outside upon the request of a publisher or a friend.[15] But Tchaikovsky hastens to explain in a letter of July 6, 1878, to Madame von Meck that the value of a score does not depend upon the category to which the work belongs. "Very often a piece that was artificially engendered turns out quite successfully, while pieces invented wholly on my own inspiration are sometimes less successful for various incidental reasons. The circumstances surrounding the composer at the time of writing . . . are very important."

When music is made to order, the composer depends primarily upon his craft to meet the task. Craft enables the composer to work within definite limitations and according to definite specifications. Countless commissioned scores throughout history are forgotten, not because they owe their existence to an outside order, but because the composer who fulfilled the order did not have the creative plus which distinguishes a Mozart, Beethoven or Berlioz from the mortal musical craftsman.

THE MUSICAL MOOD

IN THE course of their classical investigation of the psychological premises which surround the creative phenomenon, Schiller confided to Goethe: "In my case, perception occurs first without any definite or clear object. It does not crystallize until later. A certain *musical mood* precedes and only afterward does the poetic idea follow."

How illuminating is Schiller's use of the term "musical mood" in reference to his creative work: the German word *Stimmung* (which he uses) belongs to the language of music. Here it means "to tune up." Human voices singing with each other must be in tune. Likewise the instruments of an orchestra have to be tuned for harmonious performance. The poet's *Stimmung* implies, then, that he is keyed up to his inner voice. He is in the state which is characteristic of the receptive condition of all creative artists.

The musical mood can flow from many inspirational sources. It can lead to many different working methods. In this mood of receptivity, certain composers displayed highly emotional behavior, inexplicable to the unknowing observer. Ries tells[1] of a long walk with Beethoven through the countryside: "During the entire stroll, Beethoven hummed and even screamed, raising and lowering his voice. No sooner did we return to Beethoven's apartment than the enraptured composer ran without taking off his hat to the piano and there was an outburst of at least an hour on the new finale . . ." Beethoven was improvising on the last movement of the *Appassionata*.

Dr. B. (probably Breuning) reports of another excursion with the master during which Beethoven, afire with his music, "wildly

120

gesticulated, screamed and scared a team of oxen away." But these scenes were not limited to outdoor composing and also occurred while Beethoven worked at his desk. This we learn from a Conversation Notebook of the year 1820 where Schindler asks: "How far have you progressed with the Mass? You are supposed to have had terrific outrages during the night. Is this true? Was it in *cum sancto spiritu?*"

But these strong reflexes are by no means characteristic of Beethoven only. Handel and Brahms are also described by witnesses as displaying extreme emotionalism while composing: tears, raging, screaming and stamping their feet.[2] His friends stated that Schubert resembled a somnambulist while writing. Schumann says of himself: "I am all on fire," and Tchaikovsky: "I forget everything and behave as if I were mad; all in me pulsates and vibrates."

Mozart's brother-in-law, Lange, has this to say of the composer's behavior during hours of creativeness:[3] "Never was Mozart, in his words and deeds, to be recognized less as a great man than when occupied with a great work. Then he spoke nonsensically with great confusion and indulged in jokes of a kind which were not usual with him otherwise. Yes, he even purposefully neglected his good behavior." The well-meaning and naïve brother-in-law did not understand the psychological mechanism of the genius to whom he was otherwise close. Mozart's process of composition was one of utmost concentration. The resulting nervous tension required a specific type of relaxation beyond the laws of "good behavior." When Mozart had exhausted his spiritual energy in creative work, his mood swung to an extreme of uninhibitedness, to childish humor, but also to that unrestricted type of wit which we know from the jokes in his letters. All this is Mozart, too! It is not the Mozart of sublime music; it is Mozart, the human being who, between the feasts of creation, relaxes like a naughty boy.

Creative excitement during work itself is not typical of all composers. On the contrary, different creative behavior points to the differences between an emotional art and a constructive craft. It points to the contrast between an involuntary conception in which the composer depends on the forces of the subconscious and a craftsmanship where all emphasis is on the conscious pursuit of the tonal material.

What appears as the *musical mood,* then, is the beginning of the creative process. This mood can be a happy or sad one depending upon what has caused it. It can be one of mere playfulness or enjoyment of craft. But it leads to the lucky moment, to the point from which the realization of the art work starts and from which the mind begins to concentrate on the artistic goal.

THE ARTIST LIVES A DOUBLE LIFE

Once an experience is turned into art, the music starts to live a life of its own. Frequently the emotional associations become the content of the music. Interwoven in its development and growth, the initial creative mood may lend shape to a theme, to complex tonal thoughts, perhaps to a whole work. But the tonal craft also transfers the subjective influx into the province of musical tectonics. A thought may have been touched off by a certain mood, but in the process of composition, it follows intrinsic technical laws of craft. And so the artistic enterprise may lead far away from the place where it started—even into most unexpected channels of imagination. A score begins in a state of great depression; yet it may not necessarily be turned into altogether unhappy music. On the other hand, a work that has begun under bright auspices may soon glow with somber tones. Music changes as one's thoughts change. And even the initial emotions themselves can develop and change as the composer proceeds with the composition. Ideas reshape themselves constantly in the stream of creation.

In short, the act of composing can in itself create specific moods. Tchaikovsky explains this phenomenon in his letter of July 6, 1878 to Madame von Meck:

The sad or happy—are invariably retrospective. With no special reason for rejoicing, I can experience a happy creative mood, and conversely among the happiest surroundings, I may write music suffused with darkness and despair. In brief, the artist lives a double life, an everyday human one and an artistic one, and these two lives do not always coincide.[4]

Some of Tchaikovsky's best-known music serves as an illustration. Even a work so hopeless and tragic in its corner movements, the opening and finale of the Symphony Pathétique, displays moments, almost entire movements of serene charm, of playful elegance and the buoyancy of bursting life.

SURVEY OF INSPIRATIONAL SOURCES

In the composer's discovery of musical ideas, many factors play their part. But the results of these discoveries always serve an identical purpose, namely to transform the raw material gained through inspirational vision, through the phenomena of nature and through abstraction or sheer accident, into tonal construction on the high art level. The inspirational sources of these discoveries cover the whole gamut of human experiences.

The emotional spring of the composition may blend various spheres of association: the impulse stems from emotional reactions, from serene and tragic experiences. Obviously, the kernel of such experiences cannot be composed. Every experience is surrounded by a zone of emotions and reactions wherein the creative musician finds his definite points of contact. Religiosity is expressible in the age-old symbols of musical liturgy. The loss of beloved ones is sublimated in the Mass for the Dead. Wit and humor speak out in tonal corollaries. As the artist eavesdrops on Nature, he captures the song of birds, the sound of animals, the noise of the elements. Here like everywhere Nature appears as the first teacher.

The composer's admiration for the art of other musicians points to new inspirational sources. With the young talent, this admiration manifests itself in an absorption of style which the maturing composer transforms and develops into a style of his own. Even if the artistic experience is psychologically not original (since it is derived from technical deductions and the tracing of foreign structures), the final results of style transformation lead to something new and great. The new is always a new illumination of the old.

Much stimulation is also provided by theoretical analysis, by a study of material pertaining to the specific task which the composer pursues at a particular time. We will show later how the composer strives to arrive at his solution from such inspirational points just as the inventor pursues his idea—half by instinct, half by knowledge.

The role of the accident is manifest wherever musical inventions originate as a by-product of various human activities and experiences. This usually happens when the composer's imagination is firmly directed to the creative goal. At such a time, any acoustic utterance, be it musical or mere noise, enters into the imaginative circle and takes on added meaning for the composer. Yet as the quoted reports of great composers prove, this transformation succeeds only if it coincides with an intense preoccupation of the composer with a specific musical problem.[5] Here, accident is but another word for expressing the unforeseen chance of a musical flash in its various appearances. The finding of an idea is the instantaneous grasping of the musical situation. It is not based on a plan, not arrived at by intermediary logical steps, but luckily born, a chance event—almost like a lottery prize won through betting on the right number.

In short, every variety of human experience can produce the *musical mood* which bears creative fruit. The mood is invited, even courted by the artist, but it cannot be commanded. Wagner sums up the mutual action between creative power and its stimulating forces in the following comparison:

The musical creative power seems to me like a bell, which, the bigger it is, does not give its full tone until put into motion by an appropriate force. This force is an inner one. And if it is not inwardly present, it is not present at all. The purely inward force, however, does not operate until it is awakened from the outside through something related and yet different.[6]

PART TWO

CRAFT

CHAPTER SIX

WORKSHOPS

I have never pretended to belong
to those enviable beings who
possess a studio.

BRAHMS

I have been smitten with the
luxury devil.

WAGNER

MATERIALS AND TOOLS

TONE is the material of music. It is the raw stuff which the composer uses as the painter uses color or the sculptor stone. The formed material of music—its sounds moving along in time—appeals to the ear just as the forms of the visual arts appeal to the eye. Hence, it is from the basic acoustic qualities of tone that all artistic means at the disposal of the composer emerge.

Tone, then, is the root of all musical work. Its various properties and permutations carry the art work to its aesthetic goal. Everything that is art in music depends essentially upon the combination of tones and upon their concerted action. Among these tonal qualities, pitch and duration play the primary role, at least from an historic point of view.

Musical events occur in the horizontal and vertical dimensions. In the horizontal, tones occur one after the other. The differences of pitch lead here to a motif, a phrase, a theme. By contrast, the vertical dimension ties two or more tones into simultaneous sound. Here, the results are chords, and their organic succession results in harmony. These horizontal and vertical factors of music assume manifold types of mutual relationships. The composer can build his music along linear patterns in such a way that only the horizontal factor seems important and the role of the vertical is negligible. He can also reverse this procedure: then the harmonic factor of his music will appear far stronger than the horizontal one. Obviously, the two dimensional impulses can operate in close connection with each other. They may blend in the art work in such a manner that an impression of complete balance will result.[1]

In what way and to what extent the factors dominate or even cancel each other becomes an all-important characteristic of the composer's approach to his work, determining the expression and character of his music. Logically, both factors, the horizontal and the vertical, are the keys also to musical theory. In the following chapters we will learn about their function in the composer's workshop.

Music happens in time. Hence, along with pitch, the most important property of tone is its duration. In this time element lies the foundation of rhythm—the grouping of tones according to their value. Intensities of sound in their innumerable variations supply the composer with all contrasts of loudness and softness. These intensities are referred to as dynamics whereas the term agogics pertains to time and all problems of tempo variation.

The final quality of tone is its color, that character of sound called timbre. Like all the other properties and their application in the composer's workshop, tone color is best understood in the historic perspective of its different functions.

Pitch, duration, intensity and tone color (all these ingredients deducted from the various properties of tone) assume the role of elementary material in the composer's workshop. Yet, in his practical approach to work, these elements do not play an equally important part. Melody, harmony and rhythm are of primary importance: no music on the art level in our modern sense is made without their full integration into the score. But dynamics and tone color have only gradually gained an importance comparable to that of the other elements. Prior to the end of the eighteenth century, their character was accidental. The baroque composer's chief concern with tonal architecture did not warrant detailed exploration of the coloristic and dynamic qualities of his tonal material. Likewise every other style period shows its own specific evaluation of the various tonal elements. What appears to be unessential and even extraneous in one style may assume overwhelming importance in another. We have only to recall the various roles enacted by tone color throughout history in order to realize the revolutionary change that has taken place in the composer's evaluation of the different properties of his material. For example: if we study the set-up of orchestras in the first part of the seventeenth century, we find variegated ensembles, veritable conglomerations of instruments. This shows that the Renaissance musician had little or no discrimination for specific orchestral tone color. It took three hundred years to develop gradually a sensitivity for tone color which gave rise to musical styles in which timbre appears all-important.[2]

Regardless of period and style, the material of the musician always plays an essentially different role than the material in the hands of other artists. The painter paints a subject and applies the material of his colors and lines to a certain design, a landscape, a portrait, a still life. The sculptor, too, forms from his material of plaster, marble or bronze a certain object, be it a head, a body or a group. The composer, in contrast, has no such concrete subject. His work, a play of tonal sensations, always remains comparatively abstract: even if a subject shines through the text of his vocal forms or if the subject is associatively suggested by a program, the composer can never represent the content of his form in the sense that the painter or sculptor can. The musical representation of a subject matter always occurs indirectly. The direct carrier of all musical content is nothing but tone. And here lies the special importance of tone property in the musical workshop.

Like any artist craftsman, so the composer uses tools in his workshop: pen and pencils, sketchbook and score paper, a metronome (since Mälzel's day)[3] and certain instruments which aid the flow of his music on its way from the brain to the note paper. Among the various musical instruments which serve the composer in his study, the piano holds first place. The keyboard enables the composer to test his tonal combinations and to control his harmonies and contrapuntal features in the working out stage. The music stand of the piano permits convenient writing, jotting down on paper what has just been tried on the keyboard. Thus, the piano has functioned for many composers as a real working table, a sounding laboratory for their tonal combinations, sonorities and textures.

Yet the keyboard instruments of the old and new styles—harpsichords and clavichords, modern uprights and grands, harmoniums and last but not least the organ—have proved to be more than mere tools assisting the composer in the process of sketching. Some composers were also great performers on the organ or clavier, masterful executants who spent inspired hours with their favorite instruments. To them the keyboard served often as a springboard for their tonal imagination. Bach and Handel, César Franck and Bruckner on the organ bench, Haydn, Mozart and Couperin on the harpsichord, Beethoven, Schumann, Brahms, Chopin and Liszt on the modern piano were all famous for their extemporaneous playing and composing. And many of their compositions originated in this impromptu style, improvised in productive hours of instrumental performance. Later some of these fantasies were set into script from memory.

Their instruments are indicative of the composer's creative style and expression. The powerful grands, of which he received a new one every year, suggest the grandeur of Liszt's chromatic gallops. An imposing instrument conspicuously filled his worldly atelier in Weimar which consisted of two large rooms—a workshop and concert hall in one—always ready to receive an admiring and select audience.

Quite a contrast is the smaller type of piano, a little upright Pleyel, belonging to Chopin.[4] It indeed suggests the quality and tonal gentleness of the music that was composed on it. The clavichord of Rameau, the harpsichord of Haydn and Mozart,[5] the grand piano of Beethoven suggest to a certain extent the kind of music that these masters evoked on their keyboards. The severe, powerful and polyphonic quality of Beethoven's last piano sonatas is forever associated with a particular instrument which linked the last decade of Beethoven's life in so friendly a manner with England. The

master received a grand piano, No. 7362, which Thomas Broad-
wood of London shipped to Vienna on December 27, 1817.
Beethoven's letter of acknowledgment is written in his curious
French, the qualities of which lie in expressive suggestion rather
than in obedience to grammar:

A Monsieur Thomas Broadvood a Londres (en Angleterre)
Mon trés cher Ami Broadvood:
Jamais je n'eprouvais pas un plus grand Plaisir de ce que me causa votre
Annonce de l'arrivée de Cette Piano, avec qui vous m'honores de m'en
faire présent; je regarderai Come un Autel, ou je deposerai les plus belles
offrandes de mon Esprit au divine Apollon.. Aussitôt Come, je recevrai
votre Excellent instrument, je vous enverrai d'en abord les Fruits de
l'inspiration des premiers moments, que j'y passerai, pur vous servir d'un
Sourvenir de moi à vous mon très cher B., et je soutaits ce que, qu'ils
soient dignes de votre instrument . . .

Not only in domestic workrooms, but also on journeys, the piano
appears as an aid to the composer. It supplements what the abstract
imagination cannot supply alone. Mendelssohn writes on July 14,
1831, from Milan: "I finally took a Tafel Klavier and tackled the
eternal Walpurgis night with rage, so that the thing can have an
end." When the imagination is blocked by a dead-end, playing on
the keyboard can do wonders, as is borne out by many statements
of other composers.[6]

It is by no means only the performer-composer who praises the
great value of the keyboard for the progress of work. Wagner, anything but a skilled pianist, was fully dependent upon the help of
his instrument. He was truly obsessed with the sound of a favorite
piano: an Erard, manufactured in France. This instrument traveled
with the German musician in exile through the various highways
and byways of his erratic existence, crossing the Alps several times
to commute from Italy's strands to Switzerland's valleys. The grand
piano, where other means had failed, performed the wonder of
stimulating the creative stream. And so Wagner impatiently awaited
the arrival of his beloved clavier in the foreign land writing to
Mathilde Wesendonck, October 6, 1858:

Oh! If the Erard but came, it must help, have I often thought, for when
all's said, things must be! I had long to wait, but here it is at last, that

cunning tool with its lovely timbre which I won in those weeks. . . . How symbolically plain my genie here speaks to me, my daemon! How unconsciously I erst happed on the piano, yet my sly vital spark knew what it wanted! The Piano! Ay, a wing were it the wing of the angel of death![7]

Here Wagner plays on the German word *Flügel*: its dual meaning—"wing" as well as "grand piano"—symbolizes the deep relationship between the craftsman and his humanized tool. And furthering this romance between harmonious beings, Wagner christens his piano "the swan." Like that wonder bird in the tale of *Lohengrin*, the most faithful companion of his master, the piano, called "swan," shares the most crucial love experience of Wagner's life—the composer's renouncement of Mathilde and the creative sublimation of the experience in the composition of *Tristan und Isolde*. And he writes to his beloved friend:

The piano had just arrived, been unpacked and set up. While it was being tuned, I read thy spring diary through again. There, too, the history of this instrument is full of meaning . . . but this wondrous, soft, sweet, melancholy instrument wooed me right back to music once more. So I called it the "swan" that had come to bear poor *Lohengrin* home again! Thus did I begin the composition of the second act of *Tristan*. Life wove its web around me like a dream of existence. Thou returnedst; we did not speak with one another, but my swan sang across to thee.

An afterthought leads us back from this sad romance to the realities of the composer's workshop. There is more technical significance attached to the possession of a fine piano in those days of the composition of the second act of *Tristan* than Wagner's poetic metaphor would betray. Here in the chromatic realm of the love-night, in the land of fourths and ninths, where so much occurred to revolutionize romantic harmony, composition was a dangerous adventure. Here, if anywhere, the keyboard functioned as an indispensable corrective for what the composer's imagination brought forth. And on his piano, Wagner checked and controlled the unheard of harmonic progressions that lead straight from this crisis of romantic harmony to the tonality-dissolving problems of modern music.

THE INNER EAR AND EYE

Certain masters have never required an external medium, be it piano or any other instrument, for composing. They had a remarkable capacity to conceive mentally the blueprint of a complex score, and did not depend upon external sound tests for the realization of their music.

Forkel reports on the different stages through which Bach had to pass before he acquired his phenomenal craft of composition independent of an instrument:

Bach's first attempts at composition were, like all first attempts, defective. Without any instruction to lead him from step to step, he was obliged, like all those who enter on such a career without a guide, to do at first as well as he could. To run or leap up and down the instrument, to take both hands as full as all the five fingers will allow, and to proceed in this wild manner till they by chance find a resting place are the abilities which all beginners have in common with each other. They can therefore be only "finger composers" ("knights of the clavier," as Bach, in his riper years, used to call them);[8] that is, they must let their fingers first play for them what they are to write, instead of writing for the fingers what they shall play. But Bach did not long follow this course. He soon began to feel that the eternal running and leaping led to nothing; that there must be order, connection, and proportion in the thoughts; and that, to attain such objects, some kind of guide was necessary.[9]

Constanze Mozart, with characteristic naïveté, insists that her husband "never composed on the piano, but wrote his music like he wrote letters and did not try a movement until he had finished it. After this was the case, he always enjoyed to play the piece for his wife, making her sing along or to play with friends. . . ."[10] We learn from other documents that Mozart did not depend on the piano; his imagination presented the unwritten work to him clearly and distinctly in all details. But whether, as Niemtschek likewise asserts, Mozart really never referred to the piano during hours of work is more than doubtful. A letter to his father on August 1, 1781, stressed the need for an instrument: ". . . the room into which I am moving is being made ready. I am now going off to hire a

clavier, for until there is one in my room, I cannot live in it, because
I have so much to compose and not a minute must be lost."

If Constanze's contention is right, how is the contradiction to be
explained? Mozart was trained from early youth to pianistic
virtuosity; he was a professional performer who badly missed an
instrument if it were not at his disposal. His custom was to improvise and to write out later what occurred to him extemporaneously
on the keyboard. But all this does not imply that Mozart did not
prefer to work from memory. In a way, Mozart constantly composed. There is no definite borderline between hours of work and
hours of relaxation. His sister-in-law, Sophie Haibel, describes him
composing during meals. Likewise, during bowling and billiard
games, the inner work of composing keeps on. And in the midst of
"hair styling," the barber would have to follow Mozart when he
would suddenly jump up to try a passage on the clavier. If Mozart's
letters imply a certain dependence on the instrument, it simply
means that he wanted to have it handy now and then for improvising on the spur of the moment. It does not mean that he used it
constantly or even relied on it for regular work.

Czerny relates that Beethoven depended a great deal on the
piano for composition. Regarding this problem, the master's advice
to others is contradictory. In a letter to the English pianist and
composer, Philip Potter, written in 1817, he admonishes him "never
sit in the room with a piano while composing, to avoid the temptation to consult the instrument." And to his pupil, the Archduke
Rudolph, Beethoven writes five years later, July 1, 1823: "May your
Imperial Highness continue the particular training of writing and
sketching briefly on the piano. This requires a little table by the
clavier. Through this, not only is the fantasy strengthened, but one
also learns how to notate the most distant ideas immediately."
Characteristically, the following is added: "But it is also necessary
to write without a piano." We can guess Beethoven's reasons for
his somewhat conflicting statements. With the advice to the Archduke, Beethoven speaks as a master to his apprentice. But in the
letter to Potter, elements of self-observation come to the fore.
Moreover, Beethoven probably evaluated the mental capacities of
the two musicians differently.

Schumann composed on the piano approximately until 1843, yet

gradually weaned himself away from this method. He advised his
wife, concerning her own composing, never to rely on the keyboard,
but rather to fix her musical thoughts clearly on paper. In his "Rules
for Home and Life" (Musikalische Haus- und Lebensregeln) which
contains much sound advice gleaned from practical experience, he
suggested the following procedure:

When you start to compose, do everything in your head. The fingers must
do what the head wants and not the other way around. If heaven endowed you with a rich imagination, you will sit in happy hours completely engrossed at the piano, trying to speak out your inner soul in
harmonies. These are the happiest hours of youth. Beware, however, to
indulge too frequently in your talents (the fantasy) which seduces you
to give away strength and time to phantoms. You can acquire the control
of the form, the strength of a clear disposition only through the firm
signs of the script. Hence, write more than you improvise.

This, at least, was Schumann's conviction in his mature years.
And in a similar vein, he wrote to Alexander Dreyschock admonishing the composer-pianist not to write at the instrument, but rather
to proceed from the inner mental conception alone. This very
independence of composing without the instrument is called the
"sign of a clear and inner musical eye."

In analogy to Schumann's picture of an inner musical eye Weber
speaks of a "spiritual ear." Yet Weber, like Schumann a splendid
pianist, does not consider his instrument a means to arrive at creative clarity. In fact he takes an uncompromisingly negative attitude
by excluding the piano altogether as an aid to composing:

The composer who secures his work substance from it (the piano) is
almost always born poor and on the way to yielding his spirit to the
ordinary and vulgar. Those very hands with their damn piano fingers,
with their eternal practicing and mastering, finally acquire some sort of
independence and a stubborn intellect. They are nothing but conscious
tyrants and dictators of the creative power. . . . How differently he
creates whose inner ear has become the judge of the invented . . . substance. This spiritual ear comprises and surrounds, with wonderful
capacity, the tonal figures, and is a divine secret not conceivable to the
layman.

These various quotations show the inner musical imagination at
work without the auxiliary perception of external sounds played

on the piano or on any other instrument. It is through the inner eye and the inner ear that the creative faculty must be directed toward its aim. Thus imagination is liberated from all distracting outer influences which the association with an instrument might involve. It is independent of realistic considerations such as dexterity or the playful lure of passages and keys and external attractions. Imagination reigns supreme.

"I love the company of musical instruments and if I were rich enough, I would always have around me, while working, a grand piano, two to three harps, sax horns and a collection of stradivari, violincelli and violins." This desire of Berlioz might well have been expressed by other composers, though their choice of instruments would most likely have been different, and less extravagant. Instruments other than the piano were owned and played by several masters, but their role as an actual aid in composition is only a conjecture. The value of the intimate knowledge of any instrument is self-evident.[11]

Bach, the modest cantor at St. Thomas, owned an amazing number of instruments. It seems as though they were the only luxury the humble man permitted himself. The roster of instruments points to an impressive collection and includes no less than five claviers and a little spinet, a lute, two lute-harpsichords (Lauten Werk), a viola de gamba, violins, violas and violoncellos.[12] Out of this array of instruments, he could form a veritable chamber orchestra. This fact is borne out by Bach's letter of October 28, 1730 in which he sought another position. He informed Georg Erdmann, Imperial Russian Resident Agent in Danzig that his children "are all born musicians, and I can assure you that I can already form an ensemble both *vocaliter* and *instrumentaliter* within my family, particularly since my present wife sings a good, clear soprano and my eldest daughter, too, joins in not badly."

Often the ink was hardly dry when Bach's family of musicians and pupils joined in *Haus-musik* for their own recreation: the little private home orchestra and vocal ensemble was entrusted with the first performance of many of Bach's scores. His workshop was rehearsal room and performing hall as well. Out of this milieu of domestic music-making, some of Bach's instrumental compositions originated, just as most of his great vocal music unpretentiously grew from the daily and weekly needs of his job as Thomas-cantor —from one church service to the next.

WORKROOMS AND ENVIRONMENT

Workshops reflect the diversity of human nature and also of the varying fortunes of their occupants, ranging as they do, from absolute bareness to sumptuous luxuriousness. Frequently "workshop" is much too pretentious a term to describe the four walls in which some of the greatest wrote their music. How often was not poverty and misery the keynote of their earthly dwellings?

There were the humble lodgings of Mozart or Schubert; yet within the nothingness of a poor man's four walls self-sufficient creativeness triumphed. If comfort and stability of environment were the chief requirements of work, Mozart could not have written one single note. In the few years he was permitted to live with Constanze, he led a gypsy's existence, moving from one place to another, from furnished room to hotel, from apartment to friend's home, from city to village. He was at home nowhere except in his art. The quarters for which he could sometimes pay or borrow the rent were confined, cramped and hardly seemed fit to shelter a family with growing children. Yet here was the cradle of celestial music—untouched by poverty and earthliness. When we read what Mozart had to contend with we wonder how he could ever have composed at all: "Above us lives a violinist," he wrote, "below another one; next door is a singing teacher who gives lessons, and in the last room toward the other apartment is an oboist. This is gay for composing." At least the composer of the *dramma giocoso, Don Giovanni,* could discover in his own life drama, sparks of humor.

Schubert, like Mozart, was never able to free himself from the most pressing material anxiety in spite of his immense industry. He usually lived and worked in a small "cabinet" (as the Viennese call a room with only one window) containing hardly more than a bed which often had to serve as his writing desk. It was an exception when he had a table, carpet or armchair. Friends often found him fast asleep in the morning with freshly composed manuscripts strewn all about his bed and his glasses still on his myopic eyes.

When he needed a piano to try out the "Erl King," he had to run to friends at a near-by convent to play the score. The composer of some of the most beautiful music for the piano had one at his disposal only at more fortunate periods of his life. Often he did not have the necessary tools for writing music, not even enough paper. The overflowing fantasy of this impoverished schoolteacher turned everything into a manuscript that would take ink or pencil, the cuffs of a worn-out shirt included.

As to the earthly dwellings of the classical composers in Vienna, Beethoven was, by and large, more prosperous than Mozart or Schubert. And Haydn certainly was the most fortunate of them all: he lived and worked on the estates of his princely employers, and finally, when he took up permanent residence in Vienna, he acquired a comfortable house within a short walking distance of the imperial castle.

Beethoven, like Mozart, was a man of many lodgings. There were times when Beethoven, dissatisfied with the room he happened to be living in, rented, in addition, two or three others, and once, incredible as it may seem, he rented a fourth simultaneously! The requirements which his rooms had to fulfill were indeed very specific. Among them, one of the most important was closeness to nature: he wanted at least a view of the nearby Vienna woods. To the composer of the Pastoral, such a need for nature's panorama was not a mere fancy. Creative stimulation depended upon it. There was one particular view of which Beethoven was extremely fond: north of the city, the foothills of the Alps fall into a steep grade against the valley of the Danube; farther south the river flows through the green meadows of the romantic Prater with its many square miles of wild park in a beautiful natural setting. These sights were visible from certain houses in old Vienna, and so Beethoven moved into a room of a large building owned by Baron Pasqualati. As Gerhardt von Breuning, son of Beethoven's boyhood friend Moritz von Breuning, reports:

Beethoven lived on the third floor and had the widest view of the Glacis;[13] on the other side, of the Prater. But in order to see the latter view he had to lean out of the window and to turn his head right. . . . Since the neighboring house was only two floors high, a window through that wall, Beethoven thought, would transform his room into a true corner room with free view to this side. To accomplish this seemed simple enough and so he called a mason. I do not know who interfered with the procedure—whether the superintendent or the owner—but Beethoven was furious and retracted the lease immediately. Yet the beautiful view along with the warm invitation of the friendly Pasqualati brought Beethoven back after a time. Newly suffered alleged injuries made Beethoven leave the house again. Reconciliation followed and back he went (the room was still vacant). Pasqualati, suspecting that he would return, did not rent it.

The rather complete catalogue of Beethoven's workshops must trace his Odyssey through houses in the heart of the old city as well as country villas in more distant suburbs such as Mödling, where the *Missa Solemnis* was composed. Again we owe a vividly drawn picture of Beethoven's last apartment where death reached him in March, 1827 to von Breuning and we freely quote from the account:[14]

One reached the apartment by way of an attractive staircase. Entering the second floor on the left side through a somewhat low door, one arrived in a spacious foreroom with one window facing the court. From this hall one went straight to the kitchen . . . left was a very spacious room with one window facing the street.

The two rooms right off the foyer were Beethoven's real living quarters: the first one was chosen as his bed- and piano-room, the other, the "cabinet," was his study for composition.

In the middle of the first room (containing two windows) stood two pianos with their keyboards on opposite sides, arranged in this way so that the players could face each other. Beethoven preferred this arrangement for the purpose of teaching and also for performances on two instruments. With its keyboard facing the entrance stood the English piano which the Philharmonic· Society in London had presented to him; toward the other side, with the keyboard facing the study, stood the grand piano which the Austrian manufacturer, Graf, had put at his disposal.

A chest with drawers was placed agains⸢ a pillar between the two windows. On top of it was a bookcase, painted black and containing four shelves full of books and writings. Upon this chest lay several hearing aids and two violins. Everything was in pitiful disorder and usually covered with dust. Papers and music were thrown everywhere—over the bookcase, under the table, on the floor, on the piano. The rest of the furniture consisted of Beethoven's bed, his night table, a small extra table and a clothes hanger.

The cabinet room with one window was Beethoven's study. Here, on his desk, framed under glass and always in front of him, he had the following sayings written in his own handwriting:

> I am what is;
> I am everything that is, what has been, what will be;
> No mortal being has lifted my veil.
>
> He is unique in His kind and to this unique One
> All things owe their existence.

These sentences are parts of inscriptions from the ancient temple of the Goddess Neith in Saïs, found by the French Egyptologist, Champollion-Figere. Obviously, Beethoven was captivated by their mystic connotation.

His desk was rather large and also served as a table for knick-knacks. Among other things, he kept on it letter weights, silver bells, several candle holders of various forms, a figure of a Cossack and of a Hungarian Hussar and a few statuettes of old Greeks and Romans, one of them being Brutus, for whom Beethoven had deep admiration. There was more in these gadgets than meets the eye. They were tokens of Beethoven's spirit. The Brutus statuette symbolized freedom, liberation from Caesar's tyranny. The Beethoven whom we know from the Eroica, the *Egmont* music and *Fidelio* responded to the democratic hero—to Brutus who freed Rome from its dictator. These farewell living quarters of Beethoven do not show the sordidness of the surroundings in which Mozart and Schubert struggled in neighboring times and places. Here, at last, we feel that Beethoven had a certain comfort and ample space.

The proletarian living standards of some of the very greatest are in sharp contrast to the extravagance on the part of those composers who believed that they could achieve nothing unless surrounded by the material comforts of life. In every century there are examples in which composer and pauper are synonymous, but also instances in which, due to fortunate employment by the church or court, composers were protected from hardships. Such masters as Purcell, Byrd, Palestrina, Lasso, Lully, Handel and Haydn were the children of a more fortunate fate, which offered them a fair degree of security and an adequate standard of living.

In the nineteenth century there are frequent instances of composers who were able to attain all the comforts of life as free creators, working without the ties of obliging and narrow contracts. They could afford what every composer needs—a refuge from the noise of the great cities, from their superficial fashion and covetousness, an "asylum" (in Wagner's word) where they could concentrate on their task in peace and solitude. Such was the happy lot of some of the successful composers for the theater—writers of opera, serious and light. Lucky owners of idyllic places in the country or at the seashore, they did not have to stand the test of productivity under the trying circumstances of their great predecessors. The roster may start anywhere with Auber, Spontini, Rossini, Meyerbeer, Sullivan and Offenbach and may lead through a whole century of opera production to Puccini with his Mediterranean villa and his tower where he could withdraw to complete isolation and compose in peace.

THE LUXURIOUS AND THE NECESSARY

Artists try to raise additional creative power—beyond the limit of their normal working energy—by means of extraordinary stimuli. In this effort, the atmosphere and environment of workrooms play a logical part. This problem in all its psychological ramifications is vividly illustrated by Wagner:

I have been smitten with the luxury devil and I decorated my house as agreeably as possible. If I have to throw myself into the waves of fantasy in order to satisfy myself in an imaginative world, then my fantasy must at least be assisted and my power of imagination must be elevated. I cannot make my bed on straw and I cannot enjoy bad wine. I simply have to feel somehow flattered if my spirits are to succeed with bloody heavy works and in the buildup of a not existing world.

But the man who knew starvation, exile and poverty, also knew how to use the wealth of others to pay for the luxuries he claimed indispensable for his work. In a letter to Liszt, May 8, 1857, Wagner described his Swiss study and acknowledged its sponsors:

My workroom is furnished with the pedantry and elegant ease well known to you; the writing table stands at the big window with the splendid view of the lake and Alps; quiet and tranquillity surround me. Quite a nice soil for my retreat is won, you see, and when I reflect how much I have been longing for such a thing and for how long, and how hard it was even to get a prospect of it, I feel compelled to look on this good Wesendonck as one of my greatest benefactors. Next July, too, the Wesendoncks hope to be able to take possession themselves, and their neighborship promises me all that is friendly and pleasant. So, something achieved! And I hope very soon to be able also to resume my long-discontinued work.

A highly romantic environment was a necessity, at least in these and later years, for this composer of romantic music-dramas. The décors of his workrooms, too, had to produce illusion, a dream world where the composer-poet lived in the unreal sphere of his gods and demons, Rhine maidens and Amazons, dragons and swans. Nature had equipped him with the genius not only to envision his fantastic music dramas, but also with the talent to create specific surroundings where the twilight beings of his fantasy could be lured from the subconscious into artistic existence.

The relationship between the composer Wagner and the products of his art is that of a highly skilled gardener to the rare plants in his hothouse. Only under very special circumstances may orchids grow; much knowing care and tender nursing is required before they bud and blossom. And, just as the gardener's task is fulfilled as the plant unfolds its leaves, so Wagner, once his work was born, no longer required luxurious surroundings to kindle his illusion. Or is he only indulging in self-delusion when he writes in the throes of *Tristan*: "Once I am through with my work, the most important cause for this apartment disappears. In Paris I will hide myself modestly in a furnished room and will suffer this torture. Only when I think of my births—I care for a rich and noble cradle."

Luxury in Venice, frugality in Paris! Wagner rationalized that he depended on material refinements only as a creator of music, not as a human being. He drew a line between periods of creative activity and times of idleness. At any rate, in exile or in the happier days of his repatriation, he usually found means to work in ateliers carpeted, curtained and even perfumed to his sumptuous taste.

In the Venetian palace on the Canale Grande, where Wagner completed *Tristan*, he arranged "to have dark red portieres, even if they were of the cheapest material." The effect itself was more important than the true quality of the stimulant providing the illusion. Wherever he worked soft lights and a mellow interior were the keynotes of his study. No detail of decoration was unimportant. As on the stage of the opera, every prop played its part in the setting of the atmosphere in the workroom. Even the color of furnishings assumed importance during his creative seizures: "This time it has to be red. . . . Only the bedroom was green." (In Venice, in the Giustiniani Palace, during the forlorn daydreams of *Tristan*.)

The composer's attitude is summed up in these words to Otto Wesendonck (1855): "I am not in the world to make money, but to create. And I think that the world should provide the means for me to do this undisturbed." Yet "undisturbed" in Wagner's sense means not only the absence of worry, but also retirement into a luxurious atelier furnished to the most extravagant specifications. These demands reached a climax of sumptuousness during his Munich years, when they became a perfect target for a hostile clique of jealous Bavarian artists, courtiers and journalists. Their interpretation of what is necessary and what is superfluous to the work of an artist was different from Wagner's. The interdependence between inspiration and squandering was nowhere more sarcastically depicted than in these contemporary satires on the composer's ways of creating. The morning of Wagner's working day is thus ridiculed:

A valet enters with a catalogue of silk dressing gowns so that the master may select the one appropriate for the day's composition. A violet-blue one with yellow embroidery is chosen to inspire the big aria for the giant Fafner. Goldfish must be rushed from the winter garden to stimulate water music. Indian and Persian carpets, camellias, azaleas and carnations picked from royal property—all are necessary tools for Wagner's fantasy.[15]

Nevertheless, in their satirical exaggeration, there is more truth than that for which these philistine writers gambled. How can the needs of genius be measured by the banal envy of such keyhole snoopers? Wagner insisted: "I cannot live like a dog." True, while Wagner quite successfully avoided the life of a beast, the composer's salon, dressing gowns, flowers and fish cost his boyish admirer, King Ludwig II, rather handsome sums. But were some thousands of German thaler really so high a price to pay for the upkeep of tools and workshops where such bagatelles as *Parsifal* matured to challenge the musical world for generations to come?

If it is true that rooms betray the personalities of their occupants, then the musician's study, chosen and furnished by its owner, can be no exception. How significant is the difference in personality reflected in the studios of those historic antagonists, Wagner and Brahms! In contrast to Wagner's luxurious Munich villa and its splendid garden, the door of Brahms' apartment in Vienna's narrow and hilly Karlsgasse leads into the opposite world from that of the creator of magic spells. It leads into an atmosphere of bourgeois unpretentiousness displaying the modest comfort of an academic man. Here is no luxury. Through a glass door one enters into a simple furnished livingroom with piano and desk. Over his bed he had an etching of Bach; on his desk stood the well-known medallion pictures of Clara and Robert Schumann with a personal inscription.[16]

Everything in the study points to the writing of music. The furnishings are functional. Brahms liked to write in a standing posture and so a prominent place in the room is occupied by his characteristic "Stehpult,"[17] such as one would have encountered in a merchant's office for the scrupulous bookkeeper. Above the writing stand hangs a lamp with the most modern light available—an electric one! Brahms enjoyed showing his visitors that amazing bulb which worked at the turn of a switch. He proudly considered himself a pioneer of electricity. This was his idea of comfort: good light by which to study a score and an armchair in which he could relax with his cigar. Behind his desk there was an excellent and scholarly library to which he often referred, the answer to a natural desire in a composer whose own art was so deeply rooted and inspired by the past: more than half a thousand of years rises again in his works. Late medieval, baroque and classical sources contribute to the life stream of his music. It was no accident that the great theoretical treatises of the eighteenth century, J. J. Fux, Forkel and Mattheson, made up the bulk of his library. Manuscripts of classical masterworks, among them Mozart's G Minor Symphony, were considered the treasures within his walls. Using this library extensively, Brahms turned into a truly creative historian—touching old stones, he turned them into the gold of living art.

By the window stood a piano. And from the window, Brahms loved to glance at the old Karls-Kirche, the beautiful church of graceful characteristics which almost belie the baroque monumentality of its proportions. Its tall pillars are like the mighty chords opening the finale of his Fourth Symphony.

This, then, was Brahms' workshop, so closely corresponding to the artist who lived and created here. A workshop it was; no one dare name it a studio! Brahms wrote to Clara Schumann: "My studio! Good God, I've never pretended to belong to those enviable beings who possess a 'studio'!" This came from a composer who had already achieved the greatest fame and could well afford to live luxuriously if he had felt the need. The necessary and the superfluous—we have it in a perfect antithesis in the workrooms of Brahms and Wagner. (Illustrations V and VI.)

PEACE WANTED

To whatever differences the needs, tastes or idiosyncrasies lead the artists in the set-up of their workshops, one condition is desperately required by them all: peace, absence of disturbance from the outside. Countless documents relate the composers' struggle with their arch enemy—noise. Frequently, their plight appears truly pathetic. Supersensitive ears make them helpless victims of the hubbub and turmoil in the great cities where their profession forces them to live. Sad episodes illustrate some attempted escapes from this evil of all evils. Schumann fell from "the frying pan into the fire" when, in 1852, he desperately tried to avoid the horrible noises of a district in Düsseldorf. Unfortunately, he moved again to the wrong place: on one side lived "an English family whose children played the piano the whole day in spite of many pleas for neighborly consideration." On the other side a new building was under construction where from early morning to late at night the workmen hammered and sawed. A new pavement was also being made with all the accompanying noises. Finally when with great financial sacrifices, he succeeded in dissolving the lease, he was, in the words of Clara, "a nervous wreck."

Wagner often reached a similar stage of pathological irritability. When working on the first act of *Siegfried*, he hopefully moved to another flat: "I expect very much from my new apartment. In my last one, I had to struggle with five pianos and a flute. I was on the verge of insanity." How grateful he is to the people who are able to liberate him from the plague to his ears: "Vrenali is truly my guardian angel. She does everything to keep loud neighbors from the house. No child is permitted to appear on the whole floor. And Joseph plugged a mattress into the door of the next room." (Lucerne, 1859.)

Brahms, battling with what he called "beasts on the piano," finally resorts to a clever but expensive device, and escapes, at least for the summer, from plaguing neighbors. He rents an entire house in the country, living in only two rooms. The other rooms remain empty and thus, undisturbed, he is able to devote himself to his compositions.

Of course, the composer's longing for peace goes far beyond the mere absence of external disturbance. He needs inner tranquillity as a psychological premise at least for the synthetic stage of composition in all its technical ramifications. Even if music has been inspired by a soul-shaking experience, the stage of craft, the elaboration of the music requires tranquillity to the point of serenity—an inner aloofness of the artist in his absorbing task, from the potential dangers and distractions of reality. Mozart depends on this inner tranquillity and beseeches his father to help him maintain it. From Munich, where Mozart stays, on November 24, 1780, goes the request to his father for more cheerful communication: ". . . Pray do not write any more melancholy letters to me, for I really need at the moment a cheerful spirit, a clear head and an inclination to work, and one cannot have these when one is sad at heart."

And in the following year, June 8, 1781, from Vienna, father Leopold is again implored: ". . . Must I repeat it a hundred times that I can be of more service to you here than in Salzburg? I implore you, dearest, most beloved father, for the future to spare me such letters. I entreat you to do so, for they only irritate my mind and disturb my heart and spirit; and I, who must now keep on composing, need a cheerful mind and a calm disposition."

SPIRIT TRIUMPHANT

This need for outer and inner peace is perhaps the only generality which emerges from our study of the set-up that great composers have chosen for their productive lives. Otherwise, it would be hard to find a common denominator to indicate the requirements of creative personalities in respect to environment and psychological premises for work.

To a certain creative type, inspiring environments are indispensable. The artist of this type cannot successfully defy all handicaps and hurdles which life puts into his creative path. To him, flattering surroundings and friendly working conditions are an absolute necessity. Yet there is the other creative type where genius seems almost insulated against adverse currents of outer life, enabling the artist to work under unblest external circumstances. To this type belong some of the greatest masters who were denied the freedom from want. The account of their miserable quarters can only amount to an indictment of a society that permitted such poverty of those who enriched the world beyond any measure of material wealth. What additional contributions they might have made in a kindlier environment can obviously remain only speculation. Yet we have the irrefutable statements of great artists claiming frustration in their work because of their wretched environment and their economic struggle.

But sometimes the artist, unable to obtain for himself the place he desires for his work, is rewarded by fate through the gift to build a higher substitute—an ivory tower. Here, isolated in the spirituality of his art, life can only touch him so far and no further. This inner isolation is the obvious reason that some music, written under the most trying circumstances, gives no testimony of what went on in the hatchery of ideas—in the outer workshop at the time of creation. Sublime music has poured from a man working in a hovel as well as from a man working in a palace. If a cross section of workshops proves anything, then it is the consoling fact that

genius can set itself free to create in spite of the unkind earthly fate
that imprisons human life behind bars of ill-starred exigencies.
Those masters who accomplished this feat are the glorious illustrations of a triumphant spirit.

CHAPTER SEVEN

THE BONDAGE OF THEORY

> Let us turn back to the old mas-
> ters; progress will be the result.
>
> **VERDI**

SOVEREIGNTY OF CRAFT

THE road to artistic creation lies between two extremes: emotional exuberance and cool-headed reasoning. These antipolar factors of composition are readily translated into the language pertaining to inspiration and craft. Inspiration is the enthusiastic seizure of ideas; craft is their calculated setting.

The second stage of the creative process is essentially that of craft. Here the initial idea is worked out, the form is developed, the constructive elements are blended.

Inspiration flows from the subconscious. Craftsmanship is conscious. It is that part of art that can be taught and learned. Each epoch, each style in the history of music stressed one or the other of the two main factors of creation. Each individual composer tends to one of the two poles. In short, the roles of inspiration and craft have not been evaluated equally by different times and figures in the history of music. In various periods preceding the romantic nineteenth century, emphasis was placed strongly on craft and sometimes on workmanship alone. According to such convictions, the composing musician was safely carried along by craft, almost on its own momentum. The conscious will of the artist, his organ-

149

ized reasoning powers, his ability to plan and to build dominated the process of composition for centuries. By their consciously forming will and the technically acquired power to build their music, composers worked on safe ground as superb craftsmen, shaping the tonal material into the forms of whatever styles their time brought forth.

Craft is regarded as the true source of composition. The role of inspiration is minimized. No exalted environments are required by the musical craftsman. He goes about his task of making music like any artisan, knowing his job, always sure of his approach and with a clear, specific goal in mind. He is a master of composition, busy in his workshop in the medieval sense of guild crafts, rather than a son of the Muses waiting for inspiration from a mystical force beyond his control. The concern is not primarily the source of the material, not how and where to secure it, but what to do with it—a procedure which was taught by the laws of musical theory.

All knowledge springs from the craft of composition. Rules and skill guide the musician along the creative path. The point of procedure was given frequently on the basis of an already existing music. The composer borrowed, adopted or copied. Melodic loans were made from anywhere and everywhere. To borrow the music of another artist seemed natural. Young trees have to be supported and nurtured by a prop until their own strength is safely assured. Likewise newly growing music was supported by firmly established older compositions or at least by parts of them. Such procedure had no odor of plagiarism, but was the generally accepted state of affairs.

For instance: a composer would borrow a melody and transplant it into his own score. Here the loan becomes a cantus firmus and governs the texture of the score in the making. The other parts of the score were designed as new contrapuntal combinations of the borrowed chant. Such a method prevailed in the composition of sacred as well as of secular music. As to theme and substance, they were taken from anywhere: from the Gregorian chant to love songs. This nonchalance of approach explains why we might find, in the solemn surroundings of a strict Mass, some bold quotations from very frivolous music. The borderline between the two spheres, the religious and the profane, were readily transgressed. Heaven came down to earth!

We observe this technique frequently in the workshops of medieval composers. Guillaume Dufay (ca. 1400-1474), the Burgundian master, used the tune "l'Homme Armé"—a popular ditty whistled by everyone on the street—for one of his great Masses.

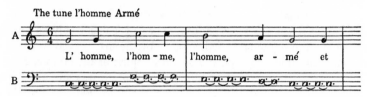

The tune l'homme Armé

A   L' homme,   l'hom - me,   l'homme,   ar - mé   et

The camouflaged cantus firmus of Dufay's Mass

EXAMPLE 12

The musical example shows the folk tune, "l'Homme Armé" which Dufay had chosen for his firm chant.[1] We observe the similarity as well as the difference between the secular model (A) and its application (B) in sacred surroundings. The cantus firmus of the Mass uses the tune, "l'Homme Armé," in augmentation and transposition. Gone is its leaping and lively rhythm. Yet its melodic profile, consisting of a raising fourth, which falls diatonically into the opposite direction, has been preserved. Countless other examples analogously show the growth of great scores from ideas that were borrowed and well camouflaged. Such a procedure is typical of the French and Netherland composers in the fifteenth and sixteenth centuries. They employ without restriction all sorts of tunes as firm basic chants for their complex compositions. Often the resulting polyphonic interplay becomes so intricate that it is difficult to recognize or to remember the model upon which the total composition was built.

The date line between the Middle Ages and modern times by no means broke up this trend of composing on borrowed inventions. On the contrary, the medieval technique was strongly intensified by the type of composition we find in the church music of the sixteenth century referred to as *Missa Parodia*. In essence, this technique consists in taking over an entire composition with its web of parts into the structure of a newly built Mass. The older score which served as a model is recomposed; it is integrated as the basic substance of a new composition.

What is the ideological basis for such an approach to musical composition?

Medieval man was not free in thinking or planning. Governed by strict disciplines, even his philosophy was regarded only as *ancilla religionis,* the handmaid of theology. All the arts served to express the catholic, that is to say, the universal spirit of the church. Music functioned as the servant of liturgy; its making was subjugated to given patterns. Dependence on these prefabricated models, their application on the basis of a strict theory and their final elaboration along scholastic rules—all this ties logically into the broader picture of medievalism. In an ecclesiastical art, where universality of faith is the sole aim of musical expression, the composer's individuality remained in the background, sometimes to the point of anonymity.

In the construction of a Gothic Mass, the source of its themes matters as little as the origin of the stones out of which the Gothic cathedral was built. Only the result counts: the architecture of the art work, its proper religious function and the relationship of parts according to accepted ideals of proportion. The cardinal point is not from where the material stems which is used to build a church or a musical composition, but how the whole is put together and what the finished product expresses. The workshop of ecclesiastical music appears as a temple of firm rules where the most decisive contrapuntal complications were solved by great musical craftsmen to the glory of God.

It is only in its projection against such cultural background that we can comprehend this tonal art—how it was created, how it functioned. In the first centuries of polyphony, countless tonal compositions were built upon themes or motifs of the Gregorian chant or upon folk songs in a manner comparable to our example of Dufay's "l'Homme Armé." The composer is not concerned with the invention of a theme. He is absorbed in his task of contrapuntal elaboration. Compositions of all kinds, Masses, motets, worldly scores, originated thus from identical thematic material borrowed from the property of a previous inventor. The ambition of the composer consisted primarily in the display of an imposing power to build and to form tonal structures.

Craft—the mastery of counterpoint and form—distinguishes the great composer in this period from a musician of minor accomplishments. Here we find the key to the otherwise incomprehensible fact that great musicians considered melodic inventiveness only an insignificant skill. Heinrich Schütz appeared reluctant to show the world such melodies of his own vintage as those in his Psalms of David. The great seventeenth century master believed that his creative message would have to be found elsewhere: in those scores where he had so admirably blended southern décor with the restrained expression of his native north, in his amazingly adventurous treatment of harmonic construction, in the spiritual works which are the antecedents of the baroque and without which the accomplishments of Bach and Handel would be unthinkable.

It may appear baffling to the modern mind that the invention of melodies was not considered a criterion for the greatness of the composer. Is it not the discovery of original and beautiful ideas that differentiates the true artist from the mere amateur? And is not that astonishing talent to create beautiful melodies the chief characteristic of the great composer? No, not according to the evaluation of this era. The high esteem of sheer inventiveness in music is a relatively recent trend. It is strongly conditioned by the romantic ideology of an inspirational art where the emphasis falls upon the creator's subjective experience rather than upon the objective architecture of the art work itself.

The talent to form themes—appealing musical thoughts—was in former centuries considered the unimportant property shared by amateurs as well as professionals. Just as the amateur painter is able to use beautiful colors from his palette with a certain effectiveness, so too the dilettante musician may easily succeed in combining his tones into a pleasing tune. The earmark of the truly professional composer was his faculty of developing music along intricate patterns, his craft of construction. And to acquire such craft through intense study of its underlying principles was the desire of every young composer. He was eager to embark on the study of the discipline covered by the Greek term *theoria* (i.e. theory) which means observation, study, contemplation of the material, its laws and regulations. Thus, the study of musical theory was the first step to acquiring craft and the only safe guide in approaching creative work.

SECRET SCIENCE

In 1595, the Franciscan monk and renowned master of composition, Costanzo Porta, saw in a bookstore in Padua the first volume of Ludovico Zacconi's *Prattica di Musica*. To his pupils who had accompanied him on the walk, Porta exclaimed: "Not for one thousand ducats would I have divulged the secrets which this friar is giving away here."

What Costanzo Porta meant was that composition should remain a secret science known only to the chosen few. He was the upholder of an old idea of preserving music as an individual craft handed down from master to apprentice—a concealed knowledge passed on by personal and verbal transmission only. Accordingly, Costanzo Porta (a church musician steeped in the centuries-old tradition), passionately deplored that Zacconi (a priest himself) should have given away, in a textbook available to any buyer, the jealously guarded laws of beauty and craft controlling his esoteric art.

But with the coming on of humanism, the medieval monopoly and secretiveness regarding knowledge yielded to the common man's right to know and to learn. When new light fell on the sciences, on Arts and Letters, music happily joined in this fresh stream of universal enlightenment. Since the Renaissance, learned works dealing with the underlying principles of musical composition have come to the fore in increasing numbers. Like Zacconi's *Prattica di Musica*, some of these volumes covered the various topics of composition from its origin and history to the problems of notation, tactus, solmization,[2] the canon, and also included practical questions of instrumentation and performance. Other books are limited to a treatment of music in a more abstract manner. Here the principles of composition are discussed apart from its practice. These are the treatises which are placed by terminology into the category of musical "theory."

What exactly is this theory, and how does it function in the composer's workshop? The value of its knowledge and comprehension must be great: masters have devoted years of extensive study to a penetrating analysis of all problems embedded in theory. Composers of all times have relied upon a theoretical explanation of musical phenomena as the true basis of their work. They have taken pains to absorb all laws which emerge from these theoretical dissertations, thus making them part and parcel of their own craft.

Different eras produced different theories. Obviously the problems that confronted the ancient musician belong to another sphere than those of the medieval composer. And the latter's orientation must differ fundamentally from theoretical results of the centuries to follow. In modern times, a division of musical theory into three categories gradually emerged.

First, there is the theory of harmony: the discipline of chords, of their function and interrelationship with regard to the melodic, rhythmic and formal features of the score. Harmony, then, teaches all laws governing the mutual relationship of chords. It does so by examining their function and sequence. The viewpoint of harmony is primarily vertical; nevertheless, the linear aspect of part-writing cannot altogether be ignored.

Second, there is counterpoint as a discipline of voice-leading. It expounds the laws and architecture of polyphony (a term derived from the Greek meaning many voices) and is based on the combination of several melodic parts. Harmony, by contrast, is an exponent of homophony (a term derived from the Greek meaning one voice). The harmonic experience is vertical. Polyphonic events occur in the horizontal. The term counterpoint, used synonymously with polyphony approximately since the beginning of the fourteenth century, is readily comprehended on the basis of its Latin etymology. *Punctus* means note: thus *punctus contra punctum* conveys a music wherein note is set against note. In a broader meaning, we refer to counterpoint as the art of interweaving independent voices in a polyphonic web where no part predominates over the rest. In counterpoint, not the chords but the melodic lines are the primary concern. The goal is to write melodies in several independent parts. The so-called "strict" and the "free" counterpoint both teach the intrinsic beauty of linear designs. They teach how voices are led to independence and yet blend with other parts, thus fulfilling the aesthetic demands of variety and unity. All contrapuntal parts, if heard together, should amount to a rich harmonic sum. The intricate technical problem, then, is to invent an aesthetic and ordered net of voices, well knit over a structure of good, lively and full progressions. The artistic end result of the polyphonic work must stand the double test of both linear and harmonic inquiry. Harmony and counterpoint work with the same tonal material and may even aim at related goals. But the road to the goal is started at different points. In his treatise on the Palestrina style,[3] Jeppesen describes the problem of this dual approach as "first the lines and then, in spite of them, the best possible harmonies or, as in the teaching of harmony, first the chords and afterwards, so far as possible, good voice leading."

Third, there is the theory of musical form. The combined technical efforts of harmony and counterpoint serve here to build the structure in music. The theory of form teaches composition per se: it studies musical architecture in its totality. It is tectonics, the art of construction involving all problems of planning, blueprinting and finally erecting a musical edifice. The means by which these ends are attained differ remarkably throughout the history of musical theory. Every era inevitably creates its own form and expression. The basic aims, however, remain similar: namely, to achieve clarity of form, variety of features and to preserve an inner unity in the art work.

This traditional triple division of musical theory makes the individual and isolated study of harmony, counterpoint and form possible. There is the danger, however, that the three disciplines may lose contact with each other in such isolated study, whereas composing necessarily occurs as a unifying procedure: the musician cannot isolate his elements like a chemist. He cannot work with disconnected harmonies, nor can he use counterpoint without the vertical component. Nevertheless, certain works strongly lean in one direction or the other: the composer's orientation may be primarily homophonic or polyphonic. Musicians are dispositionally inclined in one way or the other. Some, almost hereditarily, and certainly through the artistic climate in which they grow up, submit to the predominance of harmony. Counterpoint may be the principal source for others. The decision in favor of either factor is all-important: on it depends the composer's style, the profile of his inventions and the structure of his scores. An intimate understanding of these varying approaches to composition is unthinkable without a complete awareness of the underlying differences between the vertical and horizontal factors in the composer's workshop.

Notwithstanding their individual stylistic position, all masters agree that the study of theory is the basic source for the achievement of musical craft. The young composer's ability to organize the raw materials of his imagination can only be developed by the tested methods acquired in theoretical training. What the imagination brings to the young composer is successfully organized into an art work only if he has gradually developed a thorough technique in the three categories of theory and has learned how to employ it in the direction of his artistic aims. There can be no short cut to a secure and individual craft. The apprentice of composition must first dig into the roots of the tectonic problem; he must study the laws describing artistic effects which are common to as many art works as possible, while attempting to reduce them to as few common causes as possible. Some of the greatest original talents singularly blessed with inspirational power failed to arrive at the summit of their art because they lacked theoretical knowledge, and failed as craftsmen.

Of course, theory alone can never produce an art work. With few exceptions, the laws of theory are nothing more than abstractions from specific masterworks. They originate through empirical observation and generalization: the theorist promotes to the standard of a principle what he finds in admired scores unsurpassably formulated. Hence, the creative artist not only produces his own art work, but in addition he becomes, involuntarily, a coauthor of the theory which is deduced from his work. Palestrina (as far as we know) did not write a treatise on counterpoint. Yet the sum and substance of his polyphonic style, derived from his scores by certain theorists, is in essence the greatest single codex of strict counterpoint since the Middle Ages.

In other cases, the theorist penetrates into the production of a whole period (rather than of a single master) and even beyond such time limits, in order to find a firm pole in the constant fluctuation of artistic events. Once the theory is safely established, the contemporary musician and those of generations to follow may turn to these theoretical findings, relying upon them as the solid basis for the creative effort. The sixteenth century marks the line at which the teachings of a remote past have retained a living and practical meaning for the theoretical guidance of the present. This is particularly true of the theory of counterpoint. The conservative approach to teaching its problems is still, today, based on old methods that had long been in practical use before they were first codified by Johann Joseph Fux in his *Gradus ad Parnassum,* published in Latin in 1725, German edition in 1742. At any rate, no theory has taken on greater practical significance in the musical workshop of the four centuries following Palestrina than the technical and aesthetic laws derived from the pure style of this "savior of music." The world's undeviating loyalty to this historic doctrine may be compared to the mathematician's adherence to algebra as the science of calculations by general symbols. The study of counterpoint follows a related aim. In both cases, here in mathematics, there in music, conditions of utmost clarity and mental purity must be secured to create a state of transparent intelligibility which is the premise for the further pursuit of musical craft.

THEORY VERSUS PRACTICE

The greatest writer on theory in the sixteenth century was Gioseffo Zarlino whose unusual life started in Chioggia, the proletarian part of Venice. He survived the great plague (which carried off Titian in 1577 and other great men of this time), and in 1583, Zarlino was chosen to be the bishop of his town.[4] Zarlino's main occupation was that of conductor and church composer at St. Mark's Cathedral. Yet he lives on, not in his scores, but in his voluminous theoretical works, among which the most important is the treatise, *L'Istitutioni Harmoniche,* in three volumes, published 1558, 1562 and 1573 respectively. Zarlino shares this artistic fate of immortality as a theorist, rather than a creative artist, with other great musicians in the history of music such as Fux, Rousseau and Mattheson. Summing up his task in the service of his art in a literary manner, Zarlino explains: "There was disorder in the theory of music and also confusion. Through perseverance, labor and the help of God, I hope that the art of music, robbed of its ancient dignity for such a long time, can reinstate itself with majesty and decorum as one of the most noble and important sciences."

What Zarlino actually contributed to musical craft can best be appreciated from the fact that most preceding theorists filled their dissertations to a great extent with material which must be considered as only collateral to composition: such topics as the discipline of intervals and the church modes, of solmization and notation, which pertained only indirectly to the main problem of how music is really made. Johannes Tinctoris figures prominently among the notable exceptions whose writings on counterpoint had made a serious attempt to tackle the problem of composition in a more practical way. This Flemish fifteenth century musician in the service of the King of Naples was among the first to study, with analytical awareness of their style, the great polyphonic masters of his own and preceding times, particularly Okeghem and Busnois. The Swiss Henricus Glareanus (Born 1488; died 1563) disclosed in his famous treatise, *Dodecachordon* (1547), a gold mine of practical work material illustrated by the scores of Josquin, Okeghem and Obrecht. Yet if a student attempted to follow the principles set forth in the *Dodecachordon*, he would find that he still required the guidance of a practical teacher to supplement and elucidate the theoretical illustrations of Glareanus.[5]

Zarlino, however, went further: his treatment of the laws of theory is not only retrospective but prophetically anticipates the revolutionary change which led to the abandonment of the modes and established the major and minor tonalities. Infallible judgment led Zarlino to the choice of his examples from works of his adored teacher Willaert and other masters in the foreground of the musical past including Okeghem, Josquin, Isaac, Pierre de la Rue, Gombert and Cypriano de Rore. The scores of these composers represented to Zarlino "classical appearance and content." And how characteristic is the attribute "classical," used by this Renaissance musician in reference to the polyphonic music of the fifteenth and sixteenth century masters. Yet with all his discriminatory power, Zarlino's appreciation for contemporary art was limited. Judging from his writings, one would not know of the existence of the greatest Italian composer living at this time in Rome—of Palestrina.

Zarlino's writings display a high culture and spirituality. The author's wisdom is nourished by deep insight into the antique world, into acoustics and mathematics and history, philosophy and aesthetics. All this knowledge finally resolved in his main interest— composition. In *L'Istitutioni Harmoniche* Zarlino states:

Although every composition, every counterpoint, indeed even every harmony is chiefly and preferably made up of consonances, one also uses dissonances, but secondarily and incidentally (per accidente) in order to enhance beauty and ornamentation. . . . The dissonances, which sound somewhat unpleasant when occurring alone, are not only bearable but they actually refresh and please the ear if they are introduced in a suitable and lawful manner. These dissonances afford the musician two advantageous possibilities of significant value: the first is that a dissonance may aid one to progress from one consonance to another; the second advantage is that dissonances heighten the pleasure of the consonances which follow immediately after them, just as light is much more pleasant and lovely to the eye if it follows darkness, and just as something mild seems so much better and sweeter after something bitter. Experience teaches us that the ear which is hurt by a dissonance finds the consonance which immediately follows so much the more charming and beautiful. For this reason the musicians of old were of the opinion that not only perfect and imperfect consonances should be used in their compositions, but dissonances as well; they realized that the beauty of their compositions could be enhanced by the use of the latter. Compositions which are made up solely of consonances may themselves sound good and have a beautiful effect; but there is something imperfect about them both melodically and harmonically in that the charm which may arise from the use of contrast is lacking. And although I have said that one should for the most part use consonances in composition and that dissonances should be used only secondarily and more incidentally, one must not therefore assume that the latter can be used without any rule or order for from this use only confusion would arise.

So far so good! Yet what Zarlino promulgates in such clear language has by no means proved to be binding for the creative spirit: Claudio Monteverdi, far ahead of his time as is so often the fate of genius, throws Zarlino's theory overboard in his revolutionary music. And in his preface to the Madrigals, he claims the creator's right of progress in a manner timeless in its applicability: "Some believe," says Monteverdi, "there are no other laws of art than those pronounced by Zarlino. Yet they might be assured that as far as consonances and dissonances are concerned, still another point of view is justified (deviating from the usual opinions) which defends the modern method of composition while satisfying completely the senses and the intellect." Zarlino was no longer alive when Monteverdi's Madrigals appeared. And so it was up to one of Zarlino's apostles to reject Monteverdi's novel freedom of expression. In a pamphlet titled the *Imperfections of the Modern Music*, Giovanni Artusi discusses what has remained forever the crux of progress in the history of music: the treatment of the dissonances on the part of "modern" composers. Artusi's words have retained a curious actuality; almost every one of his lines could be written today as a rebuke to modern music branded as atonal:

The new ways are little pleasant to the ears and it could not be otherwise. They transgress all those good rules which are based partly on experience . . . culled from nature and tested by reason. Thus we deem (the new rules) as distorted and unnatural, opposed to the purpose of the composer, which is to delight. The sharpness of the dissonances strikes you unprepared as though the composers wanted purposefully to attack the ear. If they did not want to do that and if they really wished to flatter the ear with dissonances, the thing for them to do is to continue the road of the old masters . . . in the manner in which they prepared dissonances through consonances, and directly resolved them so that their sharpness disappears. Yes, it is even possible to flatter the ear through them (the dissonances). Yet appearing without preparation they cannot produce a good effect. How the dissonances are to be used is shown by Adrian Willaert, Cipriano de Rore, Palestrina, Claudio Merulo, Gabrieli and Orlando di Lasso. . . . Yet do the modernists pay attention to them? They do not realize that the instruments betray them . . . they are satisfied to produce a terrific noise, and unrhythmical chaos and mountains of imperfections.

What well-known phrases: noise and chaos are the earmarks of modern music. Violation of all rules culled from nature and tested by reason! No continuation of the road of the old masters. Mountains of imperfections! Self-appointed guardians of eternal aesthetics try to discredit the inevitable progress of art in the name of the sacred past and its unalterable rules. Since this outburst of an ultra-conservative and blind believer in Zarlino's theory, Monteverdi's music has been evaluated differently and his treatment of the dissonances in particular has been considered one of the most ingenious contributions to the progress of musical art since the beginning of the seventeenth century.

At any rate, here, at the turning point from the sixteenth to the seventeenth century, we have a complete picture of theory and its remaining function in the musical workshop. We see its usefulness and its inevitable limitations; we realize that its substance is necessarily derived from delving into the masterworks of the past which, in turn, easily leads to a neglect of the most important contemporary works.

RELATIVITY OF RULES

When the young student opens expectantly his first traditional textbooks on the theory of music, he is confronted with a firm rule: an unequivocal prohibition of parallel progressions. Parallel fifths are forbidden; similarly outruled are parallel octaves. If two intervals of the same kind, fifths or octaves, move in the same direction, upward or downward in immediate succession, then the progression is regarded to be at fault:

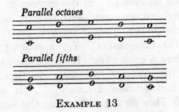

EXAMPLE 13

This inaugurating rule of theory, which takes the student back four hundred years to the strict world of sixteenth century polyphony, is a symbol of the controversial position of musical theory. In this single instance lives the historic conflict between theory and practice, between the time-bound purpose of an aesthetic law and its carefree transgressions in creative application.

Fifths are forbidden! The student of theory, if he has been

observant in reading master scores and in listening to their performances, cannot help but be puzzled with this initial lesson. Has he not heard certain of these forbidden parallels in masterworks, in the scores of the romanticists, not to mention their characteristic appearance with the French impressionists, and so many living composers?

Moreover, these "wrong" parallels do not in the least disturb his young ear. They seem impressive, even irresistible. These fruits, which he now learns are forbidden, tasted well. Why, he asks, is there this obvious conflict between theory and practice? Why this contradiction between liberties that the masters choose to take and that which the theory prohibits with its holy laws? On whose authority is based this rule of forbidden progressions, and for that matter, the whole array of other prohibitions which make textbooks, from the very beginning, appear like a censor's code, clipping the wings of imagination.

There is no denying that such a dualism exists: there is work for the purpose of learning, subject to the censorship of the teacher on the basis of agreed rules; and there is creative work as self-expression which has intrinsic rules of its own, the rules of genius. And there is still another dualism which helps to clarify this controversial situation. The student must clearly comprehend the aesthetically guiding character of musical theory: it is retrospective as well as descriptive.[6] As we have shown, theory is retrospective in that its wisdom is primarily acquired by looking backward; it offers an array of rules only as an abstraction from masterful scores of the past. As such it is the by-product of creative works which have been written before the laws of theory were formulated. The descriptive faculty of theory is limited when it attempts to formulate laws pertaining to the present. The present is too close; the necessary distance has not yet been gained to view the creative phenomena objectively. And it is this descriptive or rather prescriptive role that provokes the eternal conflict between theory and contemporary practice.

Nevertheless, from this prescriptive function of theory, certain instances occurred in which its laws really became the a priori given guideposts of composition. The so-called *ars antiqua* of the twelfth and thirteenth century motet reversed causes and effects: theory preceded creative art. One of the chief rules of this theory was the so-called Franconian law forbidding the use of dissonances on the accented beats of the bar. This rule was formulated before its practical application. In analogy, the survey of medieval theory, particularly of the thirteenth and fourteenth century, shows the prohibition of parallel fifth progressions. Yet it was not until the masterworks of the sixteenth century, primarily the sacred music of the Palestrina style, that a strict obedience to this law was put into artistic reality.

If we turn back a thousand years of musical history to consult one of the theoretical works of that time, we find in the famous treatise, *Musica Enchiriadis*, the following paragraph: "Organum is also called diaphony because it does not consist in uniform singing, but in the harmonious blending of sounds that differ. . . . Although the name is common to all symphonies, the fifth and fourth have nevertheless got hold of it." Uniform singing means singing in unison. Symphony is used in its etymological meaning: sounding together. Here the author of *Musica Enchiriadis*, allegedly the monk, Hucbald, describes under the title of symphonia the primitive form of part-writing, and he continues: "Not only may a simple voice be united to another simple one, but either the simple organum may respond to a double or a double to the simple, or you double both in the octave and you shall hear the voices of this sort of relation resound sweetly in reciprocation."

This was a primitive form of discant in which the melody of the *vox principalis* was accompanied by the *vox organalis* a fourth below or in other intervals. The text of the *Musica Enchiriadis* amounts to a precise direction on how to make music. The medieval composer in need of guidance was given a recipe on how to proceed: take a voice as a leading chant, double it up by putting the upper voice into the fifth, fourth or octave. Here we see how music originates in medieval theory according to very precise and definite patterns. Theoretical prescriptions prefabricate, as it were, the plan of the musical structure. Later, the patterns become more intricate, yet the procedure remains essentially the same. The composer invents voice parts to a given chant, according to certain intervals controlled by the rules of theory. In a more primitive procedure, this occurs note against note. From this type of part-writing, the various species of strict counterpoint develop. This cantus firmus work, where a given melody suggested to the composer the invention of all other parts according to the theoretical laws of counterpoint, remained the guiding technique for the composers of the Middle Ages and directed the study of polyphony for centuries to follow.

As to the parallel progressions, we realize that after they had served the purpose of high art, they eventually disappeared from this realm and turned up in popular music, in folklore, in primitive performances. When Leopold Mozart heard some street singers in Italy sing their little tunes, he was astonished to hear their uninhibited use of parallel fifths. This led his speculative mind to arrive at a convincing conclusion: "We might consider the parallel fifths and octaves of primitive peoples as nothing more than a more fully orchestrated unison." The fifths were applied to achieve a stronger and fuller sound, perhaps subconsciously on the part of the village musicians. But an analogous employment of parallel fifths occurs consciously in the organist's use of the full mixture when he employs full organ and adds fifths and octaves. In the music of the great son, Wolfgang Amadeus, parallel progressions once more become a means of artistic expression when he powerfully unites voices and instruments in bare octaves at the words "De Ore Leonis" in the Domine Jesu in his Requiem. Here the composer's intent is to reinforce the choral writing by a parallel use of all available sonorities.

All this adds to our understanding of the conflicting laws governing the use and prohibition of parallel intervals. Fifths and octaves are taboo in the practice of the great vocal composers of the Palestrina period. As a result all writers who based their theories on this style forbade them. And so the prohibition of parallels is an entrenched rule in the textbooks of Fux, Kirnberger, Ph. E. Bach, Albrechtsberger and others. Deeper psychological reasons for their prohibitions are rarely given. Even if the author of the text is himself an important composer such as Cherubini, he offers only an indirect motivation to explain his interdiction. In his Counterpoint and Fugue, Cherubini simply states that a "succession of fifths forms a discordance because the upper part progresses in one key while the lower part moves in another." Thus, he aims to avoid polytonality, which would occur through a parallel shift of two voices into conflicting regions. Another motive given by theorists for the prohibition claims that the use of parallels hampered the independence of part-writing. Not even attempting to offer a technical explanation, some writers simply insist that parallels "sound badly." But what is good and what is bad? Obviously such reasons based on the subjective reaction to sound are not reliable. Besides, the prohibition refers specifically to fifth and octave parallels, whereas other progressions are permitted such as those of fourths, if they are covered by thirds below. Parallel sixths or thirds are admitted freely. Yet rules forbidding fifth and octave parallels have remained entrenched.

Schumann offers the following explanation of the problem:

Different times hear differently. In the best ecclesiastical works of the old Italians, we find progressions of fifths. Thus, they could not have sounded badly to them. In Bach and Handel they likewise exist, but rarely and in a broken manner. The high polyphonic art avoided all parallel progressions. Hence, the important theorists that followed forbade them by death penalty until Beethoven appeared and wrote the most beautiful fifths, particularly in chromatic succession.

Ferdinand Ries[7] called the attention of Beethoven to two parallel fifths which the disciple discovered in the score of Beethoven's Quartet in C Minor:

At first, Beethoven refused to believe it. But when he saw that I was right he asked me: 'Well did I ever forbid them?' Now since I (Ries) did not know what to make out of this question, Beethoven kept on repeating the question several times until I finally answered: 'Well, those are the first fundamental rules.' The question was repeated several more times, upon which I said: 'Marpurg, Kirnberger, Fux—they all have forbidden them—all the theorists.' But this did not make any difference to Beethoven: 'And so it is I who permit them,' was his answer.

Beethoven taught according to the old rules. He believed in them as a teacher and broke them as a free creator. The moral is clear: a pupil must adhere to the rules, it takes a master to break them!

CHAPTER EIGHT

MASTER AND APPRENTICE

> I have had to work hard; anyone
> who works just as hard will get
> just as far.
>
> BACH

THE abstract truth of making music is taught and learned. Instinctive action becomes enhanced through guidance: the inherited talent of the composer does not suffice to build the great forms of music without the added wisdom of the experienced craftsman. The age-old art of teaching has proved to be in music, too, the safeguard of all craft. Important composers have turned their apprentices into masters equaling or even surpassing themselves. In a truly inspiring relationship, where a master takes under his wing a promising apprentice, the bond transgresses the limits of an ordinary association; it assumes a spiritual tie of a specific importance wherein the master aims at a goal beyond the mere imparting of his doctrines and knowledge. He has the eternal impulse to create his own spiritual image. And it is through his disciple that he tries to obtain this goal. Thus, teaching becomes creation of another kind. The teacher expresses himself not only in his own personal scores, but also through fulfillment in a personal successor. The master immortalizes his art in his apprentice.

The teacher becomes a model in his art and in his mode of life.

The disciple, in turn, grows through faith and emulation. He worships his master, becomes his apostle. Heinrich Schütz speaks of his master: "When I came to Venice I went ashore there where I had spent as a youth the first years of apprenticeship under the great Gabrieli. Yes, Gabrieli . . . Ye immortal Gods! What a man was he. If antiquity would have known him it would have preferred him to Amphion."[1] Giovanni Gabrieli owed his knowledge to Andrea Gabrieli, his uncle, who, in turn, was the disciple of Adrian Willaert. Emigrating from his native Netherland, Willaert transplanted polyphony to Italian soil. Here, in Venice, he introduced outstanding composers such as Cipriano de Rore, Vincentino and Zarlino into the intricacies of his art. Zarlino, who truly preserved Willaert's art in his theory, never referred to his master other than as "Excellentissimo" or "Divino." With his disciples, the Flemish musician founded the Venetian school of the sixteenth century. Thus a master-apprentice relationship developed into enduring significance for musical art.

BACH'S METHOD OF TEACHING

Probably the greatest pedagogue since these great teachers of the Willaert-founded Venetian school was Johann Sebastian Bach. Our knowledge of Bach's approach to teaching is based on various sources: there are the preparatory texts in his own hand which are supplemented by the information furnished by various pupils such as Johann Philipp Kirnberger, Heinrich Nikolaus Gerber and Bach's son, Philipp Emanuel. Kirnberger's text, *Die Kunst des reinen Satzes* (*The Art of Pure Writing*) is in fact an elaborated commentary on Bach's manner of teaching. In Kirnberger's words:

His (Bach's) method is the best, for he proceeds steadily, step by step, from the easiest to the most difficult, and as a result even the step to the fugue has only the difficulty of passing from one step to the next. On this ground I hold the method of Johann Sebastian Bach to be the best and only one. It is to be regretted that this great man never wrote anything theoretical about music, and that his teachings have reached posterity only through his pupils. I have sought to reduce the method of the late Johann Sebastian Bach to principles, and to lay his teachings before the world to the best of my powers.

Kirnberger obviously assumed that Bach had written down nothing pertaining to his method of teaching. Yet in addition to the
rules of thoroughbass which Bach wrote for his second wife and
former pupil, Anna Magdalena, there has come down to us from
Bach a scholarly work on thoroughbass written at the age of fifty-
three.[2] The instruction book shows how Bach guided his pupils in
the study of counterpoint up to the fugue by teaching them the
accompaniment of short fugal movements. A series of preludes and
fugues, sixty-two altogether, written throughout on one staff with
figured script, supplemented Bach's teaching of the thoroughbass.
Here, too, the more advanced pupils learned how to improvise a
polyphonic movement on the keyboard and how to combine an
extempore execution while faithfully attending to figures. Of great
interest is the fact that Bach did not start his supervision of counterpoint with two-part writing, but with simple counterpoint in four
parts. We must realize, however, that the preceding supervision had
prepared the pupil in such a manner that he could solve the more
advanced problems. The same approach occurs with Kirnberger,
who states that "it is best to begin with four-part counterpoint."
Forkel's On Johann Sebastian Bach's Life, Genius and Works
(cf. Chapter 7) also provides us with a substantial account of Bach's
teaching. We learn from it that Bach's method in essence was conservative. It did not aim at the exploration of new ways but at
the transmission of good and solid craft.

It is also noteworthy that in learning as well as in teaching, Bach
relied upon an earlier work for his point of departure. He resorted
to Friedrich Erhardt Niedt's Musikalische Handleitung and in some
of Bach's teachings the original arguments of Niedt are merely
abridged and compressed. Even Bach's musical creed was essentially a variation of the beliefs of Niedt:

The thoroughbass is the most perfect fundament of music, played with
both hands in such a way that the left hand plays the prescribed notes,
the right hand however plays consonances and dissonances so that the
whole might result in a well-sounding harmony to the honor of God and
the enjoyment of the soul and thus should be the final aim and end of
the figured basses as well as that of all other music to the honor of God
and recreation of the mind. Where this is not taken into account, there
will be no real music but devilish yowling and yapping.

GENIUS AS APPRENTICE

The master's attempt to recreate himself, to continue his spiritual ego in the work of an apprentice cannot always succeed. Among the most subtle of human ties, the relationship is frequently steeped in complication and conflict. It involves two different artistic temperaments, men usually belonging to different generations with all that such disparity between the young and old, between the inexperienced and the mature implies. The eternal clash between the past and the present, between the storm and stress of youth and the conservative rigidity of age, is often inevitable. A young genius is not necessarily the best, that is to say, the most willing, mentally adjustable and technically plastic student. A high degree of inborn originality resists the dictatorship of rules yet the act of learning requires as much elasticity as that of teaching. To imbibe knowledge, just as to impart it, requires talent.

Moreover, not every composer who found himself in the role of teacher really enjoyed the occupation. It might have been a mere means of livelihood to him. A great composer who is equally great as a teacher is an exception. Yet studying the behavior of great composers in their dual role as teacher and student always provides illuminating insight into the musical workshop: it shows how craft grows out of learning.

An involved relationship was the fate of that historic tie which started when the young Beethoven left his native Rhineland to become Haydn's pupil in Vienna. At the end of 1790, Haydn departed from the Austrian capital on his way to London and stopped, on Christmas Day in Bonn, where one of his Masses was performed. The visit turned out to be one of those accidents that changed the course of musical history. Here, in Bonn, Haydn met among the other musicians in the service of the Elector, a twenty-year-old composer named Ludwig van Beethoven whose greatest desire it was to move to Vienna and to study with the admired Mozart. Fate decided otherwise. Mozart died the following year. When Haydn in July, 1792, on his journey back from England to Austria, again spent some time in Bonn, Beethoven begged to be accepted as his pupil. A cantata, submitted by the young Rhinelander to the famous master, won Haydn's warm praise and the

incorruptible man could now encourage Beethoven with full conviction. In November of the same year, Beethoven left Germany and
moved to Austria, destined to become the third figure in the trinity of
the Vienna classical school.

By December 12, Beethoven had already taken his first lesson
from Haydn for which he paid the nominal fee of eight groschen.
The lessons were in strict counterpoint and the textbook used was
Gradus ad Parnassum by J. J. Fux. Of Beethoven's exercises in
simple counterpoint alone, two hundred and forty-five have been
preserved. Haydn corrected forty-two of those which have come
down to us.

At this time Haydn was no longer a young man. In his varied
life of inner struggles (of which we can guess more than we know)
he had achieved philosophic resignation along with an unsurpassable mastery of his classical art. Moreover, he still had a great deal
to give: Haydn belongs to those chosen few who created best in
old age. On the threshold of Olympic serenity, Haydn dreaded the
volcanic fire of the young apprentice as a distraction from his own
peace of mind and still-envisioned productive tasks. The inevitable
happened—Beethoven became dissatisfied. He felt he was progress-
ing too slowly and that his exercises were corrected somewhat
cursorily. Neither could the young genius understand Haydn's
Austrian nonchalance, the relaxed manner of his approach. The
wish for a new teacher grew slowly in Beethoven's mind, but he
did not dare to break openly with his famous master. He secretly
took additional instruction from Johann Schenck (a Viennese composer of considerable skill and experience, whose comic opera, *The
Village Barber*, is still occasionally performed). At the same time,
Beethoven continued his lessons with Haydn and even accompanied
him to Eisenstadt as late as 1793. When Haydn left for his second
trip to England on January 19, 1794, Beethoven felt free to make
an open change.

Now his choice did not fall on Schenck but on Johann Georg
Albrechtsberger (born February 3, 1736; died March 7, 1809), the
organist of St. Stefan's Cathedral. This musician, a prolific composer
and a great scholar of counterpoint, seemed to be just the man
Beethoven wanted. For in spite of all his years of intense learning,
the young apprentice considered his knowledge of counterpoint far

from adequate. The instruction started auspiciously and Albrechtsberger's own *Gründliche Anweisung zur Composition* served as the
textbook. We can follow the course of their lessons, since no fewer
than 263 exercises belonging to this period are in existence under
the following headings: "simple strict counterpoint; free composition
in simple counterpoint; imitation; simple fugue, fugued choral,
double fugue; double counterpoint in the octave, decime and
duodecime, triple counterpoint and triple fugue; canon." This
amounted to a thorough supervision in all possible topics. Particularly, Albrechtsberger's fugal technique remained a strong influence throughout Beethoven's life. But the personal relationship
of the men did not develop successfully. After Haydn's equanimity,
young Beethoven was now exposed to the scolding and fault-finding
of the strict and ultraconservative church organist. Hence when the
lessons terminated in March, 1795, it was not a happy end. "Have
nothing to do with him," warned Albrechtsberger to an inquiring
musician, "he has learned nothing and will never do anything in
decent style." Nottebohm has proved that Albrechtsberger was
not at fault. Beethoven's exercises display the accuracy and pains
which the teacher took to guide his disciple, who in turn worked
with great industry and conscientiousness—essentially all premises
for good progress were given. The reason for their eventual break
lies deeper—in Beethoven's indomitable spirit of independence. He
was born to create the new. He was an iconoclast to whom the
dogma meant nothing. The student Beethoven was never detached
from the true creative drive. He regarded most laws which his
teachers promulgated, like that of the consecutive fifths, an open
question.

In spite of these inner difficulties to adjust himself to the codex
of a disciplinarian, Beethoven's insatiable desire for perfection
prompted him again and again to seek the supervision of different
teachers. He was never ready to give up. Thus we find Beethoven
also among the pupils of Antonio Salieri, the court-conductor of the
Imperial Opera. Salieri's daily contact with famous singers and his
conductorial experience promised valuable insight into the problems
of vocal expression and their application in oratorio and opera
scores. The maestro, highly critical of Beethoven's bad treatment

of Italian texts, taught him the correct division of the syllables and countless other features of practical composition.

The list of Beethoven's teachers which starts with the Rhenish musician, Christian Gottlob Neefe, must include still another name, that of Alois Förster, whom Beethoven consulted especially in his early attempts at quartet writing and to whom he remained long and closely attached. It is not so much the length of the list of his teachers, but the tenacious, stubborn search for the best obtainable guidance which makes this phase of Beethoven's artistic growth comparable to his creative procedure itself. Here, as there, he knows no rest in the pursuit of the highest ideal. Everywhere there is that unbroken drive for the instinctively felt goal. It is impossible for Beethoven to compromise short of its fulfillment.

After Beethoven's death, some of his personal belongings were auctioned and five parcels marked "contrapuntal essays" were found. These contained six hundred pages of work on the figured bass, on harmony and counterpoint. The studies on the figured bass and on harmony were derived from a series of texts which Beethoven compiled in 1809, the year of Haydn's death. The contrapuntal studies belonged to the time of his apprenticeship with Haydn and Albrechtsberger. The important pendant to these studies in theory is another batch of contrapuntal exercises which Beethoven wrote and edited after his role of apprentice was reversed to that of teacher. The contrapuntal theory accepted here is in reality that of Fux and his *Gradus ad Parnassum*. The rules are simply taken over and arranged for the practical purpose of his individual teaching. In keeping with the pedagogic purpose of this unique collection, we find that the musical examples are written with utmost care. Whether Beethoven approached the problem of theory in the role of apprentice or master, he always threw himself with unconditional fervor into the conquest of the problem.[3] (Illustration VII.)

STEPS TO PARNASSUS

The three classical masters—Haydn, Mozart as well as Beethoven —followed the famous textbook of Johann Joseph Fux, *Gradus ad Parnassum*, as the guiding star of their theoretical studies. When Fux published this work in 1725, he was a man of sixty-five who looked back to Palestrina as the source of all spiritual and technical wisdom: "that splendid light in music to whom I owe everything I know of this science" were his words of worship referring to the sixteenth century master. Fux had no use for contemporary music which he thought had become "almost perverse." He was the type of savant who turns with disillusionment from a problematical present to what appears to have been a better past. Hence his theory if profound retrospectively; it is devoid of insight into contemporary art.

Fux anticipates the goal of his Grades to Parnassus in the opening imaginary "Dialogue" between the apprentice Joseph and the master Aloysius:

Josephus: I come to you, esteemed master, so that I may be initiated into the laws and fundamentals of music.
Aloysius: Do you want, then, to study the art of composition?
Josephus: Yes.
Aloysius: But do you realize that this study is like the infinite sea which one cannot exhaust in the life span of a Nestor? You are indeed taking upon yourself a difficult task, a burden heavier than Mt. Aetna.

A difficult task it is indeed and in its methodical clarification lies the great contribution of Fux: in his systematic approach to this vast contrapuntal substance and in its enlightening unfolding to the student. With the organizing mind of the born pedagogue, Fux starts with the simple and typical. He leads the student through grades that are steadily and almost facilely climbed, to the more complex and atypical features of higher polyphonic forms. As all counterpoint is written for a specified number of parts, the grades commence with counterpoint for two voices and later proceed to the analogous problems for three and four voices. Five different species are devised in regard to the style in which the added part (or parts) is written against an assigned cantus firmus:

First Species.......Note against note (all of equal value)
Second Species.....Two notes against one
Third Species......Four notes against one
Fourth Species.....Syncopation ("tied over" notes, causing a shifting of accents)
Fifth Species......Florid (a mixture of all species, with some additional ornamentation)

This system is only a means to an end. In the words of Fux: "With this training, later on, when the restraints of the cantus firmus are removed, and the student is, so to speak, released from his fetters, he will find to his joy that he can write free composition almost as if it were play." The clear and consummate treatment of the material in conjunction with the fact that these were, indeed, the grades which led the great classical masters to Parnassus is the best endorsement that posterity can bestow on this eighteenth century treatise.

The young Haydn studied Fux along with the texts of Mattheson and Ph. E. Bach. From Haydn's mature years, a manuscript has come down to us dated Esterház, September 22, 1789 and bearing the title, *Elementary Book of the Different Species of Counterpoint, Condensed from the More Comprehensive Work of Kapellmeister Fux,* by Joseph Haydn.

In the Mozarteum in Salzburg, there is a copy of *Gradus ad Parnassum* bearing the name of Leopold Mozart. Padre Martini, the famous teacher in Bologna who also taught the child Wolfgang Mozart, insisted that there was no other system than that of Fux. It is not surprising, then, that Wolfgang as a teacher continued along the same traditional principles of Fux that his father and Padre Martini had taught him. Mozart was an innovator only in his own creation. As a teacher he adhered to the principles of tradition and only on occasion deviated from the accepted path. Of his practical method in teaching composition, the correspondence with his father gives a vivid picture. From Paris, May 14, 1778, Wolfgang describes how he taught a young girl:

. . . If she gets no inspiration or ideas (for at present she really has none whatever), then it is to no purpose, for God knows I can't give her any. Her father's intention is not to make a great composer of her. "She is not," he said, "to compose operas, arias, concertos, symphonies, but only grand sonatas for her instrument and mine." I gave her her fourth lesson today, and so far as the rules of composition and harmony are concerned, I am fairly well satisfied with her. She filled in quite a good bass for the first minuet, the melody of which I had given her, and she has already begun to write in three parts. But she soon gets bored, and I am unable to help her, for as yet I cannot proceed quickly. It is too soon, even if there really were genius there, but unfortunately there is none.

Everything has to be done by rule. She has no ideas whatever—nothing comes. I have tried her in every possible way. Among other things I hit on the idea of writing down a very simple minuet in order to see whether she could not compose a variation on it. It was useless. "Well," I thought, "she probably does not know how she ought to begin." So I started to write a variation on the first bar and told her to go on in the same way and to keep to the idea. In the end it went fairly well. When it was finished, I told her to begin something of her own—only the treble part, the melody. Well, she thought and thought for a whole quarter of an hour and nothing came. So I wrote down four bars of a minuet and said to her: "See what an ass I am! I have begun a minuet and cannot even finish the melody. Please be so kind as to finish it for me." She was positive she could not, but at last with great difficulty— something came, and indeed I was only too glad to see something for once. I then told her to finish the minuet, I mean, the treble only. But for homework all I asked her to do was to alter my four bars and compose something of her own. She was to find a new beginning, and use if necessary the same harmony, provided that the melody should be different. Well, I shall see tomorrow what she has done.[4]

Briefly, the pupil is given a melody and must then proceed to write out the other parts, or must work on the invention itself and continue the melody. A certain progressiveness, however, emerges from the fact that Mozart admonishes his pupils to bring the bass to its simplest line. Mozart calls the plain bass line "the fundament of the general bass." Working out such a texture, the pupil had to write this reduced part on a third staff below the bass proper. Since the middle of the eighteenth century, the theory of the fundamental bass had found an increasing number of admirers among musicians in central Europe. The principle to form such a fundamental bass line (as distinguished from the real bass of a composition) was proclaimed first by Jean Philippe Rameau. The great French composer, equally great as a theorist, laid down in his epochal *Traité d'Harmonie* (and elsewhere) the inversion of the chords, the 6 and $\frac{6}{4}$ chords as deductions from the triads in the root position. Toward the end of the century, Rameau's theory, first promulgated in 1722, was firmly entrenched outside of France. There is no doubt that Mozart, with his intimate knowledge of French music acquired on French soil (he lived in Paris in 1778), was influenced by this technique. Moreover all problems of theory

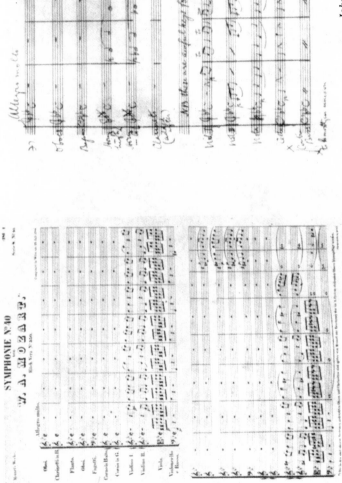

I. Mozart: Symphony in G Minor, K.550

Mozart's Werke, Series 8
Breitkopf & Härtel, Leipzig

II. Elgar: Manuscript of Symphony in G Minor

John Lane The Bodley Head,
London

III. KIRCHER: MUSURGIA, VOLUME I

IV. Drawings by Mendelssohn

V. The Workrooms of Brahms in Vienna

VI. Wagner's Library in Wahnfried

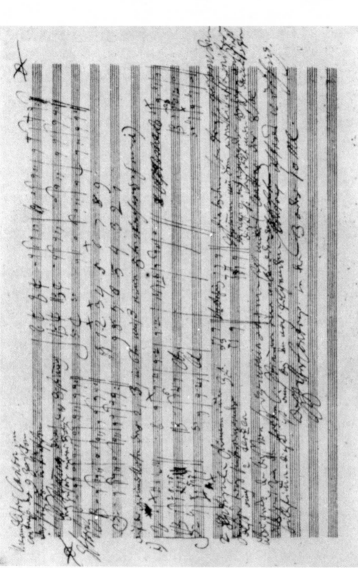

VII. Beethoven: Studies in Counterpoint

Handel's Werke Vol. 22 Ed. of Händel-Ges.
Breitkopf & Härtel, Leipzig

VIII. HANDEL: MARCH FROM JUDAS MACCABAEUS

Handel's Werke Supplement 5 Ed. of
Händel-Ges., Breitkopf & Härtel, Leipzig

IX. MUFFAT: COMPONIMENTI MUSICALI

X. HANDEL: ODE FOR ST. CECILIA'S DAY

Handel's Werke, Supplement 5, Ed. of
Händel-Ges., Breitkopf & Härtel, Leipzig

XI. MUFFAT: COMPONIMENTI MUSICALI

Handel's Werke, Vol. 16, Ed. of
Händel-Ges., Breitkopf & Härtel, Leipzig

XII. HANDEL: CHORUS FROM ISRAEL IN EGYPT

Primo Crocchio.

Secondo Crocchio.

Concertino.

Concerto grosso.

Handel's Werke, Supplement 3, Ed. of
Händel-Ges., Breitkopf & Härtel, Leipzig

XIII. STRADELLA: SERENATA

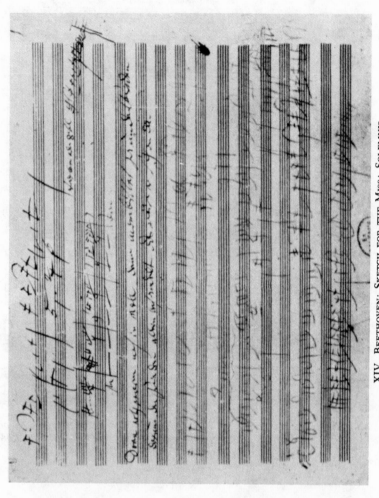

XIV. BEETHOVEN: SKETCH FOR THE MISSA SOLEMNIS

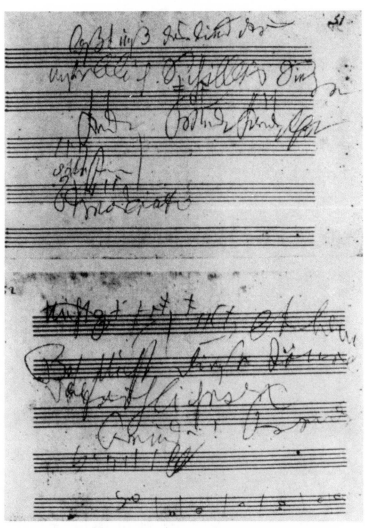

XV. Beethoven: Sketches for the Ninth Symphony

XVI. Schubert: Seventh Symphony

Gesellschaft der Musikfreunde, Vienna

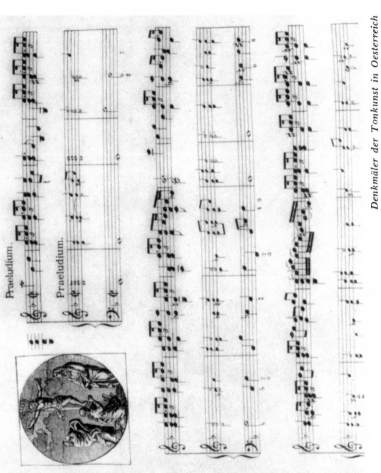

Denkmäler der Tonkunst in Oesterreich

XVII. BIBER: SONATA FOR VIOLIN (CRUCIFIXION)

and teaching interested Mozart.[5] He assured his father: "I would like to write a book, a small musical criticism with examples, but *nota bene*, not under my own name." Among Mozart's more important pupils are Stephan Storace, Thomas Attwood and Johann Nepomuk Hummel.

CONSTANT LEARNING

Young Weber, like Beethoven, led a varied life during his apprentice years. There were two periods of theoretical study with Michael Haydn (Joseph's brother who lived in Salzburg). From 1798 to 1800, Weber studied with the Munich court organist, J. N. Kalcher. Weber explains the reasons for the unsatisfactory relationship with his early teachers: "There was too large a distance between the child and the serious man. I learned little and only under great effort." The decisive turn in Weber's theoretical training occurred when he met in Vienna (1803) Abbé Georg Joseph Vogler, one of the most celebrated musical theorists of the time, a man endowed with a colorful personality, who played an important part in the creative lives of many musicians. Among others, Abbé Vogler taught Meyerbeer. Johann Gänsbacher stated that "the mere association with Vogler was a kind of a school." Weber was by no means a beginner when he took up his studies with the priest and had already completed three operas. Yet such accomplishments did not change Vogler's principle which demanded that every student start from scratch. "Not without a struggle," Weber relates, "did I abandon all creative enterprises." He had to dedicate a year to intense study of the various scores of the great masters—their ideas, their structure and their artistic means. Vogler's teaching was chiefly a method of analysis whereby the teacher interprets the groundplan of great scores and thus prepares the way for the student's own approach.

In his unfinished novel, *A Musical Artist's Life,* begun in 1820, Weber takes issue with the pitfalls of theory and attacks the negativistic attitude by which "we only forbid and dictate without saying why and showing how. They say Bach did it that way! Handel did not do this! Mozart took particular liberties. If one has an idea which differs from the way they did it, one had better scratch it out immediately, for there is no proof that it could be right. What a pity!" But Weber came to the conclusion that in spite of all its deficiencies and the shortcomings of its interpreters, the conscientious study of theory remains indispensable: "How foolish it is to believe that the serious inquiry into the means crushes the spirit and clips the wings of imagination. It is only from the mastery of these means that free creation can emerge. Only the familiarity with roads that have been already trod, enables the fantasy to find new ones." After Weber had achieved mastery and fame, young musicians turned to him for advice and consultation. Alois Fuchs, a government employee, found himself in a dilemma—so frequent in the lives of young people—whether or not he should embark professionally on a musician's career. Weber's answer penetrates to the technical and psychological roots of the crucial problem:

I do not know the talent which God has given you, but I do know that even the most extraordinary one needs happy circumstances to produce important works and also to be esteemed in the world. At your age (twenty-five), when the critical powers have already gained the upper hand, it is very difficult to make up for the technical and grammatical part of art, in such a way and with such success that one does not become handicapped because of exertion and discouraged over one's talent. One already knows too much about what and how the art operates to carry it on naïvely for its own sake. It is this innocence alone which enables one to master the means. The matter goes from the outside to the inside instead of as it should, according to its nature, from the inside to the outside.

In Weber's judgment the subconscious factor of composing is held to be decisive. Instinct is superior to reflection. Realizing his great responsibility in a decision so crucial for the life of this young man, Weber hesitates to play fate and realistically warns Alois Fuchs not to overlook the all-importance of the "lucky break." With all his talents, the young artist needs fortunate circumstances if he is to be successful: "Please consider the whole neither as advice against or for," Weber continues. "In such cases which are decisive for the whole life, only the inner voice is the sole judge." This correspondence of Weber with his young friend belongs to that category of letters in which great artists have taken time and thought to advise young people on the brink of their career. Note-worthy among these letters is the correspondence between Schumann and a high school student, Ludwig Meinardus, who later became a composer and musicologist, between Bruckner and Leopold Hofmeyer and, with wide spiritual implications, between Tolstoi and the then unknown Romain Rolland.

Young Berlioz changed teachers when his viewpoint changed. It is understandable that such a strikingly original artist as Berlioz would resist the conventionalism of his early teachers: "I quit the broad road in order to take my way through valleys and mountains, through forests and meadows." Among his teachers were Joseph Reicha, Beethoven's colleague in the Bonn Court Orchestra and the brilliant Jean François Lesueur who anticipated concepts of program music so important to Berlioz's later development. Yet they did not teach him enough, Berlioz complained. The fact remains that he learned a great deal from them in an amazingly short time. At first young Berlioz refused to acknowledge the validity of old rules. Later, he discovered the truism that all theoretical laws were derived through careful observation and analysis of past masterworks. What inevitably causes the trespassing of the old laws are "new desires and a new spirit which forces the ear to seek new roads. Certain forms are already so worn-out that one can hardly admit them any longer. Everything is good or everything is bad depending upon the use one makes of it."

Schumann's whole life can be regarded as one continuous quest for learning: he never considered himself finished with the study of theory. At different stations of his life, he took up the study of counterpoint. The early studies with Heinrich Dorn lasted not much longer than a year. "With Dorn I shall never see eye to eye, and he will never bring me to the point where I will see in music only a fugue," reads the outrage of the young romanticist against the formalistic dryness of an academician in a letter of 1832, to his father-in-law, Wieck. Nevertheless, Schumann admits "the theoretical studies had a good influence upon me." (His iconoclastic ideas on the fugue and the whole world of old forms were thoroughly revised in mature years.) Kindhearted and considerate by nature, young Schumann is very careful not to hurt his teacher's feelings. We sense his inner conflict, when he tries to make the inevitable break appear as nothing final and pleads with Dorn: "Please don't believe that I stood still since our separation. . . . From where we stopped, I comfortably kept on going according to Marpurg, and I do not abandon hope still to resume lessons with you on the canon. . . . I badly miss your assistance. . . . Marpurg is truly a most remarkable theorist, otherwise Bach's Well-Tempered Clavier is my grammar, the best one whatsoever."

This devotion to The Well-Tempered Clavier remains with Schumann throughout his life and becomes evident in numerous references, such as the following: "I, myself, have analyzed the fugues even unto the very smallest detail. The value of this effort is great. It has. a morally strengthening effect upon the whole human being—everything here seems written as though for eternity." In spite of such boundless admiration for Bach, Schumann circumvents onesidedness in his education. Hence, at thirty-five, he pursues contrapuntal studies according to Cherubini. But it is Beethoven who remains the last word for Schumann: "If you want to know what can be done with a simple thought through industry, love and particularly through genius, then study Beethoven and see how he developed it to its summit and ennobled it, and how the original common word is transformed in his mouth into a universal proverb." And again: "Yes, I do love him (Beethoven) very much, but do not forget that it was only through years of long study that he achieved his poetic freedom."

Such a conquest of craft through constant study of theory is held to be an absolute necessity. As Schumann asserts, the laws of theory must be obeyed unconditionally before creative license is possible: "Do not detach yourself from any rules until you have conquered them in hard work." It is not necessary, however, to go back centuries in the search for the fundamental laws: their application is firmly embedded in the works of the masters following the great polyphonic era of the sixteenth century, from which the essence of all theory stems. "In the course of time the sources came closer and closer to each other. Beethoven did not have to study everything that Mozart had already absorbed, Mozart not Handel, Handel not Palestrina, because the predecessors had already consumed the technique. It is only from one single man that we can again and again draw—Bach." But the study of the music prior to the eighteenth century is of highest value and that of Palestrina's counterpoint a must, because "one learns to move within narrow limits, to get along with scarce means. This in one way or the other will reward you." Only from limitations can mastery emerge. Therefore Schumann's insistence that every young musician must thoroughly study the old masters even though "they may not convey the same message which their music did centuries ago." The tolerant and progressive outlook, always characteristic of Schumann's thinking, comes to the fore in his attitude to teaching: "Do not interfere with the course of time. Make youth study the old masters but do not ask the young musician to carry simplicity . . . to the point of affectation."

A constancy of learning which we observe with Schumann likewise prevails with other great composers. Beethoven, Schubert, Brahms, Tchaikovsky, Bruckner never considered their studies completed. They did not bestow upon themselves graduation certificates in composition. In years of maturity, these masters eagerly learned like schoolboys. They considered every age to be the right one for theoretical studies. Hence, intense learning was resumed long after they had achieved—in the opinion of their contemporaries—full proficiency of technique.

Bruckner, at the age of thirty-six started, once more, to study musical theory with a zeal that would put any young student to shame. He traveled from Linz in Upper Austria once or twice a year for six or seven weeks to Vienna where he "spent the whole day with the professor." The authority who exerted such an attraction was the famous theorist, Simon Sechter, a contrapuntalist of the old school. Touched and amazed by Bruckner's incredible diligence, he paternally writes: "I have looked over your seventeen notebooks containing work in double counterpoint and I justifiably marveled at your industry and at the progress you make therein. . . . However, I must ask you to take better care of yourself so that you will be in good health upon your arrival in Vienna . . . I feel compelled to assure you that I never had a more industrious pupil."

Not torn by doubts and wavering trust in his teacher, Bruckner's belief in his theory was that of a pious man in the dogma. He regarded Sechter's system as "the expression of the highest logic, consistency and law, not only of nature but also of all ethical beings and divine righteousness." Here, the teacher takes on an almost religious significance. He functions as a model: he sets the example not only in the craft of music, but also as a human being. Years later, after Bruckner himself had achieved fame as a teacher and had become a lecturer at the University of Vienna, he would start his classes with the following sentence: "Well, here is what Sechter says and you pupils must most carefully keep it in mind." Thus Bruckner initiated his apprentices in the sacrosanct name of his own master, into the laws of musical craft. Whatever problems would turn up later would eventually be solved by Sechter's word as the final authority.

Yet there was one thing wrong with all these laws of strict theory, namely that Bruckner, their rigid guardian, would occasionally break them himself in his compositions. Pressed by students to confess his own sins, he would just grin and say: "It is I who am allowed. You are not." Creation was one thing, learning another. As a teacher, Bruckner permitted no deviation from the law; he expected full obedience from his disciples. Again, the tremendous industry which he imposed upon himself was equally expected from his pupils. Friedrich Klose reports that Bruckner made him write 180 different counterpoints to one single cantus firmus and no less than 300 canons! Similarly astonishing figures are disclosed by other disciples of Bruckner. He considered three years obligatory for the study of harmony alone, provided the student was acquainted with the elements of music. It may seem paradoxical that a composer would declare that for the study of "composition a few months suffice." But Bruckner believed that composition proper was not teachable at all. Such differentiation obviously points to the teachable factors of craft and the unteachable factors of inspiration. The latter comes from above. Craft, however, must be learned in systematic work. After the thorough study of harmony and counterpoint, there still follows extensive analysis of musical form. Even at this late stage, free creative expression is altogether excluded. Only studies are permitted. Bruckner followed here the same principles that we encountered in the method of Abbé Vogler. This was also the way Sechter reared Bruckner.

Can musical craft be acquired in an autodidactic manner? Bruckner denies it emphatically and expresses himself against any method of self-teaching. We learn from his letter to Leopold Hof-meyer that "one absolutely needs in this field an efficient teacher because even the treatises . . . would remain incomprehensible or wrongly interpreted without a good teacher."[6] It must be assumed that a rather heavy teaching load at the university (and otherwise) distracted valuable energies from Bruckner's life task of composing. Teaching, however, proved to be creation of another kind for him. The great disappointments he had to take as a composer in the competitive concert life were strongly offset by the moral success and unbending loyalty he found with his students. Here, in the self-created environment of his workshop or the classroom, he ex-perienced warmth and friendship instead of the hostility which made the concert halls of Austria and Germany dreaded places. With his students, Bruckner had peace instead of struggle. Success was less dramatic and glorified, but sure and lasting. The childless old man was happiest among his spiritual children.

THE DISCIPLE AS SPIRITUAL SUCCESSOR

Fate provided Brahms with a teacher singularly equipped to acquaint him in early youth with the tonal world of the classicists. The Hamburg musician, Eduard Marxsen, from whom Brahms took a systematic course in theory, proudly considered himself a "grand-son-pupil" of the classical masters: he had studied with Mozart's disciple, Ignatz Seyfried and also with Karl Maria von Bocklet, an associate of Beethoven and Schubert. Thus, Marxsen had learned the classical craft from first sources. An inner affinity of spirit led Brahms to Marxsen. And an association of constancy and stability resulted which lasted and retained its original character much in contrast to the erratic relationships between other composers and their numerous teachers. Brahms' achievement of fame altered neither the warmth of the friendship nor the desire to have his scores corrected by his old teacher. At the height of his mastery, Brahms sent Marxsen the manuscript of the German Requiem for critical perusal.

When Marxsen celebrated his golden jubilee as an artist in 1883, Brahms felt the urge to pay an unusual tribute to him. He had Marxsen's One Hundred Variations on a Folksong printed at his

own expense. The seventy-seven-year-old man wrote to Brahms
with gratefulness:

What a surprise, what a great pleasure you have given me! In my old
age it has been granted to me to see a second day of triumph in my
artistic career. The first, of course, occurred when Seyfried, in regard
to my first symphony, called me 'his son.' The second is caused by my
faithful pupils, headed by you, the pride of my life and professional
career. I want to clasp you to my heart—the loyal friend who has employed his heavenly gifts for the true welfare of art. May the Lord continue to protect you, may He lavish his love upon you, to the joy of all
those who render homage to what is lofty and noble in art . . . your
enraptured Marxsen.

This touching letter of the old musician discloses the true bond
of a teacher-pupil relationship. Marxsen's words literally expose
the father-son tie as it lives in the aging artist's desire to attain
immortality through his disciple. Indeed, Marxsen achieved this
goal as the teacher of Brahms. Here, in the art of a greater musician
than he was himself, Marxsen's spirit has been tangibly trans-
mitted into specific features of the Brahms' style—its deep roots in
classical expression, its passion for the folkloristic and the form of
variation, and, last but not least, its polyphonic character. All these
traits distinguish Marxsen's music and were inherited by his disciple
Brahms. The everlasting pursuit of theory emerges as a chief
interest throughout the lives of both men.

A CORRESPONDENCE COURSE IN COUNTERPOINT

Unique in the history of counterpoint studies is the long-distance
venture upon which Brahms embarked with Joseph Joachim. The
overture for the enterprise was made by Brahms in a letter from
Düsseldorf, February 26, 1856:

I would like to remind you and to request that we finally put into practice
what we had agreed upon so often, namely, to send each other studies in
counterpoint. Let us every fortnight exchange our exercises which will
be returned with our respective comments—until we have both become
very smart. Why should not we, being rather intelligent and serious
people, teach each other better and much more beautifully than some

Philistine would? . . . Let us be serious about it. It will be beautiful and useful indeed!

Brahms was twenty-three, Joachim was two years older and at that time concertmaster in Hanover. After he had sent his approval, Brahms happily started the wheels rolling on March 24:

. . . I send you herewith two small pieces to start our common studies. If you still like our plans, then I will tell you some of the rules of the game which I consider useful. Every Sunday, exercises must be exchanged. . . . Who misses the day, that is to say, who doesn't send anything, will be fined a taler, with which the other one is entitled to buy books. The only excuse is if one sends a composition instead of an exercise. . . . You must return to me, by next Sunday, all the pieces . . . and send others such as counterpoints, canons, fugues, preludes or whatever they might be.

Joachim's reply contained a series of fugal themes with the request that Brahms should "scratch out with a red pencil all errors." The correspondence included examples such as a canon, a circle canon in the octave and so forth. Brahms, in a letter of April 27, 1856, did not like the work of his friend: "There is nothing I can do with your fugal themes." He then explained why the themes were not suited as subjects for fugues: they did not lend themselves to further contrapuntal development. One theme was considered bad because "there can be no thought about a stretto. It would be probably difficult to find a fluid and invertible counterpoint." The strict Brahms denied one of the exercises even the name of a canon: "too many empty spots occur in it." The studies were also returned with pertinent aesthetic questions: "If the artfulness therein is discounted, are they good music? Does the artful, the expert craftsmanship make them more beautiful and more valuable? What occurs to you?" Technical complications, such as only highest skill can solve, were not shunned but eagerly sought as welcome challenges. "I enclose exercises which I consider very difficult and which I ask you to complete," Brahms writes. "The canonic imitations (rather free) are on a cantus firmus. The intervals are still missing. Just try it. It is difficult. Hereafter we will attempt to treat the theme more beautifully and freer if you care to do it. In reference to the canon I think of string instruments because their tone vibrates whereas it would not sound well on the piano."

Joachim's answer dealing with the exercises amounted to a thesis four printed pages long. Yet this was exactly the sort of reply for which Brahms craved—industrious, conscientious, critical. And his response was jubilant: "I have to run to open country fields because in my room I cannot jump for joy. I am so happy that you like the fugues. You are right in all your objections, and they are going to be changed by the time you see them again."

The strict counterpoint! The solution of some of its difficult problems (on the part of the friend) warmed the cockles of Brahms' heart. He certainly had counterpoint in his blood. We hear and admire in his music this deep-seated and lifelong inclination toward the polyphonic style.

Five and a half years after its inception, this long-distance correspondence in counterpoint came to an end. Part of the studies later turned into completed compositions and were published.[7] Here was truly a teaching method on the highest level. Every rule, every note was tested conscientiously as to its external place and its inner meaning. The tonal material was carefully weighed on an aesthetician's gold scale. The treatment of the problem always led to the very roots of craft and aesthetic philosophy. The potential master of music spoke out of every line in these studies written in years of apprenticeship. And ever after, like a cantus firmus, the search for craft flowed through Brahms' musical life. Its deep significance came to the fore in Brahms' last creative period which was devoted, once again, to theoretical studies. At the close of his life, Brahms elaborated a series of canons and set them for women's chorus. These were later published as Op. 113. Brahms' whole attitude is pertinently summed up in his words referring to the task of writing notes: "Whether they are beautiful is not your affair, but perfect they must be." This perfection he sought all his life and found it through the conquest of craft.

TRADITION AND PROGRESS

The pedagogical question in all its ramifications is answered by Verdi in several statements which convey a clear picture of his position as an inspirational artist and a craftsman. In a letter to Giuseppe Piroli from Genoa, February 20, 1871,[8] Verdi places all emphasis on the analysis of old music, both sacred and profane. A severe initial course of contrapuntal training is indispensable for the young composer to achieve his own style. Then, if he sees fit, he can study the old scores and he will no longer be in danger of turning into a mere imitator. But the study of moderns is taboo. "Many people will think this strange, but today, when I hear and see so many works put together the way a bad tailor puts clothes together on a standard model, I cannot budge in my opinion. I know, of course, that many modern works could be cited which are as good as the old, but what of that?"

Noteworthy is Verdi's conviction that instrumentation and the theoretical aspects of composition proper do not belong to the regular curriculum. They must be taught by the composer's "own head and heart, if he has any." And in a letter written to Francesco Florimo (January 14, 1871) rejecting the offer of the directorship of the Conservatory in Milan, Verdi expresses himself in unequivocal terms:

It would be an honor for me to instruct the students in the weighty, vigorous and lucid teachings of those fathers (referring to Alessandro Scarlatti, Durante and Leo who had occupied the post). I should have been able to stand, so to speak, with one foot in the past and the other in the present and future. . . . And I should have said to the young people: "Practice the fugue constantly and particularly until you are weary of it and your hands are supple and strong enough to bend music to your pure will. Thus you will learn assurance in composition, proper part-writing, unforced modulation. Study Palestrina and some few of his contemporaries, then skip everybody up to Marcello, and pay particular attention to the recitatives. Attend but few performances of contemporary opera, and don't be seduced by the profusion of harmonic and instrumental beauties, nor by the chord of the diminished seventh, that easy subterfuge for all of us who can't write four measures without half a dozen sevenths."

When they have gone thus far and have achieved a broad literary background, I would finally say to these young students: "Now lay your hands on your heart and go ahead and write. If you have the stuff of artists in you, you will be composers. . . . But to apply these few deceptively simple principles, it would be necessary to supervise the instruction so closely that twelve months a year would be almost too little. . . . I hope you may be able to find a man who is above all learned

and a strict teacher. Liberties and mistakes in counterpoint can be con-
doned and are even sometimes quite good . . . in the theater. But not in
the conservatory!

In both letters, the intense study of the old masters is regarded
as a must. Furthermore, Verdi insists on a broad literary education.
This plea is most significant if we consider that even today the need
for a general college education is not always recognized as an
obligatory part of musical studies. But the essence of Verdi's
pedagogic philosophy is expressed in the concluding exhortation of
the letter to Francesco Florimo: "Torniamo all antico: sara un
progresso." "Let us turn back to the old masters: progress will be
the result."

CHAPTER NINE

ARS INVENIENDI

> The greatest genius is the most
> indebted man.
>
> **EMERSON**

THE "SPECIALTIES"

EVERY era lives in bondage to its own theory. The sixteenth century, however, produced the music as well as the theoretical laws to which composers up to our day turn as the source of tonal craft. Accepting Verdi's slogan, "Torniamo all antico: sara un progresso," musicians pursue the wisdom and technique of Palestrina which is comparable only to that of Bach in its far-reaching and seemingly timeless message to posterity.

The sixteenth century is also the time of Zarlino and his encyclopedia of musical craft. A steady decline of medievalism and its worship of dogma terminates the era of unquestioned theoretical truth and of a scholastic obedience to rules and laws. The fact remains that since the Middle Ages, every great composer was a master of his craft in the sense of the old guilds. He had learned his métier as an apprentice in long and hard training. He was a highly skilled artisan in the setting of tonal material. But with the turn from the seventeenth to the eighteenth century, the time approached when a reaction to the centuries-long emphasis on craft was bound to set in. The role of inspiration in creative work begins to make itself more strongly felt in the treatises on composition; references to its function occur in increasing numbers. But still the procedure does not depend on mere imagination (in terms of the romantic artist and his inspirational sources). To wait for inspiration, for the gifts from the Muses would contradict the whole ideology of this realistic and practical era of music-making. The trend is still to aid the imagination by means of solid craft. "If the inspiration does not come, then the teaching of the invention and imagination must help." So reads the prescription in Johann Mattheson's *The Perfect Conductor* (*Der vollkommene Capellmeister*). And in this famous thesaurus of musical knowledge, a difference is made between the unteachable inspiration and the learned invention. Significantly, craft can substitute for inspiration—as shown in this volume published in 1739.

A term occurs in Mattheson's treatise which characterizes a whole trend of composition. This term is, in its original Latin, *ars inveniendi*. Yet what it actually connotes is less an inspirational art than a specific craft of invention as taught by the contemporary schools of composition—an all round method of developing given tonal material along certain established lines. *The Perfect Conductor* demonstrates, in the chapter on "Melodic Invention" how without the aid of inspiration, the tools of workmanship must assist the composer. He must resort to a reservoir of "specialities such as modulations, small phrases, turns, skillful and agreeable tunes, melodic leaps—all of which are to be collected through much experience and through intense listening to good music." Whatever pleases the composer by way of sentences and modulations, he should write down, in order to have them at his disposal for future reference. In short, the composer goes about his task by devising a system of musical material according to topics— a musical filing system, as it were. Its organization is guided by association of thought pointing to a certain type of performance in church, the theater, or to chamber music.

Does not *The Perfect Conductor*, with this advice to collect and revise material, invite the would-be composer to downright plagiarism? Not at all, since Mattheson rationalizes with typical eighteenth century dialectics, that the new is never anything but a novel permutation of the old. What does it matter if the *specialties* were already employed by previous composers? "They still could be arranged in such a way that the result can be considered an invention of one's own." Mattheson warns the disciple not to expect a rain of beautiful ideas from this method. Who does not bring along a natural talent will find little to gain from his guide to musical craft. Who has talent must still make every effort to assemble all possible auxiliary means to composition. "Although invention cannot easily be taught or learned, one can assist and show the way in such a manner as to lend a hand to one's native gifts." Mattheson's illustrations show some of the methods to secure inventions: "I have known a conductor who sought a way to invention in the belfry tower of St. Peter's which at certain hours would strike a tetrachordon or a sequence of fourths by way of a clockwork." Another way of obtaining new melodies is to adapt variations from well known songs, from sacred hymns and folk tunes. Here and there a phrase may be borrowed and newly developed with success.

The following is one of Mattheson's characteristic illustrations. It shows how an old German evening song of calm contemplation is turned into a passionate expression of love:

EXAMPLE 14

Evidently the points of contact between model and variation lie in the melodic curve which both tunes have in common. The transformation from the tranquil mood to the passionate expression occurs chiefly through a change of rhythm: the quiet and solemn half-notes of the model, "Now rest all the forests," are transferred into an affetuoso variation: a lively $\frac{6}{8}$ rhythm carries the fiery message, "With delight to press you on my heart."

Even from the "smallest things," claims Mattheson, the sources of melodic invention may spring. To be on the alert for them is part of the composer's task. If he is sensitive enough, he will hear music everywhere.

Whether an invention flows freely from the composer's imagination, or is pumped from strange wells, is of no consequence. For it is in the following stages of composition—the working out and synthetic stages—that the composer's genuine craft must unfold itself. The most beautiful ideas, Mattheson warns, are of poor value if they are not accompanied by three inseparable companions. These partners of melodic invention are:

dispositio..................the skillful organization
elaboratio................. the industrious development
decoratio..................the clever embellishment

In a systematic and orderly way, Mattheson leads the apprentice through all of these stages.[1] On his way, he is guided by the so-called *loci topici* which are about a dozen means of invention directing the composer to a particular problem of his score.

HANDEL: ON BORROWED TUNES

"Borrowing is a permitted matter, but one has to pay the loan back with interest. One must arrange imitations in such a way that they acquire a better and more beautiful appearance than those models from which they are taken." These are Mattheson's words, and they sum up a whole trend and attitude of music-making with a realism characteristic, not only of the author, but also of his century of rationalism.

Composition was taught as a process of reproduction in conjunction with the composer's own train of thought. Hence, composers borrowed tonal substance without any hesitation, even as a sign of mutual admiration. The mere fact of a loan did not detract from the value of a score. Only what the composer had done with the borrowed material really counted: its artful disposition, elaboration, decoration. We have found roots for this procedure in the religious soil of the Middle Ages. Now in the eighteenth century, such tolerance toward re-using musical substance was rationalistically tinted. It emerged from the realization that memory, voluntary as well as involuntary, is always at work in artistic creation.

Whatever music the composer has heard before takes possession of his mind and makes a high degree of involuntary borrowing inevitable.

Among the great masters, it was particularly Handel in whose workshop the procedure of reworking borrowed material played an enormous part. Moreover, never in history was this technique treated with such superb mastery. Handel's music stands as a monument of that whole era, where, in its own terms, artistic greatness emerged not from melodic invention, but from elaboration and disposition.

Handel's method of re-using already existing compositions[2] was by no means an accidental or an occasional procedure. It appears rather as a basic device of composition permeating many of his great works. He borrowed from composers such as Muffat, Kerll, Dioni, Erba, Urio, Stradella—some of them are almost forgotten; their names would have remained in obscurity had the light of a greater master's glory not fallen upon their scores.

In the scores of the Austrian composer Gottlieb Muffat,[3] and particularly in his Componimenti Musicali per il Cembalo (published 1734), Handel discovered a veritable gold mine of tonal material. Muffat's work is one of the finest contributions to keyboard music made by any of Handel's contemporaries. Obviously it had a wide circulation since numerous copies dating from Handel's time can still be found in old European libraries. Observing Handel's borrowing from the Componimenti Musicali, we will gain a first insight into the baroque technique of borrowing. The most direct instances occur in cases where the main thought of a composition is taken over almost in its entirety. Such is the case in our example of Muffat's Air in G Major which Handel turned into the March of his great oratorio, *Judas Maccabaeus.*

If we compare Handel's March with Muffat's Air (Illustrations VIII and IX), we will not fail to recognize the stamp of the greater composer. We see how Handel alters the curve of Muffat's melody: three times instead of twice, Handel's theme reaches for the ornamental third on the tone B. Muffat, after a simple repetition of his motif, proceeds conventionally toward the fifth of the broken triad on which he built his tune. In contrast, Handel, with characteristic tenacity, embellishes and emphasizes the B as the marked point of the melody. He eliminates Muffat's light pauses in the second and third measure of the Air and dots the half-note in the March. The difference between Handel's orchestral arrangement and Muffat's keyboard setting (inspired by Couperin's graceful textures) is evident. Handel's instrumentation calls for a pair of horns, strings and the "continuo"[4] (which is taken for granted in baroque orchestral performances). Tying in with the change of the melodic line, the violins play, emphasizing trills on the accented beat of the second, third and fourth measures. The immediate result of these various alterations is a distinct change of expression—a ·firm and determined march originates from the playful air. Handel's lively and breezy *alla breve* rhythm supplants Muffat's $\frac{4}{4}$ *vivace*. The bass line is reinforced throughout by Handel's firm quarter-steps. The French horns add a touch of martial color.

This first comparison of a model and its baroque transformation already demonstrates that whatever Handel touched became his own at the initial point of contact. In other cases, Handel dealt still more freely with his models, imprinting on them a higher degree of his own originality. This technique is frequently developed to such a point that the transformation retains only a very remote similarity with the original. In his *Ode for St. Cecilia's Day*, Handel utilized, among other foreign material, the Fuga a quattro in B-flat Major, again borrowed from Muffat. Comparing the model with its Handelian metamorphosis, we see how brilliantly the master has transformed the decorative keyboard polyphony of his contemporary into one of his greatest choruses. After a profound prelude, Handel introduced the fugue with the words, "The dead shall live, the living die," developing it into a truly baroque piece of one hundred and fifty-two bars as compared with Muffat's thirty-six measures of limited elaboration.

How is the problem solved this time? We see from our musical illustrations X and XI that Handel divides Muffat's ornamental theme into two forceful phrases of a quality different from the model. Handel breaks the ornamental line of Muffat's two-measure subject into a highly contrapuntal design of a double fugue that spins its web of voices from the first couple of bars: such a division gives the music immediately a feeling of space, a character of depth. "The dead shall live," proclaims the soprano and, two octaves lower, the bass announces the eternal fate of all creatures, "The living die." The alto now introduces that motif of running eighth-notes suggested by Muffat's sixteenths. Granted that here (as well as in our previous example) most of Handel's notes are undeniably Muffat's; still Handel's music emerges as something entirely new. New is the set-up of theme and answer, and totally different is the expression: out of Muffat's decorative lines and ornaments emerge the granite blocks of Handel's resurrection scene.

Our last highly characteristic example shows how the famous chorus of the hailstones in Handel's *Israel in Egypt* is almost entirely borrowed from the Sinfonia d'Ouverture of the *Serenata* by Alessandro Stradella (Illustrations XII and XIII). If we compare the two musical profiles, we have to admit that they are almost identical. No doubt, Stradella's main idea which Handel has transposed from D Major to C Major displays almost the same notes. In both cases, we see the short initial motif with its upbeat of an eighth and the $\frac{3}{4}$ rhythm with its characteristic pauses. Stradella, as well as Handel, continues after this intrada of chords, with a theme of broken triads in equal eighth-notes, shifting this pattern to the other voices. All this Handel has literally taken over from Stradella. Moreover, the most important suggestion is derived from the set-up of the model: from its arrangement of two ensembles answering each other in the antiphonal style.

Yet the spirit of Handel's music has nothing to do with Stradella's overture. The light *Serenata* with its instrumental passages is turned into an intense and threatening thrust. There is no playful division into Concertino and Concerto Grosso[5] as in Stradella's *Serenata*. If we learn that certain measures of Stradella's overture are quoted from the buffo tune, "Piu sequir non voglio piu," then the secret of Handel's approach is given away. Comedy has been turned into tragedy. The musical expression has been changed from one extreme to another, the bright tone color of the *Serenata* has been darkened to the black of the hailstorm. As in the previous instances, the notes alone can show how this has been accomplished: Handel's vision steered the light setting of Stradella's play into a rushing stream of polyphonic power. Where Stradella loosened his music for light caesuras of breathing, Handel firmly continued the onrush of tones. His full orchestra, with organ and double chorus, transformed Stradella's leaping quarters and eighths into the hailstones which roar and tumble without a stop.

What formerly was a pleasant setting of a fine craftsman became the terrific and overpowering tableau conceived by genius. No one had a deeper comprehension of the creative process here involved than Romain Rolland[6] who explained that Handel saw in the music of others that which was not there. Not only did Handel create his own music, he recreated that of others. He made his eyes and his ears discover in the serenades of Stradella the cataclysm of the Bible.

A SIDELINE ON SHAKESPEARE

Composers' indebtedness to the music of others has its parallels in all the arts. The liberties which Handel took in his creative procedure correspond to the license of artists in all times who consider a good thought the common property of those who adequately know how to re-use it. These artists do not see their mission in the discovery of strikingly novel material; they rather function as the carriers of the thoughts and artistic substance surrounding them. Their distinction lies in the strikingly original use they make of common material and in the range and extent of their work.

When Shakespeare left Stratford to join the London theater, with its audiences clamoring for dramatic entertainment, he found there countless plays of all dates and sources, from the Greek and Roman histories to English, Italian and Spanish tales. All these comedies and tragedies on Helen of Troy, on Julius Caesar or the Kings had been written and rewritten, enlarged upon and altered in various ways for the English theatergoers. Facing this wealth of dramatic raw material, Shakespeare's intuitive mind quickly discerned the sparkle of the true stone. Whatever he could use, he took unhesitatingly and shaped it into the jewels of his own fantasy. His varying roles as playwright, actor and director suggest the blend in Handel's activities of creating and performing, one hundred years later on the old cultured soil of London. The works of these practical artists emerged from adaptation, adjustment and minute changing of foreign material. Deeply steeped in the world of dramatic performance, poet and composer always coped with its ever-changing laws and demands. They keenly observed the

:ffects of other writers and composers only to improve upon them.
Glorious results justify the means: borrowing serves here a truly
:reative purpose.

The quantity of loans and the great variety of sources is a further
)oint of comparison. Thus, Shakespeare, like Handel, owed debts
n all directions. And both seemed to be able to use whatever they
ound. The examination of the extent and substance of Shakespeare's
)orrowings has been the intriguing problem of research. The fol-
owing comparison of a section from *King Lear* with excerpts from
Montaigne, who was Shakespeare's source, is an illuminating
)arallel to the procedure of Handel:

Shakespeare	Montaigne
s man no more than this? Con-ider him well. Thou ow'st the vorm no silk, the beast no hide, the heep no wool, the cat no perfume. Ia! here's three on's are sophisti-ated; Thou art the thing itself; naccommodated man is no more ut such a poor, bare forked animal s thou art. Off you lendings! Lear, iii 4, 107	Miserable man; whom if you con-sider well what is he? Book II, 172 Truely, when I consider man all naked . . . and view his defects, his natural subjection and manifold imperfections, I finde we have had much more reason to hide and cover our nakedness than any creature else. We may be excused for borrowing those which nature had therein favored more than us with their beauties to adorne us, and under their spoiles of wooll, of haire, of feathers, and of silks to shroud us. And that our wisdome should learne of beasts, the most profitable documents, belonging to our chief-est and most necessary parts of life . . . Where (with reason) men have done, as perfumers doe with oyle, they have adulterated her with so many argumentations, and sophisticated her. III, 310

Allow not nature more than nature needs, Man's life is cheap as beast's.

Lear, ii 4, 270

If that which Nature doth exactly and originally require at our handes for the preservation of our being, is over little (as in truth what is it, and how good cheape our life may be maintained, cannot better be known or expressed than by this consideration)

III, 263

In analogy to our tracing of Handel's work on borrowed tunes, we learn that Shakespeare, too, has freely integrated the material of others into his poetry. The extent of Shakespeare's indebtedness throughout other works has been widely investigated. Thus, Malone's detailed figures in regard to *Henry VI* show that "out of 6043 lines, 1771 were written by some other preceding Shakespeare; 2373 by him, and on the foundation laid by his predecessors; and 1899 were entirely his own."[7] Research proves that hardly a single one of his plays can be claimed as the absolute invention of this greatest of all dramatists. He had, in terms of musical theory, developed his own *ars inveniendi* and based his dramas on borrowed poetry.

As to Handel, it is again from figures that we can judge the extent of his borrowings and adaptations. Focusing on our already quoted examples, altogether eighteen clavier pieces of Muffat have found their way into the *Ode for St. Cecilia's Day*. They have been distributed throughout thirty movements of Handel's work. And out of seventy-nine printed pages of the score, forty-three contain—that is to say more than half of the entire score—material borrowed from Muffat's music. Out of about thirty numbers which comprise the score of *Israel in Egypt*, at least seventeen are borrowings from Kerll, Stradella, Erbe and Urio. These figures speak for themselves: more than half of Handel's work grew on foreign soil!

Yet we have observed in the three musical illustrations from *Judas Maccabaeus*, from the *Ode for St. Cecilia's Day* and finally from *Israel in Egypt* that Handel never copied his models with mechanical imitation. They were taken over as raw material and used in the construction of ingenious blueprints. The relationship of

Handel's music to its model is that of Shakespeare's play to its original source.

The following list shows eighteen compositions of Muffat and their respective adaptations in various scores of Handel. (According to Friedrich Chrysander's supplementary volume to Handel's Collected Works.)[8]

Muffat's Model	*Handel's Utilization*
1. Courante	Overture, *Ode for St. Cecelia's Day*, also Fifth Concerto Grosso
2. Air	Aria with Flute, *Ode for St. Cecilia's Day*, also adagio and allegro in the Eighth Concerto Grosso
3. Rigaudon	March in *Joshua*
4. Adagio	Introduction in *Joshua*
5. Finale	Chorus, "From Harmony" in *Ode for St. Cecelia's Day*
6. Courante	Allegro of the Tenth Concerto Grosso, also courante of the last movement of the Overture to *Theodora*
7. Trio	Third movement of the Overture to *Theodora*
8. Fantasie	Aria with organ in *Ode for St. Cecelia's Day* and elsewhere
9. Allemande	March in *Ode for St. Cecelia's Day*
10. Minuet	Minuet at the end of overture in *Ode for St. Cecelia's Day*

11. Finale	Finale of the First Concerto Grosso
12. Fantasie and Adagio	Tenor recitative in *Ode for St. Cecelia's Day*
13. Fugue	Fugue in the finale chorus in *Ode for St. Cecilia's Day*
14. Courante	Overture, *Salomo*
15. Hornpipe	Hornpipe in Seventh Concerto Grosso
16. Fantasie	Second movement of First Concerto Grosso and elsewhere
17. Adagio	*Ode for St. Cecilia's Day* also largo in Twelfth Concerto Grosso
18. Air	Melody of March in *Judas Maccabaeus* also end of an organ concerto

BACH'S CIRCLE AND THE CRAFT OF INVENTION

The creative procedure of most composers in the baroque era fits into the broad picture of the *ars inveniendi* and its various devices, particularly the technique of borrowing. Yet that masterful integration of foreign material into music of his own which Handel achieved can be compared to only one of his contemporaries—to Johann Sebastian Bach. He and Handel were born in the same year and both were contemporaries of Mattheson.[9] We find in Bach's workshop many features closely related to the creative procedure of Handel. Bach, too, built much of his music on the basis of borrowed material, and was attracted by the same models as his greatest contemporary. Thus, music of Muffat appears as a loan in his Italian Concerto in F.

Bach's superb craft could make great works grow on seemingly insignificant and unpretentious themes. The creative emphasis lies, with Bach as with the whole era, on the disposition and elaboration of the tonal substance. Herein, his working method was deeply rooted in the past. Bach approached his tonal blueprints like the great musical architects of the Gothic era, who conceived in advance all the details of the building in due proportion to the whole structure. But he generated old themes with the seed of new life. As the music unfolds from the initial theme it develops with the naturalness of an organic being. Some of Bach's lasting scores were written merely for the purpose of demonstrating craft and work. He hoped that his two- and three-part inventions for the clavier would teach the student "a clear manner of securing good inventions and how to develop same." A minute analysis of every note and its function in these scores will indeed guide the apprentice on safe roads toward his own goal. He can look straight through these glass-clear constructions and see how ingeniously they were built. He can proceed by tracing and copying the lines of the contrapuntal web as the basis of his own inventions and can follow the logic of plan. Thus he learns what Bach wanted to show him: how a variety of contrapuntal types is developed in the framework of a specific task.

The men surrounding Bach's creative life in Leipzig stood firmly on the ground of invention as a teachable craft. The trend to employ reason in composition rather than anything resembling romantic inspiration was promulgated by Bach's pupil, Lorenz Christoph Mizler. This scientifically-minded man altogether dismissed in his main work, *The Critical Musician*, the role of imagination. Reason alone leads to the making of music; composition results from the methodical work of craft. Such an ideology was fostered in Mizler's Society of Musical Science in Leipzig, to which his master, Johann Sebastian Bach himself, officially belonged. But it would be foolish to infer from this fact more than sympathy of the master with the enterprise of his apprentice. Obviously Mizler's ideology is an exaggerated one. No further step was possible in the direction of an estrangement between inspiration and invention, between the forces of the conscious and those of the subconscious creation. And who would deny the power of inspiration in the works of Johann Sebastian Bach?

Johann Kuhnau (1660-1722), Bach's predecessor in the service of the St. Thomas Church, advocated a less extreme approach to composition. He did not discourage reliance upon inspiration. For instance, composers of biblical texts were advised to seek stimulation by reading the Bible in other languages rather than the German translation. "It is proved that foreign tongues reflect more its inner spirit." In this admission, the eighteenth century German favored Hebrew for its closeness to the world of the *Old Testament*.[10]

The problems of invention in sacred music have much in common with those of secular music: here, as there, an association of thought derived from the text but outside the absolute musical element will aid the imagination. This we learn from Johann David Heinichen (1683-1729), a disciple of Kuhnau, when he discusses inventiveness in composing an opera score in his *Neu erfundene gründliche Anweisung zum General Bass*. Suppose the composer is faced with the following text

Chi ha nemica la fortuna	He who has fortune for an enemy
Si vedra sempre penar	Is bound to suffer

and he finds himself at a loss how to put the verse into music. In order to stimulate his imagination, he may ask himself how fortune can be interpreted metaphorically; he can, for instance, envision fortune as the goddess of fate, changeable, illusive, or even persecuting in her actions. Whatever he chooses will incite his fantasy to a definite association of thought. A picture thus originates which can easily evoke a musical idea. Once this process is complete, the clockwork of invention starts to tick—word and tone can meet. Yet with such advice to the composer, Heinichen is on the borderline: no longer is careful elaboration the musician's sole concern. His approach is admittedly determined by an initial stimulation from the outside. Once the opening thought has been established, the course of the composition is assured. From this point, the procedure follows the established laws of organization.

IMPROVISATION

Mattheson refers to an invention "on the spur of the moment." Thus he points to all springs from which music flows freely in contrast to the calculations and efforts of conscious brainwork. Among these spontaneous sources, the most important one is im-

provisation in its various garbs. Making music extemporaneously
has truly proven to be an ageless craft. In fact, the entire history
of music shows the urge of composers and performers to improvise,
to express themselves on the spur of the moment.

In its early beginnings, musical utterances and improvisation were
almost synonymous.[11] In later phases of history, we encounter improvisation in one form or another in the different categories of
performance. There is vocal and there is instrumental improvisation.
Terms such as faux-bourdon, cantus supre librum and contrapunctus
al mente point to the varying forms of improvising polyphony.

Almost every renowned composer and organist, from the Renaissance to the Baroque, was also lauded for his skill of improvising
on the keyboard. Such great organists as Frescobaldi in Italy and
Froberger in Germany gained fame as improvisators. Handel set
London afire with his extempore on given themes or fugues. Bach's
accomplishments in extemporaneous performances were legendary.

The improvising artist usually starts from given themes, perhaps
from something conventional and familiar and elevates his performance through contrapuntal elaborations into the realm of high art.
The form of variation or the polyphonic types such as the fugue are
the typical starting points. Old terminology differentiated between
improvisation and free fantasy. *Improvisation* proper was more confined to closed types of form. *Fantasy*, by contrast, was not restricted
to a definite pattern, but often indulged in kaleidoscopic change of
tonal pictures. In neither case did the artistic result depend on the
invention of a motif by the improvising composer, since themes were
frequently given to him by his audience. What mattered in this
atmosphere of extemporaneous music-making was the player's
presence of mind, the readiness of his contrapuntal knowledge and
the firm concentration on his task.

Bach when improvising usually confined himself to a single theme.
Often, he treated a theme for hours—according to Forkel who also
describes how the master went about his plans. "He would start
with a prelude," Forkel reports, "followed by a fugue in all registers.
This could be alternated by a trio, also by a four-part counterpoint
or a choral prelude. He finally concluded with a new fugue of
highly complicated character." The most significant example of an
improvisation that has come down to us in Bach's notation is the

Musikalisches Opfer (Musical Offering). Bach dedicated this score to Frederick the Great with the following statement:

Most Reverend King! . . . with fervent pleasure, I remember the very special Royal Grace when you condescended, at my stay in Potsdam some time ago, to play for me the theme for a fugue on the piano and ordered me to execute the same in your very highest presence. To obey this order was my most humble duty. Yet soon I realized that, due to the lack of preparation, the execution did not succeed as well as such a splendid theme would have called for. Thus I decided to work out more perfectly the truly royal theme and to acquaint the world with it. . . .

Bach differentiates here between the results of extemporaneous elaboration on the keyboard and the synthetic work on a score written at his desk. That even such a past master of improvisation as Bach could not achieve extemporaneously the finishing touches of a precise note script does not need any explanation. His comment in the dedication to the king can be taken quite literally though it also bespeaks the humility of the St. Thomas cantor in addressing the Prussian king. Bach's highly contrapuntal extempore was different from the spirit of improvisation as it lives in the works of his great son, Philipp Emanuel. The younger Bach's music is simpler, less artful. As it flows from the "spur of the moment," the hands follow primarily the inner feelings. Construction is not the principal concern. Philipp Emanuel plays for the sake of mere playing and not for the sake of an highly abstract art and its polyphonic intricacies. Yet, what all composers in this sphere of improvisation have in common is that they are inspired to a high degree by the specific instrumental imagination. The instrument, as it were, helps them to compose. It suggests ideas in terms of its keys, pedals, stops. It becomes the lively spring of the tonal fantasy.

For Haydn, improvisation was one of the chief means to stimulate the tonal imagination in early hours of the day. In his own words: "I sit down, I start to play, to improvise, depending upon whether my soul is sad or gay, serious or playful. If I succeeded in catching an idea, then my endeavor is directed to an elaboration of the work according to the rules of art." Haydn's loyal servant Elssler[12] was well aware of the importance of this playing as a prelude for actual composition. Under no circumstances would he admit, during these hours, a visitor to Haydn's study, no matter how urgent the business. Sometimes he would eavesdrop at Haydn's door and announce: "He will be through soon. My master is already working in the rough." Old Elssler had observed that it was Haydn's habit to rush, at the end of his improvisations, toward the bass and to conclude his extempore with a "rough coda."

Leopold Mozart, with his infallible instinct for effect and his knowledge of audiences, trained Wolfgang as a child in the skill of improvisation, and other teachers developed this talent. A program of the "Academy" where Mozart appeared in 1770 at Mantua promised:

First a symphony of his own composition; secondly a pianoforte concerto which he will play at sight; thirdly, a sonata just placed before him, which he will provide with variations and afterwards repeat in another key. Then he will compose an aria to words given to him, sing it himself and accompany it on the clavier. Next, a sonata for the cembalo on a motif supplied to him by the first violin; a strict fugue on a theme to be selected, which he will improvise on the piano; a trio in which he will take the violin part improviso; and finally the most recent symphony of his own composition.

This was certainly a program of quality and of a quantity which only those old audiences could endure! The striking skill of the fourteen-year-old composer in improvisation turned into a working method on which Mozart relied forever. Niemtschek relates[13] how Mozart spent nights improvising on the piano, and the biographer seeks in those hours the true origin of Mozart's inspiration: "In the silent peace of night . . . his fantasy glowed in fullest power unfolding the whole wealth of tones. He created an infinite store from which he later organized and constructed immortal works with a light hand." As an old man, Niemtschek confided to Alois Fuchs: "If I could be granted one more privilege on this earth, it would be to hear once more Mozart improvising on the piano. Who did not have that privilege did not know what Mozart was able to do."

A systematic description of improvising composition was attempted by Carl Czerny. His essay demands special attention because of the author's proximity to Beethoven, whose personal friendship and teaching he enjoyed for many years. Czerny's *Anleitung zum Klavierphantasieren* was published in 1836—only nine years after Beethoven's death. The author defines the purpose of his work: to teach the musician to spin out, without any special preparation, during his playing any idea (his own or given) into a composition of aesthetic value. The various approaches to improvisation are divided into six different types:

1. The development of one single theme
2. The development and combination of several themes into a whole work
3. The potpourri, i.e. the juxtaposition of favorite motifs without a special development of each single one
4. Variations of all kinds
5. The fantasy in a strict style and in that of the fugue
6. Capriccio in a very free style

The first type is described as the most difficult one. In particular reference to Beethoven's fantasies on the piano (the mastery of which was also extolled by other witnesses), Czerny states that it would have been next to impossible even for the master himself to put into notation that wealth of ideas and harmonies which he displayed in his extempore. But Beethoven developed some of his extemporaneously conceived compositions into finished scripts. The Choral Fantasy, Op. 80 (which functioned as a study for the finale of the Ninth Symphony) is a lasting monument of Beethoven's improvising genius.

"Only by not paying any attention to what one plays can one really improvise. That is the way one plays best and most truthfully in public, leaving oneself spontaneously to what one likes best." With these words, Beethoven stresses the subconscious source of inspiration as well as artistic truthfulness as its guidepost.

With many other composers, improvisation emerges as an aiding technique for the stimulation of new thoughts and as an independent creative enterprise. Since its products are not entrusted to elaboration on the note paper, but to instantaneous playing on instruments, a certain alfresco of execution is always inevitable: the finishing touches of elaboration are eliminated. But what is lost on the polishing of details, is gained through the vitality of the spontaneous element in such a performance. It is a type of composition in which only the inspirational factor is in full force. Obviously, synthetic work is stressed least; its results can be achieved only in approximation.

CHAPTER TEN

SKETCHES

> The artist should follow all traces
> leading to the secret workshop of
> the master.
>
> SCHUMANN

THE PURPOSE OF SKETCHING

ALL artists sketch.[1] To all of them their sketches have the meaning of a tryout, of initial planning. The painter chalks out form and space on the canvas, and distributes tentatively the colors of his palette. Certain sculptors first make a sketch in clay or wax, experimenting with the qualities of mass, contour and flow which they expect to integrate into the envisioned work. The architect plans his areas and dimensions on testing drafts before he can entrust them to the final blueprint, and later proceeds to the real stage of building.

The musician, too, feels his way through similar stages of testing. He sketches his tonal ideas in terms of melody, harmony and rhythm. He outlines the form and marks the tone color. To him, as to all artists, the sketch is a means of seeking and finding: it serves the purpose of a preliminary orientation prior to further and final stages of synthetic work.

The method of sketching differs widely with the individual musician. His ways and means of sketching, like other features of his work, depend upon a specific, personalized process of inner elaboration. The first draft is normally a memorandum of finds and flashes for the composer—the beginning of the working out stage, often done in haste and excitement. Thus Beethoven explained to his pupil, the Archduke Rudolf: "When you were in town the other day, the chorus occurred to me. I rushed home to make a note of it, and since that took me longer than I originally expected, I missed your Imperial Highness, to my regret. . . . A bad habit since my childhood, forcing me to write down my first flashes immediately, did me some harm here." Beethoven's apology for a missed appointment shows the procedure and purpose of the first sketch as a memorandum; it is a short record, marking the borderline between the inspirational and the testing stage.

The sketch, then, fixes a motif or a larger tonal idea in the early stage of its origin. It might give the composer only a point upon which to hinge his musical thoughts later—when he continues his tonal plan toward a definite creative end. Thus, many first sketches are primitive, abbreviated, notated in a kind of musical shorthand. Some sketches betray an ease of work, a seemingly continuous flow of thought, a methodical and gradual procedure. Only with certain composers is what comes to light in the sketching script no longer an embryonic thought, but rather a matured and clear idea, almost ready for its integration into final form. Other sketches reveal the arduously searching artist. He must undertake the casting of the form again and again. His procedure is one of intense search and inspired labor. We shall come to know Beethoven as the great representative of this creative type.

Not many sketches of the preclassical masters are preserved and those that we have usually refer to rather extended enterprises. It was only an exception if a smaller composition required any drafts at all. A master like Bach prefixed his ideas firmly in his memory. The actual writing of the manuscript, without the aid of preliminary sketches, was a routine procedure. So precisely had Bach decided upon the thematic work and the groundplan of his music that changes after the manuscript had been written down were rarely necessary. It is particularly in the workshop of the baroque composer that the various phases of conception, sketching and synthesis appear in close proximity to each other. The reason is clear: in the polyphonic style, the initial choice of possibilities anticipates a great deal of the work otherwise relegated to the synthetic stage. Once the main concept (the themes, their counterpoints and the form of the music) has been decided upon, the score unfolds itself on the strength of logical procedure. A prelude, a fugue, a chorale or any other contrapuntal form, be it vocal or instrumental, evolves on its own momentum. The composer follows the laws of its musical architecture. Theme and form are the unmistakable points of crystallization. In the fugue, for instance, the choice of the form contains the clues as to how the work is going to start as well as to how it will continue, where and how the chief subject and its counterpoints will return and which possibilities of combinations and complications it will offer in episodes between the entries of the themes.[2] It is a method of preconceived building. It anticipates the complete evolution of the score, making it possible for the composer to write intricate works without intermediary steps. Everything is pre-established in his mind. Great tonal pillars and blocks have been built from memory without any or with very sparse sketches, safely carried along by a great composer's craft and working experience.

HAYDN: MELODY AND FIGURED BASS

The creative procedure and consequently the type of sketching changes with the intrinsic differences of period and style. Certain styles of composition necessitate the notation of specific features in the composer's early drafts. A contrapuntal sketch will obviously stress design and architecture. In a sketch of romantic music, a tone color, a specific timbre or a mere dynamic feature can assume decisive importance. Due to the stylistic analogies in the creative approach of composers living in the same era, we find certain similarities in the sketches of musicians who were contemporaries. There are numerous features which bear out the tectonic relationship not only in the music but also in the drafts of Haydn and Mozart.

In spite of such similarities based upon common background and stylistic principles, it is their individual differences that make the study of sketches a fascinating experience: they open the door to the composer's workshop in its most personal aspect. In our interpretation of the composer's sketches, an element of caution must always be present. We must realize that sketches do not necessarily lead in direct and even steps to the final shape of the art work. Often they are a mere abbreviation of the composer's train of thought, perhaps understandable only to the artist himself. By and large, however, many fruitful results are obtained from studying and comparing these intimate musical elaborations of the masters.

Haydn's sketches display a marked tendency toward economy. Only essentials are notated. The melodic lines are always given. Where the accompaniment results naturally from the melody (i.e. where it is the self-understood vertical result of the horizontal design) Haydn omits any special references to chords. Yet where the harmony presents deviation from the obvious, he does not rely on his memory alone, but notes the harmony in figured bass script. Significantly, there occur also memos on instrumental details; with Haydn's ingenious innovations in the instrumental sphere, tone color assumes growing importance, a fact which is reflected in the sketch. Haydn's preliminary drafts generally belong to that type upon which visible traces of work are left. We can compare what has been preserved with what has been eliminated. We realize at what point the master felt the need to condense his material, and where to build joining bridges between loose parts. Thus we can usually follow the thought process which preceded the final crystallization of the art work.

The sketches bear out[3] that Haydn always made a precise plan of the melodic lead, adding here and there a minimum of figures for his harmonic orientation. After this, he breathed into the dry skeleton spirit and life, equipping the music with accompaniment, secondary voices and skillful transitions.

MOZART: "BLIND" COMPOSITION

Mozart, like Bach, belongs to the creative type who strongly relies on brain work alone—detached from notation. He frequently did not feel it necessary to make special notes of first flashes. He relegated many initial thoughts to his phenomenal memory, as safe a one as any musician ever possessed. Here Mozart could keep complex thoughts for a long time—even without writing down a single line as a reminder. He was a past master in the remarkable faculty of composing "blind," that is to say, he frequently worked out his scores without the help of the seeing eye and the written notation in front of him. As a boy, he had already accomplished that feat of hearing complex music and later reproducing it in score. When listening to Allegri's *Miserere* in Rome (and not being permitted to write in church during the service), young Wolfgang reconstructed the religious piece from memory.[4] This he was able to do as the outline of the music was fixed unmistakably in his mind—recalling melodies, harmonies and tectonic play with a seemingly superhuman certainty. In Mozart's mental storeroom remained much of the material which other composers entrust to their sketchbook, awaiting a later phase of work. To be sure, only a limited number of Mozart's sketches have come down to us, and we do not know how many he threw away once they lost their usefulness for him. This, in turn, implies that much work was done by Mozart without leaving the visible traces of sketches. If this were not so, a statement written by Mozart, December 30, 1780, to his father would be incomprehensible and paradoxical: "Everything is already composed, but nothing is yet written down." The sentence is easily understood in the light of Mozart's particular type of creative process. Many of Mozart's musical ideas already displayed a high degree of maturity when they first appeared on paper and they did not require any further elaboration. Beautiful forms shaped themselves inside the composer's brain as though they sprang like Minerva from the head of Zeus.

We know from various documents that the crystallization of Mozart's music succeeded often without any external medium. The shift from the inspirational stage of the composition to the evolutionary one occurred rapidly and uninhibitedly. The road from the subconscious to the conscious was freely traversed. Herein lies the intrinsic difference between the procedure of Mozart and that of other composers who depended on voluminous sketches.

All these particularities of Mozart's creative procedure lend themselves to that widely spread but erroneous belief that his music was facilely shaken out of his sleeve, without earthly toil. But quoted documentary evidence suffices to destroy such a myth. Moreover, the actual notation of his music often meant to Mozart nothing more than the mechanical reproduction of a tonal form which had shaped itself with complete certainty in his mind. There are also a few of his sketches which show extended and laborious work—the distance traveled from the first flash to its final shape is considerable.

Mozart not only thought out and firmly remembered entire scores, but he did not have the least trouble in composing several compositions simultaneously. When sending (April 20, 1782) his sister "Nannerl" the Three-Part Fugue with Prelude (K. 394), he explained to her the strangely reversed order in which the manuscript was written: "The prelude belongs first, then the fugue follows . . . I had already made the fugue and while I was writing it down, I thought out the prelude." Such mental maneuvering with his tonal thoughts has a similarity with a certain imposing procedure of a masterful player of chess: both the composer of music and the player of the royal game have so trained their minds that they are able to think "blindly"—without looking at a score or the chessboard. Both engage themselves in the simultaneous enterprise of independent tasks. The musician can work on several scores just as the chess master plays "blindly" and simultaneously several games. Schooled in this synchronized undertaking of independent problems, the musician takes care of the mechanical part of composing during another activity. Mozart's Duo for Two Violins, written July 17, 1786, bears the remark, "while bowling." In Prague he wrote the trumpet and tympani parts for the second finale of *Don Giovanni* "blind," i.e. without having the orchestral score before him. After having done so, Mozart warned the players that there might be an error, that he might have written four measures too many or too few.[5]

Mozart usually first notes the melody in his sketches, writing it in full and later adjusting the bass line. Just as in the drafts of Haydn, the figured bass script acts as a reminder wherever irregular modulations or exceptional details occur. Counterpoints and accompanying motifs are also jotted down. In the sketches of his two great uncompleted vocal scores, the *C Minor Mass* and the *Requiem*, the voice parts and the bass line are completely written out. But in the unfinished section of these works, the accompaniment is only suggested by characteristic clues, as for instance, in the *Requiem*, from Dies Irae to Quam olim Abrahae of the offertory. For his orchestral works Mozart sketches first the violins (provided they carry the theme) and next the bass line. Woodwinds and brass are recorded briefly, provided they are prominent. From this economic stage of sketching, Mozart completes later what still remains to be done. In the drafts for the Piano Concerto in C Major, one page contains the remark "Mittel Gedanken" (thought for the middle part). With the tonal picture clearly in his mind, such a simple direction is a further clue for his imagination.

In the whole manuscript of the Jupiter Symphony, not more than five corrections occur. This seems like a feat of imaginative power and constructive providence, and it certainly is one—even if we take for granted that Mozart must have made some sketches for the intricate work. Be this as it may, his miraculous accomplishment can only be understood in view of the already mentioned fact that Mozart was trained from early youth to think out complicated musical ideas without the aid of instrument or note paper. He is constantly composing; that is to say, the shaping of musical forms occupies him wherever he may be—in the coach, in the opera, bowling, eating. He himself pokes fun at the circumstances under which he manages to write. While we may assume that Mozart made additional sketches for the Jupiter Symphony, we know that he did sketch certain complicated details which confronted him while composing the first finale of *Don Giovanni*. Mozart outlined on a special sheet that famous scene in which a minuet occurs and the offstage orchestra unites with the main orchestra in the pit. It is indeed a complex enterprise: the whole scene is an ingenious musical juxtaposition of court and peasant dances, while the trio of masked aristocrats arrives at the party for the merry country folk. This colorful scene is the classical prototype of modern polyrhythm by contrasting the $\frac{3}{4}$ rhythm of a minuet with the $\frac{2}{4}$ and $\frac{3}{8}$ steps of other dance types. The whole results in a rhythmical permutation most audacious and prophetic for a score written in 1787. Obviously the solution of such intricate rhythmic problems was difficult even for Mozart: it called for advanced sketching. Probably Mozart drew drafts also for passages in other works of complex character.

Mozart's sketches are the brief record of what his fantasy brings to him; they do not reveal a struggle of tectonic forces, and they show no long road ahead to the final goal. From such "memos," Mozart proceeds to the last and final stage of writing. If changes are still necessary, he does not hesitate to make them here. But so plastically has he anticipated the total groundplan and the place of all details that alterations after the completion of the manuscript are an exception.

BEETHOVEN: VARIOUS TYPES OF SKETCHING

It is one of the fortunate facts in the study of the creative process that a very substantial number of Beethoven's sketches have been preserved. Many of these sketches have come down to us in the form of notebooks which contain not only drafts of initial suddenly occurring thoughts but also the elaborate development of ideas. The credit for having made these sketches available to the musical world goes to a poverty-stricken scholar, Gustav Nottebohm, a friend of Brahms, who probably had a hand in this important enterprise. The first of these *Skizzenbücher* were published in 1865. These sketchbooks were Beethoven's permanent companions: "I always carry around a sketchbook like this, and if an idea occurs to me, I make a note of it instantly. Even during the night I get up when something occurs to me, lest I forget the idea."[6] And a contemporary witness, Anschütz, describes him during the throes of creation as follows: "I saw a man lying in the field, rather disheveled, leaning his head on his left hand—a head heavy with thought, very spiritual and beautiful in a wild sort of way. His eyes stared at a sheet of note paper, on this he wrote with his right hand heavy mystical figures, meanwhile tapping with his fingers."

We have only to look at these sketches to see what sort of scribbling went on. The mute signs on the paper eloquently bespeak excitement, reflection, vacillation, stormy pushing onward. Every stroke is the sign of an inner struggle. Countless motifs come, are caught in hurried script, whirling through each other. All this is only raw material, mined rapidly from the subconscious. Arduous work is required to polish the crude material into beautiful, shining stones. But the way from the first flash to the elaborated idea is long in space and time. The main theme of the first movement in the Seventh Symphony is found only after six pages of untiring efforts. Six pages of trying, rejecting, testing. For other solutions,

Beethoven required weeks, months, years of inspired labor before his music finally reached the form dictated by his inner vision.

This was the way Beethoven created from youth on. Rapidly he jotted down and sketched the sounds which raged within him. In the creative excitement, it made little difference what sort of paper he used. The special notebooks (as Nottebohm published them), or regular loose sheets, were not always at hand. And so Beethoven resorted to any kind of paper he could grab: bills and correspondence, individual pages in almost any size, papers which had piled up on his piano or desk. He snatched household notes of which one side had been left empty, free pages from his calendar, and all possible and impossible sorts of loose leafs which he folded together and carried around with him in his pocket on walks.

In these books and notes of Beethoven, various types of sketching can be discerned. One type aims at the conquest of motifs, themes, melodies. Another type tests the usefulness of a theme which has already been chosen for the later development of a movement. Sketches for the second movement of the Ninth Symphony leave the theme unchanged and deal only with the development of this scherzo. In the sketchbook of the year 1803, a theme of the Eroica appears with its finished profile. Beethoven explores with it the further development, and possible contrasts, in a most extensive web of sketches. This is the type of sketching which Beethoven himself describes as "changing, reflecting and testing."

In other cases, Beethoven aims specifically at form—accepting and rejecting thoughts with a final blueprint clearly in view. For the sake of the form of a movement, or of a whole cycle, themes are exchanged, one thought is substituted for another. Here not the shaping of motifs, but the formation of a unified groundplan appears as the purpose of sketching. Different parts are weighed against each other; their inner balance is sought. Sometimes a certain detail is the focal point around which all sketches rotate. Along with the primary elements, dynamics and tone color also have a part in these experiments. The envisioned orchestration is often made evident by such directions as "violin," "bassoon," "oboe" or "with blowing instruments." In the sketches for the *Missa Solemnis* Beethoven notes the instrumentation: "The Kyrie of my new Mass only with blowing instruments and organ."

In the Agnus Dei of the Mass, Beethoven reminds himself of the stylistic attitude: "Utmost simplicity, please, please, please." It is in the drafts for this final movement that we note the intimate tie-up between Beethoven's aesthetic speculation and the tonal vision. We see in our Illustration XIV how Beethoven first jots down a melody and reminds himself of its harmonization with a few figures. Below he writes the following words: "Dona nobis pacem noch in moll denn man bittet ja um den Frieden darum der Frieden allein behandelt als wäre er schon da." (Dona nobis pacem, still in minor, since one prays for peace and therefore treats peace as though it were already granted.) This remark is an important psychological clue to Beethoven's approach. Originally he had planned two contrasting sections in major and minor respectively. He pursued the tonal idea in the immediately following pencil sketch. The idea is derived from aesthetic thinking which is further in evidence on another leaf on which Beethoven notated: "Es kann auch Stärke der Gesinnungen des innern Frieden über alles sein (Sirach!). (Strength of the convictions of inner peace can be above everything.) Beethoven, the intense student of philosophy and ethics, apparently thought here of the book, Ecclesiasticus or The Wisdom of Jesus, the Son of Sirach,[7] a work teaching humility and love of peace. The allegretto vivace of this movement in the Missa Solemnis bears the motto: "Prayer for outer and inner peace." The tonal figuration which builds its music is already visible in the sketch. (Cf. Illustration XIV.)

In general, Beethoven's various types of sketches freely overlap. His approach is always different, not subordinated to any pre-established scheme. Once the seeds are planted, Beethoven searches for melodic lines, counterpoints and forms. The draft might pertain to an exposition, a development, a whole movement, a cycle. Throughout the sketches, we realize how, from a mere skeleton, from sporadic notes and remarks, the work is gradually built and finally reaches its superb synthesis. We witness that amazing and tireless "elaboration in the broadness, in the narrowness, in the height or depth," as Beethoven himself describes his approach. The stupendous spiritual effort does not cease until the last creative possibility is reached, until the onrushing flood of ideas is conquered and the distant goal is reached. This is usually a process consuming a great deal of time. As already mentioned, years may pass before a work emerges from such elaborate search in its final shape. The growth may also occur in installments—broken up by other creative experiences, interrupted by new enterprises.

Certain observers have claimed that this titanic struggle in Beethoven's work is nothing more than an indication of intrinsic difficulties which blocked an orderly and direct approach to the execution of his material. This "difficulty," in turn, has frequently been contrasted with the prodigious facility apparent in the work of Mozart or Schubert. The difference is undeniable. But it lies not so much in a difference in the method of procedure as in the composer's final goal. Beethoven could produce with great facility, too: in one single night a complete work such as the Sextet, Op. 71, or the Fidelio overture originated. His thoughts streamed in infinite waves to him just as thoughts did to Haydn, Mozart or Schubert. But Beethoven's very nature was one of strife. As he struggled for inner and outer peace (as indicated by the motto of the Agnus Dei in the Missa Solemnis), so his creations, too, reflect the constant self-imposed struggle for artistic truth, the right, the good.

CLASSICAL THEME-BUILDING

Some of the most striking and characteristic features of Beethoven's music—those in fact that especially bear the stamp of his genius—were by no means the fruits of a first inspiration, but became part of his scores only after much effort and continuous search. The following pages trace the genesis of certain of Beethoven's tonal ideas.[8] They show how their first appearance was often insignificant and commonplace, and in no way betrayed the beauty and character of these thoughts as we know them today.

The funeral march of the Eroica emerges after a measure for measure struggle with the thematic substance. The ten measures of the initial draft (A) are not yet welded into the periodic units and closely knit balance of primary elements which is so characteristic of classical theme-building. (Cf. Example 15.)

While Beethoven was working on the sketch, his affinity with classical form ideals came to the fore: after the first occurrence of the march theme in its still unorganized state (A), he recognized the need for a different disposition. He reorganized the melodic substance and harmonized it in a strong and poignant way (B), projecting it against a bleak, slow march rhythm. One must compare the original with the final version to see how everything has become "properly" placed, how the structural interdependence of harmony, melody and rhythm serves the expression of this tragic music. Consider how the A-flat in the sixth measure of version (B) has now risen to the crest of the melody, simultaneously appearing as the dynamic climax of what is now an eight-measure phrase. Compare this with the position of the A-flat in the first draft (A), and its problematic role in the cadence of the melody. In the final version—after the pathetic sforzando of the A-flat, carried by the diminished seventh chord—the melodic curve swings back, diatonically, stepwise. Reaching the tonic C, the theme dims into its opening *sotto voce* and the oboe starts its sad complaint.

EXAMPLE 15

In the drafts for the Eroica, we find a theme called "minuet." Today we know it only in a metamorphosis: it has become the scherzo of this symphony. What motivated Beethoven's revisions? We find the answer by tracing the embryonic stages of this music, on its way from the original minuet idea to the form which best lent itself to Beethoven's vision of the whole work. The first draft (a) consists of an ascending motif: a scale of almost two octaves, climbing complacently the earthly steps of the minuet. In contrast, the next motif (b) sways back and forth on two notes only, while a third draft is marked presto (c). With such differentiation in tempo, the theme has been fully stripped of its minuet attire and visibly assumes the character it has in the final score (d): rocking on two tones, B-flat and C, pianissimo and staccato, the phrase now runs up only one octave (touching the upper auxiliary note) and merrily descends to its starting point. It now appears in the shape of a true scherzo which follows the marcia funebre; life is astir

EXAMPLE 16

again after the lament of death. It is the blueprint of the total symphony which forced the change. Once Beethoven had chosen a definite symphonic course, the early thematic version fell and the metamorphosis of the minuet became inevitable.

The pure beauty and diatonic simplicity of the andante con moto from the Fifth Symphony seems to be the outcome of a single stroke of genius. Yet the sketches show that not only did Beethoven make repeated revisions of the theme until he arrived at the desired version, but also that in the course of the symphonic composition, the whole character of the theme and subsequently of the entire second movement underwent considerable change. As we see from our musical example 17 the phrase appears first in a rather insignificant form. The initial draft (a) refers to an andante quasi menuetto, a piece of dance character, in three-quarters, with suspensions on the downbeat of the second and fourth bars respectively. The theme is built on a rising sequence from the tonic to the second degree.

The next version (b) replaces the $\frac{3}{4}$ of the minuet with $\frac{3}{8}$, lightening up the character and leaning toward a different combination of the rhythmic patterns. The third version (c) like the second version has abandoned the dotted rhythm and appears as an ascending spiral based on the tonic triad (which in the final score plays its part in the coda of the movement).

In the finished draft (d), the former minuet melody (a) is stripped of its suspensions and some of the passing notes disappear. A classical melody of pure diatonism emerges. It shows a thematic profile displaying the search for a pure unadorned and diatonic line, typical of Beethoven's melody building in this creative period.

Why did Beethoven reject his original thought?

According to the heading of his first sketch, andante quasi menuetto, the music was intended as a minuet. Just as in his sketches for the Eroica, so in those for the Fifth, Beethoven aimed at a symphonic stylization of that centuries-old French court dance which, since the days of Lully, has played, in changing raiment, so considerable a role in classical sonata cycles. Hence, the first version of the theme is conceived in $\frac{3}{4}$, connoting the typical minuet step. Beethoven, who showed his preference for the minuet form in piano and chamber music works, hesitated to apply it in symphonic cycles. The still conservatively named minuet of the C Major Symphony displays already the characteristics of Beethoven's newly created type, the scherzo, in unmistakable manner. Only once in his nine symphonic scores (in the Eighth) does the old type of minuet occur.

In the classical drama of the Fifth, as Beethoven ultimately conceived it, there was no room for the leisurely tripping steps of the minuet. Between the work's fateful opening and its conclusion—with that uninterrupted sequence of a tense scherzo and triumphant finale—the minuet was out of place. It had to be sacrificed to the higher considerations of the total symphonic course and a different type of music had to be created for the second movement. To this end, the original minuet contributed certain features which were transformable into a lyrical and contemplative character. And thus, the andante con moto finally appears as a second movement of the symphonic cycle, lending itself to the heavier accents, which certain variations of the final A-flat major theme strike in the later development of the music.

Noteworthy is the resemblance between the minuet in the first version (a) and the second subject (e) of the symphony's opening movement. In both cases, there are the characteristic suspensions on accented beats and the rising sequences as the means of spinning forth the motif. Again, the ascending and descending intervals of the fourth and fifth are markedly evident in both themes. All this suggests the derivation of the one from the other, whereas the final version of the andante con moto (d) betrays no likeness to the

EXAMPLE 17

theme (e) from the first movement. Thus the hidden substance—common even to themes of different movements—appears as another salient feature which only the sketches could bring to light.

LIFELONG PURSUIT: BROTHERHOOD OF MAN

The choral finale of Beethoven's Ninth Symphony is the coronation of a lifelong artistic pursuit springing from a tonal vision which already the young composer had tried to realize. Since his youthful years in his native Bonn, Beethoven had been impressed with the poetry of his great contemporary, Friedrich Schiller. It was more than the beauty of his verses and the rhythm of a truly musical language that early attracted the composer: he felt a deep affinity with the idealism of Schiller's poetic world, and artistically responded to the classical balance of form and content.

On January 26, 1793, Schiller's sister, Charlotte, received a letter from a friend in Bonn, Fischenich, who inquired about her reaction to the musical setting of Schiller's "Feuerfarb," "by a young man of this place whose musical talent is becoming known and whom the elector has just sent to Haydn at Vienna. He intends to compose Schiller's 'Freude,' verse by verse."[9]

It is through this letter that we learn for the first time of young Beethoven's intention to compose Schiller's "Hymn to Joy."[10] The theme of joy was already the driving force behind Beethoven's cantata, On the Ascension of Leopold II (September 30, 1790). It is jubilant music; choruses sing joyfully for the happy occasion. Moreover, the evolution from darkness to light, which is the psychological curve of the Ninth, underlies also the structure of the cantata: the music first mourns the death of Emperor Joseph, and then turns to the jubilant greeting of his successor. Here, too, the fugato technique is integrated in the enthusiastic chorale. The exuberance of the "Heil" chorus sounds in D Major just as the finale of the Ninth. When the basses intone "Stürzet nieder Millionen" in the cantata, this passage anticipates, in mood and text, the phrase "Ihr stürzt nieder Millionen" of the Ninth. In the cantata, the people are urged to "look up to the Master of all thrones" and the analogous invocation of God occurs also in the symphony.

Beethoven was twenty years old when the coronation of the
Emperor inspired him to a score forecasting artistic events of para-
mount importance. But it needed a deeper message and a stronger
experience than the enthronement of a monarch to stimulate the
imagination of Beethoven—the greatest republican of all the artists
—to a work of immortal significance.

Yet the cantata proves that the young Beethoven already envisioned masses joyously marching along and singing together: a
tone-poetic conception, which decades later culminated in the
choral scene of the Ninth Symphony. While the actual composition
of the symphony is biographically relegated to the years 1817-1823,
more than two decades after the quoted letter to Charlotte Schiller,
we have, however, tangible evidence of Beethoven's occupation
with the problem (known to us as that of the Ninth) in sporadic
notes dating throughout all the intervening years.

What lies between such creative beginnings and such ends is a
fascinating interplay of sketches, studies and enterprises—of subconscious and conscious work. Already in a sketchbook from 1798,
we find a reference to the great unison passage, "Brüder über'm
Sternenzelt muss ein lieber Vater wohnen." The sketch, however,
hardly permits a clue to the final shape of tones to come. Only the
words point to their later tie-up. This early flash occurs most unexpectedly between drafts for two piano compositions, namely the
Rondo in G, Op. 51, No. 2 and the Sonata in C Minor, Op. 10, No. 1.
As we have already seen, such a process of interrupting one work
and suddenly shifting to another occurs frequently with Beethoven.

From about the year 1803, Beethoven was engrossed in the
composition of his only opera, *Fidelio*, first performed in Vienna,
Theater an der Wien, November 20, 1805. Here, too, the way to
its final conquest is one of long search and struggle. The finale of
the opera (originally laid in the prison, later on the outside) is
again a tone picture of joy, of an hour of gladness; an outburst of
suffering people into jubilant singing. The minister, Don Fernando,
liberates the oppressed: "I seek my brethren as a brother." We face
here again pillars upon which the choral scene of the Ninth was
built: a score for soli, chorus and orchestra in jubilant expression,
a text based on the theme of brotherly love—a culmination of all
preceding music into a finale of overpowering joy.

In 1808 Beethoven wrote his Fantasia for Piano, Orchestra and Chorus, Op. 80. This work appears, in retrospect, as the chief study for the form of the choral scene in the Ninth. Beethoven himself interprets the close relationship between these two scores, Op. 80 and Op. 125, in a letter on March 10, 1824, to his publisher, Probst: "The Ninth Symphony is in the style of my Choral Fantasia but very much more extended." While the Fantasia is less complex in character than the Ninth, it clearly anticipates the musical contours of the Ode to Joy. Both scores introduce their vocal sections with recitatives which are followed by variations on a theme of a simple diatonic character. And even the themes resemble each other in their construction upon neighboring tones.[11] There are numerous other analogies, which the stylistic comparison of Op. 80 and Op. 125 readily yields.

In the years 1811 and 1812, Beethoven planned the composition of three new symphonies. He finished the manuscripts of those in A Major and F Major (the Seventh and Eighth) in May and October, 1811, respectively. As to the third in this series of symphonies, little progress was made at this time. Yet its key was settled—D Minor, which indeed remained the key of the Ninth. Between sketches for the Seventh and Eighth, appears the following draft and comment:

EXAMPLE 18

"Finale, Freude schöner Götter Funken Tochter aus Elysium. The symphony in four movements; but the second movement in $\frac{2}{4}$ time like the first. The fourth may be in $\frac{6}{8}$ time—major; and the fourth movement well fugued."

But the integration of Schiller's Hymn into the planned symphony could not have been definitely established in Beethoven's mind because his sketches for an Overture in C, called Namensfeier

(published later as Op. 115) and finished in October, 1814, surprisingly refer to the Schiller verse, "Freude schöner Götter Funken"
with the remark "vielleicht so anfangen" (perhaps begin thus).

When Beethoven in 1817 contemplated plans for a new symphonic
composition of great dimensions, he entertained various and, as we
shall see, conflicting ideas. The sketches show, under a headline
"Zur Sinfonie in D," rather extensive work pertaining to the scherzo.
Yet the plan at this date did not call for the characteristic feature
which distinguishes the finished Ninth from all symphonic works
written before, namely, the use of a choral finale. Like Beethoven's
preceding eight symphonies and the preceding movements of this
new one, the finale of the planned score was to be a purely orchestral movement based on a fugal theme which is preserved as the
theme of the scherzo. In 1818 the drafts for the symphony again
occupy Beethoven's mind. Yet they are soon repressed by extensive
work on the Hammerklavier Sonata. In spite of the intense effort
expended on this great polyphonic score, Beethoven shows, at this
time, enough strength to plan his pair of symphonies:

Adagio Cantique:—
Religious song in a symphony in the old modes (Herr Gott dich loben
wir—Alleluja), either independently or as introductory to a fugue. Possibly the whole second symphony to be thus characterized: the voices
entering either in the Finale or as early as the Adagio. The orchestral
violins, etc., to be increased tenfold for the last movements, the voices
to enter one by one. Or the Adagio to be in some way repeated in the
last movements. In the Adagio the text to be a Greek mythos (or) Cantique Ecclesiastique. In the Allegro a Bacchus festival.

In these words, Beethoven sets the stylistic attitude of his never
completed Tenth Symphony. It was to be a thanksgiving in archaic
colors, an alleluia, a polyphonic adoration of Deity. The idea of
blending the symphonic with vocal expression is now in the foreground. The point at which the human voice was to enter the
symphonic cycle might have been the adagio or the allegro finale.
The planned festival of Bacchus points to orgiastic expression and
jubilation, the ecclesiastic song to the mood of thanksgiving.

In 1822, Beethoven again refers to his pair of symphonies.
Rochlitz relates in his *Für Freunde der Tonkunst* Beethoven's
confession that he had "two grand symphonies round his neck,

different from each other and different from any of the preceding ones." The first of the symphonies is referred to as "Sinfonie Allemande." And in the preliminary work, the irrefutable evidence of the diatonic D Major theme, "Freude schöner Götter Funken," appears and variations are mentioned as the underlying form-scheme. Schindler reports how Beethoven walking up and down his room suddenly exclaimed: "I have it, I have it." What Beethoven "had" was the solution as it appears in our Illustration XV, which shows two pages of his sketchbook. The first page contains the exclamation: "Lasst uns das Lied des unsterblichen Schiller singen." (Let us sing the song of the immortal Schiller.) "Freude, Freude, Freude" (Joy, Joy, Joy). And on the next page, Beethoven notes the beginning of the bass recitative: "Bass nicht diese Töne, Voce[12] fröhlichere Freude!" (Bass not these tones; let us sing something more pleasant and full of joy!)

In spite of all these powerful proclamations, the plan for a choral finale was still not firmly entrenched in the master's mind. Facing one of the conflicts so characteristic of Beethoven's creative life, we find in the sketchbook as late as the summer of 1823, in the middle of drafts for the Ode to Joy, a plan for a "finale instrumentale." Yet the basic thought of this sketch eventually found its place in the finale of the String Quartet, Op. 132. Such a shifting of material has already been shown as a typical procedure with Beethoven: the tonal substance of important inventions is preserved. If not used for a current enterprise, the material is stored for future work. Often it was not until after extended experimentation that Beethoven found the proper environment for his ideas.

The draft of the second movement of the new symphony was finished in August, 1823—the notebook from May to July contains sketches for the first, second and third movement. Two fugal themes written in 1815 and 1817 are transplanted into this new environment and their prolongation eventually becomes the theme of the scherzo. But the second of the planned pair of symphonies did not materialize in spite of a new and intense period of planning. He gave the project up although he had already sketched extensive parts of the symphonic score. The scherzo, in particular, had taken on form. But the following note expresses his decision: "instead of a new symphony, a new overture on Bach, intensely fugal with three."[13] The negative decision to postpone or definitely reject a tenth symphony turns into a creative opportunity: from the moment the Tenth is given up, the idea of the choral finale is available for the Ninth. And this plan seizes Beethoven's mind, excluding all other possibilities, at a time when he is intensely occupied with the idea of choral variations on the Ode to Joy. Gradually the vision emerges with a sufficient degree of clarity and gains final impetus. It is the plan which triumphs in the Ninth as we know it today.

This then is the life story of the choral symphony: the budding of a tonal vision in the mind of the youth, its slow ripening in the early venture of the Cantata for Emperor Leopold and in the later one of the Choral Fantasia. Passing through stages of trial, the youthful vision finally reaches a new form in the jubilant singing of the opera, Fidelio. But it is not until the human voice is transplanted into the symphonic realm that the lifelong tonal vision of the Ninth is truly fulfilled. Beethoven, the creator, who had set his art free, crowns classicism in its greatest human message: the Ode to Joy lights the way to the brotherhood of man as a still unfulfilled promise of a better tomorrow.

SCHUBERT: CRAFTSMAN AND MUSIKANT

The friends of Schubert describe the composer in a frequent state of somnambulance. His first important interpreter, the baritone Johann Michael Vogl, speaks of Schubert's "truly divine inspiration," of "utterances of a musical second sight," and thus characterizes the prodigious flow of beautiful inventions from Schubert's musical brain to his manuscripts. After two weeks, Vogl asserts, Schubert would not recognize his own songs which he had written in a trance, as though they had been dictated to him by an outside force.

Another of Schubert's friends, Joseph von Spaun, relates: "Whoever saw him in the morning, his eyes glowing, sparkling, even talking another language like a somnambulist will never forget it." Spaun describes how the "Erlkönig" came into being: one afternoon he went with Mayerhofer to see Schubert who, at this time, lived with his father in the Himmelpfortgrund, a section in old Vienna. The friends found Schubert glowing with enthusiasm reciting the verses of Goethe's "Erlkönig," excitedly pacing the room with the book in his hand. "Suddenly Schubert sat down and, in the shortest time one can imagine, the magnificent ballad was on paper. We ran, since Schubert had no piano, to the convent close by, and it was there that the 'Erlkönig' was sung the very same evening." Again his friends relate how the composer, sitting with them in the garden of an inn with a glass of wine, was reading Shakespeare's *Antony and Cleopatra.* Suddenly the spark of inspiration took fire, and Schubert jotted down a drinking song without delay.[14] Note paper lacking, he grabbed the menu card and in a few minutes the list of good Viennese dishes contained on its reverse side the new song.

These accounts (and many others) bear witness to the composer's impulsive creation on the spur of the moment. There is no reason to doubt the reliability of Schubert's friends who corroborate his creative spontaneity. Very much like Mozart, Schubert has always been credited with a process of creation completely beyond anything that resembles work in slow and systematic stages. Both composers turned out an abundance of scores in short lives terminated in their thirties. How could they have accomplished such stupendous work if their ideas had not gushed forth like springs from a glacier—clear, fresh, light! And it is such uninhibited inspirational flow that lent itself to a one-sided view of their creative process. It is one-sided in that it ignores all aspects of systematic work and the role of craft.

But did some six hundred songs with which the impoverished Schubert enriched posterity really originate in a state of creative intoxication as his friends describe it? Certainly not, as proven by the fact that no less than two hundred of these songs are different settings of specific tonal projects. There are cases in which Schubert abandoned his initial version in a second or third sketch. Sometimes a fourth or fifth trial occurs. Schubert even felt compelled to resort to a sixth version if all preceding attempts appeared unsatisfactory. The trance in which Schubert jotted down the "Erlkönig" did not settle the issue. Later it was reset, altogether four distinct times. As we hear the ballad in the fourth (and final) form, we are immediately struck by its characteristic accompaniment and dramatically threatening tense triplets. In the third version, however, the triplets are missing. Instead, there is an even row of eighth-notes—to be played in octaves. Why? We know that Schubert anticipated with eagerness Goethe's approval of the musical settings of his poems, "Erlkönig," "Heidenröslein" and the "Lied der Mignon." In 1817, Schubert had sent these songs with a dedication to the great poet in Weimar. Yet he knew that Goethe's musical taste was not independent: it was strongly guided by the composer, Friedrich Zelter, an excellent musician but of ultra-conservative leanings. Schubert, apprehensive about Goethe's reaction to the romantic deviations of the music from the classical line, revised the manuscript accordingly and abandoned such features as the romantically pictorial accompaniment of the "Erlkönig." Hence the triplets fell by the wayside.

Likewise Schubert reset numerous of his other songs. Among these revisions are "Geistesgruss" (four versions), "Dem Unend-lichen" (three versions); "Die Forelle" (four versions). There are two versions each of "Der Musensohn," "Willkommen" and "Abschied." In the Winterreise, Schubert made two versions of "Rast," "Einsamkeit" and "Der Leiermann."

For eleven years, from 1815 to 1826, Schubert sought an adequate musical expression for Goethe's poem, "Nur wer die Sehnsucht kennt," in no less than six different settings. Such incessant pursuit of a problem is a trait which could well be likened to Beethoven's working method, to his search for a steadily growing improvement from one draft to the next. With Schubert, as with Beethoven, the succeeding sketches usually condense and concentrate the content. This process of concentration reveals itself in a characteristic way in the repeated settings of Matthison's poem "Der Geistertanz" (1812); Schubert set this song four times (if one counts the version for male chorus, 1816). The first pair of attempts remained in the sketching stage. Significant are the verbal clues—Schubert's remarks which read like those of a scenario: "Midnight," "The Howling of the Wind," "Solemn Quiet," "Dance." These clues point to the pictorial element of the music and guide its stylistic attitude. This specific technique is reminiscent of Beethoven's sketching.[15]

The original version of the Winterreise shows an approach to work typical also of Haydn and Mozart: it is work first on the melody and then on the bass line and the piano accompaniment. Such a procedure is a natural one in the composition of songs, in which all invention is borne from the vocal idea; the tune carries the music along on its own strength. In the sketch of the song, "Einsamkeit," the melody runs for several measures without any accompaniment—Schubert hearkens to the inner drive of the melody. Otherwise, the accompaniment is noted and continued for several lines. If Schubert changes his mind concerning the value of the sketch, he scratches out the whole page and starts anew on another leaf. Mere altering of details will not solve the problem. Thus, the song "Nähe des Geliebten," exists in a complete version which Schubert later crossed out and marked: "Gilt nicht"—not valid! There are many instances in which Schubert rejected altogether what did not strike him as being satisfactory. Two different copies of the Winterreise exist; the one is a writing full of corrections, erasures, of minor or major changes; the other copy has the appearance of a finished manuscript.

Schubert's various tonal ideas do not necessarily call for one specific medium of performance. The tonal picture may lend itself to different negatives, various arrangements, settings and instrumentations. What was first conceived as a Lied for solo voices and piano accompaniment may suggest a different raiment at a later time. Thus, the "Gesang der Geister" is created in four different arrangements. The list in chronological order and type of setting appears as follows:

1816	song with piano
1817	four male voices
1820	male chorus with piano
1820	with string accompaniment

These settings appear as four different interpretations of one tonal vision.

There are features in Schubert's creative procedure which definitely set him apart from his classical predecessors. There is a certain nonchalance and freshness in his work which at times is unguarded by the inhibitions of the mere intellect. Eusebius Mandyczewski, the editor of Schubert's collected works, shows how Schubert keeps changing his ideas as he writes. While proceeding along his chosen path, he continues to rearrange until his thoughts have taken the desired shape. These changes occur not only in the sketches, but frequently in the final stage of composition where other masters are already occupied with smaller details pertaining to the final version of the work. With Schubert, however, the various stages frequently overlap and herein lies a basic difference of approach: the culminating stage of work is wide open to new trials and attempts. Schubert's inspirational power lends itself to a facile and untrammeled start. Often, there is a tendency to shorten the second stage of composition, the stage of sketching, which is followed by a carefree, optimistic handling of the third stage. For instance, all afire, Schubert sits down and begins to write the "Frühlingstraum" in the key of G. He had already written the introductory measures when he suddenly decided to brighten up the song and to transpose it a whole tone higher to the key of A major. In short, he approached the writing of the song before he had a definite idea of certain of its essential characteristics. Schubert did not hesitate to choose the higher key once he felt that the one in which he had started did not suit the expression.

In the Second Symphony, Schubert altered the themes of the opening movement after important sections had already been developed. The andante of the Tragic Symphony (the Fourth) was originally conceived in $\frac{3}{4}$ time. Again, after he had proceeded with the composition, Schubert renounced the original $\frac{3}{4}$ and wrote into all the staves of the orchestral score the new time signature of $\frac{2}{4}$.

The manuscript of the Seventh Symphony shows that Schubert had already completed the first movement when he reconsidered the shape of the main theme. His original motif obviously did not seem sufficiently important to him, particularly in view of the splendor of its brilliant C major environment. And so Schubert decided upon that change which we see on our facsimile page of his manuscript (Illustration XVI).

Schubert did not regularly make sketches, not even for more extended compositions. We have no evidence of drafts for the symphonies one to four (inclusive). But he did sketch the two symphonies in the key of C—the Sixth and the Seventh. The B Minor Symphony was first minutely sketched, the whole written in a sort of piano score. Not until after such preparatory work did Schubert approach the orchestration. The sketches for this symphony also clarify a problem of great interest to posterity, namely, how Schubert had planned the third movement. Unfortunately, the manuscript becomes, soon after the beginning of the scherzo, very sketchy though the melody is always well enough indicated. In the trio, neither the bass nor the harmony is given; only the melody is carried on. There is only one score page of the finale. The whole manuscript consists of thirty-nine pages altogether; the last four pages are empty. Thus we have at least some notion of what the scherzo of the great work would have been like although fate did not permit its completion.

What are the deeper reasons for the particularities of Schubert's creative approach? Schubert is, in the highest sense, the artistic type characterized in his native land by the word, *Musikant*. This term refers to that full-blooded artist who makes music uninhibited by intellectual restrictions, drawing happily from rich tonal sources of his imagination. Music flows from his heart and brain as naturally as the apple grows on the tree. His musical learning and his great technical accomplishments only help him to keep the stream dammed and to direct its course into works of real art. Such a *Musikant* was Schubert.

This explains much of what is in the sketches. At times, Schubert approaches the execution of his scores with a not too clear idea of the content and character of the music in all details. It is like going for a walk in beautiful country with a general direction in mind. But, by chance, an attractive view leads to a detour or per- haps even to a change of destination. He changed unhesitatingly all-important features of a major work, even its theme, after he had proceeded with the composition and had even gone quite a distance. All this is characteristic of Schubert, the man and his human traits: a naïve *Musikant* working ahead unworried about the thematic material.

There is, however, the other side to his creative endeavors, and this shows a different picture. Here we see Schubert as a hard worker aiming with intense self-criticism at his artistic ideals. If the products of his fantasy do not live up to his expectations, he throws them back into the melting pot of tectonic work, recasting the shape again and again. And this places Schubert's approach into the realm of craft, on the highest level of art.

THE "STENOGRAPHIC" SKETCH

In addition to the problems that we have already surveyed in
the composer's various methods of sketching, certain specific questions pertaining to the interaction between fantasy and the mechanical part of writing down the notes arise. The composer can hardly
write a score at the speed with which his music first occurs to him.
Yet while writing, he cannot eliminate the work of his imagination:
it is his fantasy that dictates to him whatever he sets out to
write. Here a conflict arises. If the sketching cannot keep pace with
the flowing imagination, it must be somehow slowed down to the
tempo of writing.

Berlioz resorted to a system of musical shorthand based on a
figured script, supplemented by additional features understandable
only to himself. He applied this device the first time during the
composition of the *Requiem*:[16] "It seems as though my head would
burst under the pressure of bubbling thoughts. The plan of the first
piece was not yet sketched when the next one would push itself
forward. Unable to write so rapidly, I had to avail myself of stenographic signs which were of excellent service particularly at the
Lacrimosa."

In nineteenth century Europe, as war-torn then as in any other
time of its history, the composer's business of sketching had its
complications and made trouble for young Berlioz, whom a love
adventure had led from Rome to Nice in 1831. The French pearl
of the Riviera belonged at this time to the kingdom of Sardinia.
Here on the Mediterranean, inspired by the beauty of the Côte
d'Azure, Berlioz composed, strolling or lounging on the beach,
eagerly making notes in a sketchbook. But he did not enjoy the
romantic setting for long; the behavior of a wild-maned man, first
loafing, then suddenly sketching and writing hieroglyphics on paper
caused suspicion. The chief of police himself took an interest in the
matter, and Berlioz reports the following dialogue:

Chief of Police: You are seen everywhere with a sketchbook drawing
industriously. Are you perhaps occupied with the drawing of plans?

Berlioz: Yes, I am planning an overture to *King Lear*, that is to

say, I did already score it: the groundplan and instrumentation is finished.

Chief of Police: What do you mean by instrumentation?

Berlioz: That is just a musical term.

Chief of Police: Always those pretexts. I know very well, Monsieur, in
music you cannot compose without a piano—certainly
not with just a sketchbook and pencil. And in doing so,
it is just on the embankment that you have to go for a
walk? This will never do. You cannot remain in Nice
any longer!

And back to Rome Berlioz went, "to keep on composing without
a piano with the kind permission of the chief of police."

THE CONDENSED OPERA SCORE

How does the composer sketch an extended and complex score
such as that of a great opera or oratorio with its multiple parts for
vocal and instrumental groups, for soli, chorus and orchestra
in combined ensembles? Is it at all possible to concentrate its content on a few lines, as one might note the composition of a small
score? Wagner's method of sketching at least gives a positive answer.
We must realize, however, that the chief problem is the intrinsic
complexity of the idea itself, rather than the problem of its external
realization. Polyphonic complications and even composite tone
colors may prove more difficult to sketch than an idea which, while
intended for a large apparatus, may be reducible—in its tectonic
content—to only two lines.[17]

Wagner's approach normally consisted of extreme condensation.
He reduced all tonal thoughts to their lowest common denominator:
even the drafts for his more complex score pages contain only one
or two staves. But Wagner himself felt that this procedure was not
always efficient. Thus he was handicapped when he was outlining
the score of *Rheingold*. He had already finished the piano sketch,
which means in this case a simplified and condensed piano score.
Yet as he stated, he was "at a loss to sketch, in his customary way
of using two staves, the orchestral prelude." And he came to the
following conclusion (in a letter to Franz Liszt of March 4, 1854):
"No, I will have to write *Rheingold* directly into score with (com-

plete) instrumentation. I could not find a way to distinctly notate the prelude as a sketch. I tried it directly into the score."

In other words, with the beginning of work on the *Ring*, an important change in Wagner's mode of sketching took place. Until *Lohengrin*, Wagner made separate sketches for the musical structure and later for the final score. But now starting with *Rheingold*, he proceeded from the first pencil sketch to the final score without intermediary drafts. The sketches for both *Rheingold* and *Walküre* contain, in addition to scenic remarks, directions for instrumentation, proving that Wagner must have heard inwardly the various tone colors and found it necessary to notate them at their first conception. In *Siegfried*, Wagner returned to his earlier method. His primary sketches, he confessed, appeared to him like "altogether strange signs." He did not remember any longer what he had intended. As a result, Wagner interpolated once again a full orchestral sketch between the first outline and the finished manuscript.[18]

Many other of Wagner's first drafts are drawn on a single staff. A second line on the paper is left free to note certain harmonic successions and other details, particularly of the instrumentation. The sketches of *Rheingold*, *Walküre* and most of those following are first written in pencil and later retraced in ink.

Wendelin Weissheimer[19] tells of Wagner in the crucial days of *Die Meistersinger*—sitting at the piano where he wrote the prelude in a very detailed sketch. This draft resembled a normal piano score with its duplications and the notation of accompanying voices. While he was sketching, the piano remained the important tool: Wagner would consult the keyboard again and again, thus testing the actual sound and never depending only on his tonal fantasy alone. During this work, Wagner left the lid of the piano completely closed—in Weissheimer's opinion in order to write on it more comfortably (but perhaps also to hear the clearest possible tone without acoustic distraction through the more powerful sound of the open instrument). Wagner usually played with his left hand, simultaneously writing the sketch with the right one. Yet he would frequently test complex chords with both hands until he was sure of the harmonic result. His steady search for the new, for the harmonically audacious, his pursuit of the infinite melody did not make for fast progress. As to his working tempo, Wagner stated that he could write six score pages a day without effort. Yet the dependability of the result compensated for the relatively slow pace. Unlike other composers, Wagner made his decisions once and for all, with few exceptions.

Beyond these technicalities, the study of Wagner's sketches permits most revealing glimpses into the more intimate strata of the creative experience. In the left upper corner of one page of the drafts for *Walküre*, Wagner wrote: "I l d gr!!" (Ich liebe dich grenzlos!!). Likewise at sixteen different places in these sketches for the first act of *Walküre*, he made similar confessions all referring to his love for Mathilde Wesendonck. Wagner, while writing the great scene of Siegmund and Sieglinde (which leads to the fulfillment of their forbidden desire) must have thought constantly of Mathilde, the object of his own unfulfilled love and eventual renouncement.

On June 22, 1857, he turned from the composition of *Siegfried* to *Tristan*. Already at the beginning of the second act of *Siegfried* (June 18, 1857), we find a note: "already decided on *Tristan*." And in the *Siegfried* sketch, Wagner addressed his hero (June 27, 1857): "When are we going to see each other again?" On the next day, he wrote to Liszt: "I have accompanied my young Siegfried into the beautiful solitude of forests but I will let him rest under the linden tree and bid him farewell with tears." On August 20, 1857, Wagner threw himself completely into the *Tristan* world. After the completion of the prose writing, he turned immediately to the composition. On November 30, in the middle of sketching the first *Tristan* act, Wagner approached the composition of the Fünf Gedichte for Mathilde Wesendonck. He started with "Der Engel" and composed, four days later, "Träume." In its published form,[20] this song like the fifth, "Im Treibhaus," bears Wagner's eloquent inscription, "Study for *Tristan und Isolde*."

Brahms, when composing a large work, sketched some sort of a piano score: the contours of the two outer voices are sharply delineated while the middle parts are never neglected, thus giving the sketch a truly polyphonic aspect. This procedure characterizes the genesis of the great vocal scores such as the *Requiem*. Characteristic is the sketching on triple staves. Only the primary elements are in focus, while directions for dynamics and instrumentation are

missing. Divorced from its association with the text, the play of
tones is in the foreground. In such a procedure Brahms' affinity
with the classical and baroque masters becomes apparent. In his
sketching of large works, the approach is not essentially different
from that of smaller enterprises. Here as there, the pursuit of the
melody prevails, followed in importance by the marking of the bass.
The figured bass script retains its function as an expedient device.
Along with the melody, the words of the text are frequently written
down. Not until he had completed the outline of the song in such
alfresco manner, did Brahms direct his attention to the details of
the accompaniment. In contrast to the composer who works only
on the spur of the moment and ties the tonal idea definitely to the
uniqueness of the experience, Brahms was in the habit of letting
his scores lie untouched in a drawer, sometimes for years, and then
at a later date resuming work on them. He let his music mature,
as good wine mellows with age.

SUMMARY: ARTISAN OR AMATEUR

Madame von Meck asked Tchaikovsky (July 6, 1878), somewhat
naïvely, whether he could describe to her his method of work. He
answered the prize question in so simplified and summarizing a
manner that his comments are applicable to the creative approach
of most musicians:

I write my sketches on the first piece of paper that comes to hand,
sometimes a scrap of note paper, and I write in very abbreviated form.
The melody never appears in my head without its attendant harmony.
In general, these two musical elements, together with the rhythm, cannot be conceived separately; every melodic idea carries its own inevitable
harmony and rhythm. If the harmonies are very complicated, one must
indicate the voice parts in the sketch. If the harmony is very simple, I
often jot down the bass, or write out a figured bass; at other times I
do not need even that. It stays in my mind. The preliminary sketch of a
work is extremely agreeable to do; sometimes it affords a quite in-
expressible delight, but it also means anxiety and nervous excitement.
One sleeps badly and often quite forgets to eat. But the actual execution
of the project is done very calmly and quietly.

Thus Tchaikovsky clarifies the difference between inspirational

ardor and the calm approach to craft. Art may flow from both
sources. The raw material is mined in exciting hours of inspiration,
and is later worked out with the tranquillity of the skilled artisan.
Tchaikovsky throws more light on the complex interaction of the
two main factors in the creative process—inspiration and craft—by
shifting the focus from his own work to that of the main figures
in the contemporary Russian scene. The musical art of Russia
showed, in Tchaikovsky's time, a division into two camps—the one
wide open to western European influence, the other dogmatically
insisting on the orthodox Byzantine-Slavic orientation, stressing
also in music the religious background and the history of its
motherland. Inevitably, the leading composers were drawn into
one or the other spheres of influence. And the two greatest
composers in nineteenth century Russia belonged to opposing
groups. Tchaikovsky blended most attractively his cosmopolitan
technique and substance with the melancholy chants of old Russia,
while Mussorgsky portrayed the soul of the Russian people in all
its profundity, breaking to this end with Western tradition. Such
isolation from central European influence was the battle cry of the
so-called group of the Five to which Mussorgsky belonged along
with Rimsky-Korsakov, Cui, Borodin and Balakirev. But Tchaikovsky, little interested in the ideological undertones of their music,
examined the complex problem technically on a "l'art pour l'art"
basis. In January, 1878 in a letter to Mme. von Meck, he argued
that the Five were essentially bad craftsmen, dilettantes, who had
convinced themselves that theoretical training was destructive to
all inspiration and dried up their creative power. The interesting
correspondence deals individually with the deficiencies of these
composers: Tchaikovsky shows that lack of training is at the root
of all their evil.

Rimsky-Korsakov (Tchaikovsky admits) was overcome by despair once he realized how many unprofitable years he had wasted
following a road which led nowhere. But changing his mind he
began to study with tremendous zeal.

During a single summer, he finished innumerable exercises in counterpoint and sixty-four fugues, ten of which he sent me for inspection. From
contempt for schools, Rimsky-Korsakov suddenly went over to the cult

of musical craft. Shortly after, his symphony appeared and also his quartet. Both works are full of obscurities and—as you will justly observe —bear the stamp of dry pedantry.

César Cui is dismissed as a gifted amateur. Tchaikovsky derides his manner of composing which consists of tediously picking out his melodies and harmonies at the piano. This process was so laborious that it took him ten years to complete his opera, *Ratcliffe*. As to Borodin, he likewise never had a systematic training and thus his great talent was unhappily wasted. His technique was so inadequate that he could not write a single bar without help. Prophetically, Tchaikovsky diagnosed the case of Mussorgsky as the most remarkable of the Five but doomed to an early end. Mussorgsky had no aspirations to correct his own deficiencies. "He writes just as it comes to him, believing blindly in the infallibility of his genius." Balakirev is seen as the greatest personality of the entire circle, but also as its main sinner. He is discredited as the inventor of all the theories in this circle which united so many undeveloped, falsely developed or prematurely decayed talents.

The lesson which Tchaikovsky teaches in the review of his fellow Russians is that theory is all-important. Those who evade its bondage must pay a high price. In an exemplary manner, he shows causes and effects, proving how men, endowed with great creative gifts, failed to reach artistic heights because of their lack of craft which in turn was due to their negligence of theoretical studies. Some of the highly gifted Russian composers belonged to other professions. Cui's specialty was not music but fortifications which he taught in a military school. Borodin was a professor of chemistry in the Academy of Medicine. But all of them were almost purposefully detached from a professional inquiry into musical theory. The Five were obsessed with the idea that academic training would clip the wings of their artistic imagination. Theory, they thought, offered nothing but enslavement to dead rules.

But in Petersburg as anywhere, derision of craft on the part of the musician led to dilettantism. Not equipped with the tools of theory, Cui required years to complete a work that the skilled craftsman might sketch in several weeks. Great talents wasted precious and irreplaceable time and energy which they could have so successfully employed in other productive enterprises. In their amateurish struggle with craft, the buds of inspiration did not unfold. Only Rimsky-Korsakov, after he had realized that his indifference to theoretical systems led nowhere, swung to the other extreme. But in doing so, the one-time amateur talent turned into a grim, bearded, bespectacled professor who censored and changed the production of Mussorgsky's powerful fantasy mercilessly with the red pencil of an academician.

The deficiencies of the creative teamwork, in spite of intuitive talents, were already apparent in the case of Glinka, the true inaugurator, the prophet-patriarch of the national Russian school. With his clear insight into the creative process, Tchaikovsky raised the question of what would have happened to his countryman had he worked as an artist who recognized his power and felt it his duty to perfect his talent rather than to compose music as an amateur. In reference to craft, Tchaikovsky wrote:

One must acquire this, one must conquer oneself and not fall into dilettantism from which even so colossal a talent as Glinka suffered. That man, endowed with great original power of creation, lived to a mature age, yet wrote amazingly little. Read his memoirs and you will see that he worked only as a dilettante, at leisure, when the mood came. We are proud of Glinka, yet we must admit that he did not fulfill the task his genius put upon him. Both his operas, in spite of marvelous and quite original beauty, suffer from striking inequality of style. Pure and gracious beauty is followed by childish naïveté and insipidity.

With this critical comment, Tchaikovsky lets the cat out of the bag! He himself, an artist blessed with high imaginative powers, significantly claims craft as the criterion of the professional composer. The musician who can only produce in the inspirational trance is a dilettante. In artistic work on a high level, all three stages must be perfectly welded into each other with no breaks at any point. A true art work can only result from thorough organization and domination of the material through craft—in a perfect teamwork of synthesis. That is the reason the truly great composer always proves to be a thoroughly trained craftsman. In analogy to the talent and failure of Glinka, it would be worth-while to examine why and how other extremely talented composers did not succeed in producing works of lasting value. It would be challenging to prove that their shortcomings usually lay in their inability to attain a higher degree of synthetic co-ordination. In this sense, a study and analysis of the three stages of composition shows not only the story of creative success, but also that of failure. Some highly gifted composers invent melodies more beautiful perhaps than those of the great architects of music. Yet to have a beautiful theme is not enough to build a great work of art. Inspiration must be followed by solid craft, by the exact knowledge of what to do with beautiful inventions. The inspirational raw material must be worked out with skill and profound artistry in the second and third stages of the creative process. Tectonic work, carried safely by dependable craft into successful synthesis, must resolve in the total effort of composition. The analysis of the creative procedure shows that certain scores which start out auspiciously do not materialize into the promised perfection because the composer lacks control over the multiple factors of craft or because he cannot conquer the form. What differentiates the professional from the amateur is not the power of inspiration, the faculty of having ideas at all, but the composer's command of craft. In the true composer's workshop, a team of all his creative faculties must be at work. The conscious and subconscious, intuition and intellect, instinct and technique must permeate each other in an ever varying permutation.

There is no art without craft and no craft without theoretical learning. Obviously, it takes much more than both craft and theory to produce a true art work. The most loyal apprenticeship and fanatic obedience to the rules can lead, in the best case, to a satisfactory piece of craftsmanship. Yet great music is always the sum of inspiration, plus craft, plus creative synthesis.

Richard Wagner, in his variations on the theme of musical creation in *Die Meistersinger*, delved deep into the roots of the whole problem. When in the first act, David, the apprentice, enumerates the infinite trouble he has taken to learn the craft of shoemaking and poetry, his humorous dialogue with Walther discloses the real truth.

David: Shoemaker's craft and poet's art,
      Both daily I learn by heart;
      First all the leather smooth I hammer,
      Consonants then and vowels I stammer;
      Next must the thread be stiff with wax,

Then I must learn it rhymes with Sachs.
With awl and thread I make stitches neat,
And then I learn about time and heat.
With lapstone and last, the slow and fast,
The hard, the light, the gloomy and bright,
The scissors and snippings and word clippings,
The pauses and corns, the flowers and thorns,
I learn all such things with care and pains:

And at this point the industrious apprentice finally asks:

"To what now think you all this attains?"

And Walther, the exponent of inspiration in the drama (who knows
nothing about the tabulature, the rigid and past-bound theory of
the masters), quite rightly guesses the answer:

"Say, to a pair of right good shoes!"

It is in this sense that we may now conclude: art starts where craft
ends. A greater force than mere craft is needed to carry the artist
to the new and true fulfillment. Wagner points to the nature of
this force in the last act of *Die Meistersinger*: what power that is
is shown when Walther composes the prize song in the workshop of
Sachs. The good shoemaker-poet warns Walther that his dream-
inspired vision will violate the theory of the mastersingers:

Ihr schlosset nicht im gleichen Ton:	Your closing key is not the same:
Das macht den Meistern Pein;	This gives the masters pain;
Doch nimmt Hans Sachs die Lehr' davon,	But Hans Sachs draws a rule from this,
Im Lenz wohl müss'es so sein.	In Spring it must be so, 'tis plain.

It is plain, however, to Hans Sachs, the only man in the opera who
knows what it is all about: he draws the rule that in art it must
always be spring. The primeval power must reign which creates
all things anew. Spring! That arch source of nature's budding as
well as the springboard of all young art.

PART THREE

SYNTHESIS

CHAPTER ELEVEN

FORM

> The way I am accustomed to write
> I always have the whole before my
> eyes.
>
> **BEETHOVEN**

THE MEANING OF FORM

NATURE carries the artist to an inner unity. Goethe came to this conclusion after a lifelong study of all the arts. The great creative artists were unifying natures, endowed with the power of synthesis—of that force which binds all separate elements of substance into the wholeness of the art work.

Every great composer is possessed with this inborn drive toward an entity. In the synthetic stage of composition, he eliminates all unessentials, closely links the factors of the art work and firmly organizes his music to the inner unity of its creative form.

Synthesis implies the act of composition in its most literal meaning: it is the putting of parts together, the tectonic combination of all details within the whole. It is the casting of the form, the total organization of all individual parts. Synthesis, as a synonym for the last stage of composition, pertains to all work following the previous stages of inventing and sketching. It also comprises the mere externalities of writing the manuscript in a final copy.

Creative synthesis is always the result of inner order. It succeeds only if a spiritual center has guided the organization of the tonal material. In this organization, the great composer clearly recognizes the principles of musical design. He balances all ideas included in the total score and tests their function. In this sense everything is teamwork; everything is co-operation to achieve the end purpose of form.

The idea of musical form has frequently been defined mechanically: theorists have shown the form of a fugue, sonata or song to be something like a prefixed pattern—like a form used for the casting of a chime or for a piece of sculpture. The shape of the tonal substance originates as though the composer would cast his form in a musical bell foundry. The soft tonal material is poured into a rigid, hard framework. It flows into given patterns, limiting the composer's inventiveness within a chosen, pre-established form-scheme. But if this were true, form in music could never be a freely swinging, released force, springing from the permutation of primary musical elements, from an expression which newly creates the form with every new work.

This notion of musical bell casting is disproved by the practice of composition in every era. The medieval and baroque working methods show how new forms readily emerged even if the composer employed previously existing form patterns. In the nineteenth century, Schumann rejected the claim of contemporary theorists that the fluid material of tones must be poured into traditional tonal forms: ". . . as though there were only one or two forms to which the spiritual features would have to be adjusted. As though not every idea would bring into the world its very own form by itself. As though not every art work must have a different content and therefore a different form." Schumann, schooled in the forms of the past and deeply admiring their design, still desired to free himself from the tyranny of ultraconservative formalists and law-makers.

In the twentieth century, Busoni—likewise a great scholar of historic masterworks—expressed the same skepticism toward the theorists who retained form as a symbol and made it a fetish, a religion:

Is it not singular to demand of a composer originality in all things and to forbid it as regards form? No wonder that once he becomes original, he is accused of "formlessness." Every motif—so it seems to me—contains like a seed its life germ within itself. From different plant seeds grow different families of plants, dissimilar in form, foliage, blossom, fruit, growth and color. Even each individual plant, belonging to one and the same species, assumes in size, form and strength, a growth peculiar to itself. And so in each motif there lies the embryo of its full developed form: each one must unfold itself differently, yet each obediently follows the laws of eternal harmony. This form is imperishable, though each be unlike every other.[1]

ARCHITECTURAL FORM

A great composer's aim to achieve pure form is timeless. Yet form means something different in every era and style. A projection of certain form ideas against the cultural background of their time best explains this problem in all its ramifications. Of all the concepts in the composer's inner workshop, his form types demand the broadest interpretation. They are not isolated musical phenomena; they are inherent in the cultural expression of their time.

"Music is fluid architecture and architecture is frozen music." The commonwealth of these arts, which Schlegel thus defines, contributes to the understanding of musical tectonics. We have shown (Chapter II) how the composer builds his tonal structure along horizontal patterns and at the same time considers the vertical aspect of his plan. He hears and views certain features of his work separately and yet conceives the whole as something cohesive and unified. The architect approaches his work in a related manner. In his mind, groundplan and frontal view occur together. His sketch has something contrapuntal in it: what he conceives horizontally, he also projects against the vertical component.

In turn, the musical fugue can be viewed as an architectural form. The fugue is, in the literal sense, the product of tonal building. The architectural principle never leaves the composer out of its grasp. His thinking in every measure is structural. Hence, the plan of a strict fugue can be shown in a graph of geometric precision. The fugal pattern is the musical pendant of the canopy in the Gothic cathedral. Fugal themes as well as architectural motifs climb here into the polyphonic development, there into the web of arches in the naves of the church. In both cases the design starts with a theme alone. In a later development it forms an organism of tonal polyphony or of architectural features. In the fugue, the essential thematic material is introduced by the exposition. In Gothic architecture, the motif (namely the crossbeam traverse section) amounts to an anticipation of the whole space. Mounting from the floor, losing itself in the canopy, the design appears to be in its whole stretch, the consequence of one single theme.[2]

The fugue is not the only musical form that reflects Gothic architecture. We can observe a structural similarity between both arts in the Franco-Flemish chansons of the fifteenth century. Here melodies developed into a contrapuntal play of architectural artfulness. For instance: a tenor[3] would hold the given chant in long values while the other voices above varied and shortened the notes into the patterns of diminution.[4] All this suggests the form play in Gothic cathedrals where the gallery is a copy of the nave but reduced in size.

The Gothic fugue is a form of pure construction. Yet the purely architectural character of the fugue has not been preserved throughout the whole course of history. The fugue has not remained solely a piece of rigid structure in which the form dictates its place to every feature. We have already studied (in Chapter I) the modified status of the fugue in the workshop of the classical masters and have observed how Beethoven continued in young years the fugal style of Haydn and Mozart. He turned in years of maturity to the baroque fugue of Bach and Handel for reorientation. To most nineteenth century romanticists, the fugal form offered only a general plan for polyphonic construction; at the same time, it permitted a liberal deviation from the strict path.[5]

The fugato[6] finds its way frequently into the opera. Its service to the stage obviously does not help to preserve the purity of form. In Wagner's *Meistersinger*, a brawl climaxes in a fugato, in which theme fragments come and go with the turbulent action of furious Nürnbergers awakened from their sleep. In the opera *Falstaff*, the fugue becomes the musical frame for a last laugh of Verdi, the great tragedian. In the romantic solo sonata, chamber music and symphony, the fugal form loses most of its strict qualities. The trend is to personalize the content of all form types. As a result the objective character of the fugue is dimmed by the subjective expression of the romanticist. In his workshop, the sharp fugal contours become less discernible. His polyphonic products are far removed from a form type which once was likened to the dogmatic principles of Gothic architecture.

"A genuinely artistic work of music," says Schumann, "always has a certain center of gravity toward which everything must tend, and from which the spiritual radius emerges. Many place it in the middle in the manner of Mozart, others to the end, as Beethoven. In any case, the total effect (of the work) depends on its forcefulness (of the groundplan). If one has first listened to the music with tension and torture, then the moment must come when one can, for the first time, breathe freely. One has mounted to the peak—the view stretches brightly and contentedly forward and backward."

The point of gravity, or rather the spiritual center of the score decides, then, the distribution of all tonal balance—in the individual movement as well as in the cycle of an entire work. It is the crux of the design. It directs the whole course of the music. The chosen center is the magnet toward which all spiritual and tectonic elements of the music are drawn. Schumann, when referring to Beethoven's plans, thought of scores such as the Fifth Symphony: its curve from the dramatic opening to the liberating finale bears out perfectly Schumann's metaphor. The transition from the scherzo to the finale marks the point where, after the preceding tension, one can "breathe freely" again and serenely enjoy the outstretched view. Such an experience is typical of the classical cycle, which is one of a gradual loosening of tension. There is frequently a decrescendo of the expansive forces as the cycle unfolds from the opening to the last movement. Tonalities in minor lead to finales in major. The expression turns gradually from the serious to the light, from the problematic to the playful, from the closed to the open forms. Already the baroque suite with its austere beginning and its happy ending follows such a course. So do most sonata cycles of Haydn, Mozart and their contemporaries. By and large, this order continues until the revolutionary finale of Beethoven's Ninth Symphony.

Nottebohm justifiably divided Beethoven's sketches into one

group in which the total form appears as the aim from the beginning, and another, in which thematic work predominates, with the form only distantly in mind. Psychologically, however, the origin of ideas is closely related, no matter how Beethoven elaborated upon them. A flash occurs and brings a motif, a harmony, or suggests an idea pertaining to form. Nevertheless, the various examples show the different function which such inspirational occurrences have in reference to the architecture of the finished music. The differences lie in the composer's evaluation of his tonal substance—where and how the various thoughts fit into the plan of a specific work.

The drafts for Beethoven's Fifth Piano Concerto in E-flat Major are stamped from their very beginning by a conception of form rather than by a pursuit of melodic and other tectonic elements. Already in the initial sketches, the form idea unfolds itself. The piano introduces the concerto with a brilliant passage, without a pronouncement of the main theme. Along with this unusual opening, and likewise clear from the inception of the music, we observe its familiar harmonies. Yet the main theme of the concerto is not evident at all at this early stage of composition. Motifs come and go; they are accepted, rejected and newly cast. Obviously, they are of lesser importance for it was not a theme or rhythm which untied the flow of Beethoven's imagination. It was rather a definite idea of a form, given a priori, which inspired and remained the decisive factor throughout all stages in the composition of this movement.[7]

An analogous procedure is shown in the sketches to the first movement of the Piano Sonata in D Minor, Op. 31, No. 2. Again, Beethoven is primarily concerned with the form. He envisions a recitative to be interpolated in the blueprint of the sonata movement at the recapitulation of its main thought. As in the case of the Fifth Piano Concerto, the melodic lines as such are only of secondary importance in relation to the pattern of form. In the early sketches, in which the usual form of this movement is already established, the thematic material itself is still in a problematic stage and shows little resemblance to its final shape. Without any decisions as to main or secondary themes, the form alone lives clearly in Beethoven's mind. He seeks and finds the blueprint first. In the piano concerto as well as in the sonata, the composition does not originate from thematic flashes. Waves of form decide their course.

A comparison of the different blueprints of Beethoven's work pertaining to the same genre proves the wealth and variety of his plans within the related form-scheme. How varied is the organization in the blueprints of the ten sonatas for violin and piano! Not two groundplans are identical. Of course, all of these sonatas are built on the basis of main themes. Yet the form that follows their initial statements, displays in each case striking differences of development. Again, all recapitulations in Beethoven's nine symphonies differ from each other in specific features. They differ here in the way the theme is reintroduced, there in instrumentation as in dynamics. Everywhere with Beethoven a high degree of newness is born with each new work. It is remarkable how Beethoven succeeds in accomplishing this variety, in spite of his emphasis on the classical sonata-scheme as a supreme guide.

In his synthetic work, Beethoven frequently utilizes previous ideas while he fuses new ones into his form: the old and the new attract each other in the playful teamwork of tectonics. The problem as to where to place an idea is often solvable only in later stages of creation. Thus, between work on the second and third movements of the Quartet in C Major, Op. 59, No. 3, there occur preliminary sketches for a highly characteristic theme. Had it at that time been intended for the quartet? We do not know. The theme disappeared for six years from the surface of traceable planning. Yet when Beethoven worked on the Seventh Symphony, he must have discovered that this forgotten idea functioned well in the framework of its allegretto: the melody of the elegiac A minor movement in the Seventh Symphony is nothing but the formerly discarded theme from the sketches of the C Major Quartet.

TOTALITY AND DETAIL

"The way I am accustomed to write, I always have the whole before my eyes. I carry my thoughts a long time, often very long before I write them down. Therein my memory remains loyal to me, since I am sure not to forget a theme even after years, once I

have conceived it. Some things I change, reject, try all over again
until I am satisfied."[8]

From these words of Beethoven, the total pursuit of work clearly
emerges. The total idea of the planned work, then, gives direction
to the creative imagination. With the specific goal and definite blueprint in mind, the composer has a selective attitude toward all the
products of his tonal fantasy. He rejects as well as accepts. Censor-
ing, he chooses those ideas which fit specifically into the framework
of his plan, or he transforms earlier thoughts which he might
originally have chosen for a different score.

Even if the artist envisions a great form in its totality, ideas pertaining to details naturally occur. At times, such work on smaller
sections occupies the composer's full attention. This happened, for
instance, in Beethoven's work on the first movement of the Eroica.
Of all the passages in Beethoven's works, few caused so much
bewilderment and stirred such heated arguments as the horn call in
the first movement, four measures before the recapitulation. When
the symphony was first heard following its completion, contemporary listeners thought this passage absurd—either an obvious error
of notation, or the idea of an altogether mad musician.

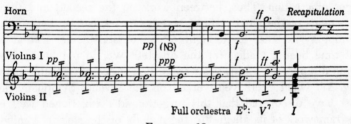

EXAMPLE 19

Even when Ferdinand Ries, Beethoven's associate and disciple,
heard the entry of the horn at the first rehearsal, he flew into a rage,
upon which (as witnesses assert) the dumbfounded apprentice
barely escaped a box on the ears from his master. Time passed, but
brought no progress in the understanding of this perplexing passage.
To make matters worse, J. J. Fétis, the esteemed professor of theory
of the Paris Conservatory, actually changed in his Beethoven edition the tonic form of the horn passage to a dominant form. The

ultraconservative theorist rationalized for his willful correction by pretending that Beethoven, in his hasty score writing, must have committed an error and put the part in the wrong clef.[9]

No doubt, Beethoven's conception was revolutionary. These measures, bridging the development and the recapitulation with a most original superimposition of the dominant and tonic harmonies, were something unheard of in 1804. Turning to the true meaning of this passage of trials, the sketches establish the fact that Beethoven had the quoted horn call firmly in mind while working on the rest of the great movement. He considered the audacious transition at an early stage of planning. The development section was far from finished when he concentrated his attention on this particular problem. Soon after the end of the exposition, it apparently became clear to Beethoven that the main motif ought to be reintroduced in a specifically daring way. And the sketches show how he planned first to bring the horn call in the remote key of D major. This would have been a sharp contrast to the E-flat tonality of the approaching recapitulation. Still another draft establishes that such a combination of dissonant tonalities was by no means a passing flash. Adhering stubbornly to this unusual conception, Beethoven finally arrived at the desired solution. The terrific excitement and fury of the development gradually calms down. With overlapping tonalities as its harmonic background—and four measures before it would have entered "normally"—the horn motif sounds. At this point, most of the instruments have already become silent, the dynamics have decreased from fortissimo to pianissimo. Only the violins remain in softest tremolo, on the B and A flats of the suggested dominant harmony. Now playing unexpectedly the main theme in the tonic, the horn calls like a voice from real life into the depths of a dream. The E-flat major motif restores the daylight of the oncoming recapitulation. This stroke of genius, so much ahead of its time and therefore so incomprehensible to contemporaries, might have been "heaven-sent." Its elaboration was certainly earthly: the result of human toil.

Generalizing, we can assume that nowhere in the development of great music can the tie-up between the total work plan and the details be ignored. In fact with many of Beethoven's scores, the first movements are commentaries on what happens in the first measures. No motif in any score in history incites the entire cyclic motion of an extended symphony as does the opening of Beethoven's Fifth. Like a turbine, the famous four notes generate the motion of the music. The structure of the inciting theme is one of utmost simplicity. It uses a design which is the favorite of all classical composers, consisting of tonic and dominant forms, reductions and cadential condensation. Yet as this scheme unfolds, we become aware of the unshakable logic of Beethoven's symphonic architecture.

As to the andante of the Fifth Symphony, we have traced the reasons which led to Beethoven's intense reworking of the theme: the onetime minuet had to be fused into the symphonic groundplan in its entirety. Even seemingly isolated ideas—striking modulations and unusual instrumentation in the Eighth Symphony, the various bird calls interpreting the voice of nature, the bubbling of the brook, lightning and thunder in the Pastoral—are all associatively inspired by the total idea. All these ideas are unthinkable detached from the fundamental plan.

The approach to the wholeness of work is again strikingly exemplified in Gluck's description of his creative procedure: "Once I am clear about the composition of the whole and about the characterization of the main parts, I consider the opera finished, although I have not yet written one single note." The whole composition occurs as a vision of the work in its totality, anticipating the total conception of the music drama. The pursuit of total ideas from memory also develops from inspiration through elaboration to synthesis. The difference lies in the fact that nothing is written down on paper. Gluck explained how the plan first fully matured in his mind and how the writing of the manuscript was but the after effect of an already completed mental elaboration:

First I go through each individual act, later through the whole work. The plan of the composition I sketch in my mind while sitting in the parterre (of the theater). Such a preparation usually takes one entire year and not rarely do I contract a severe disease upon such effort. Yet people call this composing light songs.

Gluck's comment points to will power and imagination as prerequisites of his method to compose "blindly" an entire dramatic work.

This procedure of Gluck is closely related to that of Weber. And the affinity of their dramatic ideals and operatic reforms is characteristically reflected also in their process of creating. Weber, as Gluck, preconceives the entire opera:

Before I approach the execution of the detail, I figure out the great plan of the tonal picture through determining its main colors and its individual parts; namely, I outline for myself the exact sequence of the keys . . . and I strictly weigh the use of the instruments. The emotion of human nature . . . its expression through melodies is the subject of my next attention. . . . So, my dear friends, here you have my report: how my head and my heart act, and with which colors I try to paint. Yet how all this happens is a gift from above and only the world can judge.

His music, once it had matured, became fixed in unmistakable lines in Weber's mind. As his son Max reports: "Without any intermediary stage, the whole score would flow out of his pen from the flute to the double bass like an etching."

Weber's repeated reference to tone color is not surprising. In his workshop the coloristic elements of composition achieved great significance. As a master of instrumentation who revolutionized the role of the orchestra in dramatic music, Weber was bound to integrate vocal timbre and instrumental color in a novel manner into his scores. To the composer of *Der Freischütz*, instrumentation could not have been a matter of mere detail or routine. In a letter to his friend Liebich (1818) Weber makes this revealing statement: "There is nothing that I consider of secondary importance. In art there is no such thing as a secondary matter."

A direct line leads from Gluck and Weber to Wagner, not only in the development and reform of the music drama but also in the technique of its planning and building. Wagner, too, stresses the total approach: "The new form of dramatic music must display the unity of a symphony and of a symphony movement. This we can accomplish by reaching for the whole drama in an inward connection, not by engulfing individual parts only." And as Wagner shows at length, if unity is to be achieved, the dramatic work with all its details must be conceived as a whole.

MEMORY AND SYNTHESIS

Mozart has defined his approach to composition in words almost identical with those of Gluck: "Composed is everything, written not yet a single note." This remark, in a letter of December 30, 1780, turns up in all possible variations in Mozart's correspondence. As he explained, he became accustomed early to have "the whole in my head as it occurs in all parts." This type of brainwork remained his favorite mode of composing throughout his life. Leopold Mozart vehemently disapproved of his son's working procedure. Being a schoolmaster (though an excellent one and otherwise a pedagogue of the highest type), Leopold Mozart saw everything through the spectacles of a strict disciplinarian. Nagging, charging Wolfgang with "lack of industry," the systematic and precise father could see nothing but procrastination in such a method: no planning, hardly any sketching of the form. Nothing but the final manuscript!

But Wolfgang could not help it. His genius not only provided him with boundless inspiration but also dictated to him a specific and unchangeable approach to work. He did not, as his father complained, leave everything to the last minute. In reality, Wolfgang constantly composed. Thus he wrote to his father, July 31, 1778: "I am with music all the time, go around with it the whole day." Yet the mere final writing down into the score of already completed thoughts was to Mozart the least enjoyable part of composition. His phenomenal memory made it possible for him to postpone this job as long as possible. He felt that it was too mechanical, the least inspiring phase of his work. And what was worse, it consumed so much time—time which otherwise would have been available for new creative work. As Jahn shows[10] in his biography, such aversion to writing down his works lasted throughout Mozart's life.

The technique of total planning and elaborating was obviously not a monopoly of the masters whose own comments we have just perused. Other composers developed their technique of work to the astonishing degree where they could not only write scores without the aid of preceding sketches, but could also put their music directly into the different parts without relying on a full score. This procedure accounts for many cases in which music has come down to us in the form of individual parts only. If full scores are missing, it does not necessarily mean that they have been lost. They may never have been written! A conductor's score was not considered indispensable at a time when the composer himself was, as a matter of routine, personally in charge of the performance of his music, frequently directing a symphony, an oratorio or an opera from the clavier. The composer knew his score; only parts for the individual instrumentalists or singers were necessary. The historic European libraries contain many manuscripts not written by the composers themselves but assembled to a full score (often at a later time) from the individual parts and by foreign hands.

CONTRASTS AND EPISODES

Music happens in time. As the tonal events of the score unfold in sequence, the distribution of variety assumes added importance. Monotony is a mortal danger to the art work. The unbroken sameness of design, a similarity of acoustic experience decreases the listener's capacity for attention and may even kill his enjoyment of the music.

Variety then is an aesthetic postulate. Yet variety must not be superimposed or overdone. Too much diversity spoils the type of unity which is likewise an axiom of artistic planning. Too much of the best material leads to the unformed and chaotic. In every great art work, variety grows from its main features by way of logical development and organic contrast.

The composer achieves variety in his musical blueprint through the appropriate integration of contrasts and episodes. The painter distributes the chief contrasts of light and shadow on his canvas into the simultaneousness of visual form. But the composer must meet this problem of variety in a different manner: he has to apply his contrasts in time, placing them one after the other. In doing so, he employs contrasts to every feature of his composition.

Variety pertaining to the general organization of parts occupies the composer's attention at an early stage of synthesis. Such planning is concerned with contrast in the sequence of movements in a suite, sonata or symphony or with contrasts in the scenes and acts of an opera. Everywhere unity and variety are interdependent. They necessarily balance each other in a masterful blueprint.

Episodes are a chief means of obtaining the necessary contrast. This is so in the framework of every type of form. In contrast to the main theme, episodes are made up of material of lesser significance. They are transitory, leading from one section to another. In the fugue, the exposition of its theme is followed by an episodic transition to the next sequel of subject and answer. In dramatic music, the episodes are of particular necessity, taking on added meaning in the service of the stage action. Important episodes were often incorporated into the blueprint of an opera after the scheme had been designed in its main sections.[11]

The order of contrasts and episodes may be firmly pre-established in the composer's mind. Yet the planned sequence of sections does not necessarily coincide with the order in which the composer actually proceeds with his score. Beethoven, by his own admission, wrote entirely out of order. Yet the result is one of unsurpassable unity. The finished score appears in a state of being one, leaving no trace of the multiple and separate attempts that led to the impressive singleness of form. Originally Beethoven concluded the scherzo of the Fifth Symphony with an authentic cadence, with a typical sequence of dominant and tonic chords in the last measures. But this version was not satisfactory: Beethoven desired a different transition through which the contrast of the oncoming finale and its tremendous strength would produce an overpowering effect. The sketches aim repeatedly at such a solution. But it was not until a late stage of work that he succeeded in finding the famous transition.[12]

The homogeneity manifest in Mozart's opera scores would never betray the irregular procedure of composition to which they owe their existence. But the tightly knit sequence of such master scores as *Figaro, Don Giovanni, Magic Flute* came into being by the synthetic combination of independently written recitatives, arias and ensembles. The manuscript of *The Magic Flute* shows the role of instrumentation in the service of coloristic variety. Mozart had originally used trumpets and tympani not only in the overture but in the opening number of the first act as well. When he approached the composition of the brilliant scene in which the three Ladies-in-

Waiting of the Queen of Night appear, Mozart desired the color of trumpets and tympani as a specific effect of splendor for this moment. He erased the respective brass and percussion parts in the preceding number, obviously to save the color of such festive instrumentation for its more fitting place. In the manuscript of *Don Giovanni*, Mozart originally employed tympani and trumpets in addition to the other instruments which accompany Leporello's Catalogue Aria. But Mozart, for reasons corresponding to those in *The Magic Flute*, later eliminated the tympani and trumpets. Neither Leporello's aria nor Tamino's opening number (in *The Magic Flute*) required these instruments. Mozart felt that they were more essential in later scenes of both works—to produce the instrumental contrast of added splendor.

THE WINTER JOURNEY

In the entire song literature there is no more perfectly drawn cycle than Schubert's Winter Journey with its superb balance and poignant contrasts. It is of particular interest to observe that these songs were by no means composed in the order of lyric and dramatic episodes which we admire today. The sequel from "Good Night" to "The Organ Grinder" might have been in Schubert's mind as a final plan but it did not determine his approach to the composition of the individual songs. Here again, the unsurpassable unity of the music is an aftereffect. To achieve his end, Schubert did not follow the sequence as it appears in the original *Winter Journey* as written by its poet, Wilhelm Müller. The comparison of Müller's order with Schubert's version enables us to trace the composer's reasons for his changes: Schubert considered the contrasts which his own sequel of songs produces more effective in a primary musical sense. It is for such intrinsically tonal reasons that Schubert changed not only the succession of songs, but also individual verses and words.[13]

The two lists are self-explanatory. We see how Schubert follows Müller's order for the first five songs up to "The Water-Course." The greatest deviations from the original occur toward the end of the cycle. But the twenty-fourth song, "The Organ Grinder," concludes the poet's as well as the composer's sequel with a melancholy note.

THE WINTER JOURNEY: COMPARISON OF SEQUENCE

Poet Wilhelm Müller	Composer Franz Schubert
Good Night	Good Night
The Vane	The Vane
Frozen Tears	Frozen Tears
Benumbed	Benumbed
The Linden Tree	The Linden Tree
The Post	The Water-Course
The Water-Course	On the River
On the River	Looking Backward
Looking Backward	Will o' the Wisp
The Gray Head	Rest
The Raven	Spring Dreams
The Last Hope	Solitude
In the Village	The Post
The Stormy Morning	The Gray Head
Illusion	The Raven
The Guide-Post	The Last Hope
The Wayside Inn	In the Village
Will o' the Wisp	The Stormy Morning
Rest	Illusion
The Mock Suns	The Guide-Post
Spring Dreams	The Wayside Inn
Solitude	Courage
Courage	The Mock Suns
The Organ Grinder	The Organ Grinder

VOCAL FORMS

When the composer projects certain form types against a given text (or vice versa, if the composer adjusts a text to a chosen form idea), numerous problems are bound to occur. What should be accorded sovereignty, the musical form or the text? A history of the opera, of the oratorio, the cantata and of the art song could

e written on the basis of the various answers which composers
ave given to this problem in vocal composition throughout the
ges.

The study of the inner workshop of the song composer yields
isight into the struggle for pure vocal form. Schubert, Brahms,
Volf, Fauré—all these composers of song, no matter how different
ieir stylistic position and their linguistic expression, had in common
 glowing will to master their small forms, to control their laws
ithin the text and very often in spite of the text.

The song composer's approach to the so-called strophic form
nows the problem in its simpler state. Here he faces the task of
utting into music a repeated group of verses which the poet had
rdered according to a definite meter. In the strictest kind of
rophic Lied, the composer employs the same melody for different
anzas of the poem while he may also retain the same accompani-
lent. The editor's report[14] on Schubert's complete works reveals
ertain aspects of the composer's work on strophic songs. Schubert
sually wrote first a melody which would fit to the text of the
litial strophe. Next, he changed the melody for the sake of a
ifferent text in a later strophe. At this point, Schubert tested the
ecast melody: would its new shape also fit the first strophe? He
light then decide on a revised form—even if the original flash
emed more appropriate for the first strophe.

There are two autographs of Schubert's "Nähe des Geliebten."
he first version bears the composer's remark "gilt nicht." What did
ie composer consider "not valid"? After Schubert had written the
rst version, a second one occurred to him. In this new version,
chubert paid special attention to the third strophe of the poem.
: we read the verses of the poem, "Nähe des Geliebten," we note
ie great variety of pictures in its text. This could have led to
angerous diffusion in the composition. But Schubert, circumventing
ie peril, designed a simple melody only a few measures long.
his melody is a strong tonal reflection of the text as a whole. If
iis were not so, it could not be explained that every new strophe
f the Lied seems to say something new, although the notes are
he same. And so we understand why Schubert did not employ both
ersions individually wherever they best fitted the text. His art
itellect told him that the total effect would be enhanced by the

unity resulting from the use of a single strophic form. Therefore he
abandoned the original idea even though it seemed to suit the text of
the first strophe, and finally chose what corresponded ideally to
the wholeness of the vocal form.

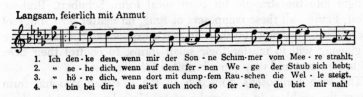

Langsam, feierlich mit Anmut

1. Ich den - ke dein, wenn mir der Son - ne Schim - mer vom Mee - re strahlt;
2. „ se - he dich, wenn auf dem fer - nen We - ge der Staub sich hebt;
3. „ hö - re dich, wenn dort mit dump - fem Rau - schen die Wel - le steigt.
4. „ bin bei dir; du sei'st auch noch so fer - ne, du bist mir nah!

EXAMPLE 20

The strophic design is obviously not always the most fitting
musical expression for all song texts. Many considerations can
oppose strophic treatment. But it is in their employment of this
form with its limitations that the great masters of the Lied showed
their superb achievements. "I prefer my small songs to my big
ones," said Brahms referring to his ability to express a maximum
of thought within a minimum of measures. It was an accomplishment of which he was proud—as an artist and as a craftsman.

In the greater vocal scores of Brahms, the idea of form guided
the main approach to composition. His desire to submit to the
sovereignty of the primarily tonal design could lead to an extreme
position where the composer took far-reaching liberties with
the interpretation of the poet's text. This is illustrated by Brahms'
choral score, the "Song of Destiny." The beautiful "Schicksalslied"
by Hölderlin evokes in its opening verses the serenity of the Elysian
spirits. The section that follows (polyphonically developed) is a
pessimistic commentary on the fate of all human beings: man is
doomed to fall down into the unknown abyss. . . .

But Brahms did not accept—tonally—this hopeless ending of the
poet. Instead, he designed an epilogue in which death is followed by
transfiguration. This postlude recalls, in the hopeful key of C major,
the Elysian music of the introduction in E-flat major. We do not
have to interpret the composer's organization of the text and
music as an optimistic contradiction of the sad ending of the poem.
But his arrangement obviously serves the idea of form: it gives the
whole "Song of Destiny" the appearance of a great A-B-A scheme

in which placid and tranquil corner sections afford a lyric contrast to the drama expressed in the middle part.

In extreme cases, the text becomes for certain composers almost a pretext for writing music. The score lives completely on its own momentum, the development follows its independent laws. Evading altogether the dictatorship of the word, the composer is guided by tones alone.

THE PROGRAM

On the crossroads of music and the other arts, there originated early in history a specific blend of tone and extramusical thought. Ideas underlying certain music were associatively derived from sources beyond the tonal realm. They frequently emanated from Arts and Letters, leading to a type of composition which has been characterized as program music. But this term covers a rather wide range of working methods.

Program music may imply simply the type of descriptive composition which tries to tell a subject matter in tones. This kind of music had already reached a highly developed state at the end of the Middle Ages. The previously discussed medieval scores of Jannequin contain a program: they portray the song of birds, still more realistically the street noise in Paris or wars with their battles. Each of Jannequin's scores, conjuring up idyll or terror, was followed by a whole literature of imitations. In most of these attempts, a text appears the indispensable means to the listener's comprehension of the program. The meaning of the music is carried by the underlying words; the music always originated on the basis of the text. A further step in the evolution of program music is the disappearance of the text from the score. This occurs when the program becomes an integral part of instrumental music. If verbal substance appears at all in the score, it is prefixed to the music as a mere commentary explaining what the music is all about. In such cases, the text still sets the course of the music. Often it decides the form-scheme of the score, not only in broad outlines, but also in countless details.

Johann Kuhnau introduced certain of his scores with such prefaces in which he clarified the programmatic implications of his music. Without these commentaries, Kuhnau felt, the meaning of his music would remain unintelligible. We readily understand such a claim from a perusal of Kuhnau's *Musical Representation of Some Biblical Histories in Six Sonatas for the Clavier*. These scores are important also as the first sonatas written for keyboard and were published in Leipzig, 1700.[15] Here, the composer embarked on the task of tonal illustrations of familiar biblical scenes such as the cure of Saul through David's performance on the harp or the fight between David and Goliath.

How can these stories be told in tones? Kuhnau answered the question by expressing certain aspects of the action in naïve tone-painting. For instance: a movement called La tristezza ed il furore de Ré describes Saul's sadness and madness, and the transformation of the king's melancholy by means of music. Saul is insane. This can be illustrated musically through an "insane" passage which no normal composer would write, namely a parallel progression of fifths:

EXAMPLE 21

Since every contemporary musician knew that such fifths were considered an elementary error, he could also be expected to grasp immediately the programmatic inference of the music pointing to the insanity of the king.

From this somewhat humorous example, we learn that Kuhnau did not organize his tonal material according to an intrinsically musical logic, but to an extramusical one: what would be non-sensical according to the laws of musical theory, takes on sensible meaning through the specific association of tones with their under-lying thoughts. The listener must actively participate in the musical play with double connotation of its tones and thoughts. He must bridge the gap between the music and whatever it is supposed to portray programmatically.

In the biblical sonata, *The Combat between David and Goliath,* Kuhnau furnished his score with the following detailed program:

1) Goliath's bravado
2) Fear and prayer of the Israelites
3) David's courage, his ardent desire to destroy the enemy's arrogance, and his faith in God
4) The combat, the stone is hurled, and Goliath is overthrown
5) The flight of the Philistines and their pursuit
6) Triumph of the Israelites, the women's fanfares in David's honor
7) General dancing and rejoicing

The course of the music is directed in each of these movements by its underlying story. In the second of the pieces, the German Protestant chorale, "Aus Tiefer Noth," expresses the supplication of the old Hebrews—an obvious anachronism! But it served the purpose well; Kuhnau expected his listeners to know the choral melody and therefore to understand immediately his message.

This then is psychological program music: a working method which applies the associative forces of the listener's mind to the composer's specific goal. Such a technique has developed greatly since the days of Kuhnau, but its intrinsic devices have remained essentially the same.

In another noteworthy and slightly earlier example of psychological program music, pictures take the place of a text: the original edition of Heinrich Ignaz Biber's Solo Sonatas for Violin (1681) is decorated with small woodcuts. These pictures show scenes from the New Testament—such as the Annunciation, Birth, Crucifixion and Resurrection—which had inspired Biber's composition. Our Illustration XVII shows the "Crucifixion," a praeludium of sadness and meditation. With sighing intervals, the violin intones its complaint; poignant dissonances evoke the scene on the cross. We note that the composer has modified the normal tuning of the violin for the fourth string and lowered the E string a whole tone. Biber was the first composer to venture this device. Throughout all of these sonatas, he aimed at a reflection of those tone pictures which his subject had created in his soul. The composer was not concerned with realistic paintings; his scores are true psychological program music. In this sense, they clearly forecast a mode of composition which in a century-long evolution finally led to the stylistic position of the "impressionists."

THE POETIC IDEA

When Beethoven, more than a century after these early essays in psychological program music, created for his Pastoral the style which he himself characterized as "more expression of feeling than painting," he was not altogether conquering new land. His chief contribution is a classical grasp of the material in which all programmatic elements are resolved in the great idea of nature. Everywhere in Beethoven's blueprints, form emerges as the central factor. Even the expansive forces of his poetic ideas are subjugated by the power and purity of his form ideal. The classical drama of the Eroica, the summer day dream of the Pastoral reveal such poetic ideas in forms of purest music. The groundplans remain, at least in their fundamental conception, those of the classical symphony. Glorious conquests of poetic substance in the classical scheme are the piano sonata, Les Adieux, Op. 81, the three overtures to *Leonore* and the overtures to *Coriolanus* and *Egmont*.

Beethoven's *Egmont* overture anticipates and fulfills prophetically the possibilities of dramatic expression within the blueprint of the sonata movement. Its features, kept in the iron bondage of form, concentrate on the very core of Goethe's five-act drama. The overture starts with the strong lament of the people of the Netherlands, oppressed and enslaved by foreign tyrants. In the allegro section, revolution rages. A coda of tumultuous rejoicing in liberation concludes the work. Beyond his overwhelming tonal imagination, Beethoven's greatness and guidance to posterity lies here in a self-imposed confinement. The symphonic plan reveals the sovereignty of music. The concise dramatic expression immortalizes Egmont, the liberating hero.

The symphonic harvest of romantic seeds started in the autumn of classicism; the opening horn solo of Schubert's Seventh Symphony is an herald call of romanticism. The warm colors of an expressive brass, where even the trombones sing, the gentle romantic harmonies and their sighing suspensions and a slight loosening of form show the trend. The poetic factor becomes more and more entrenched, and the constructive factor loses its iron grip in the composer's workshop. In the romantic atmosphere, the purely abstract, the absolute conception of form is bound to assume a less important role. The composer's inspiration is nourished by extramusical sources in symphonic creation, too. Poetic ideas gradually take on more tangible content. Mendelssohn, Schumann, Weber and Spohr still tried to reconcile the romantic with the classical in their attempts to keep tone poetry behind the bars of traditional plans and cycles. The one-movement symphony and the four-movement symphony without break are typical products of the proverbial romantic conflict between form and content. Such works as Schumann's D Minor Symphony and Mendelssohn's Scotch Symphony preserve the traditional framework of a four-movement plan without interruption: "attaca" instructions at the end of the movements call for unbroken sequence of the main parts. Along with such steps toward a unification of the blueprint, there occur several changes in the symphonic structure such as alteration of the exposition and of the development. Mendelssohn blends the scherzo with the sonata form. In contrast to its vigorous predecessor (as Beethoven created it), the scherzo and other related types take on a sylphlike lightness. Pianissimo ensembles of woodwinds, embedded in tender brass sonorities, compete with the light and fast bowing of the strings in the irresistible spriteliness of romantic instrumentation—fairyland is entered through the middle movements of the symphony.

The scores of Weber and Spohr also show how tone poetry may benefit from the classical sonata-scheme. Still under disguising titles, a truly new form dawns—the symphonic poem. In the final romantic metamorphosis, the classical structure is overthrown. The tables are turned. Not the form, as in Beethoven's inner workshop, but the poetic content triumphs in romantic music.

SYMPHONIC DRAMA WITHOUT WORDS

The great event in the evolution of orchestral program music during the early nineteenth century was the appearance of Berlioz's Symphonie Fantastique. It is a score incredibly audacious for 1830, the time of its completion—only three years after the death of Beethoven. In this work Berlioz blended the psychological and the naturalistic factors of program music into a unique style which he interpreted in his memoirs. A characteristic instance of his new

approach is the third movement of the Fantastique, The Scene i
the Country. Berlioz intended "to render the distant roll of th
thunder in the middle of a peaceful atmosphere. This is not don
in childish pleasure, aiming at imitation of the majestic noise. O
the contrary, the deep peacefulness (of this country scene) is mor
intensely emphasized by way of this contrast." In other words, th
naturalistic imitation of the thunder on the tympani serves her
only as a means to the poetic end of tranquillity and has no purpos
in itself. The written word—the program attached to the score a
verbal comment—fills the gap between the musical expression an
the dramatic thought. As Berlioz admits, in reference to anothe
of his program symphonies, Harold in Italy:

The author knows only too well that music cannot substitute for word
or pictures. Hence, he never had the absurd idea to express (in tones'
abstract or moral qualities, but only emotions or moods. He did no
want to paint mountains—he simply wanted to suggest the style an
the melodic form which pertains to the songs of their inhabitants or th
impressions which the view of these important massives evoke.

The underlying "story" of a programmatic work may be derivec
from the composer's own imagination or it may stem entirely from
a work of Arts and Letters. What is the influence of such a program
on the groundplan of the music? When Berlioz sketched his own
scenario for the Symphonie Fantastique, he retained the classica
frame for this score of hyper-romantic emotionalism and feveris
dreams. His approach to the "instrumental drama without words"
is based on leit-instruments and leit-melodies. Berlioz called the
latter idée fixe, by which he meant a thematic token calling for ä
fixed association of thoughts tied to a frequently recurring theme
Thus the idée fixe functions as a psychological signal—ready to
direct the listener to a definite meaning within the tone poetic
program.

Liszt later transplanted this symphonic-dramatic technique of
Berlioz from France to Germany. What Liszt called the symphonic
poem finally became the form par excellence of all orchestral
program music. The blueprint of such scores as his Torquato
Tasso is a typical example of a poetic program condensed into the
one-movement form—with subdivisions suggested by the poem.

The treatment of the leit-melody here shows how a principal theme lends itself to a constantly changing expression—ranging all the way from the hero's despair to his awakened hope and final triumph.

The drama of the symphony also speaks through the eternal symbols of tension and relaxation, tonally embodied in the cyclic curve. Such a symphonic curve may start in a dark and tragic minor mode, gradually leading up to the triumphant finale of a liberating major. The old Latin message, *per aspera ad astra*, is the poetic connotation in works like Beethoven's Fifth and Ninth, Brahms' First, Tchaikovsky's Fourth, Liszt's Torquato Tasso and in many other romantic scores which all lead "through darkness to the stars." In the sense of Schumann's definition, these symphonies are finale symphonies. All threads of the preceding music lead to the last movements. This design also underlies the symphonies of Gustav Mahler. Here, too, the finale holds the key to the comprehension of the entire work. The message of the symphony emerges in retrospect, be it through the resurrection scene of the Second, the angelic idyll of the Fourth, the happy rondo of the Seventh or the "Farewell" in the Song of the Earth.

THREE TIMES FAUST

Few works of literature have been set to music more frequently than Goethe's drama, *Faust*. Composers of different generations and nations have interpreted in tones the poetic substance of this medieval legend. It has been turned by Berlioz into an oratorio, by Gounod into an opera. Schumann wrote Scenes from Faust, for soli, chorus and orchestra. Of particular interest is the manner in which numerous composers have organized and expressed this literary work in the symphonic medium. The following synopsis of three treatments of the Faust material on the part of Wagner, Liszt and Mahler brings to light important aspects of its symphonic organization:

I   Wagner: A Faust Overture

Wagner's struggle with the poetic substance forced the composer into repeated revisions of the original plan. The final form excludes the figure of Gretchen and concentrates on

Faust in his solitude. A bleak symphonic picture is the result. "Life is a curse and death a longed for rest"—this Faustian motto—appears as the key to Wagner's approach.

II Liszt: A Faust Symphony

Liszt's symphony with choral finale is a tableau of the three main figures: Faust, Gretchen, Mephistopheles. The following synopsis indicates the relation between symphonic form and dramatic content:

Faust movement: a lento of solitude and skepticism
an allegro agitato of aspiration and activity
an andante of belief and ideals
a grandioso of the scholar's search, of his accomplishments and pride

Gretchen movement: a gentle woodwind music of the flutes and clarinets reflects Gretchen's lovable qualities
a combination of the Faust and Gretchen themes expresses the fulfillment of their love

Mephistopheles movement: the devilish spirit of negation satirizes and botches the Faust themes of ideals

Epilogue: the vocal setting of the "chorus mysticus" concluding the Goethe drama, sung by tenor solo and male chorus: "All transient earthly things are but symbols"

III Mahler: Eighth Symphony

Mahler's symphony is based upon two heterogeneous texts. The Latin hymn, "Veni Creator Spiritus," underlies the first part of his symphony. The second part comprises the final scene of Goethe's *Faust* which in its wealth of moods suggests a tonal kaleidoscope in a great alfresco frame. Mahler chose this most difficult task, namely a composition of Goethe's verses complete from the scene of the Anchorites to the "chorus mysticus" (which already Liszt had chosen for the vocal finale of his otherwise purely instrumental Faust Symphony).

Mahler's blueprint aims at a strict parallelism between his symphonic and Goethe's scenic design. This is accomplished within the framework of the traditional classical groundplan: first movement; adagio; scherzo (fragmentary); finale (starting with the appearance of "Mater gloriosa"). Yet it is the final verses of Goethe's drama that gave Mahler the tone-poetic clue

for his symphony of love: "The woman-soul e'er leads upward
and on!"

We realize from the three examples that none of these composers
aimed at an all-embracing interpretation of the poem. Their music
establishes only certain points of contact with the literary substance. Common to all three *Faust* scores is the fact that they are
intelligible in terms of musical logic alone; they can be appreciated
apart from the inspiring text.

TITLES

Form and content of his music have guided the composer's search
for the proper titles of his scores. Already a denomination such as
sonata or symphony contains a certain characterization of the
content of the work.[16] Trio or quartet as titles of chamber music
simultaneously indicate the performing ensemble as well as the
number of participants. The same procedure prevails in vocal
music. And the differentiation between terms such as duo and duet
or trio and terzetto also points to differences in instrumental and
vocal ensembles respectively. A trio is a chamber music work; a
terzetto is a vocal number in an opera or an oratorio.

Yet in the specific tie-up with an underlying program (be it
psychological or naturalistic) the choice of a title presents the
imagination of the composer with a different kind of a problem.
The nomenclature becomes, in a measure, also an exponent of the
composer's style. It often gives away, anticipatingly, a taste of his
creative approach.

Couperin points to the tie-up between the title and content in
his Collection of Piano Pieces:

In the composition of my pieces, I always had a definite objective before
my eyes. The occasions . . . which suggested such an objective were of
various natures, yet the titles of the pieces correspond to them . . . The
pieces pertaining to these titles were portrayals which were considered
rather good likenesses, and most of the advantageous titles were to
express the amiability of the originals rather than the success of my
copies.

Couperin appears here as a champion of the pictorial, aphoristic
and witty statement in tones. The inspiration of some of his pictures

were the charming ladies of the French court, some of whom were his pupils. Other examples of Couperin's titles refer to abstract subjects such as the French national virtues and faults. Couperin's playful portrayal of concrete and abstract subjects on the keyboard points to a working method where, as the composer himself explained, the title determines the shaping of the music. The title guides the course of the work in the sense of an a priori given idea from which the composer approaches the total form and all details.

Frequently the situation is reversed: first the music and second the caption. The title may be only an afterthought which follows the completion of the score. The composer often finds himself in a conflict as to the proper formulation of titles:

I have arranged the Nachtstücke—what do you think of calling them: No. 1, Funeral Procession; No. 2, Droll Company; No. 3, Nightly Carousel; No. 4, Round with Solo Voices? While I was composing I kept seeing funerals, coffins and unhappy despairing faces; and when I had finished and was trying to think of a title, the only one that occurred to me was Funeral Fantasia. I was so much moved by the composition that the tears came to my eyes.

Schumann, in these words to Clara, asks her advice concerning the choice of headings for his completed music. Elsewhere he explains, however, why he considers titles desirable at all: "There are secret states of the soul where a hint of the composer through words can lead to a faster understanding and must be gratefully accepted." Yet Schumann makes it unmistakably clear that no title can ever add to the quality of the music itself. And he suggests an easy test: one has only to leave out the titles in order to examine the effects and value of the musical product. Yet the programmatic intent of a considerable part of Schumann's music remains beyond doubt. Fanciful titles such as Carnival, Scenes from Childhood, Forest Scenes, Bird as Prophet, Kreisleriana point to Schumann's romantic brand of psychological program music. Often, as in Carnival, the program is hidden in mystification while the tonal play achieves an absolute beauty far beyond the need of a nomenclature. The stylistic position of Schumann as a composer of program music is idealistic: he creates his scores quite differently from the naturalistic musician who relentlessly unveils the essence of his program. This latter type is represented best by the programmatic works of Liszt and his scores of decorative realism. Liszt captures his content through the pictorial craft of naturalistic imitation and tonal suggestion.

The relationship between title and tonal content presents a specific problem in the workshop of the "absolute" musician. Due to his stylistic position, he will frequently consider a title a mere superimposition on his music—an extraneous feature, forcing upon the work and its listener a definite extramusical association. But this contradicts the intent of the composer who wishes to remain "absolutely" free and sovereign in his play of beautiful tonal sensations. The composer of this type of music is apt to avoid all romantic nomenclature and resorts to headings which are mere generalities.

In the light of these observations, it is not surprising that Brahms, whenever confronted with the task of christening his music, found himself in a dilemma. Already as a young and romantic composer (1854), he wanted to give a work the long and involved title of *Leaves from the Diary of a Musician Edited by the Young Kreisler*. But Joachim convinced Brahms that such pseudonyms and mystifications had become hackneyed. As late as 1880 Brahms consulted with Elisabeth Herzogenberg: "Do you know a better title than Two Rhapsodies for the Pianoforte? The alternative would be Klavierstücke, a term which betrays nothing." The advice of the friend was to let it go with the "foggy dress" which Brahms gladly accepted. In the same year, Brahms asked his friends Deiters and Scholz for a more attractive name than Academic Festival Overture and a "prettier title" than the Tragic Overture. Yet, as we know, nothing "prettier" suited the heavy-hearted man. Referring to some of his latest works, the piano pieces, Op. 116 and 117, Brahms was "not clear whether to name them Monologues or Improvisations." He was finally persuaded to abandon both titles and chose Fantasias for Op. 116 and Intermezzi for Op. 117. The scores, Op. 118 and 119, he called in a more neutral fashion, Klavierstücke. As always, Brahms preferred the understatement. He would rather say too little than too much in order not to steer the listener's imagination into any pictorial sidetracks.

CHAPTER TWELVE

MANUSCRIPTS

> The music of certain composers
> resembles their handwriting: diffi-
> cult to read, curious to look at,
> yet once you understand it, it is
> as though it could not have been
> otherwise.
>
> SCHUMANN

CREATIVE sources spring from inspiration. They pass the river bed of elaboration, gradually grow through the tributaries of new ideas and finally flow into the manuscript as the last basin of synthesis. The manuscript contains the ultimate resolution of all preceding work, of all vacillation and struggle. This is true, at least, for many composers: what has been decided in the final manuscript has been decided for good. With few exceptions, once the handwritten score has been taken to the publisher, it is on its fateful way to the world for better or worse.

The study of manuscripts has for a long time occupied only a select group of scholars who realize that no note-print, no beautiful edition of engraved music could ever substitute for the living impression which the manuscript alone conveys. In the composer's workshop the study of the manuscript logically follows the study of the sketches. The handwritten text contributes its share to the understanding of the creative conquest; it shows how every detail

274

finds its proper place and setting in the totality of the written work.

"The music of certain composers resembles their handwriting: difficult to read, curious to look at, yet once you understand it, it is as though it could not be otherwise. The handwriting belongs to the thought, and the thought to the character." These succinct words of Schumann in a letter to Henrietta Voigt point to an issue for which our time is slowly acquiring a deeper understanding.

The manuscripts of masters—with all their unique qualities which Schumann so well formulated—had particular fascination for Brahms. He collected, as precious treasures in his workshop, the beloved scores of other composers. The most outstanding pieces in his possession were Mozart's Symphony in G Minor, Haydn Quartets, two sheets of music showing on the front page Beethoven's, on the back page Schubert's handwriting, various songs and dances by Schubert, numerous sketches by Beethoven and the first version of Schumann's Symphony in D Minor. Brahms also owned—of all works—Wagner's prelude to *Tristan und Isolde*.[1]

Not all manuscripts lend themselves unconditionally to a study of the creative process. Some of them seem to hide whatever has taken place before the final script: no trace of creative struggle is visible. What preceded is the composer's secret. Now that the work is finished, it appears in objective signs before the reader—a clear-cut score for the performer, like the blueprint for a building or a bridge, directing the architect or engineer how to proceed.

MANUSCRIPTS FOR PERFORMANCE

A cross section through the manuscripts of great composers indicates that their final texts fall into different groups. There are Bach's scores for his personal use only: they were obviously written for the purpose of performances which he might have believed to be ephemeral. In contrast, there are those copies which he wrote out with utmost care, with diligence in every detail. Finally, there are manuscripts which were not penned by Bach himself; they bear either the handwriting of his former pupil and second wife, Anna Magdalena, or of his older children and pupils. For Bach's home was a true musical workshop where he composed as a master craftsman, aided by his family and apprentices. Everyone in this group of music makers was adept in the external skills of copying or arranging; some became truly original also in the invention of tonal products.

Johann Sebastian Bach himself was a phenomenal note writer. From early youth on, he had to copy out music for all kinds of occasions and performances. What hard work the sheer physical side of this task involved! And not only did he have to copy out his own compositions in all required parts, but frequently those of other composers whose works he performed. He wrote until his eyes and hands hurt. Young Bach did not seem to mind it; a great deal could be learned that way. After all, copying meant also tracing another master's work in every musical line. Already in his early days in the village of Ohrdruf, Bach copied, by moonlight, the organ book by Johann Pachelbel[2] which was withheld from him, but the knowledge of which he deemed priceless. A long life followed, a life of writing, writing, writing! In his old age, with diminishing eyesight, Bach was forced to copy numerous lengthy parts of his passions and cantatas. In the last three years of his life, almost blind, he had to depend on the assistance of his various apprentices.

These varying circumstances surrounding Bach's lifework account for the lack of uniformity in the master's manuscripts. Yet in spite of all external difficulties—of the pressure of work and daily toil in his duties as a practical musician—many of his manuscripts are marvels of calligraphy. There is the beautiful manuscript of the *St. Matthew Passion*—every line bespeaks the undivided devotion which guided Bach throughout the composition of this work. The manuscript is a precious achievement of creative genius as well as of a craftsman's skill. Not only the structural blueprint is ingenious, but also its manifestation in notes and staves. All parts are weighed and balanced to the smallest detail. It is an aesthetic experience to see with one's own eyes how the organizing hand of this superb score writer has integrated the various lines and ornaments into the texture of the great score.[3] The words of the Evangelist are written entirely with red ink. The orchestral accompaniment of these spiritual passages is entrusted to the string quartet only; Bach felt that the tone color of other instruments was too material. We grasp his simple but irresistible symbolism: the color of the script, as well as the tone color of the instruments reflects the inner meaning of this music. Aside from these recitatives of the Evangelist and a few other places, only the choral "O lamb of God," in the opening chorus, is written with red ink.

Yet the *St. Matthew Passion* is not the only score in which Bach's meticulously written pages display a striking contrast to the erratic and irregular manuscripts of other great masters. In the Brandenburg Concertos, bar lines are drawn with a ruler, notes are placed and spaced with the skill of an engraver. These are copies ready for practical use, perfectly suited for immediate performance.

With his numerous activities, Bach could not turn every manuscript into a show piece of beautiful handwriting. In the *Christmas Oratorio*, the script is rapidly flowing, giving the impression that the score was written hurriedly in an attempt to have it ready for the approaching holidays. Hence, various corrections became necessary after the completion of the score, pointing to a procedure of revising which otherwise was not a favorite with Bach. To the student of his manuscripts, however, these corrections are a welcome encore. They indicate the parallelism of traits in writing and creating—Bach's desire for utmost clarity. The whole manuscript is one single striving toward precision. Where changes are inevitable, Bach scratches out notes, adding letters to keep the order unmistakably clear. If letters do not suffice, he writes short comments further clarifying the meaning. Lucidity first! Such thoroughness aims at clearness at any price—even at the price of pedantry.[4]

Bach had to be very economical with paper, using every page to the end. A half-used sheet was a luxury he could ill afford. If a composition did not fill the whole page, he started the next work on the same leaf, immediately following the preceding composition. The paper, of which he had so little and which he was so eager to conserve, was thin, and frequently the ink was too thick for it. This led, in spite of Bach's great care in writing, to many blots and other little mishaps. Normally, he used a goose feather; a special pen served him for the ruler-drawn bar lines. In the "Coffee" Cantata, a rapid pen frequently supplied too much ink. Sometimes Bach pressed hard on his goose pen, and the ink would eat through the paper and cause tears. It happened that in the eagerness of writing, the ink bottle toppled over, leaving a large ink blot.

The type of a most carefully hand-written score, ready for all practical needs, for rehearsing and performing, as we find it with Bach, is also represented by the manuscripts of Gluck. The two composers worked in opposite spheres—Bach in the church, Gluck in the theater. Their manuscripts, however, aim at the same goal of clarity. Reflecting the exactness of his reformatory demands in the performance of opera, the scores of Gluck are precise, unmistakably expressing the composer's intent. His innovations aim at the faithful execution of the music drama; rejecting all willfulness on the part of the singers, eliminating their extempores and embellishments. Only a meticulous score script could guarantee a conductor's enforcement of all these innovations. It is no accident that scripts of similar exactness are found with all composers who were related in spirit and purpose to Gluck's dramatic reforms—such masters as Mozart, Weber, Spontini, Verdi and Wagner.

OUTER AND INNER ORDER

When Mozart, in spite of his aversion to score writing, finally made up his mind to tackle this tedious task, he achieved in his manuscript the elegance and gracefulness which truly reflects the important traits of his music. Classical order is the key te of these pages, too. The extreme clarity of his spirit, the charm and facility of his personality are overwhelmingly reflected in his manuscripts. Everywhere, Mozart's genius is integrated in the form and content of the score's picture. Certain of his manuscripts are true show pieces of calligraphy.

Like Bach, Mozart included verbal directions in the music, addressed to the copyist (wherever such instructions were necessary). Mozart used almost exclusively note paper of twelve or less staves. As we can easily see, this size did not suffice for the greater ensembles and scenes as they occur in his various operas. The limited space forced him, when he did not have enough room for his instrumentation, to write on special leaves the parts for wind instruments, and most of these sheets have disappeared in the course of time. Thus, in the scores of *Figaro, Don Giovanni* and *Cosi Fan Tutte,* most deplorable gaps occurred. In Mozart's letter of July 20, 1782 to his father, we read about trouble with the score of *The Abduction from the Seraglio*:

. . . The opera was performed just as you now have it; but here and there the parts for trumpets, drums, flutes and clarinets and the Turkish music are missing, because I could not get any music paper with so many lines. Those parts were written out on extra sheets which the copyist has probably lost, for he could not find them. The first act, when I was sending it somewhere or other—I forget where—unfortunately fell in mud which explains why it is so dirty.

Other manuscripts escaped this fate and are preserved in their entirety from the first to the last note. When composing *Idomeneo*, Mozart had at his disposal paper of fourteen and sixteen lines which enabled him to write out in full the orchestration of such large ensembles as the double chorus No. 5 or the final chorus.

There are autographs of Mozart which contain pages obviously not written by his own hand. Others are incomplete: pages are missing and sometimes important sections are irreplaceably lost. Again certain scores were written at great speed because of an approaching deadline. Slips of the pen and minor errors due to hastiness and oversight occur occasionally. But these mistakes are obvious and easily corrected. The scores of *Idomeneo*, *The Magic Flute* and *The Impresario* are completely preserved. As to other opera scores, such as *The Marriage of Figaro*, *Don Giovanni*, *Così fan tutte* and *The Abduction from the Seraglio*, parts of them are irretrievably lost.[5] This is partly due to the fate of the manuscripts which did not remain in the hands of one owner after Mozart's death. Smaller and larger portions fell from one collector to another . . .[6]

In Beethoven's manuscripts, genius does not appear orderly in an external sense. There is intrinsic order in his thoughts, but not in their manifestation in the notescript. The manuscripts bespeak the monumental struggle of creation—the general impression already conveyed by Beethoven's sketches is repeated in his manuscripts. It is the impression of a slow conquest of the tonal material which Beethoven builds, revises, corrects, until finally everything is put together and the whole emerges as a perfect unity, as though it would have been cast from one single mold. Sometimes Beethoven's notes are large and written far apart, with no concern for space and paper. At other times, they are small and follow so closely together that the page seems insufficient to hold the overwhelming stream of thoughts. Pen and pencil are used alternately. Certain manuscripts are written with a pencil only, perfunctorily, with the speed of the wind. Often Beethoven used a fine pen point. Nevertheless, his script is usually thick and broadly expanded. He scratches out and combines, writes above and below, with black or red pencil. At the last stage of writing on the manuscript, the eraser becomes as important a tool as the pen or pencil. But this eraser does not always work as it should, and Beethoven resorts to a razor blade or even a knife, using it so frequently and strongly that holes appear in the paper. At this point the damage may be beyond repair: whole pages have to be pasted over with sealing wax. Again and again the score becomes marked with such deeply interfering changes. Whole parts are transferred and corrected; whole pages are destroyed and replaced. Ink blots, egg spots, burnt spots appear. But what does it matter? Only the music counts.

More and more, Beethoven examines, retests the score with the pitiless self-criticism so characteristic of his strife toward the highest ideal of perfection. Nature endowed him with the indefatigable perseverance of the creator, but, at the same time, denied him the patience and external calm of a neat note writer. While one would not compare the collected order of Bach's manuscripts with the creative excitement manifest in those of Beethoven, both masters have in common the desire for utmost clarity through devices beyond the employment of mere notes. They use all means auxiliary to the note script to direct the reader as clearly as possible: they resort to gigantic notes, to additional remarks with pencil, to numbers and, last but not least, to footnotes. Beethoven particularly relies upon a system of special signs and a glossary of clarifying phrases. Words like "aus" (out), "bleibt" (remains) and "mellieur" (better) appear. In order not to be misunderstood, Beethoven notes at the beginning of the molto adagio in the String Quartet in A Minor, Op. 132: "NB: this piece always has a B natural, never as usual B flat." The warning refers to the *Sacred Thanksgiving to Deity of a Convalescent, in the Lydian Mode.* Comments of this kind are frequently communications for Beethoven's copyist.

COMPOSER AND COPYIST

When the *Missa Solemnis* was about to be printed, Beethoven sent the score from Vienna to his publisher Schott in Mainz and enclosed a list of corrections and apologies in his letter (January 26, 1825):

The old score was too messy to send you. But this one has been gone over most carefully. Truly not a small pain with a copyist who does not understand what he writes—and therefore I put in new pages for what was written worst, from which you can see what sort of a copyist I now have. That guy is an arch-Bohemian, a gangster and does not understand one.

Was the thus complimented Wolanek, the copyist from Czechoslovakia, really such a bad person? He had succeeded a man with the name of Schlemmer, a loyal soul whom Beethoven considered his best copyist. But when Schlemmer died, Beethoven had great difficulties in finding a good substitute. What he needed was a musician who could not only read his handwriting (considered to be hieroglyphics by the average copyist) but one who would also be able to stand Beethoven's terrific outbursts of temper. Under such circumstances, the task of being a copyist for the demoniacal genius was certainly not the easiest.

But Wolanek was a man of philosophical resignation. He tried to "retain his smile at the disagreeable behavior" of the composer, reminding him that "in the ideal world of tones, so many dissonances already exist—is it any wonder that there are some in the real world?" Beethoven was not willing to take such lessons from his copyist, and he flew into a volcanic rage: "Such a gangster who robs one of his money, and who perhaps expects one to bestow compliments upon him. Instead of this, one pulls his donkeylike ears." And somewhere else, the composer addresses his copyist:

Dirty scribbler! Stupid guy! Do correct your mistakes caused through ignorance, haughtiness, cockiness and stupidity. This suits you better than to try to teach me, which is rather as though a sow would teach Minerva. . . . Already yesterday and still earlier, it was decided not to permit you to write for me any longer.

Not every copyist was a Wolanek. Beethoven found, in crucial times, helpers who stuck to their difficult job and suffered through the tirades and curses of their employer as though they felt the history-making implications of their service. It seems as though there were always musicians who undertook this ungrateful but indispensable assignment of copying music for a greater mind, and thus contributed their share to art.

Handel, in his London years, depended on the services of a copyist who was familiar with all of the idiosyncrasies of his manuscripts. This faithful and capable musician, Johann Christoph Schmidt, had come like Handel himself from Germany to England and secured his place in history by knowing how to deal with innumerable problems and ramifications in his master's manuscripts and how to make them ready for the world. Under these favorable circumstances, Handel indulged in ample use of all sorts of abbreviations, his so-called "Faulenzer" (the lazy man's way of writing). Handel, the genius of industry as well as of inventiveness, need not be defended against his own charge of laziness. But it is obvious that he was able to accomplish much more through such time and energy saving devices. His abbreviations refer to many features of the score, for instance to parts doubled by other voices. They also refer to instrumental scores which Handel did not bother to write out—except in the principal part. If instruments reinforced the vocal parts, he would merely indicate his intention with an opening note. We face here the type of manuscript that the composer has written only for the preliminary team work between himself and his well tested personal copyist. It was up to the amanuensis to prepare certain features of the score for performance and print. Neither Handel nor Beethoven was able to get along with a routine copyist who merely traced the tonal pictures without hearing them inwardly in actual sound. The manuscripts of Handel and Beethoven display indeed a decided contrast to the exactness which Bach or Mozart demanded of their scores.

Wagner, like Mozart, detested the burden of final manuscript writing and the painstaking elaboration which a large work required. With the sketches, he could proceed economically, writing on two staves only, "in pencil, illegibly upon individual leaves" and, as he further accused himself, "incurably confused—so that no one except myself could find his bearings." In 1854, he asked Liszt for "a human being who would be able to make a clean score out of these wild pencil sketches." But there was no way out: "The final writing of *Rheingold* murders me! I lose a lot of time which I could preciously use elsewhere. Besides, so much writing unnerves me very much—it makes me sick." Never at a loss to find others at his service, Wagner had in the roster of his copyists no less a musician than Hans Richter, the great conductor. His task required the capacity to read those enigmatically sketched pages of his master's writing, to know Wagner's complex procedure. The following request in a letter of June 17, 1870 from the master to his apprentice is typical:

I have some work for you. I must make a birthday present to the King of Bavaria. For this purpose, I thought of the copy of the first act with prelude of the *Götterdämmerung*. . . . Often, I am not cautious enough and give only two systems for the orchestra, where three to four systems would facilitate the record very much. You would have the liberty of changing that so that the whole looks like something.

INSTRUMENTATION

Like all tools and materials in the composer's workshop, so tone color too is best understood in the historic perspective of its different functions. This is so because constant changes have occurred throughout the centuries in the method and manner in which composers have applied color and hues, light and shade to the tone rows of their musical scores.

In its technical realization, the application of color to tone is intimately connected with the craft of instrumentation—with the task of distributing music among the various instruments of an ensemble which the composer has chosen for a particular work. To that end, the composer prescribes in his manuscript an individual part for each player. The score is the sum total of these parts. It is put together in such a way that what sounds simultaneously can at a glance be read together and ordered according to its synchronized meaning in performance.

Yet such a state of affairs in the composer's workshop is a relatively new accomplishment. Instrumentation in our modern sense began only after vocal polyphony had reached its zenith—at the turning point from the sixteenth to the seventeenth century. The meaning of this statement is readily understood if we look at the title pages of scores from this period and find such directions as the Italian "buono da cantare e sonare," or the German "zu singen und auf Instrumenten zu gebrauchen." The English meaning of these instructions indicates that the music in such scores could be either sung or played. This ties in with our knowledge of the performing practice in this time as it emerges from treatises, from pictures and other documentary sources.

The definite relationship between tone and color was obscure. An orchestra in our sense did not exist. There was no precise notation which would determine the role of instruments in a binding score script. Its absence corresponded to the practice of performance which treated the tonal material freely in regard to color and instrumentation. Hence the employment and grouping of instruments followed no preconceived scheme. The approach was an extemporaneous one: whoever was present played or sang. This resulted in a conglomerate instrumental make-up which was natural to musicians prior to the seventeenth century. If the vocal and instrumental forces were combined, the procedure was simple enough: the orchestra members mechanically doubled the parts of the singers. But with the decline of high polyphony in vocal art, the hitherto hidden tone qualities of the instruments were gradually discovered. Now musicians were ready to seek new and different timbres; they hearkened to the unfolding of specific orchestral tone values. A new differentiation of instrumental sonorities came to the fore.

Claudio Monteverdi appears as the first great reorganizer of the instrumental body. This pioneer of modern instrumentation was born in 1657, in a city destined for the making of superb instruments—in Cremona, the home of many generations of famous violin builders: Stradivarius, Amati and Guarnerius. Yet the full coloristic potentialities of the violin as the leading melodic instrument of the orchestra were not realized until Monteverdi augmented its compass from the third to the fifth position.[7] The accidental combinations of the older orchestra usually resulted in a prevalence of wind instruments. Since the seventeenth century, however, various members of the string family assumed increasing importance within the instrumental ensemble. The homogeneity of an instrumental group with strings as the nucleus permitted a part-writing of balance, a careful distribution of tonal weight to an extent which was previously conceivable only in vocal scores. In Monteverdi's opera, *Orpheus*, the sonorities of a specific orchestra in our modern sense are in evidence: for the performance of every scene those instruments were chosen which seemed most appropriate to the dramatic content. Variety of light and shade, of decoration and bareness was painted with distinguished skill and taste. The composer from Cremona preferred to call himself "Claudio Monteverdi Venetiano," and a Venetian artist he truly was: a colorist in music who painted his tone pictures in transparent hues and Venetian splendor like the great painters creating in the fair city of the Lagoons—Tintoretto, Titian and Paolo Veronese.

Viewing the task of instrumentation anew, Jean-Baptiste Lully (1632-1682) supplanted the Renaissance splendor of his forerunners with the baroque simplicity of his era. Such a development in the composer's workshop recalls the evolution of techniques in the painter's atelier. We see in the history of painting how Titian's multicolored palette was replaced by Rembrandt's somber colors of simple and strong contrasts. With the inborn sense of the Mediterranean artist for tone color, Lully contributed decisively, as Monteverdi did before him, to the development of instrumentation into an organized tonal craft. Gradually other masters raised orchestration to a level where it became truly an art of its own. The problem was no longer one of just putting an instrumental vestment around a given structure of tones. It was rather to hear tone and color as an entity. In a later phase of evolution, color appeared as an intrinsic element of the tonal invention. In such a role, color clarifies and characterizes the individual musical thought. Finally instrumentation emerged as that specific task of composition which requires the finest ear for the subtle and precise differentiation of all coloristic values.

Certain phases of this development can be further traced through artistic events of first magnitude in the French capital. Almost a century after Lully, Gluck fully integrated the instrumental factor into his epoch-making reforms of the music drama. In his preface to *Alceste* (composed in 1767, published in 1769) Gluck stated "that the instruments ought to be introduced in proportion to the degree of interest and passion in the words . . . and to be employed according to the dramatic property of their tone." Here, all tone color is derived from the drama, enhancing its action and interpreting the character of the main figures.

With instrumentation coming of age, it functioned more and more as a carrier of musical tectonics: joining in the teamwork of the other elements, tone color served in the building of the structure. It helped to distribute the weight and quantity in the score. With that aim in mind, the composer chooses a particular combination of instruments and selects them according to tone volume and sonority. Herein his distribution follows the laws of acoustics. Practical experience teaches the composer where quantity must be added or subtracted in order to increase or decrease the volume of the music. Such a technique, applied generally since the second half of the eighteenth century, is illustrated in the familiar case of Beethoven's Fifth Symphony, where the most powerful sonorities in the score, the trombones, are not used until the last movement. At their entry in the opening of the finale, extreme dynamic force is wanted and achieved by this obvious device of adding the three trombones to the sum total of the instruments. Here, Beethoven is not concerned with the individual color, but with the dynamic effect of all available orchestral power—from the piccolo flute down to the double basses. At the other extreme, the choice of instruments can aim at utmost pianissimo, then the scoring is suggested by those orchestral registers which can best express the tone qualities of softness and gentleness.

Next to such distribution of tonal weight, orchestration may serve to emphasize the inner structure of the score. Tonal light or shade stresses here a melodic line, there a harmony or a rhythm. By specific means of timbre, a section of a score may be brought to a prominent position or may be embedded in the accompaniment. A melody may be gently announced by a flute solo or by a blast of the trumpets. A theme may be played in unison or in full harmony by the whole orchestra. As all this happens, the orchestral instruments assume more and more an individual message expressing definite melodic values. We can trace, in the scores of the eighteenth century, the steps in the development of orchestration from the dynamic to the tectonic coloring. And only in the light of this historic evolution, can we understand the preface of Berlioz's *Traité d'Instrumentation,* the most important treatise on orchestration that ever came from the pen of a creative musician. Berlioz refers to an art of which "one knew nothing whatsoever at the beginning of the preceding century and the growth of which was fought even by the true friends of music approximately sixty years ago." Since Berlioz published his *Traité* in 1840, his statement implies that instrumentation proper has existed only since the last third of the eighteenth century. In the mature scores of Haydn and Mozart, there occurs characteristic solo writing for woodwinds, brass and percussion—a scoring which takes into account the possibilities and individualities of these instruments. Yet they are still far from saying things of their own as they do in the romantic music of the nineteenth century.

As everywhere, Beethoven appears also in the evolution of orchestration as one of the greatest innovators. He more than any of his predecessors invents his themes out of the very nature of every instrument. This is true of his early works, of his chamber music as well as of his symphonies. In the Septet, Op. 20, the scherzo is a typical horn theme. In the C Major Symphony, Op. 21, the first theme is a string theme, the second is a specific woodwind theme. In the opening of the Fifth Symphony, the melodic thread runs from the second violins to the viola, and from here to the first violins.

EXAMPLE 22

Beethoven frequently builds his themes in this manner: he takes into account the specific timbre of the different instruments to which each single phrase is entrusted. In the Violin Sonata, Op. 96, the chief theme integrates the varying tone qualities of the string instrument and the piano. As we have already observed in Chapter X, the great importance of the coloristic element is unmistakably reflected in the sketches which not rarely note the instrumentation along with the first flash.

In the early nineteenth century, the specific association of tone with color is an accomplished fact. Musicians attach a definite color to their tonal thoughts. Such a tie-up of the romantic imagination with the coloristic sphere is indicated in a work by Ernst Ortlepp called *Beethoven: A Fantastic Characterization*. We see from the following list how the author views the colors of the spectrum as reflected in the tone qualities of specific instruments:

Flute	serene	heavenly blue
Clarinet	fresh	morning red, light blonde
Bassoon	flattering, thoughtful	dark brown
French Horn	soft, full of guesses	shady-green
Trumpet	martial	bloody-red
Trombone	religious, awakening the depth	snow-white

The trend is not new: the associative and suggestive power of chosen instruments in relation to color and mood was known before.[8] In Western music the decisive step from aesthetic theories to a diversified and subtle practice became possible only through the technical advancement of instrument building as it developed since the classical era. Intensely characteristic for the romantic approach based upon this suggestive power of instruments are Weber's comments on his dramatic workshop:

In the *Freischütz*, there are two main features: the milieu of hunters and demoniacal powers. Hence, when composing the opera, I had to seek the most characteristic tone colors for each of these two features. (Once I had them) I tried to adhere consistently to them. The instrumentation for the forest and the hunter's life was easy to find: the sound of the French horn suggested it. The second of the two features presented a more involved problem. Its most important clue was given by the words of Max, "Dark powers have befallen me," which indicate the dramatic kernel. The tone poetic symbol had to remind the listener as often as possible of these dark forces of Hell: for a long time I had to think and contemplate on the right sound for this uncanny subject. Obviously, it had to be a dark and bleak tone color. As a result the deep registers of the violin, viola, celli and basses, then particularly the lowest tones of the clarinets seemed to me appropriate for this weird picture. The carrying tones of the bassoon, the depth of the horn, the deep tremolo of the tympani and even isolated tympani strokes helped to complete the effect. If you go through the score you will hardly find a number where the use of dark color is not somehow noticeable.[9]

It is in this symbolizing concept of tone color that Weber applies an epoch-making feature to the music drama; the composer characterizes the state of the human soul through a combination of sonorities—rather than through a certain type of melodic expression as his predecessors would have done. In the *Freischütz* overture, we hear the muffled sound of tympani. They are accompanied by the ghostly tremolo of the shivering strings. Low tones of the clarinet are threateningly held, while the celli sigh in the high registers. All this marks the appearance of Zamiel and his evil world. In these few bars the composer proved to be a master of concise dramatic expression by means of tone color, and forcefully anticipated Wagner's approach to the music drama. While Weber does not work with leitmotifs, he employs what we could call leit-tone colors directing the listener's imagination associatively to the various spheres of the drama.

With such a procedure, a phase in the centuries-long historic evolution is reached where orchestration emerges as the logical result of the musical content. A separation of the tonal idea and the tonal color (as it occurred in former periods) is no longer possible. That is why Weber rejects those musicians who speak of Cherubini's "beautiful instrumentation." The composer of *Der Freischütz* insists that

it is absurd to divide the art work into two halfs: a true master has in the moment of conception all artistic means, including color, at his disposal. Just as a painter would not think of a nude figure and later clothe (his model) with splendid raiment and little stones, so (in the musical composition) the whole must be thought out in its entirety; otherwise it brings only half results.

Of course, these lines express not only Weber's convictions: all great masters of the orchestra share his belief. A musical idea is manifest not only in the primary elements of melody, harmony and rhythm; it is also intrinsically tied to the specific timbre, to a definite quality of tone.

THE STRUGGLE WITH INSTRUMENTATION

Instances are rare where the specialized craft of instrumentation reaches into the region of high art. Certain great composers—great as inventors of new styles—have not displayed a comparable degree of originality and accomplishment as instrumentators. Is it that such composers lacked a special orchestral ear, or is it rather the lack of orchestral experience which was responsible for their limitations?

The great orchestrator, Haydn, considered instrumentation a craft which had to be self-taught. In reference to his activities as Kapellmeister in Esterház, he stated:

. . . As conductor of an orchestra I could make experiments, observe what produced an effect and what weakened it and was thus in a position to improve, alter, make additions or omissions and be as bold as I pleased; I was cut off from the world, there was no one to confuse or torment me and I was forced to become original.

We know from all available documents that Haydn's daily routine as a conductor suggested many of his orchestral ideas as he rehearsed or performed his scores. Some of the most original features in Haydn's works were the result of musical events and experiences through which he lived in the artistic isolation of Esterház with its festivities at court, its landscape and nature. The charm and blend of typically Austrian folklore in that German, Hungarian, Slavic tristate corner contributed greatly to the coloristic wealth of his music.

Similar convictions, which regard instrumentation primarily as a self-taught craft, were shared by Berlioz: "My two instructors, Reicha and Le Sueur, did not teach me anything in instrumentation." Berlioz explains in a formulation reminiscent of Haydn's how he felt his way to instrumental mastery through experiments and observation of other masterworks. Whatever he accomplished as an orchestrator, Berlioz ascribes to the "discovery of the secret ties which blend musical expression with the special art of instrumentation. The study of the procedure of the masters—Beethoven, Weber, Spontini—and the detached examination of traditional as well as of not traditional combinations, visits with virtuosos, experiments with their different instruments and a little instinct did the rest."

Only a few chosen composers solved every part of their creative problem with equal success. Other masters, who made signal contributions to orchestral literature, considered instrumentation a mere by-task of synthesis. To them it was labor, sometimes almost a burden which had to be carried in the last stage of work. It was never a welcome part of the total creative enterprise. An artist of Schumann's stature freely admits these difficulties (letter of December 17, 1832): "Frequently I consider this task so laborious that only years of study will lead to security and perfection." Errors of judgment easily happen as the composer uses his tone colors like the painter his hues and tints. In Schumann's words: "I often take yellow for blue." His instrumental world was primarily the piano and not the orchestra. He loved, played and knew intimately the keyboard in all its expressive and technical ramifications. Yet his dealings with other instruments have often been regarded as sojourns in neighboring, if not in foreign lands. But who would deny that these travels brought rich rewards? Considering that Schumann wrote four beautiful symphonies, these excursions into an instrumental realm beyond his clavier cannot be underestimated. Nevertheless Schumann's symphonic scores must be considered imperfect from the instrumental aspect. Ever since they were first performed, conductors have felt the need to present them with extensive retouching. Regarding Schumann's Fourth Symphony, Brahms reveals the source of its problematical orchestration (October, 1886):

It is (the enclosed score) an exact compilation of the printed score and of the original concept of Schumann's D Minor Symphony—modestly and I think unjustly described by the composer in his introduction as a rough sketch. You are of course familiar with the state of affairs, which

is quite simple. Schumann was so upset by a first rehearsal which went
off badly, that he subsequently instrumentated the symphony afresh in
Düsseldorf where he was used to a bad and incomplete orchestra. The
original score has always delighted me. It is a real pleasure to see anything so bright expressed spontaneously with equal ease and grace. It
reminds me (without comparing it in other respects) of Mozart's G Minor
Symphony, the score of which I also possess. Everything is so absolutely
natural that you cannot imagine it differently; there are no harsh colors,
no forced effects and so on. On the other hand, you will doubtlessly agree
that one's enjoyment of Schumann's revised score is not unmixed.

But Brahms by no means considered himself an expert on any
instrument except the piano. It was his custom from early years
through maturity to call upon experienced musicians for guidance
in problems of orchestration. Acknowledging this indebtedness to
his consultants, Brahms admitted with humility: "I know less about
instrumentation than my scores would indicate. It is to Grimm[10]
that I owe the best therein." And the friend to whom so much
credit is given advises frequently and sometimes facetiously: "Why
do you begrudge the violas their sixteenths, right there where the
kisses and cooing starts? And I also do not understand why you
do not let the fiddlers fiddle more. For example, they would be
delighted if they would be permitted to use their bows once in a
while."

One could compile a thesis on instrumentation on the basis of
the correspondence, questions and answers which were interchanged
between Brahms and his "staff of consultants." We observe elsewhere the helping hand of Joseph Joachim correcting the final
writing of the Violin Concerto. In the two piano concertos, the solo
instrument was no concern to the experienced player that Brahms
was, but the orchestral instruments were a constant source of
worry. After a performance of the D Minor Concerto, Brahms turns
to Joachim: "I am confused about the horns. Do they have to be
low B-flat horns and is it not perhaps possible to use them more
in D toward the end?" This question takes on more meaning
through the fact that Brahms adhered to the early practice of
employing two pairs of differently keyed horns. Although at the
time of the Concerto, Op. 15 (written between 1854 and 1861),
the valve horns were already firmly established, Brahms preferred

the more beautiful timbre of the "open tones" on the older horns.

"I would still like to ask you," Brahms wrote to Joachim, "whether or not the horn solo in the first movement ought to be played both times primo horn? The third hornist may often be a Schofler[11] (as he is in Hamburg or in Elberfeld). Will two horns be enough?" Again these questions are noteworthy: they prove that when Brahms instrumentated he did by no means have an ideal orchestral sound in mind. On the contrary, when scoring, he thought of the ensembles which would actually play his music and even took into consideration the deficiencies of certain German orchestras. This is an important point, as it suggests that Brahms might have orchestrated differently for the virtuoso orchestras of our day.[12]

Along with the horn, the other brass instruments, trumpets and trombones, contributed their share to Brahms' dilemma. In December, 1859, he wrote regarding the D Major Serenade: "You are going to scratch out, no doubt, several high G's in the trumpets; it hurts me already just to think about it." In short, Brahms is ready to accept his friend's corrections and even anticipates the censure of music which he would have preferred not to sacrifice. When Brahms had no organ at his disposal in the small town of Detmold (October, 1858) and wanted to perform Bach's cantata, *Christ Lay in Death's Dark Prison*, he asked: "Can one add trombones to the voice parts (particularly with a weak choir)? Can one arrange this in another way? Trombones would sound too crude, wouldn't they?" Brahms later found out that they did not; he developed in his own great choral works and in his symphonies a confident relationship to this instrument.

The noblesse and imaginative sonorities in Brahms' use of the woodwinds seem to belie that element of doubt which pervaded his treatment of flutes, oboes, clarinets and bassoons: it took Brahms a long time to develop a free rapport to that orchestral family. In the First Symphony (completed as late as 1876) there is not one measure scored for woodwinds alone. One would never surmise from Brahms' wonderful chamber music and his expert part-writing in his symphonies that the treatment of the string instruments vexed the composer almost as much as the brass or woodwinds did. Concerning a new violin sonata, he wrote to Clara

Schumann in August, 1887: "I should have yielded the idea to someone else who knows the fiddle better than I." And again he stated with great frankness, summarizing, as it were, the whole relationship of the keyboard composer to the problems of orchestration: "It is one thing to write for instruments the sound of which I have only approximately in my head and it is another thing to write for an instrument (the piano) where I thoroughly know what I write and why I write it in just such and such a way."

But with the persistence of the true artist, Brahms always discovered safe detours to instrumental achievement: for instance, he would rehearse and thus hear the actual sound of his music prior to its completion. Revising after such test performances, the conscientious comparison between the merely imagined and the actually realized sound effects led eventually to great accomplishments—in spite of the composer's limited orchestral experience. This method remained a favorite with Brahms in years of maturity. Thus, referring to the Double Concerto for Violin and Cello, Op. 102, Brahms wrote to Joachim in 1887: "Could you not plan to try out the score with Hausmann and myself on the piano somewhere? Any city with an orchestra will do. For the time being I cannot make up my mind and score the thing in orderly fashion."

The correspondence between Brahms and Joachim also shows that neither of the two musicians considered the task of instrumentation as mere routine. This fact is evident in the following confession:

I have already changed certain places in the instrumentation and would like to do it with piety. I would like to rewrite particularly the tutti parts, but to that end, it is necessary that I still keep them (the parts of the score). I would like to do it with inspiration. Hence I must not be pressed for time: instrumentation, too, calls for inventiveness.

CHAPTER THIRTEEN

REVISIONS

I am going to make changes on
the Polonaise until I die.

CHOPIN

REVISIONS

IN THE course of synthesis, the composer constantly readjusts
the products of his tonal fantasy. He changes and polishes
his music to such a degree that finally everything seems in
place and adequately related to the whole. One would assume
that the more meticulously the composer has worked, the less he
will feel the need of revisions or be willing to comply with any
remodeling suggested to him. After all, he has taken scrupulous
care to perfect his music, he has left nothing to chance. Once the
score is sent to the publisher, the composer has finished his task—
not only in the technical, but particularly in the psychological
sense: the creative experience is over.

Yet an inquiry into this topic of revisions shows that such an
attitude is by no means common to all composers. Some of the
most conscientious workers are also chronic changers, hypo-
chondriacs to whom their brain children never appear healthy.
As the composer looks them over with worry and critical concern,
they always seem to require change and improvement. A certain
type of artist is never really finished with his score. What he has
written down in a seemingly conclusive manner is only another

step toward the envisioned goal. He never feels satisfied with the manner in which he has set his inner music into the graphic signs of notescript. The inevitable incompleteness of the notation is felt as pain. Thus the desire to correct, to alter, to improve is ever present and irresistible. Self-criticism gnaws at the artist and makes him feel that his inner vision is never truly attained.

Composers' revisions and alterations cover a wide range: they can involve small or very sizable sections of the work, referring to a detail or to the totality of the score. They can occur as the work progresses, offhand as it were, without structurally changing the general course of the plan. They can also amount to thorough revisions after the whole score has been finished. Sometimes such rebuilding follows close upon the completion of the original version. Yet it may take years, perhaps almost a lifetime, before the composer can see a once-finished work anew, and recast its form in the light of broadened experience and matured wisdom.

A certain limited number of corrections is normal; it can be reasonably expected as part of the process of composing. After the printer returns the proofs, the composer eliminates errors pertaining to isolated notes or passages, to nuances of dynamics, phrasing, instrumentation, and returns the revised proofs once more to the printer.

ALTERATIONS IN OPERA

Revising is not necessarily work on paper. It can be part of the "blind" process of composition—falling into the same psychological pattern which we have already observed in connection with the procedure of certain masters. We learn about the revisions of Weber's *Freischütz* from the composer's son, Max:

Between the beginning of the mental work of the composition on February 23, 1817, and the writing down of the first notes on July 2, there were four months of constant occupation with the score. There is not one single musical piece in it which he would not have altered ten times in his mind until it sounded the way that prompted him to say: "This is it," and then he would write it down almost without changing a note, quickly, safely and neatly.

This statement supplements our knowledge of Weber's independence of the written record for his work: without the external medium of a piano, note paper and sketching, the composer, in an evolutionary process, turned his ideas into final shape.

Gluck's own reports concerning his process of composition also entail similar aspects of "blind" revising. Obviously, special problems arise when an opera is translated. Thus Gluck felt the need for thorough alterations of his scores when they were performed in another language. His opera, *Iphigénie*, was originally composed on a French libretto. Upon the request of the Austrian Emperor Joseph, in 1779, Gluck revised the opera into a German version. The adaptation of the text was made by the poet Alxinger, and necessitated a different distribution of accent and phrasing, due to the great differences in the two languages. But Gluck decided on a thorough revision; not satisfied with simple resetting of the words, he insisted first upon a completely revised script which would take into account all peculiarities of the German vernacular and word rhythm. On the basis of this new text, Gluck proceeded with his musical alterations. This conscientious approach is quite a contrast to the countless existing opera translations which are mere makeshifts, lacking the complex effort that goes into real art work.

Scores written for the stage have proved to be the particular objects of revisions and alterations. In the opera, external factors enter into the work plan, factors which are often beyond the composer's foresight at the time of the writing. The actual experience of the performance on the stage plays a tangible part: the laws, but also the whims and tricks of the theater decide issues which even some of the most routine composers could not anticipate while absorbed in the writing of the score. It is often only the practical experience on the stage itself which teaches the musician how to blend dramatic and tonal sources into the confluence of the operatic technique. But alterations do not end at the premiere of the opera. On the contrary, once a series of performances has been completed, further pitfalls in the work are revealed, calling for additional revisions. Ever since literati invented the opera with their renaissance of the antique drama at the beginning of the seventeenth century, the composer for the theater has been the easy prey of all kinds of circumstances in the performing world.

The manuscripts of Mozart give repeated proof that he corrected and changed his music until the very final stage of composition. On one occasion, he explained to his father the reason for so many alterations in the manuscript: "You are going to find a lot scratched out therein. This is due to the fact that I knew that the score is being copied here immediately. Thus, I gave free reign to my thoughts and before I sent it away for copying, I made my changes and abbreviations here and there." Mozart's practical sense is always in evidence. For instance, he aims at more music than is actually needed: "I made it (the aria) on purpose somewhat longer since one can always cut away, but not so easily add." In his work for the theater, alterations and adjustments to specific circumstances occur as a matter of routine. Allowances are made for possible changes of the cast. An aria must fit the singer like a suit of clothes. Thus according to a letter of February 28, 1778, Mozart accommodates the tenor Raaff as follows: "I told him that he should just tell me if it doesn't fit him and if he doesn't like it. I will change the aria for him as he wants it, or else make another one." Two years passed, and the voice of the aging singer had not changed for the better. On November 15, 1780, Mozart writes in reference to *Idomeneo*:

The aria is excellent now, but there is still one more alteration for which Raaff is responsible. He is right, however, and even if he were not, some courtesy ought to be shown to his gray hairs. He was with me yesterday. I ran through his first aria for him and he was very well pleased with it. Well, the man is old and can no longer show off in such an aria as that in Act II, "Fuor del mar ho un mar nel seno." So, as he has no aria in Act III, and as his aria in Act I, owing to the expression of the words, cannot be a cantabile as he would like, he wishes to have a pretty one to sing (instead of the quartet) after his last speech, "O Creta fortunata! O me felice!" Thus, too, a useless piece will be got rid of—and Act III will be far more effective.

The friendly consideration for the gray hairs of the once celebrated but now deteriorating singer is typical of Mozart. Kindness became part of his creative realism. While tailoring an aria to order, Mozart attends first to the artistic features, but the human ones are not neglected.

As everywhere in Mozart's workshop, so in his revisions, the traces of his father's influence appear. Three days after the last quoted letter regarding the aria for Raaff, Wolfgang received a letter from his father, who with his usual pedagogic strictness enumerated the necessary changes or alterations in the opera, *Idomeneo*:[1]

First of all, there is an alteration in Act I, Scene I, No. I, where Ilia in her recitative must say Achivo instead of Argivo. This occurs again in Act II, Scene II, No. 4, as you will see on the other side of Varesco's page above. The reason is that Achivo is a word which can be used of any Greek, but Argivo can only be used of the Greeks of Argos. But you must not be confused when you find the word Argivo in another place. There it is perfectly correct. But in the two places I have marked, it ought to be Achivo because the reference is to Greece as a whole. Now for alteration No. 2. This is in Idomeneo's speech to his retinue, after they have left the ships, and when he dismisses them. There you will find at the end the word, e al ciel natío, etc. This natío, which stands for nativo, has an accent on the i, which is long. The verse shows this. Alteration No. 3 is a very necessary one, and the idea of it only came to me after I had read the text carefully. Idamante must not say (as Varesco makes him) that he has witnessed the glory of his father, he must say the exact opposite, that is, that he regrets not to have been able to witness the great deeds and the glory of his father. You must note all these points in your copy immediately so that when you are composing the music, none of them may be overlooked. Alteration No. 4 is what I have said above about Achivo. Alteration No. 5 is to substitute for the duet a recitative.

Such philological thoroughness on the part of the pedantic father served as a corrective for the exuberance and impetuousness of the son. With the precision of a scientist and the dryness of an academician, Leopold Mozart criticized all of Wolfgang's libretti up to that of da Ponte's *Don Giovanni*. And with the same solidity of approach, the father trained his prodigious son from earliest youth to the profound stature of a great artist.

It is of great significance that some of the most melodious arias and scenes in Mozart's operas show a great amount of revisions in the manuscripts. Thus, in the *Abduction*, the aria No. 15, "Wenn der Freude Tränen fliessen," caused Mozart much thought and concern. He changed the great scene of Belmonte after the scores of the opera were already available to the public in various cities. In the manuscript Mozart would paste over whole passages,

erase others and constantly work on the improvement of the earlier
version. Writing *Figaro* he pondered long over Susanna's duet with
the Countess and over the aria, "Deh vieni, non tardar." It took
Mozart a long time until he succeeded in giving this graceful and
lucid piece of music that perfect balance which we now enjoy and
admire. Particularly the ending worried him a great deal: he
changed, enlarged and then shortened it in his manuscript score.
The elegance of Susanna's cadence and the following coda belies
all the effort which went in to the making of these mellifluent lines.

The most thoroughly altered portion of *The Magic Flute* is the
duet, No. 7 of Papageno and Papagena.[2] Originally Mozart conceived the following metric structure:

EXAMPLE 23

On the basis of this phrase, starting on the downbeat, the duet
developed. But Mozart changed his mind in favor of a rhythmic
scheme starting on the fourth eighth-note. And incidentally, when
Mozart made this alteration in the manuscript, he forgot to put
the tones of the dominant and tonic chords into the clarinet and
horn parts. His first version had included such instrumentation.
One may safely assume that Mozart overlooked them in the hurry
of revising.

EXAMPLE 24

Of great interest are Mozart's alterations in the service of
psychological characterizations. Originally, the aria of the Count
in *Figaro* ended with the following cadence:[3]

EXAMPLE 25

But a crucial measure was erased and replaced with the now familiar coloratura:

EXAMPLE 26

What a striking comment on the hurt ego of the count! With the energetic triplets (which had been missing in the first version) Almaviva pulls himself together; in this proud passage, he tries to meet his unruly subjects with controlled dignity. Here Mozart's deep insight into human nature produces new nuances in the musical portrayal of the count. Equally in the aria of the Countess, alterations of psychological import occur.

In the *Figaro* overture, one of the most interesting revisions in the entire opera score took place. This enchanting opening was written last, like most of Mozart's other opera overtures. As always, Mozart was in a hurry when working toward a deadline, this time for the scheduled premiere in Prague. Nevertheless, he indulged in far-reaching alterations, which proves that even at the last writing, Mozart still yielded to new thoughts. The manuscript shows how Mozart had originally planned the blueprint for the introduction to the comic opera: he conceived a music wherein the serene would blend with the elegiac. Before the recapitulation of the chief theme and its frolicsome climbing eighth-notes—where the orchestra holds firmly the chord of the dominant seventh—the rapid movement comes suddenly to a standstill. At this point, Mozart had first intended to interpolate a contrasting middle section in the parallel key of D Minor. It would have been an oboe solo, an andante con moto in $\overline{8}$, swinging gently above the siciliano rhythm of the pizzicato accompaniment on the part of the strings:

EXAMPLE 27

But Mozart changed his mind. He eliminated the leaf upon which this andante con moto was sketched. He crossed out those measures with the sign marked VI-DE[4] to allow the interpolation and returned to his original plan of an unbroken presto. He threw the music into the turbulent mood of the Beaumarchais comedy of marriage, into a whirlwind of a hurling and laughing presto. The planned $\frac{6}{8}$ siciliano was too contemplative. Mozart obviously decided in favor of singleness of expression, of a pellucid, continuous mood: let the opera buffa be started in uninterrupted gayety!

Mozart's conflict over the two alternatives for the *Figaro* overture is again of utmost psychological interest. He had already used the form type A-B-A (a presto contrasted by a contemplative middle section) for the overture of the *Abduction*. In his Overture to *Don Giovanni* (which followed *Figaro*) he decided upon a slow introduction with a subsequent sonata movement. An intricate form-play blending the sonata-scheme with fugal exposition was appropriate for his last opera overture, *The Magic Flute*. In short, every overture created its own specific form. Hence, the mercurial statement of two themes in the *Figaro* score, one jubilant in the tonic, the other with a slightly lyric undertone in the dominant. In this overture there was no room for thematic and harmonic development. Out of two hundred and ninety-four measures, which the total overture comprises, one hundred and nineteen bars are based upon an organ point. The form is open, fleeting, never static. Here is tonal movement in its highest potency.

REVISING AS A ROMANTIC TREND

It is characteristic of the romantic composer to rely upon his inspirational flashes. What, then, causes his constant concern with his findings, causes doubts which lead, in turn, to endless changes and revisions?

"Composing goes lightly and rapidly," Schumann stated, "but later I start to polish and this usually brings me to a state of despair." This confession bespeaks the dual approach to composition on the part of a deeply romantic artist. The products of his fantasy are accepted with security and self-assurance. Yet a critical trait of artistic conscience operates in the composer's mind, creating conflicts and interfering with a blind dependence on his inspirationally found material. At a later stage, he tries to look with growing detachment on the musical outpourings of subjective moods. Eventually, he faces their integration into the art work with piercing objectivity. And the conflict between the belief in his inspirational discoveries and his self-criticism leads inevitably to frequent alterations. As a result, many of Schumann's major works underwent complete revisions, among them his symphonies, his Piano Sonata in G Minor and his *Faust* music.

The romantic Mendelssohn was a reviser of first rank: he did not hesitate to recall a manuscript from the engraver's shop to make alterations in a score which was all set for print. This occurred, for instance, with some of his songs. The Italian Symphony was completed in March, 1833. But already in June, 1834, Mendelssohn began to revise the score. In the next year, February 16, 1835, he confided to his friend Karl Klingemann that he was biting his nails over the opening movement and simply could not conquer it, but that he would have to turn it into something different, perhaps into something altogether new. It was not until 1837 that Mendelssohn managed to complete the revision. The genesis of the Violin Concerto is a story of constant changes. Mendelssohn's correspondence with Ferdinand David, who functioned as the sponsor of the concerto, is replete with references to the composer's many alterations. The Hebrides Overture, the symphony cantata, Lobgesang, the first Walpurgis Night and other scores were all rewritten and subjected to thorough revisions.

Alterations are likewise a typical procedure in the workshop of Berlioz. In regard to the Symphonie Fantastique, he writes in his memoirs: "I applied as usual my corrections and modifications. The Scene in the Country had no effect at all (at the premiere). . . . Thus I decided to work it over." Was then the lack of external success the decisive factor for his revisions? Pointing to Harold in Italy, the composer asserts the contrary: "I kept on changing for fully six years some of the details in the March of the Pilgrims which took me only two hours to sketch by the fireplace. I believe (the changes) were very much to its advantage. And this in spite of the fact that it had great success even in its first version." In addition, the statement proves that even minor revisions (quantitatively minor) are by no means a simple matter. No true artist throws off lightly his corrections in the final score. As Berlioz insists, only through yearlong revisions did he succeed in conquering the faults in his work.

In 1873, Bruckner twice revised his Third Symphony, after it had already been completed in full score. Regarding his Fourth Symphony, he admitted to a friend with his typical modesty (October 12, 1877): "I have become fully convinced that my Romantic Symphony urgently requires a thorough revision." A short time after its completion, the Eighth was also completely revised. And it seems as though the fate of alterations remained closely tied to the Austrian composer's work even after his death: his symphonies are haunted up to this very day by constant alterations. But the tables have turned, and musicians claim the "Urfassung," i. e. the original setting of his symphonies, to be the only acceptable version; they demand a restitution of the original texts according to Bruckner's unaltered manuscripts.

THE MANIA FOR CHANGING

In keeping with his psychosomatic make-up, Chopin was a most erratic worker. At the mercy of his moods and his fragile health, the composer appeared frequently at odds with the world, with himself and particularly with the products of his Muse. Chopin characterized himself as the reviser *par excellence* and offered this extreme formulation: "I am going to make changes until I die."

Even if a new work would first meet with his approval, the composer was later tortured by doubts:

I finished four new mazurkas . . . they seem pretty to me as one's newest children usually do. I do not know myself yet because it is too new . . . during the work one thinks it is good, otherwise one could not write at all. . . . It is not until later that reflection comes, rejecting or keeping the work. Time is the best censor and patience the best teacher.

George Sand, who was in a position to know the peculiarities of Chopin's artistic constitution and who, as a writer, knew well enough the problems involved in the creative process, gives a vivid account of the composer's manner of work. "His creation was amazing," the poetess says of her friend, "he formed thoughts without seeking them or anticipating them. On the piano an idea suddenly occurred to him . . . and during a walk it was singing in him. Then he was in a hurry (to get to the piano) to play his new thoughts." After such facility of invention, the struggle started with the elaboration:

Then, however, began the most painstaking work that I have ever witnessed. There was no end of impatient and undecided essays to fix certain details of the theme as he had heard it inwardly. He analyzed very much when writing down what was conceived as a whole, and his regret that he could not represent it perfectly made him desperate. For days, he locked himself up in his room running up and down, breaking pens, repeating, changing one single measure a hundred times, writing, scratching it out and the next morning starting all over again with painstaking and desperate efforts. He would work for six weeks on one single page, to write it finally exactly the way he had sketched it in the original draft.

Bearing out George Sand's vivid account of a typical romanticist at work, Chopin's manuscripts show the continuous search for a better solution far beyond the sketching stage. Just as with Mendelssohn, even the manuscript copy destined for the printer had nothing final for Chopin. He saw in it just another version of his music, another passing stage. And so, even while the manuscript was being printed, Chopin made matters difficult for the publisher, the printer and himself, by insisting that last minute changes must still be made—made at any price! The result of such vacillation is often traceable in his manuscripts, for instance in his Valses, the Mazurkas and other scores which appear in the original editions to be very different from the autograph. In the manuscript of the Second Ballade, the last measure is written in two versions. Chopin could not make up his mind, and, when he corrected the final proofs, he changed the measure a third time.

AGAINST ALTERATIONS

"Children! make new things! New and always new!" Thus Wagner revolted against revisions when he learned that Berlioz was remodeling his opera, *Benvenuto Cellini*.[5]

If I am not mistaken the score is twelve years old. Did Berlioz not develop further? Do these people have no life in them? As far as I am concerned, it is only with reluctance that I still pay any attention at all to the *Holländer*, *Tannhäuser*, *Lohengrin* and this I do only because I know they have not been understood yet . . .

While Wagner makes his point clear enough, he is not free from his proverbial contradictions. After all, he was willing to revise his *Tannhäuser* score for Paris, more than fifteen years after its Dresden premiere in 1845. Moreover, the composer praises revisions elsewhere as highly beneficial: from an artistic point of view, he insists, certain problems remain unsolved in a work of youth. Only the mature artist can successfully interpret them.

Comparable to Wagner's dual attitude is that of Mussorgsky who repeatedly rejects the very thought of remodeling his music once it is finished. In a letter to Balakirev, who was about to perform A Night on a Bare Mountain, Mussorgsky states his unequivocal position against changes of any kind:

Whether you agree to produce it or not, dear friend, I shall alter neither the plan nor the elaboration, for both are in close relationship with the content of the scene, and are carried out in a spirit of genuineness without tricks or make believe. Every author remembers the mood in which he wrote and that remembrance does a good deal toward helping him to abide by his own standards. I have fulfilled my task as best as I could.

But with the inconsistency which seems to be the prerogative of genius (not in his art work, but quite often in his actions as a human being), even such strong convictions are themselves subject to alterations in the course of years. And so it happened that the violent antirevisionist, Mussorgsky, turned up in the camp of remodelers when he finally decided to change A Night on a Bare Mountain in 1867. In the same year, however, he warned in reference to the opera, Boris Godunov: "Let it be clearly understood, that I shall never start remodeling it (the opera). With whatever shortcomings it is born, with them it must live, if it is to live at all."

Rimsky-Korsakov, whom Mussorgsky addressed in this solemn and philosophical way, was far from following such admonishments. On the contrary, Rimsky-Korsakov went to the other extreme and made the most uninhibited alterations of the original Boris Godunov score which anybody ever dared to impose on Mussorgsky's masterwork. The technical aspects of the revisions have often been described. Psychologically, they were rooted in a strange obsession: Rimsky-Korsakov believed that fate had chosen him to newly cultivate the wild flowers of Mussorgsky's fantasy, and to replant them in the proper vases of academic moderation.

ADVICE OF FAMILY AND FRIENDS

Acute self-criticism is a chief source of artistic improvement and of constant growth. We have seen that a persistently watchful attitude toward his work prevents even the romantic composer from relying blindly on what his imagination brings to him. Equally, a musician of firm confidence in the results of his craft, may test, revise and change until he feels that the merits of his work can fully stand the strongest censorship of the outside world.

The most striking monument of a piercing and merciless self-criticism in the service of his art was set up by Beethoven. No malevolent eye could have looked with more disapproval upon his scores than did that of the composer himself. No harsher diagnosis of the ills of the music was ever made than by the brain which caused it. Recasting his work again and again in the synthetic foundry, polishing, filing, checking and counter checking his completed scores according to the most uncompromising standards of workmanship and spirituality, the master of masters declared: "The true artist has no pride: he realizes that art has no limits. He feels how far he is away from the goal, and whereas he might be admired by others, he mourns that he has not yet arrived where the better genius lights the way like the sun."

If a score was taken from Beethoven's workshop, ready for the printers on its way to publication, that moment of completion was reached which implies perfection. It was perfection though perhaps not to the humble genius who alone knew his ideal vision and felt that he could never reach it. In the judgment of posterity, however, it is supreme achievement. The trials and probations to which Beethoven had subjected his work made the final product withstand the severest test of all—the test of time. The lack of false pride, along with all the intrinsic ramifications that Beethoven's quoted words imply, has induced every truly great artist to seek perfection above all and at any price. To this end, he submits to self-criticism brought to the highest pitch.

But not every artist is capable of Beethoven's piercing insight into his own work. Nor does he have at his command Beethoven's boundless mastery of craft. In spite of all efforts to acquire an objectivity toward his own creation, his view remains limited. Detachment from the subjective sphere can never fully succeed. Moreover, no two artists create alike. Thus, even with comparable ideals and aims or certain similarities in the working method, Beethoven's road to perfection is not open to others. They must take detours: an obvious path leads to trusted friends for advice and constructive criticism. Great masters have eagerly listened to the judgment of other artists and have accepted their appraisal and censure.

Life provided certain great composers with such advisers in their own family circle. Mozart's chief counsel was his father Leopold, who united in one person all requirements of teacher,

friend and artistic confidante. The samples indicative of Wolfgang's reliance upon his father's wisdom are numerous. In the
following letter, written November 29, 1780, referring to the opera,
Achille in Sciro, Wolfgang asks Leopold Mozart questions concerning the text by Metastasio:[6]

Tell me, do you not think that the speech of the subterranean voice is too
long? Consider it carefully, picture yourself in the theater and remember
that the voices must be terrifying—must penetrate—that the audience
must believe it really exists. Well, how can this effect be produced if
the speech is too long, for in this case the listeners will become more and
more convinced that it means nothing. If the speech of the ghost in
Hamlet were not so long, it would be far more effective. It is quite easy
to shorten the speech of the subterranean voice and it will gain thereby
more than it will lose.

With such piercing and pertinent questions, "Tell me . . . consider it carefully . . . picture yourself in the theater . . . ," Mozart
must have addressed his father often. But we also see in his letter
how the strong mind of the advice seeker comes to the fore. While
Wolfgang wants his father's criticism of the libretto, he provides,
in a way, his own answer and finally does not hesitate to criticize
Shakespeare: young Mozart had an opinion of his own which the
greatest name in the world of the drama could not intimidate.

Like Mozart, other composers, too, had the opportunity of advice
and artistic counsel given by their close relatives. Proverbial is the
intimate artistic understanding and co-operation in the Bach family.
We may think of the musical tie between the Scarlattis, father and
son, or of that example from the early seventeenth century: the
Gabrielis, uncle and nephew. There is that precious artistic bond
between husband and wife: Clara and Robert Schumann.

Mendelssohn's favorite sister, Fanny, boasts of her role as adviser
to young Felix with justified pride: "Up to the present moment
I possess his unbounded confidence. I have watched the progress
of his talent step by step, and may say I have contributed to
his development. I have always been his musical adviser and
he never writes down thoughts before submitting them to my judgment. I have known his scores by heart before a single note was
written." This statement of Fanny is no exaggeration; the composer's own letters prove that his relationship with his highly

gifted sister was by no means a negligible factor in his creative life.

Long before Bizet married Geneviève Halévy in 1869, he had enjoyed the guidance and most generous encouragement of her father, the French operatic master, Jacques François Halévy. The latter taught the composer of *Carmen* many features in which this pearl of French opera excels—the art of graceful and refined ensemble building, the setting of a stage abundant with folkloristic pageantry and the effective yet always noble treatment of the human voice. In the camaraderie of Parisian art life, mutual stimulation always played its creative part. Berlioz disclosed and acknowledged the contribution of friends and colleagues with frankness and gratitude: "Ferdinand Hiller . . . gave me excellent advice from which I reaped all benefits." Such willingness to listen to trustworthy criticism was ever present with Berlioz. After all, he was a professional critic himself and knew the value which an honest and critical appraisal of a work might have for an artist. On journeys, the different viewpoints of musicians from other countries proved a stimulating corrective. Mr. Frankoski, a newly made acquaintance in Vienna, 1846, called the composer's attention to the bad and sudden ending of the Queen Mab scherzo. "I then wrote a coda for this movement . . . and destroyed the first version." And it is in this revised and prolonged setting that we hear this piece so delightful in form and sound.

Advice is not always for the best: just as in the varied conflicts of life, so in the artistic dilemma, suggestions of well-meaning friends do not necessarily produce the best solution of a problem. This is demonstrated in Chopin's relationship with his various consultants. Nervous and gullible, frequently lacking confidence in his own convictions, Chopin invited and sometimes followed pernicious advice. And here a vicious circle started: after having consulted his friends and accepted their suggestions, Chopin would later regret the recommended alteration. Sorry that he had not adhered to his original plan, he would revert to it again only in order to throw it overboard once more. In comparing the original manuscript of the Ballade in G Minor with the later version, Camille Saint-Saëns discovered a measure in which Chopin had first written down a D and later changed it to an E-flat. "This

supposed E-flat gives an expression of pain which would be in
keeping with the character of the piece. Was it a printer's error
or was it the original intention of the composer?" Saint-Saëns
questioned Liszt on the matter but could obtain nothing except
that Liszt preferred the E-flat. "So do I," admitted Saint-Saëns,
"but that is not the point. The conclusion at which I have arrived
is that Chopin, when playing the Ballade, sounded the D, but I
am still convinced that the E-flat was his first inspiration and that
the D was adopted on the advice of timid and maladroit friends."

Wholeheartedly following the advice of his loyal friends and
not showing any signs of regret was Anton Bruckner. How upset
the humble man would be over today's heated arguments around
the previously mentioned Urfassungen of his works. Now all the
blame for deviations from the original scores is on his favorite
disciples, Ferdinand Loewe and Franz Schalk. Loyal to their master
beyond a shadow of a doubt, these practical conductors certainly
had no other motive than to serve a greater cause when they made
changes in instrumentation, supplementing Bruckner's orchestral
knowledge with their wide practical experience. Bruckner was
always eager and grateful for any suggestions. A remark like the
following is typical of his attitude: "There is hard work going on
in the symphony. You will be amazed how I followed your advice
in the andante."

BRAHMS AND HIS CONSULTANTS

The most distinguished example of a great artist who widely
opened his inner workshop to the criticism of chosen friends is
set by Brahms. The distinction of his attitude lies not only in the
perseverance with which the composer sought objective evaluation
of his new works, but particularly in the caution and wisdom with
which Brahms judged the judgment of his critics.

Those whom he acknowledged as arbiters were freely consulted,
here on a mere technical question (a problem of counterpoint or
instrumental performance), there on a deeper aesthetic problem
as it underlay the creative task. Brahms really meant it when he
wrote to his friend, Julius Otto Grimm: "Do not hesitate to insult
my work. I am so much in doubt about its value—that I cannot

make up my mind one way or the other without knowing your judgment."

Insults, not compliments, were invited. Brahms needed and wanted unrestricted, constructive criticism. A free and uninhibited interchange of aesthetic views and technical opinions with selected friends was, for him, a natural procedure which had started in young years. Maturity and full mastery by no means put an end to it. Speaking up with enlightened frankness, never inhibited by conventional politeness, friends gave Brahms that for which he asked. In a letter of 1857, Joseph Joachim criticized the young Brahms for his basic approach to composition:

Forgive me if I express myself in a rather curt and dry way. Yet my violent reaction springs only from deepest love for you. I blame your impatience for everything. You simply wanted to get your score finished— but this hurried job cannot be done with work of your profound nature. Poets often let works lie dormant for years, after a happy start, until renewed imagination returns to them. Not even a Goethe or Schiller could command at will his power to create. How could it be different with the composer of music? On the contrary, he depends on the creative mood to a higher degree. Industry can mean to him only his readiness to follow promptly that invitation and to turn with enthusiasm wherever his genius directs him.

In essence, this admonishment of the friend involves the ageless conflict between inspiration and craft. Brahms is here reproached for, and found guilty of, offending the sovereignty of inspiration— he had relied too much on his craft.

In reference to his Variations, Op. 21, Brahms demanded that Joachim tell him his doubts concerning every piece and every variation with a "clear yes or no." Responding to this request, Joachim showed himself disturbed by the triviality of a particular measure, or by the close of a variation impairing the beauty of design. In addition, he worried about a certain academic dryness in the style of Brahms: "You can feel so tenderly, so warmly. I wish that this part of your nature would express itself in its full depth." Such a plea was not made in vain. Changing the shape of his music, Brahms proved that he took to heart the advice of his friend.

Often the roles were reversed: not only did Brahms appear as

the advice-seeking composer, but he particularly enjoyed the role
of consultant. Now Joachim, an ambitious composer in his own
right, became the target of the criticism of Brahms. Again a theme
with variation was the problem. The comments of Brahms assumed
general import: they were not mere offhand remarks, but expressed deep convictions which Brahms later put into sounding
reality through numerous scores based on this form:[7]

I ponder over the form of variation, and feel that it ought to be more
strict and pure. The old masters always retained the bass of the theme
throughout. Beethoven beautifully varies melody, harmony and rhythm.
We cautiously preserve the melody, but do not treat it freely. We do not
create anew and only burden it.

Tying in with this observation is Brahms' letter (1869) to Dr.
A. Schubring:

In a theme with variations, only the bass is really important to me. I
consider it altogether holy. It is the firm ground upon which I build all
my floors. Whatever I do with the melody is a play or an ingenious game.
But it is over the given bass that I invent my new melodies. It is here
that I really create.

Still later, in 1876, Brahms expressed a desire for more specific
differentiation between the terms variation and fantasy-variation
which would clarify the artistic goal. In his words: "I wish one
would distinguish in name what is different in kind."

The study of the correspondence between Brahms and his
friends shows not only how wisely the composer discriminated
between his various advisers, but particularly on what grounds he
did so. As one would expect, Clara Schumann was frequently consulted. In 1857, Brahms sent her a rondo: "I beg you, just like the
other time, for a very strict criticism." But Clara's taste was conservative, her aesthetic orientation, limited; Brahms did not always
cope with her suggestions unconditionally. Moreover, the nature
of their deep and involved relationship did not successfully lend
itself to the type of detachment and distance which is the premise
for an objective and critical appraisal of all art.

It seems as though no one dared to be quite as harsh in criticizing the music of Brahms as his friend, the singer, Elisabeth Herzogenberg. When Brahms sent her in September, 1888, the newly

composed songs and choruses, Op. 104 and 107, she certainly did not hold back what she really thought in her letter of October 28, 1888:

Alas, believe me, dearest friend, those are not your true followers who break out in jubilation at the appearance of each of your volumes without even looking at them. I know *Brahmsians* who do not discriminate—who fall into a trance by merely reading your name! Those people tend to fetishism. They lack a more intimate relationship, yes, and frequently even a notion of whom they adore. (The song) "Manns Bild," Op. 105, No. 5, seems to me out of order—it really throws me out of all heaven. How you could have considered the poem worthy to be set to music, I do not understand—so charmless, so dry, so cheap does it appear to me.

In this emotional outburst, there remains enough feminine diplomacy to divert the blame to the text that Brahms had chosen rather than to his music. The merciless criticism implies that no great music could possibly spring from such a poem. Significantly, this correspondence belonged to a time when Brahms had already achieved full mastery and fame. But he did not mind in the least to accept such criticism of his music, provided he believed in the censor's judgment and musicianship.

Into a special category fall technical problems primarily concerned with the practice of performance. Brahms sought frequent advice pertaining to instrumental as well as to vocal technique. Thus, the Violin Concerto originated under the sponsorship of friends who helped him specifically in the shaping of the solo part. The original score shows the comments which Joseph Joachim wrote into the manuscript. Here, the onetime consultant for counterpoint functioned as a specialist on problems for his instrument, the violin. Brahms enlisted Joachim's aid on August 22, 1878, with: "Now I am content if you just say a word and perhaps write in: difficult, uncomfortable, impossible." Yet something typically Brahmsian happened. In spite of Joachim's unquestioned mastery as a violinist, the composer did not rely on the opinion of one man alone, regardless of how competent he might be. Hence, Brahms called upon other experts, among them the violinist, Hugo Heermann, in Frankfurt. Yet a favorable reaction to the Concerto by the kindly musician only instilled further doubts in Brahms' mind: "I am afraid you are not frank and strict enough with me,"

he complained and sought still other guidance—only in order to
return eventually again to Joachim as the final authority.

With his new vocal works, Brahms resorted to the simple and
safe procedure of testing the music in private performances prior
to publication: he would first rehearse with friends, later giving
the score an informal tryout from the manuscript. Then, depending
on reactions and suggestions, Brahms would revise the composition,
perhaps try it out once more before a friendly but critical forum
and then finally send it to the publisher for print. He relied upon
this method in younger years and continued it throughout his life.
From 1854 to 1858, as director of the court concerts at Detmold,
Brahms had ample opportunity to write at leisure and to rehearse
his new music "with the ink still wet." In Hamburg, he conducted
a chorus of girls "who always sing joyfully—and what I feel like
writing." Vocal scores were carefully tried out, rehearsed at length
and corrected again. In 1859, he reported enthusiastically about his
forty charming singers who helped him to find better solutions for
his vocal settings. In Vienna, this method of experimental performances continued. The Joachim Quartet, occasionally younger
organizations such as the Rosé Quartet, participated in these try-
outs of the chamber music of Brahms. He would take the piano
part and also accompany singers at the first hearing of his new
songs. The audience consisted of critical connoisseurs and friends:
Hanslick, Kalbeck, Brill, Epstein, Billroth, Goldmark and a few
others. These performances resulted in frank discussions on the
qualities and failings of the work. Subsequent revisions followed.

From all this, it becomes clear that Brahms knew how and where
to choose the proper advisers and performers for the purpose of
leading his works on a safe path through various phases of creative
synthesis into the outside world. His chief adviser, Joseph Joachim,
is consulted primarily on problems of instrumentation and composition. Brahms does not rely on him for vocal orientation and
even cautiously counterchecks Joachim's advice on violin performance. Vocal scores are tested by experienced singers; choral works
are informally tried out with various ensembles. And for the experimental hearings of his great choral and orchestral scores,
Brahms managed to arrange trial performances. Sometimes, concerts in a small town served this purpose best: while the occasion

was less exposed, it still offered the opportunity to test the new work prior to its printing. Thus, with the collaboration of specialists in each field and friendly organizations, Brahms always secured the best guidance obtainable, satisfying his inborn sense of artistic responsibility. In addition to such specialists as Joachim, Grimm, Herzogenberg and Clara Schumann, Brahms also regarded the opinions of other musicians who did not belong to his circle, once he was convinced of their sincerity and good judgment. This is shown in an instance like the "Schicksalslied." Hermann Levi, the Wagnerian apostle, had seen the manuscript of this work before Brahms had finished its composition. It was Levi who discouraged the composer from his original groundplan.

Everywhere in Brahms' desire for advice, we encounter his artistic and intellectual integrity. Violent disapproval did not irritate him in the least. All that mattered to him was the growth of the work. All that he sought was the right tone. Only the wrong note could hurt, not the harsh word pointing to it. Brahms and his circle of friends were not a mutual admiration society.

CHAPTER FOURTEEN

CLASSICAL AND ROMANTIC GUIDEPOSTS

> I thought that I should employ a
> maximum effort for the sake of
> beautiful simplicity.
>
> **GLUCK**

> With every piece I come more and
> more to the point of writing only
> as my heart dictates. This is the
> only guidepost I know.
>
> **MENDELSSOHN**

ETERNAL DUALISM

"HAYDN conceives romantically that which is distinctly human in the life of man. Mozart discerns the superhuman, the marvelous which emanates from the imagination. Beethoven's music engenders a haze of dismay, dread, sorrow and expresses the timeless yearning which is the quintessence of romanticism. He may, therefore, be looked upon as a profoundly romantic composer." This picture drawn by E. T. A. Hoffmann shows how the works of Haydn, Mozart and Beethoven convey the spirit of romanticism to the remarkable poet-musician whose competent word and aesthetic judgment Beethoven himself trusted. Indeed, the romantic element in Haydn's oratorios, the *Seasons* and the *Creation*, can be as little overlooked as the decisively romantic contributions of

Mozart to the musical theater in his operas, *Don Giovanni* and *The Magic Flute*. Again, the voice of nature in Beethoven's music as well as the poetic ideas integrated into numerous of his scores bear further testimony to the romantic factors in classical creation.

History proves that classical impulses as well as romantic ones live throughout every era. We may go so far as to claim that no true art work is altogether free from the romantic: one of the tangibles that truly differentiate the work of the artist from that of the mere craftsman is the specific element called romantic— provided we define it as something that pertains to nature and romance, to the fanciful and the remote in contrast to the cold, mathematical factors of science and calculation.

Romantic music symbolically speaks the language of the feelings. Music springing from emotions must flow as freely as the emotions themselves. Hence, the subjective communication of the unique experience cannot remain behind the bars of formal schemes. The romantic composer throws traditional forms overboard; if he uses them, they turn out to be technically far below the level of baroque and classical standards. The romantic composer pushes the subjective, the associatively inspired moment into the foreground of his creation. To the radical romanticist, the sheer play of the emotional and fantastic means everything.

By contrast, there is the type of composer who believes primarily in an art of precise tonal building, in a truly plastic organization of all employed material. As a result of such aims and convictions, various attempts to arrive at a systematized, even mechanized method for composition have come to the fore throughout history. Since antiquity, composers have sought and found intense support in science and philosophy for their attempts to invent new thoughts out of already existing ones. Philosophers have promulgated inductive methods of discovering the truth, founded upon empirical observation and upon an analysis of all observed facts. Analogously, composers have attempted to find the underlying structure of their music and the development of their tonal material through a comparison of instances and by a scientific study of accompanying variations. Descartes, the great French thinker, distrusted the work of fantasy to the extent that he insisted on its complete elimination from science. He even reproached ancient geometry for having relied upon the imaginative faculty. Every branch of science—Descartes demanded—must be reduced to the pure understanding of mathematics. The musical corollaries of such thinking are the various methods of composition based on mathematical conception, on tonal building in terms of figures and numbers. The rational approach of the *ars inveniendi* is related to such a scientific trend of making music. Significantly, key terms used in certain musical theories are culled from the antecedent philosophy. The mechanistic approach to musical composition reaches a climax in the middle of the eighteenth century in the teachings of the Leipzig Society of Musical Science. Its founder, Lorenz Mizler, appears as the most radical exponent of the anti-imaginative school. Here the role of the emotional fantasy is nil; the "romantic" in music is killed.

Following its eternal course, the pendulum swings back again to the other extreme. A centuries-long spell of reason in musical creation is gradually broken under fresh impulses emanating from contemporary aestheticism and philosophy. Early signs of the turn are discerned in statements such as the revolutionary formulation in the treatise, *Scienza Nuova* (1725) by the Italian, G. B. Vico: "The weaker the rational thinking, the stronger the fantasy." A generation later, in France, that famous appeal sounds: "Faites de la musique Française!" Here, in behalf of a truly national art, Jean-Jacques Rousseau pleads for the enraptured genius whose creation springs not from the intellect, but from exuberance and emotion, "from a heart pounding with joy and from eyes filled with tears of sorrow." The philosopher-composer, so close otherwise to rationalism, rejects reason as the chief guide in the composing of tonal works. Music must be produced out of deep emotional experiences, not like chemicals in the test tubes of laboratories—resulting from formulas and prescriptions.

A survey of the aesthetics and theory around the middle of the eighteenth century shows how the new impulse for an emotional creation is gaining ground while the old rational conceptions are still in evidence. Already in 1739, the conservative Mattheson could no longer ignore antirationalistic trends which started to sweep the musical world. Hence, we have from his pen the compromising reference to "an invention on the spur of the moment, springing from musical enthusiasm as if one were devout, enamored, angry, sarcastic, melancholy." In these words, the romantic approach to musical creation is clearly recognized: the extemporaneous and emotional factors mark the unmistakable contrast to Mattheson's otherwise rational approach to invention. But how difficult it was for theorists to reconcile the old with the new is evident as late as 1774 in Johann Georg Sulzer's profound aesthetic work, *General Theory of Fine Arts*. This treatise still deals with Mattheson's chapter on invention as the basic reference to composition. At the same time, however, the author asks the composer "to leave himself to his emotions alone. Then whatever he desires to express, will lie clearly before his imagination."[1]

Retour au Nature! Rousseau's back-to-nature principle led to a shift of emphasis also in musical creation: naturalistic imitation becomes for the composer a rediscovered point of departure. The musician turns back to nature in many ways. His melodies imitate the inflection of human speech and the accents of language. His expression follows the happy shouts of joy or the cries of pain. All passions are among the composer's resources and take on musical meaning. Rousseau explains in his *Dictionnaire de Musique*: "It is necessary to observe that the charm of music does not consist alone in sheer imitation, but in a sweet one. The declamation itself must be subordinated to the melody in order to make an effect." The emotions, then, remain the spring of inventiveness. But in their integration into music, the composer must follow the laws of his tonal material: the superiority of the intrinsic musical element is acknowledged. The study of nature and its abundant reflection in art proves to be a French trait which is expressed almost everywhere in the treatises of this rationalistic era. The greatest contemporary French composer, Rameau, concludes that "it is necessary to have studied nature for a long time in order to be able to paint it as truly as possible. One must also know one's self in all great emotions and in all great suffering."

Sparks alighting from the Latin countries are soon kindled by musicians further north—in spite of the inborn trend of the Germans to crafts and guilds and their traditional obsession with mere workmanship. Artistic individualism, nourished by the young humanism of modern times, finds its musical counterpart in a strong emphasis on the emotional sources. As we have shown, the composer not only expresses his personal emotion, but it is in the state of emotion that he creates. Musicians are encouraged to make their intensely subjective experiences the true content of their works.

"O Fantasy! Thou highest treasure of the human being, inexhaustible source from which artists and savants come to drink. O remain with us, though recognized and admired by the few, and let us beware of that so-called enlightenment, that ugly skeleton without flesh or blood."[2]

Thus prays Schubert to his Muse. What is "that ugly skeleton" from which Schubert seeks refuge and what sort of "enlightenment" does he so violently reject? The answer is readily suggested by the rational and mechanistic approaches to composition which reach deep into Schubert's time. It is, of course, the method of composing by sheer calculation, that technique furnished by cool reason which has been held in high esteem for centuries. Yet nothing but a bloodless structure of bones (as Schubert pleads) can be put together by the musician who composes detached from fantasy and follows only the rules of tonal mathematics.

In the year of Schubert's birth, 1797, a young writer published a piece of prose under a rather involved and revealingly romantic title: *The Outpourings of the Heart of an Art-Loving Cloister-Brother*. Wilhelm Heinrich Wackenroder, the author, was, just as Schubert himself, destined to early death after a meteoric life of signal contribution to his art. In these *Outpourings*, Wackenroder newly defined the role of intuition in a manner which proved prophetic for a century to follow. The revolutionary, that is to say, antirationalistic character of his art philosophy emanates from the cloister-brother's eloquent lines: "Whoever tries, with the magic wand of a functioning reason, to find that which is felt only within the soul, will never discover anything but ideas on feeling, not feeling itself." Instead, the artist must be intuitively guided by a mysterious sympathy in his creative search. A powerful feeling, an elated mental state creates for him. Wackenroder the poet, and Schubert the composer, both believe in soulful creations, in an art that expresses what the heart dictates. Intuition, not calculation, is the source and aesthetic guide of their art products. The miraculous and the magic triumph over reason and science. Here, in the artist's evocation of supernatural power, lies the crux of romantic creation.

THE FUNDAMENTAL IDEA

In 1781, Immanuel Kant published his epochal inquiry into the resources of reason as the basis of experience. In his *Critique of Pure Reason*, the great philosopher investigated the universal and necessary function of reason and classified its stimuli into an orderly world.

We have seen that throughout history varying and conflicting roles have been assigned to reason as a factor in musical creation: at times, musicians have called upon reason to be their sole guide. At other times, they have excluded reason and tonal geometry in favor of the sheer play of emotions and sensations. A compromise between both trends was sought. Thus, Rousseau expressed the interaction of the emotional and the mental factors in the assertion that "in music an emotion is represented in my heart and a picture in my mind." But Kant's *Critique* rejected any art that awakened or represented human emotions. Instead, Kant emphasized the *fundamental idea* as the guiding light of the creative process.

Already Plato had employed the expression "idea," by which he meant archtypes of things themselves, not merely keys to possible experiences. Ideas are conceptions furnished by reason and suggesting the form of the whole. Kant shows how the idea conceives a priori the totality of a form as well as its content. Hence the idea accords to every part the specific place which it must finally occupy in the total structure. The idea suggests the end as well as the form of the whole which is in accordance with that end. The unity of the end communicates unity to the whole system. The whole is thus an organism, and not an aggregate; it grows from within. It is thus like an animal body: as it grows, it does not add any limb. It makes each in its sphere stronger and more active.

What is the significance of this philosophy for the creative technique of the artist?

Twenty years after the publication of Kant's *Critique*, a notable correspondence between Schiller and Goethe reveals their perception of the creative process. Both of these great exponents of literary classicism express likewise their belief in a fundamental idea as the guidepost of artistic creation. And in this light, the statement of a great musician, contemporary to Kant, Goethe and Schiller, takes on added significance. It reads:

I alter a great deal, discard and try again until I am satisfied. And then, inside my head, I begin to work, broadening here, restricting there, deepening and heightening; and since I am conscious of what I am trying to do, I never lose sight of the *fundamental idea*. It rises up, higher and higher and grows before my eyes until I hear and see the image of it molded and complete, standing there before my mental vision.

These are the words of Beethoven and with them a circle closes— rounding out our understanding of the deeply knotted spiritual tie. We now realize that philosopher, poet and musician are spiritual allies in their pursuit of the fundamental idea. As Beethoven expressed it: for the creator of music, too, the fundamental idea emerges as the life cell, as the organic center of the envisioned work. His statement is truly classical in the dual sense of the word. While it superbly describes his own creative· process, it also designates the stylistic position of the creative type which can be justifiably called classical.

With their kinship of ideologies, the philosopher, poet and musician all stand firmly on common soil. In classical creation, reason prevents the artist from leaving his work in a subjectively unconnected, unformed state. Reason requires that the sum of the composer's talents, of his knowledge and musical craft builds a well organized tonal score.

Schiller and Goethe, practicing as poets what they preached in their aesthetic prose, restricted all associative implications of the art work still further. This is the meaning of Schiller's comment in a letter of August 7, 1797 to Goethe, criticizing Diderot's famous essay, "Sur la Peinture:" "He (Diderot) sees in the aesthetic works too much foreign and moral purpose. He does not seek it sufficiently in the very subject and in its representation. The beautiful art work must always serve him for another purpose." In this criticism, Schiller indirectly pleads for a style of purity and opposes other modes of expression in which foreign purposes or implications play a decisive role. The classical musician on his part aims at a state of form, wherein his ideas are perceived as symbols, entirely pure. He does not depend on associative help of a poetic idea, of a program or of the representation of emotions. The classical composer always transforms naturalistic feelings and sensations into the abstraction of musical language.

Obviously, this pure language is spoken most fluently in the realm of absolute music. Yet to preserve its purity also in the sphere of the opera was the historic accomplishment of Gluck. He succeeded in creating a music drama wherein the lofty aesthetics of tonal expression could live in the sphere most hostile to it—in that of the theater. Gluck explained his aesthetic tenets to the Duke of Toscana as early as 1759: "I thought that I should employ a maximum effort for the sake of beautiful simplicity. I have avoided everything such as splendor or complications which would endanger clarity." Such artistic ideals of intrinsic simplicity above all were deeply steeped in Gluck's nature: of course, no man can respond to what is not latent in him. Yet one cannot overlook the coincidence between the date of Gluck's statement and what it otherwise implies in the history of music. In 1759 Haydn wrote his first symphony in Lukovec. It was the year in which Handel died—the grandiose art of the baroque had fulfilled itself. The classical ideal of a beautiful simplicity, promulgated two thousand years earlier by Greek aesthetics was taking on new meaning. Again, a turning away from monumentality and complication occurred. The classical formula of unadorned beauty, which Gluck expressed as an individual, gradually appeared as the artistic slogan of his generation. Classical thought was in the air and artists breathed it. It was like the air from a new planet to which musicians were drawn, abandoning those guiding stars which a preceding era and its artists had followed.

In the Paris of Diderot and of a nationalistic French opera tradition, Gluck tried to eliminate the naturalistic spontaneity from his music dramas. He chose to speak in tonal symbols only. His dramatic style carried a symbolization of musical ideas to the highest degree: the external and associative moments were banned as something that lay outside the territory of the pure tone language.

These noble and classical guideposts explain the phenomenon of Gluck's style as well as of his building of dramatic form and melody. They also explain the reasons why so many contemporaries

failed to grasp the deep symbolism of Gluck's art. Boyé, an exponent of the French naturalists, accused Gluck of "indifference
toward a true musical expression." Even the music for such dramatic highlights as the tragic scene of *Orpheus*: "I have lost my
Eurydice," might just as well (in Boyé's judgment) convey exactly
the opposite meaning of Orpheus' sad complaint:

J'ai trouvé mon Eurydice	I have found my Eurydice
Rien n'égale mon bonheur.	Nothing equals my happiness.

che fa - rò sen - za Eu - ri - di - ce!   do - ve an-drò sen - za il mio   ben!

EXAMPLE 28

A composer of naturalistic tenets would have interpreted the
despair and emotional distress of the young widower, Orpheus, in
quite a different way. There would have been a passionate outburst, a more obvious correspondence of tone and word somewhat
in the manner called for by the *Doctrine of Affections*. Yet in
Gluck's classical lines—written in C major of all keys—the supreme
grief of the stricken Orpheus attains an inner purity of expression
and disdains theatrical display. And it is exactly because of its
symbolic strength that this eighteenth century music drama has
become timeless.

Gluck referred to the great difficulties which the composition
of his scores entailed. When asked by his colleague, Piccini[3] how
many operas he had written, Gluck answered: "Not many . . . and
those with much study and great effort." Obviously, it was not
the craftsman's job and the routine procedure of opera writing to
which Gluck referred as the source of his trouble; the accomplishment which took so much of his time and effort was rather the
striving for style, the exclusion of unpure material, in short, the
struggle toward the realization of classical ideals. The conquest of
such aesthetic tenets of purity into real sound emerges as the
hardest of all creative tasks.

What takes place in the inner workshop of the musical classicist
is therefore the spiritual struggle and tectonic labor for his visionary
idea and for its spiritually pure realization in the art work. Among

the sketches of Beethoven's Pastoral Symphony, there is a particular
one from the year 1803 bearing the title, Murmur of the Brook,
and there is noted the following melody in two different positions,
a high and a low one:

EXAMPLE 29

As we see, Beethoven wrote below the sketch: "Je grösser der
Bach, je tiefer der Ton"—the greater the brook, the deeper the
tone. In such a naturalistic way Beethoven first recorded the
sounds of the murmuring brook—his hearing at this time was still
good enough to permit such sketching from nature. Yet from this
point of departure to the finished B-flat major andante, the master
followed a typically classical road. Beethoven's motto of the
symphony, "more expression of feeling than tone painting," served
as the aesthetic guidepost: the idea of nature shines through the
music only as a highly stylized expression. In contrast to the
realistic sketch, Beethoven transformed the original murmuring
of the brook into a tectonic play of softly flowing melodies and
counterpoints. The texture of the andante is now much more than
imitation of nature. It makes the hearer relive the delightful time
which the composer had spent on the green banks of the brook.

"The most important and rarest quality of our composer," stated
Schindler interpreting Beethoven's creative technique, "consists in
his being inspired to composition through an idea—and putting it
at all times into definite form." We see, throughout Beethoven's
entire lifework, how such fundamental ideas take an iron grip
upon his sketches and blueprinting. The idea of nature in the
Pastoral is that of an inner program; it determines the attitude of
the tone language and gives the symphonic form its curve. The
synthesis is guided by deep aesthetic thinking. Nature, as the basic
idea, leads Beethoven to the organization of the tonal material.

But the form remains classical—in spite of the fact that the Sixth Symphony borders on a real program.

FIRST CONCEPTIONS AND ORIGINALITY

Widening our knowledge of intrinsic differences between the classical and romantic working methods, we will contrast further aspects of the technique of Beethoven with that of Robert Schumann. "The first conception is always the most natural and best one. The intellect commits errors, the feelings never. Frequently, two versions seem to have the same value, but the original one is usually the better." Obviously, this claim of Schumann is the complete reversal of everything we have come to know as typical in the approach of Beethoven. And the difference between two opposing approaches to composition emerges from this single quote. With the romanticist, the emphasis is on the first flash of inspiration. For Schumann there is often something unique and irrevocable in his initial drafts. Such an obsession with the finds of "lucky moments" prevents him, in the later stages of synthesis, from touching the shape of his initial ideas. The sketches of Schumann prove this attitude quite conclusively. For instance, the notebook for the piano pieces, Album for the Youth, shows that the first occurrences, admirably noted in the haste of an inspired flow, bear already the stamp of finality—melodically, harmonically, in many details of the texture. The sketches of Schumann's songs often show a finished state even in details of the accompaniment. In the stage of synthesis, Schumann only polishes the music here and there, adjusting some minor points. But he rarely alters an inspirational idea as it first occurred to him. Thus he arrives in a relatively short time at the final stage of composing. If Schumann reworks a score, he does so after the completion of the whole work. But the evolutionary process of Beethoven from one sketch to another has no place in Schumann's workshop. This is true not only of Schumann, but of any romantic composer. Hence Mendelssohn's admission to Rietz: "Since one's thoughts can never be polished nor sharpened, one has to take them as they come, as the good Lord sent them." Or another statement like the following in a letter of July 30, 1838: "With every piece I come more and more to the point of writing only as my heart dictates. This is the only guidepost I know."

The metamorphosis of raw material in slow progress as we observed it so frequently with Beethoven, plays, then, a negligible part in the workshop of the truly romantic composers. And what must be considered the rule with them appears as the rare exception in the case of Beethoven. Gustav Nottebohm observed when editing Beethoven's notebooks that the original features of the master's individual style were by no means original in the sense of a primary invention. On the other hand, the sketches of Schumann lead us to the opposite observation. What is here original in the sense of Schumann's individual style is also original in the sense of primary thought. It is from such facts that not only the creative contrasts between Schumann and Beethoven, but also between two styles and in a measure between two eras in the history of music, come to light.

YOUTH AND AGE: THE ROMANTIC AND THE CLASSIC

The insight into the workshop of Schumann and Beethoven points to essential differences in the procedure of classical and romantic creation. Yet if we compare the style of a master in its lifelong evolution, intrinsic changes in the creative procedure become evident which similarly express the duality of the classical and romantic approach. Particularly if a composer wrote two different versions of the same score with a considerable span of time separating them, a unique opportunity is presented for the examination of his creative development.

One of the most remarkable cases in the history of revised masterworks is displayed by the two versions of the Trio in B Major for Piano, Violin and Cello, Op. 8, by Brahms. As we shall see, a comparison of these two versions shows the change of aesthetic guideposts as it occurred at distant points in the life curve of the composer.

The complete revision of the Trio, Op. 8, occurred at the occasion of a new edition of Brahms' works (1891). The original version of the Trio was composed during the years 1853 and 1854. Its reworking dates from 1890: no less than thirty-seven years separate the two versions, an interval which, measured in years allotted to a Purcell, Pergolesi, Mozart, or Schubert, was more than their entire life span. Brahms, viewing his thirty-seven-year-old chamber music score from the other end of his life, approached the work once again as a new enterprise of achieved maturity. He revised the work thoroughly, with a merciless self-criticism exposing all the weaknesses of the youthful score. From the first movement, he kept only sixty-two bars, namely the exposition (and even that not without subjecting them to censure). The second movement, the scherzo, is least touched by changes. The adagio is given a new subsidiary subject. But here as throughout the whole score, not what Brahms added, but what he eliminated is truly revealing.[4] Brahms quoted in his first version a song from Schubert's "Am Meer." Its lines, "By the ocean we sat in front of the lonely fisher house," point with subtlety to a youthful romance. In the mature version this quote is eliminated. Already this single detail discloses the secret of the mature approach. Brahms censored the romanticism of his youthfulness. Whatever he considered too personal, too subjective and emotional fell to the self-criticism of the now mature and objective artist.

The first adagio (1853) contained close to its coda an episode which arose through a sudden fluctuation of mood. This device is typical of the romantic composer who indulges in frequent shifts of expression from one extreme to another. But it interferes with the laws of classical unity. Appropriately, the mature Brahms rejected the contrasting episode. In the first version of the finale, a free and expressive thematic play took up much space. The richly nourished imagination of the young Brahms distributed his melodies generously over the whole movement. Moreover in 1853, the young composer was not too much concerned with a strict formal balance of his plan. He was overcome by the enthusiastic, naïve playfulness of youth. Thus, he introduced in his happy state of tunefulness a third subject—although he had already designed a form-scheme essentially based upon two themes. But in 1890, Brahms corrected whatever bore the stamp of such youthful romanticism. His approach was now basically changed. For the sake of form, Brahms even sacrificed the beautiful cantilena which the cello so expressively sang in F-sharp major. He forsook the passionate song of love that he had written as a young man: it lacked the veiled expression, the sombre discretion which characterizes the personal style of the mature, resigned artist. Balance between content and form is the chief guidepost of the second version. But Brahms could recognize and follow it only after he had acquired a lifetime's knowledge and deep appreciation of the classical approach.

In all details, as well as in the total plan, the two versions of Brahms' Trio, Op. 8, show in an exemplary manner the differences between the romantic and classical working methods. The mature artist, the classicist, enhances the expression of formal beauty. He aims toward unity in variety. He condenses and digests, he sacrifices everything for the sake of the unified and objectified art work. The score of the young composer shows the quality of the typical romanticist. There is a wealth of moods, a texture aiming at beauty of tone, too varied a content at the expense of form. The mature Trio is classical; it is logical, a powerful conquest of form and displays unity of content. The composer himself explains the character of his revision to Julius Otto Grimm: "I did not put a peruke on it (the Trio), but combed its hair and somewhat ordered it." Well, this facetious remark to his old friend is a typically Brahmsian understatement. When the wild hair of youth lies well combed, the storm and stress has subsided and maturity is reached. A classical artist does not show his face with the peruke of mere formalism, but with that of a truly changed human being. The second version of the Trio is the work of an artist with the same heart and nerves, but older, restrained and resigned. The composer has in the course of his life developed from a romanticist to a classicist. From a conquest over the romantic in himself Brahms emerges as a classicist in the evening of his life.

EPILOGUE

THE LAST WAVE

BRAHMS and Gustav Mahler, walking along the bank of an Alpine river, discussed the impending crisis of musical culture. It was the summer of 1896, the last in Brahms' life. The tone of the conversation was pessimistic, the accent on decline: Brahms believed that with the close of his century a final climax had been reached and that the downfall of musical art was imminent. A twilight of tonality and form seemed to darken the musical horizon. "Here flows the last wave!" Mahler suddenly exclaimed and pointed to the green water's unending stream.

Today Mahler's parable proves prophetic. Many more waves flow down the rivers of the world, and the stream of art has not receded. Old forces have died but new ones have come to life. Such is the eternal law of man's destiny and likewise of his work. Mahler's symbolic words point to the fate of all musical creation which will flow on as an ever-changing counterpart of fluctuating human thought. There will always exist, as an eternal by-product of historic evolution, the conflict between the newborn art and the old. New ways of thinking will lead to new ways of hearing. Counterrevolutions will set in against the onetime revolutionary and resolve into a change of aesthetic fundamentals as well as of the tectonic principles of composition. Thus modern music may seem to the contemporary ear to be reduced in its standards of craft and beauty and to suffer from a comparison with the alleged superior quality of past achievements.

The creative search of youth, however, does not stop. It always continues on its own momentum. It persists as a function of the inner nature of creative man. The forces which govern his nature

333

equally force the artist to express himself creatively. The born composer is impelled to write his music in terms of his individuality and of his era. In his work, he speaks as a craftsman, as an artist, as a human being. His style reveals his character, is the mirror picture of his spiritual personality. His taste and temperament participate in the ordering of his tonal material. Converted into tones, this order appears as the expression of that which lives and is implicit in man: of the merely playful and emotional, of the spiritual and banal, of the sacred and profane. Depending then upon our appraisal of music in our time, it may seem again as though "the last wave" has finally arrived, or we may hopefully believe in those other waves which are still sure to come.

We have reviewed in the foregoing chapters some of the historic struggles between a past-bound theory and a forward-storming creativeness. The relationship of the great master to the music of his time may be viewed as a problem of age. With naïve exuberance, the young composer makes ample use of working methods which the past and present supply to him. In this sense, the youthful creativeness of even the most original composer appears as the river bed through which the great waves of all art uninhibitedly flow. At a later stage, however, the truly original musician experiences a conflict between his inner nature and the ruling styles of his era. To liberate himself creatively, he now tries to direct the streaming waves of a voluntarily accepted art into a basin which he newly builds with his gradually personalized craft. This problem of artistic emancipation is characteristically reflected in the relationship of the apprentice to his master. Here, too, absorption appears as the initial phase. A freely chosen and sometimes worshiped teacher becomes the accepted model, setting the standard for all work and sometimes for life itself; the disciple's individuality is overshadowed by that of the master. But later, striving for the discovery of his own style, the onetime apprentice must free himself creatively from the bondage to which he once so eagerly submitted.

The learned craftsmen of the Renaissance resorted to time-honored laws, eager to disprove the dissonant progress of a contemporary music which sounded forbiddingly audacious to their ears. Four centuries that followed witnessed many battles that were lost by the theorists and won, at least posthumously, by creative pioneers. Never have the self-appointed guardians of the past succeeded in turning back the clock of their time and its creative progress. The ardent Artusi attacking Monteverdi's daring dissonances, the great theorist Fux calling the art of his baroque era "perverted," the rigid organ master Albrechtsberger hopelessly disillusioned with that unruly apprentice, Beethoven—all these excellent musicians, looking back for orientation, fought the progress toward a still unexplored future. They defined their convictions in sharp formulations, in biting words which have lost nothing of their striking actuality and read as though they were written here and now. Today again, the orthodox musicians feel sure that they see the last wave of music. But now, as always, the imagination of the young artist newly discovers and follows the unending stream of music. His courage reaches out beyond all theory and contemporary craft for a far-distant, envisioned goal. His instinct drives him onward and the future acknowledges this strife as prophetic.

THE ARTISTIC DISCOVERY

The study of the musical workshop suggested a division of its problems into general and specific ones. Certain factors govern the work of every artist as basic components of the creative process. Other factors prove to be of only individual import: they change with the approach of every individual artist. Our inquiry started with a test of those age-old beliefs which envision musical composition as a mystery: the inventive power of the composer is the gift of the Muse, a faculty derived from supernatural sources. But our investigation brought at least part of this miracle down to earth. Composers' own testimonies throughout the ages indicate how their scores originated, very much like other productive achievements of the searching human mind, from a methodical approach. Their music appears as the result of a highly specialized craft. The creative approach is directed by technique and order. It is often a conquest of the tonal material in an almost objective way. Composing is a knowledge, the precise knowing how to put tones together—definitely a rational process.

Moreover, the starting point of work is not necessarily an

original invention. We observed how composers have produced lasting artworks merely by borrowing and adopting already existing tonal substance. For centuries, mere inspirational power received a lower evaluation than the high art of musical construction. From the Middle Ages up to the baroque, it was considered much more important to work extensively on the available material with a distant creative goal firmly in mind than just to be able to receive ingenious flashes. The discovery of new possibilities in old material equals, as in the great example set by Handel, the composer's original inventiveness. The musician proceeded somewhat along the famous principle of Archimedes who said: "Give me a point on which to stand and I will move the earth." This point of procedure was given to the composer on the basis of an already existing music which could be anything from a motif to an entire composition. Borrowing of ideas substituted successfully for original conception. Priority was unimportant. The result alone mattered. Unsurpassable masterworks originated in this manner from foreign substance. Here art springs primarily from craft, from the expert manner and method in which the experienced and skillful musical architect builds his new tonal structures.

In contrast to such systematic building in terms of craft, there appears the inspirational approach to creation. It shifts the emphasis from the object of tonal building to the subjective experience of the inventing artist. Here, the making of music occurs through an involuntary act of the fantasy which overpowers the artist and creates, as it were, all ideas for him. A subconscious drive for which the artist can hardly account is the generator of the art work. The composer creates from an irrational, emotional urge rather than from a conscious will of tonal abstraction. The formerly revered theoretical knowledge and careful observation of working methods can function only as the humble handmaiden of the inspirational approach.

It was Voltaire who convincingly claimed that the marvelous imagination of Homer must have been equaled by that of Archimedes. The imaginative faculty of the poet as well as that of the scientist worked through lightning flashes, through raptures of inspiration. "Eureka! Eureka!"[1] cried the famous Greek mathematician jumping out of his bath and running down the streets of

Syracuse. What had happened to him and what was it that he had found? A sudden flash had brought to Archimedes the desperately sought discovery of a basic law of physics. His specific problem was to find out whether the pure gold of a crown had not been mixed with inferior metals. Stepping into his bathtub, Archimedes noticed that the water rose in proportion to his immersion. He figured that the cubic area of the rise must be equal to the cubic area of his immersed body. He also deduced that the cubic area of the golden crown could be measured by dipping it into water. Since Archimedes knew the weight both of gold and of baser metals, he could now easily compare the result and solve the rest of his problem by logical conclusion.

These were the stations on the road to the scientific discovery: a long and intense search of a problem, a sudden flash, deduction and final conclusion. Artistic problems are often solved through a process analogous to that of science. Composers vividly describe how they traverse a similar road from inspirational flashes by way of rational deduction to successful synthesis. The musician's "Eureka" is the inspirational flash which brings subconscious raw material to light. This usually occurs at a time when the mind is intensely occupied with a specific tonal task. Next, craft joins the work of fantasy. Reason sets in: it takes over the conscious development of all musical elements according to their intrinsic laws. The composer's final synthesis corresponds to the conclusion of the scientist. On the road to such creative ends, the musical flashes play the part of discoveries. They are the inventions of the musical imagination and are pursued by certain schools of composition in an almost scientific manner.

The two main factors in musical creation—inspiration and craft —are not necessarily irreconcilable partners. They may join in harmonious teamwork, constantly aiding and supplementing each other. Even such a proverbial romanticist as Schumann who always created under the inspirational spell of the subjective experience conceded the fact that "where the fantasy does not suffice, the intellect can still accomplish amazing feats." After all, what might have been received as a mere flash from unknown sources can finally evolve only from rational planning and solid building in terms of tonal craft. Such an emphasis on craft does not cancel altogether the transcendental aspect of the composer's work. It does so only to the extent in which scientific description can try to solve the mystery of all genesis and the secret of life and death.

Aesthetic judgment is employed in every creative activity. Audible beauty—that play of sounds rendered aesthetically effective—can never result from the mere technically organized record of tonal ideas and their combinations. Nor can it be, in its final shape, the musical reflection of emotions exclusively. Everywhere, the artistic intellect enters into the work of the composer, watching the growth of his composition and leading it from the sphere of craft to the realm of high art.

The artistic creed of the composer, the answers that he finds in his search for aesthetic ideals, his taste and temperament—all help to set the creative goal and subsequently to mark the road toward its pursuit. Yet this act of aesthetic judgment does not always occur consciously. It is present, nevertheless, as part and parcel of the creative process. Hence the inquiry into the musical workshop is necessarily linked with artistic truth and beauty.

Every great work of music, that is to say, a score which expresses perfect tonal matter in a perfect manner,[2] displays that tangible plus which sets its quality apart from the raw stuff of inspiration as well as from the sheer accomplishment of craft. This quality is derived from aesthetic judgment; it is the work of the art intellect. We have observed that the inborn talent to receive inspirational flashes is not enough to create great music. But we have also found that the lack of craft prevents even the most gifted composer from the proper co-ordination of his material. On the highest art level, inspiration is carried by solid craft, while the teamwork of these two factors is constantly directed by aesthetic guideposts toward fulfillment.

Mozart has been frequently pictured as the naïve musician, as the Muse-inspired composer who only returns in his art subconsciously what has been loaned to him by unknown transcendental powers from beyond. The allegories of painters, of sculptors and last but not least of writers, have glorified and sentimentalized these heaven-sent gifts. Thus in the well known Viktor Tilgner monument near the Vienna Opera House, Mozart is represented as a figure of the playful world of the rococo. He has been portrayed with deeper insight in the foyer of the Mozarteum in Salzburg as *Apollo Musagetes*, the leader of the Muses, by the sculptor Eduard Hellmer. Countless other allegories bespeak Mozart's mythical role, from his miraculous achievements as a child up to his early death. Justifiably credited with the most prodigious inspirational powers in the history of music, Mozart judged instinctively in boyhood what he heard and what he saw with the profound aesthetic sense of an adult artist. In fact, his aesthetic appraisal of music and musicians matured as early and as prodigiously as his own tonal creations.

"I love to speculate, to study and to reflect," wrote Mozart on July 31, 1778 to his father. The instinctive action of this greatest of all prodigies became richer through the wealth of information which Wolfgang acquired through his acquaintance with the musical culture of many lands. All through Mozart's youth, there is an amazing drive to assemble aesthetic as well as technical knowledge. And this leads to a later period of intense aesthetic reflection where the mature Mozart not only observes but makes it a virtue to observe. At the summit of his mastery, the scores of the great past and contemporary masters were constantly on his desk or clavier ready for frequent study.[3] He confessed to the Prague conductor, Kucharz: "I did not spare myself pains and work to do something excellent for Prague, and I assure you, my dear friend, nobody has dedicated so much effort to the study of composition as I. There is no famous master of music whom I would not have studied from beginning to end, repeatedly and with industry."[4] All this supplements the previously quoted documents which dispel some of the mythical interpretations of Mozart's creative process. His artistry is an irrefutably conscious pursuit of workmanship and spiritual perfection. With all his inspirational wealth, Mozart's accomplishments are unthinkable without his superb craftsmanship, glowing will and keenest art intellect.

Other great composers have, like Mozart, "speculated, studied and reflected," searching for clear guideposts of creation not only in their legitimate territory of tones, but also outside the narrowing fence of their tonal craft. Proverbial is Beethoven's insatiable hunger for philosophical orientation. In a lifelong self-education, he sought broad aesthetic guidance. At the age of forty, he wrote to his publisher, Breitkopf: "There is no treatise which could be too scholarly for me. Unfortunate the artist who does not see his duty herein at least to advance his own cause."

The setting of aesthetic guideposts is always the work of the artistic intellect which shapes the critical powers of the composer and permits his choice of means to be highly selective. His artistic intellect makes him examine past and present techniques and modes of expression, brushing aside all that which does not live up to his self-imposed standards.

The art intellect can never produce music itself. The invention of musical ideas remains in the domain of a specifically tonal faculty of the creative mind. There is no substitute for the talent of musical inventiveness. But already the choice and order of the primary tonal elements is the work of the art intellect, which accepts or rejects the raw material that has been mined by inspiration. It tests the results of craftsmanship from the early stages on and suggests the organization of the material in the framework of form. And in the final synthesis the art intellect can lead to something truly new: to new working methods and to the discovery of a new musical style. In this latter sense, aesthetic thinking takes on truly creative character.

THE IMMORTAL DEED

We finally come to recognize the great creative deed as the sum total of inspiration, craft and deep aesthetic thinking. The composer's conscious will power forms all tonal impulses into the musical art work of the envisioned quality. To set the teamwork of all these factors into motion calls for utmost concentration, for a state in which mind and ear are keyed up to a climax, rounding up all individual mental forces from their diffusion into the subjective narrowness of the musical task. Thus we come to understand various types of behavior during creative hours, different choices of workshops and the desire for inspirational aloofness. Oblivious to everything around him, the artist may isolate himself from the outside world. Lost in music, tones have become the artist's reality and the real world is a dream. The composer has avoided losing himself in life, living himself out entirely in his creative work. It is through such passionate dedication to his self-given mission that a true master's work develops and is carried to fulfillment. Only if the art work was a world for the artist can it also become a world for the listener.

Man's desire for perpetuation in deeds is also a deep incentive for the musician's will to create works which will endure beyond his limited earthly journey. And it is because of his creative deeds that the composer hopes and believes that he has not lived in vain. In tones will rise again what he has loved and suffered. The threat of death is overcome if the resurrection of his spirit is promised by his music. In the liturgical frame of a Requiem the composer may conjure up the timelessness of the human soul. But in a free and wider sense, all of his works, tragic or serene, become memorials to his own thoughts and experiences. A soul-shaking emotion or an abstract musical game, transformed into sound, is made to last beyond its hour. A passing event is endowed with a lasting meaning which it could not have obtained without its sublimation into music.

It is in this sense that the great masters of music have made themselves eternal—if we are permitted to use this word for the achievement of man. In his personal style, the composer has sculptured his own monument from the tonal material of past and contemporary art. He has done so with such mastery that we unerringly recognize his profile at a glance. How familiar is the spiritual face of every great master of music: we know his style immediately when listening to only a few measures of his score. This is so because the artist has expressed himself infallibly in every bar, in every note. Since he has lived himself out entirely in his creative work, he also keeps on living in his music.

A deep desire for survival beyond his earthly limit also underlies the composer's search for a spiritual child, for a successor in art as he can sometimes find in a disciple. Linked with life on earth is the artist's desire to contribute works of uplifting perfection to society. He often fears to fall short of his self-imposed standards and suffers from a sense of insufficiency. There is struggle in the inner workshop of some of the greatest: a volcanic turmoil of creation from the inspirational trance, to toil and labor in the stage of craft and finally to truly Herculean efforts of synthesis. Even composers of sweeping genius, blessed with the wings of prodigious facility and carried by technical mastery to their lasting achievement, speak of the exhausting labor and effort in their work. They are conscious of the permanent responsibility to create beyond their passing days and strive toward that ultimate fulfillment which mortals can attain. The promise of noble compensation, that of enriching the lives of their fellow men with music, has carried these artists victoriously to the end—despite all outer and inner hurdles.

No one has expressed this thought more poignantly than Haydn. A small choral group on the Baltic island of Rügen had performed his *Creation* and notified the old composer gratefully of the event. On September 22, 1802, Haydn, entering the eighth decade of a life the radiance of which spans beyond the reaches of space and time, answered the unknown singers:

Often when I struggled with obstacles of all kinds—when the forces of my spirit and body were sunken—a secret voice whispered to me: "There are on earth so few happy and content human beings, so many persecuted ones in sorrow and in pain—perhaps your work will turn into a fountain from which the downhearted may, for a few moments, at least, drink some recreation and find peace."

NOTES AND BIBLIOGRAPHY

Full titles of sources are given at their first quotation. If English translations are used, the bibliography also quotes the publisher and translator. Frequently the author has made his own translation.

PROLOGUE

1. Aristotle, *Politics*, I, 2.
2. *Gil Blas*, January 12, 1903.
3. In answer to Schlösser's question: A. W. Thayer, *Life of Beethoven* (German ed.; Hugo Riemann), English ed.; H. E. Krehbiel: Beethoven Association, New York, 1921.
4. *Zeitschrift für Musik*, 1926.
5. Schubert and Mahler made statements in almost identical words.
6. Born November 13, 354; died August 28, 430.
7. Born circa 480 A.D.; executed 525 on suspicion of treason.

CHAPTER ONE

1. Otto Jahn, *Wolfgang Amadeus Mozart*, Leipzig, 1856.
2. Max Graf, *Die innere Werkstätte des Musikers*, Stuttgart, 1910.
3. Friedrich Chrysander, *Georg Friedrich Handel.*
4. Johann Nicolaus Forkel, *On Johann Sebastian Bach's Life, Genius and Works*, 1802.
5. Ibid.
6. Cf. Footnote on Mozart's score (Mus. Illus. I) also *Sir Edward Elgar* by Robert J. Buckley; pub. by John Lane: The Bodley Head, London & New York, 1905.
7. Jahn, *Mozart*; also Alfred Einstein, *Mozart*, Oxford University Press, 1945.
8. According to Anna Fröhlich, cf. Otto Erich Deutsch, *Schubert Brevier*, Berlin, 1905.
9. Hector Berlioz, *Memoirs*, London, 1903.
10. With Haydn and Mozart, the number of thematic entrances usually equals in the fugal exposition the number of voices. With Beethoven, often an additional entrance of the dux follows.

11. Beethoven humorously boasted in a letter of 1803 that he "was born with an obligato accompaniment."

12. Analogous constructions occur in the fugues of Bach's pupil, J. L. Krebs and other baroque composers.

13. We refer to fugal works in the proper sense of the term: which applies to scores with a regular exposition of one or more fugal subjects followed by a specific form-plan in the strict polyphonic style.

14. As stated in Beethoven's Heiligenstadt Testament of October 6, 1802, addressed to his brothers.

15. As to still earlier compositions, cf. Richard Wagner, *My Life.*

16. K. F. Glasenapp, *Life of Richard Wagner,* Leipzig, 1894.

17. Gustav Nottebohm, *Beethoveniana,* II, 1887.

18. Karl Geiringer, *Johannes Brahms,* Vienna, 1933.

Chapter Two

1. Wagner, *My Life.*

2. At the occasion of the conferring of an honorary degree on Brahms by the University of Breslau.

3. The concurrence in time of the work on the two compositions does not lose its significance when we learn that the plan for the Tragic overture was much older than that for the Academic Overture, the first sketches for the Tragic Overture dating back more than a decade. Even if the idea for the Tragic Overture had been lying dormant in a sketchbook, it took the Festival Overture to reawaken its mate from subconscious slumber.

4. Of course Wagner's suffering is of a different character than the tragic losses Monteverdi, Berlioz, Verdi had to endure. Again, the deafness of Beethoven and Smetana or the blindness of Delius led to a specific kind of introversion.

5. Cf. Brahms' *Requiem,* Part 5.

6. W. Barclay Squire, in *Sammelbände der Internationalen Musik Gesellschaft,* 1902.

7. Mozart harbored feelings of gratitude toward Count Esterházy who had probably signed Mozart's application of admission to the order of Free Masons.

8. Mozart uses two oboes, one clarinet, three basset horns, one horn in E-flat, one horn in C and one double bassoon in addition to the

traditional set-up of strings. Beethoven employs only string quartet to accompany the solo voice.

9. Clara Schumann's influence lives creatively on in the music of another great composer. How Brahms evaluated her inspiring part in his work is evident in the simple exuberance of the following: "I should justly write below my melodies: truly by Clara Schumann. It is to you I owe them."

10. Robert Schumann, *Music and Musicians.*

11. *Ibid.*

12. In German usage, *Affekt* serves as a synonym for emotion.

13. Leo Schrade, *Bach: the Conflict Between the Sacred and the Secular,* Journal of the History of Ideas, 1946.

14. See letter to Eduard Hanslick, January 1, 1847.

15. The account of the story was given to the astronomer, Lalande, who retells it in his *Voyage d'un Français en Italie.*

16. Reported first in Georg Nikolaus von Nissen, *Biographie: W. A. Mozart,* Leipzig, 1828. Nissen was Constanze Mozart's second husband.

17. Clara had published the composition shortly before.

CHAPTER THREE

1. Gustav Mahler, *Letters,* Berlin, 1925.

2. The ground bass to a round. The round itself is usually called *rota.*

3. Pupil of Frescobaldi in Rome. In 1650 he became court conductor in Munich, later in Vienna.

4. Anton Schindler, *Biographie: Ludwig van Beethoven,* Münster, 1840.

5. *Ibid.*

6. *Ibid.*

7. The letters expressing Mozart's dislike of Salzburg leave no doubt of his preference for other cities.

8. Cf. Einstein, *Mozart.*

9. Felix Mendelssohn Letters, ed. G. Selden Goth.

10. Sir George Grove, *Dictionary of Music and Musicians,* Volume III, London; Macmillan, 1879-89.

11. In his role as music critic, Berlioz defended with militant zeal the original note-texts of his favorite composers, such as Gluck, Mozart and Weber.

12. Wagner, *My Life.*

13. The Second, Third and Fourth Symphonies, the Academic and Tragic Overtures, the Violin Concerto, the First and Second Piano Concertos and many of his chamber music scores were all written during his summer vacation.

Chapter Four

1. *Zeitschrift für Musik*, 1926.
2. Rossini wrote thereafter some sacred music, some medlies, (pieced together from other works and justifiably forgotten), miscellaneous hymns and a few piano pieces.
3. E. Decsey, *Hugo Wolf*, Berlin, 1919; also E. Newman, *Hugo Wolf*, London, 1907; and Max Graf, *Die innere Werkstätte*.
4. Nissen, *Mozart*.
5. Cf. letters of December 6, 1777, April 8, 1781 and October 3, 1783.
6. Handel often outlined only the structure of the score; the filling in of secondary parts occurred later.
7. Albert Dies, *Biographische Nachrichten von Joseph Haydn*, Vienna, 1810.
8. Emily Anderson, ed., *Letters of Mozart and his Family*, New York and London; Macmillan, 1938. By permission of Macmillan.
9. *Ibid.*
10. *Ibid.*
11. Berlioz, *Memoirs*.
12. Wagner, *My Life*.
13. *Ibid.*
14. *Neue Musik Zeitung*, Vol. 47, 1925.
15. For instance: Beethoven's *Fidelio* overture and sextet, Op. 71; several of Schubert's songs; Puccini's quartet from *Bohème*, etc.

Chapter Five

1. This does not include his resumption of duties with the court of Esterház in later years.
2. Einstein, *Mozart*.
3. Letter of December 12, 1771, in Ritter von Arneith, *Briefe der Kaiserin Maria Theresia an ihre Kinder und Freunde*, Vienna, 1881 (as quoted in Einstein's Mozart).

4. Anderson, Emily, *Op. cit.*
5. *Ibid.*
6. *Ibid.*
7. Cf. Tchaikovsky's letter of July 6, 1878 to Madame von Meck which deals with a similar problem.
8. K. 594, Adagio and Allegro in F Minor and Major for a Mechanical Organ, composed for Count Joseph F. Deym.
9. Jahn, *Mozart.*
10. Cf. eloquent expression of Mozart's devotion in the last letter (4-4-1787) to his father.
11. Inevitably the great artist, who experiences the loss of his parents, records it creatively—though not always in a form apparent to the outside world. Wagner's *Lohengrin* sublimated the loss of the composer's mother. As to the genesis of the *German Requiem* by Brahms see Chapter II.
12. George Hogarth, *The Philharmonic Society of London*, London, 1862.
13. From Beethoven's Conversation-Book of 1823. He had received an offer from Boston to compose an oratorio.
14. Beethoven would not allow seven bank shares to be touched; he regarded them as the property of his nephew, Karl.
15. Thus Tchaikovsky's Marche Slav was written for the occasion of a Red Cross Concert.

Summary: Musical Mood

1. F. G. Wegeler and F. Ries, *Biographische Notizen über Ludwig van Beethoven*, Koblenz, 1838.
2. As to Handel, cf. reports by Sheffield and Hawkins; as to Brahms cf. Richard Specht, *Johannes Brahms.*
3. Jahn, *Mozart.*
4. Catherine Drinker Bowen and Barbara von Meck, *Beloved Friend*, New York; Random House, 1937.
5. Julius Bahle, *Der musikalische Schaffensprozess*, Dissertation, Leipzig, 1936. Also, H. Jancke, *Musikpsychologische Studien*, Leipzig, 1928.
6. Wagner, *My Life.*

CHAPTER SIX

1. Hans Mersmann, *Angewandte Musikästhetik*, Berlin, 1926.
2. An example of an epoch-making set-up is Monteverdi's instrumental ensemble in his opera, *Orfeo* (first performed 1607).
3. In 1813, *Die Allgemeine Musikzeitung* published what was probably the first account of Mälzel's teamwork with Salieri. The inventor and the composer jointly equipped a series of master scores with metronome marks.
4. Obviously, Chopin also used larger pianos. But his own performing style definitely points to the tone of smaller instruments.
5. Mozart played the clavichord as well as the harpsichord.
6. Cf. Vincent D'Indy, *César Franck.*
7. *Letters to Mathilde Wesendonck*, Tr. by William Ashton Ellis, Scribner's, New York.
8. Bach's original word is *Klavier-Ritter.*
9. Forkel, *On J. S. Bach's Life.*
10. Nissen, *Biographie Mozart.*
11. For instance: Bach, Mozart, Beethoven were in younger years expert performers on the violin or viola.
12. The exact list is given in the *"Specification of the Estate left by the late Mr. Johann Seb. Bach*, formerly cantor at the Thomas-Schule in Leipzig, departed in God, July 28, 1750." Hans Th. David and Arthur Mendel, *The Bach Reader*, New York; W. W. Norton, 1945.
13. A natural park in old Vienna.
14. Gerhardt von Breuning, *Aus dem Schwarzspanierhause.*
15. Ernest Newman, *Life of Richard Wagner*, Knopf, New York, 1933.
16. Cf. Gustav Jenner, *Johannes Brahms als Mensch, Lehrer, Künstler,* Vienna, 1905.
17. Weber, Wagner, Johann Strauss likewise favored a standing desk on occasions.

CHAPTER SEVEN

1. Other composers such as Tinctoris or Josquin likewise used the tune, "l'homme armé" as a cantus firmus for their scores.
2. A method of teaching scales and intervals by syllables. Guido d'Arezzo (b. 990) is usually accredited with its invention.

3. Knud Jeppesen, *Counterpoint* (English tr. Glen Haydon), New York; Prentice Hall, 1939.
4. Zarlino refused the offer and remained a church conductor until his death.
5. Noteworthy is the fact that the author considers *Phonascus*, the inventing of melodies more important than *Symphoneta*, their elaboration. Such convictions contradict the contemporary ideology of composition.
6. Jeppesen, *Counterpoint.*
7. Wegeler and Ries, *Notizen über Beethoven.*

CHAPTER EIGHT

1. Amphion was the son of Jupiter and Antiope. By the music of his lyre, he caused stones to move and to form themselves into a wall around Thebes.
2. *Principles of thoroughbass and directions for performing it in four parts in accompanying for his scholars in music,* by Herr J. S. Bach, royal court composer, Kapellmeister, Director of the music and cantor of the Thomas-Schule in Leipzig.
3. The following list gives the exact titles of treatises that Beethoven studied and upon which he leaned for his teaching material:
    1. J. G. Albrechtsberger, *Gründliche Anweisung zur Composition* (First edition)
    2. Ph. E. Bach, *Versuch über die wahre Art das Klavier zu spielen* (2nd part, 2nd edition)
    3. J. J. Fux, *Gradus ad Parnassum*
    4. J. Ph. Kirnberger, *Die Kunst des reinen Satzes*
    5. F. W. Marpurg, *Abhandlung von der Fuge*
    6. D. G. Türk, *Kurze Anweisung zum Generalbassspielen* (First edition)
4. Anderson, Emily, *Op. cit.*
5. He had many unfavorable experiences with his wealthy pupils, which killed the joy of teaching. Thus, in a letter of July 9, 1778, Mozart complains that a Duke, who started to take lessons from him, later tried to cheat him out of half of his fee.
6. Correspondence from year 1875. Hofmeyer followed Bruckner's advice and later became his pupil and copyist.

7. They include Fugue in A-flat Minor, Choral Fugue with Prelude, and eleven choral preludes for organ (published posthumously).
8. Franz Werfel and Paul Stefan, *Verdi, The Man and His Letters,* tr. by Edward Downes.

CHAPTER NINE

1. In accordance with the style of this era, the final stage calls for an intricate working out of all ornamentations.
2. The reemployment of the composer's own material may be mentioned in this connection: not only the baroque masters, but musicians up to our time occasionally re-use previous material.
3. Born 1690 in Passau, Upper Austria; died December 10, 1770, Vienna.
4. Derives its name from continuous bass notes with added figures, indicating the choice of chords. The continuo was played in an improvising manner on the clavichord, harpsichord or organ (depending on the time and type of performance).
5. Concerto Grosso is the typically baroque form of a concerto for orchestra (of which composers such as Stradella and Corelli were pioneers). The concertino is the small orchestra of soloistic character in contrast to the ripieno—to the full body of all participating instruments.
6. Romain Rolland, *Handel,* 1910.
7. Edmond Malone, the great authority on Shakespeare, 1741-1812. Cf. also Percy Allen, *Shakespeare, Jonson and Wilkens as Borrowers,* London; C. Palmer, 1928.
8. Breitkopf and Härtel. *Händel-Gesamtausgabe,* Leipzig.
9. Mattheson never mentions Bach's name. As to his various experiences with Handel, cf. Handel's biography by Chrysander and others.
10. Arnold Schering, *Geschichtliches zur "Ars Inveniendi"* in Musik Jahrbuch Peters, 1925.
11. Ernest Ferand, *Die Improvisation in der Musik,* Zurich, 1938.
12. Elssler (the father of the famous dancer, Fanny Elssler) was Haydn's valet, copyist and private secretary in one person.
13. Franz Niemtschek, *Leben des Kapellmeister Wolfgang Gottlieb Mozart.* Prague, 1798.

CHAPTER TEN

1. Graf, *Die innere Werkstätte.*
2. Ph. E. Bach informed Forkel that his father, Johann Sebastian Bach, upon hearing a fugal theme, would immediately indicate all contrapuntal devices which could be applied to its development.
3. George August Griesinger, *Biographische Notizen über Joseph Haydn,* Leipzig, 1810.
4. Jahn, *Mozart.*
5. Nissen, *Biographie Mozart.*
6. Schindler, *Biographie Ludwig van Beethoven,* Münster, 1845.
7. This book dating from the third century B. C. is one of the most important apocryphal treatises; in content it resembles the books of *Proverbs* and *Job.* The ethical wisdom of the author pertains to human relations, preaching noble humaneness.
8. Gustav Nottebohm, *Ein Skizzenbuch von Beethoven,* (1865); *Beethoveniana,* (two volumes, 1872, 1887); *Beethovens Studien,* 1873.
9. Graf, *Die innere Werkstätte.*
10. George Grove, *Beethoven and his Nine Symphonies,* 1896.
11. Herman Kretzschmar, *Führer durch den Konzertsaal,* 1887.
12. The word *voce* is not clearly legible and seems to be a reminder for Beethoven to use the human "voice" at this place.
13. The "three" might refer to the employment of three fugal subjects. Grove, however, believes that Beethoven meant three trombones. The planned contrapuntal work was to be a triple fugue honoring the spirit of Bach by an extended piece of polyphony.
14. Otto Erich Deutsch, *Schubert Brevier.* Berlin, 1905.
15. This opinion is shared by Hans Holländer, cf. Ph.D. dissertation on Schubert's songs, Vienna, 1927.
16. Berlioz, *Memoirs.*
17. Glasenapp, *Wagner.*
18. Wagner, *My Life.*
19. Born, February 26, 1838; died June 16, 1810. Weissheimer, a composer and pedagogue, was a competent observer.
20. Glasenapp, *Wagner.*

CHAPTER ELEVEN

1. Ferruccio Busoni, *Entwurf einer neuen Aesthetik der Tonkunst,* 1907.
2. Karl Weidle, *Bauformen in der Musik,* Augsburg, 1925.
3. Used here in the historic sense of a cantus firmus (firm chant).
4. An embellishing variation of the melody in smaller time values.
5. Even the main characteristics of tonal and real answer in the exposition are sometimes abandoned.
6. Fugato is a free variant of the strict fugal style without considerable development.
7. Nottebohm, *Beethoveniana.*
8. Wegeler and Ries, *Notizen über Beethoven.*
9. The tenor clef, read one tone lower than the treble clef (in which the passage appears in the original score), would transpose the tonic form of the horn call into that of the dominant form.
10. Jahn, *Mozart.*
11. Such is the case with the coda of Act I in Richard Wagner's *Meistersinger* (where Hans Sachs remains alone on the stage); see also Graf, *Die innere Werkstätte.*
12. Nottebohm, *Beethoveniana.*
13. But wherever Schubert made these changes, he was sure to preserve the rhyme.
14. Eusebius Mandyczewski, Editor's report of the Schubert *Gesamtausgabe.* Breitkopf und Härtel, Leipzig.
15. Cf. Curt Sachs' comments in *L'Anthologie Sonore.*
16. Yet the changing import of these terms in different eras must not be overlooked.

CHAPTER TWELVE

1. This fact throws some reconciliatory light on Brahms' appraisal of Wagner; it suggests that Brahms was capable of a detached appreciation of the music of his antagonist.
2. Born Nuremberg, 1653; died there March 3, 1706. He was one of the important exponents of seventeenth century organ music.
3. Georg Schünemann, *Musiker Handschriften von Bach bis Schumann,* Atlantic Verlag, 1936.

4. *Ibid.*

5. For instance: in the score of *The Abduction from the Seraglio,* the sheets upon which Mozart had written the triangle and tympani parts have disappeared. In addition, the parts for oboes and clarinets of the chorus No. 5 in the score are missing. And so are the triangle, the big drum and cymbal parts in the Duet No. 14. In certain cases, the missing links are easily supplied from old music, used at the first Vienna performance of the opera. Yet in the replacing of other missing parts, there is no guarantee of authenticity.

6. Editor's Report on Mozart, *Gesamtausgabe.* Breitkopf und Härtel, Leipzig.

7. Specifically, the position of the left hand on the fingerboard of the violin.

8. Curt Sachs in his *History of Musical Instruments* (New York; W. W. Norton, 1940) shows how the ancient Chinese indulged in a co-ordination of specific musical instruments with the seasons of the year, with the phenomena of nature and the cardinal points.

9. Letter to Johann Christian Lobe; Cf. *Konsonanzen und Dissonanzen,* 1869.

10. Julius Otto Grimm, musical director in Münster.

11. Humorous synonym for an inadequate horn player.

12. The same issue points to the frequent retouching of symphonic scores by contemporary conductors.

CHAPTER THIRTEEN

1. *Idomeneo* was written for Munich and performed there in 1781. For the Vienna performance in 1786, Mozart made considerable changes. Thus, he revised the soprano part of Idamantes, the part of Elektra and the duet of Ilia and Idamantes. (Translation of quoted letters from Anderson, *The Letters of Mozart.* Permission of Macmillan Co., publishers.)

2. Mozart, *Gesamtausgabe.*

3. Jahn, *Mozart.*

4. This Latin imperative is used in older music to indicate the beginning and end of a cut.

5. Letter to Liszt, September 8, 1852 after Wagner was informed that Liszt was preparing to conduct the opera, *Benvenuto Cellini,* by Berlioz. The work was a failure at its premiere in Paris, 1838.

Berlioz promised "to thoroughly correct, polish and clean the score."

6. Born 1698; died 1782; Imperial court poet in Vienna who wrote libretti for Mozart, Scarlatti, Hasse and other contemporary opera composers.

7. This must also include movements where Brahms varies a theme without specifically referring to this form type in the title of the score.

CHAPTER FOURTEEN

1. Ernst Bücken, *Geist und Form in musikalischen Kunstwerk, in "Handbuch der Musikwissenschaften."*

2. Schubert's Diary.

3. Nicola Piccini was the historic rival of Gluck in Paris. He was born January 16, 1728 and died May 7, 1800.

4. Cf. Brahms, *Gesamtausgabe*, (Breitkopf und Härtel, Vol. 9); Hans Gál, *Revisionsbericht;* Graf, *Die innere Werkstätte;* Max Kalbeck, *Johannes Brahms*; Heinrich Reimann, *Johannes Brahms*.

EPILOGUE

1. "I have found it, I have found it."

2. Max Schoen, *The Understanding of Music*, Harper & Brothers, 1945.

3. Niemtschek, *Kapellmeister Mozart*.

4. Jahn, *Mozart*.

INDEX

Absolute music, 273, 324
Abstract expression, 76, 129, 154, 266, 324, 341
Academism, 52, 240
Accent, 194, 221, 320
Accidents, role of, 60ff, 124
Acompaniment, 29, 54, 164, 210, 212, 228ff, 237, 286, 327, 349
Acoustics 9, 72, 127, 160, 286, 324
Advice, 292, 310ff, 315. See also Friends
Aesthetics, guideposts and reflection, 9, 14, 32, 51, 91f, 107, 155, 158, 160, 162, 185f, 216, 257, 288, 312f, 319ff, 324, 326, 333, 338ff
Aeschylus, 117
Affektenlehre, 50, 345. See also Doctrine of Emotions
Agogics, 128
Albrechtsberger, Johann Georg, 28, 165, 171ff, 335, 349
Allegri, Gregorio, 211
Alleluia, 225
Allemande, 199
Alterations, 98, 194, 230f, 290, 296f, 304, 327. See also Revisions
Amanuensis, 282
Amateur, 153, 237f, 239f
Amati family, 284
Amphion, 168, 349
Amusement, as goal of music, 12
Anachronism, 265
Analysis, 26, 123, 173, 177, 182, 187, 201, 241, 305, 318
Anderson, Emily, 346, 347, 349
Anger, 49, 51. See also Emotions
Animals, 85f, 123
Anonymity of composers, 152
Anschütz, Heinrich, 214
Anthologie Sonore, 354
Antiphonal, 195
Apollo, 8, 131, 339
Ahorism, 271
Apotheosis, 45
Apprentice, 134, 154, 167ff, 170, 334
Archimedes, 336, 337
Architecture and music, 14, 24, 48, 83, 129, 152, 201, 207, 209, 241, 247f, 254, 336
Aria, 205, 258, 298
Aristotle, 3, 4, 343
Arrivabene, Opprandino, 85
Ars Antiqua, 163
Ars Inveniendi, 189ff, 198, 200, 319

Art and life, 19f, 25, 32f, 37ff, 47, 76, 328. See also Emotion, Environment, Personality, Religion, Philosophy
Artusi, Giovanni, 161, 335
Asceticism, 32
Association of thought and tone, 47, 122, 190, 202, 254, 263ff, 267, 273, 288, 318, 324. See also Idea
Atonal, 161
Attwood, Thomas, 177
Auber, Daniel, 141
Augmentation, 151
Austria and Austrian music, 22, 39, 68, 78, 81, 100, 170f, 182, 290, 304
Autodidactic, 182f

Bacchus, 225
Bach, Anna Magdalena, 169, 275
Bach, Johann Sebastian, 10, 22, 27ff, 33, 50f, 59, 70, 77, 88, 93f, 99, 130, 133, 136, 144, 153, 166f, 169, 177, 189, 200f, 203, 210, 226, 248, 275, 282, 309, 348f, 351; inspired by other masters, 23, 70; Art of the Fugue, 30; Well Tempered Clavier, Vol. I, 29, 30, 180; Well Tempered Clavier, Vol. II, 30; organ fugues, 30; cantatas, 51, 107, 276; passions, 107, 276; oratorios, 107; organ preludes, 107; at St. Thomas, Leipzig, 107, 137, 204; owner of instruments, 136; method of teaching, 168; Italian Concerto, 200; Two and Three Part Inventions, 201; Musikalisches Opfer, 204; St. Matthew Passion, 276, 277; calligraphy, 276; manuscripts, 276, 280; Brandenburg Concertos, 277; Revisions, 277
Bach, Philipp Emanuel, 25, 165, 168f, 175, 204, 349, 351
Bahle, Julius, 347
Balakirev, Mily, 239, 306
Baroque, 20, 25, 28, 31, 78, 129, 144f, 153, 194, 200, 208, 237, 246, 248, 249, 285, 324, 335, 344
Bass, 53, 65, 169, 176, 194, 202, 205, 212, 222, 229, 232f, 345, 350; figured bass, 169, 173, 209f, 237. See also Score script
Bass (vocal), 195, 237
Basset horn, 344
Bassoon, 24, 288f, 293; double, 344
Beaumarchais, Pierre de, 111, 302
Beethoven, Karl, 112, 347

355

368 INDEX